Weber, John.

From South Texas to the Nation...

64808

HD 8081 .M6 W43 2015 BEE

FROM **South Texas**
TO THE **Nation**

The Exploitation of Mexican Labor
in the Twentieth Century

JOHN WEBER

The University of North Carolina Press
CHAPEL HILL

The paper in this book meets the guidelines for permanence and durability of
the Committee on Production Guidelines for Book Longevity of the Council on
Library Resources.

The University of North Carolina Press has been a member of the Green Press
Initiative since 2003.

Portions of chapter 4 appeared previously in "Homing Pigeons, Cheap Labor, and
Frustrated Nativists: Immigration Reform and the Deportation of Mexicans from
South Texas in the 1920s," *Western Historical Quarterly* 44, no. 2 (Summer 2013):
167–86.

A few sections of the discussion of the Plan of San Diego in chapter 1 appeared
previously in "The District Deputy Supreme Dictator for South Texas Will Lead
You Astray: Reading Anglo Fears and Racial Violence in Early Twentieth-Century
South Texas," *Journal of South Texas* 24, no. 1 (Spring 2011): 22–31.

Jacket illustration: migrant workers wait outside stopped truck en route from
Laredo, Texas, to Wyoming for sugar beet harvest. Photograph by Russell Lee,
1949. Russell Lee Photograph Collection, Study of the Spanish-Speaking People
of Texas, i.d. no. rwL14233_0022, the Dolph Briscoe Center for American History,
University of Texas at Austin.

Library of Congress Cataloging-in-Publication Data
Weber, John, 1978–
From South Texas to the nation : the exploitation of
Mexican labor in the twentieth century / John Weber.
   pages cm. — (The David J. Weber series in the new borderlands history)
Includes bibliographical references and index.
ISBN 978-1-4696-2523-2 (cloth : alk. paper) — ISBN 978-1-4696-2524-9 (ebook)
1. Foreign workers, Mexican—Texas—History—20th century. 2. Migrant
agricultural laborers—Texas—History—20th century. 3. Mexican American
agricultural laborers—Texas—History—20th century. 4. Unfair labor practices—
Texas—History—20th century. 5. Mexico—Emigration and immigration—
Economic aspects—History—20th century. 6. United States—Emigration and
immigration—Economic aspects—History—20th century. I. Title.
HD8081.M6W43 2015
331.5'4408968073—dc23
2015006184

Contents

Acknowledgments ix

Introduction 1

PART I | *Revolutions* 11

   1   The Wages of Development in South Texas
and Northern Mexico 15

   2   The Revolution in Texas: International Migration, Capitalist
Agriculture, and the Interstate Migrant Stream 41

PART II | *Securing the Revolution* 73

   3   Breaking the Machines, Building the Color Line,
and Immobilizing Mobile Labor 77

   4   Homing Pigeons, Cheap Labor, and Frustrated Nativists:
Immigration Reform and Deportation 102

PART III | *Challenging the Revolution* 125

   5   The Politics of Depression 129

   6   Organization and Rebellion 154

PART IV | *The Shadow of the Revolution* 183

   7   The Bracero Program and the Nationalization of
South Texas Labor Relations 187

Epilogue 223

Notes 233

Bibliography 283

Index 311

Figures and Maps

FIGURES

Family of migrant sugar beet workers in the fields in
East Grand Forks, Minnesota, October 1937 61

Employment agency sign seeking sugar beet workers
in Corpus Christi, Texas, 1949 63

Typical corral housing in the West Side of
San Antonio, March 1939 90

Line of people waiting for free surplus clothing at the
Works Progress Administration Clothing Department,
San Antonio, March 1939 144

Braceros being sprayed with DDT at processing center
in Hidalgo, Texas, 1956 212

MAPS

South Texas 5

Agricultural Worker Migrant Stream from
Crystal City, Texas, 1938 64

National Agricultural Migrant Streams 69

South Texas Counties 81

Acknowledgments

This project began several years ago with a hazy desire to try and understand the history of a region I long called home. Born and raised in San Antonio, I knew little else before I left the area for college and graduate school. While I will never fully understand the dynamics that have shaped and continue to shape a maddeningly complicated and often objectively strange region, this book serves as the first step in explaining to myself the forces and people that have built a region I still consider home from more than a thousand miles away.

I have built up a substantial number of debts in the years since I began this project. The largest of those debts is to Cindy Hahamovitch, my graduate school advisor who continues to serve as a trusted mentor and friend. She has read and critiqued multiple iterations of this project, helping to give it a coherence it would not have without her constant prodding. I could not have asked for a better model of a committed, engaged scholar. I owe almost as much to Ben Johnson, who has also helped shepherd this project at multiple stages. He has been a constant source of encouragement and a trusted authority on all things Texas. This book would not exist without Cindy's and Ben's help, encouragement, and willingness to answer an endless barrage of my e-mails. I owe you both a beer.

But many more people also helped shape this project. At the College of William and Mary, Judith Ewell, Andy Fisher, Scott Nelson, and Cam Walker pushed me to complicate my understandings of historical causation and to strive for clarity in writing. Any complaints about this book, therefore, should be sent to them. I also received generous financial support from a number of sources at the College that helped fund much of the early research: the History Department, the Tyler Fund, the Provost's Office, the Dean of Graduate Studies, the Student Activities Fund, the Charles Center, the Reves Center for International Studies, and the Graduate Student Association. My fellow graduate students Josh Beatty, Dave Brown, Dave Corlett, Catharine Dann, Sean Harvey, Dave McCarthy, Amanda McVety, Liam Paskvan, Buddy Paulett, and, most important, Emily Moore, also helped in the long process of creating this book, though as welcome distractions more often than anything else.

After graduate school, I had the good fortune of spending a year at the Clements Center for Southwest Studies at Southern Methodist University as the Summerlee Foundation Fellow in Texas History. The time in Dallas allowed me to do additional research, begin reshaping the manuscript, and take part in a vibrant community of scholars. Particularly helpful was the manuscript workshop organized by the Clements Center that brought together several top scholars to critique and discuss an earlier version of the manuscript. Those critiques forced me to rethink and recast several parts of this project, vastly improving it in the process. Thank you to all of the participants in the workshop: Andrea Boardman, Tim Bowman, Robert Chase, John Chavez, Ruth Ann Elmore, Raphael Folsom, Miguel Angel González-Quiroga, Ben Johnson, Carla Mendiola, Todd Meyers, David Narrett, Mae Ngai, Aaron Sanchez, Sherry Smith, and Zaragoza Vargas. The Clements Center is a truly special place, and I will always remain grateful that I had the opportunity to spend a year there. I am especially glad that I had the opportunity to spend some time with David Weber, the founding director of the Clements Center and the namesake of this book series, during my year in Dallas.

Since leaving the Clements Center, I have been lucky enough to teach at two universities. At Texas A&M University–Kingsville, I want to thank Shannon Baker, Dean Ferguson, Michael Houf, Russ Huebel, Brenda Melendy, and Roger Tuller for welcoming me to the department, answering my constant questions, and putting up with my sarcasm. At Old Dominion University, I have found a supportive department of talented scholars. My senior colleagues have welcomed me from my first day and been more than forthcoming with advice on teaching, research, and where to find a decent meal in Norfolk. Annette Finley-Croswhite, Doug Greene, Maura Hametz, Austin Jersild, Jane Merritt, and Kathy Pearson have helped me navigate my first few years at ODU, as have Kelly Duggins and Sharon Metro in the History Department office. I am also lucky to be a part of a collegial group of junior faculty who have acted as support system, reading group, and drinking buddies over the last few years. Whether they wanted to or not, Brett Bebber, Erin Jordan, Anna Mirkova, Tim Orr, Jelmer Vos, and Liz Zanoni have read and critiqued much of this book over the last few years and helped me reshape parts of it. Thanks. If nothing else, its publication means you will never have to read any of it again.

Several other scholars have read parts of this manuscript and offered valuable critiques. David Rich Lewis generously suggested a series of revisions to an article that became chapter 4 that have simplified and clarified its argument. Likewise, participants in the D.C. Working Class History Research Group suggested revisions to an even earlier version of chapter 4. Thank you to Eric Arnesen, Cindy Hahamovitch, Jennifer Luff, and the other seminar participants.

A number of archivists aided in collecting the research for this book. I am especially grateful to the staffs of the Texas Labor Archives at the University of Texas at Arlington, the Texas State Archives in Austin, the Benson Latin American Collection at the University of Texas at Austin, the Dolph Briscoe Center for American History at the University of Texas at Austin, the Texas A&M University–Corpus Christi Archives, the University of Texas–Pan American Special Collections, the South Texas Archives at Texas A&M University–Kingsville, the Institute of Texan Cultures Library in San Antonio, Special Collections at St. Mary's University in San Antonio, and the Archives of the University of Texas at San Antonio.

Other sources of financial assistance have helped at every step of this project. The George Pozzetta Prize from the Immigration and Ethnic History Society and the John H. Jenkins Research Fellowship in Texas History from the Texas State Historical Association helped fund early research trips. The Summerlee Foundation and the Clements Center provided substantial financial assistance to further the research and heavily revise the manuscript. The Office of Research at Old Dominion University provided a Summer Research Fellowship Program Grant that helped push revisions further. Finally, the History Department and the Office of the Dean of Arts and Letters at Old Dominion have provided money to help finish this project.

A few others provided important help that deserves mention. Several members of the Rodriguez/Taylor family took a few days to talk to me about life in the Lower Rio Grande Valley back in 2003. Eduardo Rodriguez, Bryce and Diana Taylor, and Joe and Emma Rodriguez all went out of their way to speak to me as I tried to figure out what exactly I wanted to write about the history of South Texas. I hope this history reflects their memories of life in the Valley. David Hall took a few hours one afternoon in 2009 to discuss the case of South Texas migrant workers lured to Hawaii that opens the epilogue, helping clarify some of the finer points of legalized migrant worker exploitation over a few beers.

Michael Kirkpatrick, who tried the Wailuku case, also took time to discuss his memories of the case over the phone. Their in-depth knowledge of modern systems of exploitation helped shape my thinking in the epilogue, and their continued fight for a more just society and legal system are inspirational.

As this project has entered its final stage, it has received some much-appreciated help from the series editors for the David Weber Series in New Borderlands History, Andy Graybill and Ben Johnson, and from Dino Battista, Lucas Church, Katherine Fisher, Chuck Grench, Jay Mazzocchi, Iza Wojciechowska, and the rest of the staff at the University of North Carolina Press. Alex Lichtenstein and the anonymous readers pushed me to clarify and refine the manuscript as it neared publication. Their incisive reading and constructive suggestions have made this a much better book. Copy editor Alex Martin helped make this book far more readable. I also need to thank Rebecca Wrenn for producing the maps that appear in this book and Dave Corlett for compiling the index.

Finally, I want to thank the people who have lived with this project as long as I have. I cannot ever hope to pay back the unending support from my parents, John and Connie Weber. They have been there at every step and certainly deserve a token of appreciation more substantial than this book. But it will have to do for now. The only person who will be as relieved as me to see this book come out is my wife, Emily Moore. Thank you for putting up with me during the years that I worked on this book. Your support and companionship have made this process much easier and more fulfilling.

From South Texas to the Nation

Introduction

The year 1968 produced what many believed was a worldwide crisis of order. Protesters, rioters, soldiers, and tanks filled the streets of Washington, Chicago, Paris, Prague, Mexico City, and dozens of other cities around the world. In response to this seemingly dire situation the leaders of San Antonio, Texas, did what they do best. They threw a party.

Envisioned as a celebration of the commonalities of the nations of the Western Hemisphere, San Antonio's World's Fair, dubbed HemisFair, opened on April 6, 1968. Ninety acres of previously residential land on the southern edge of downtown were used to construct the ultramodern fairgrounds in a celebration of both the "confluence of civilizations in the Americas" (the fair's official slogan) and the economic possibilities of San Antonio and South Texas. The year 1968 was chosen for the fair because it was the 250th anniversary of San Antonio's founding by the Spanish. More than just a birthday party, however, HemisFair was a "vivid recognition of the growth potential of a particular region and its peoples."[1] Fair organizers claimed that "San Antonio lays claim to a lustrous heritage spun from the colorful threads of many cultures. On that foundation, HemisFair 68, in the truest sense, is the outcome of visionary, 20th Century pioneering."[2] On opening day, April 6, the *San Antonio Express-News* happily stated, "With the flags of many nations whipping in the breeze, San Antonians and people of the nation and the world poured into what was once a haven for winos, stray dogs and junked cars," where now "money flowed like water."[3]

The timing of this civic and regional boosterism was unfortunate, however. Two days before the fair opened, Martin Luther King Jr. was killed, setting off a wave of urban rebellions across the nation. With inner cities across the nation still smoldering, HemisFair advertised San Antonio as a place of ethnic and cultural harmony, a city that embodied social peace. According to the official souvenir guide, the fair "intended to demonstrate the actual life-giving process of cultural confluence. It sought to show how diverse threads had been woven into a strong, new social fabric."[4]

Much was made of San Antonio's Spanish heritage by the fair's organizers. "In a Europe that was beginning to question the feudal system and seeking new ways of life, Spain took the lead as a Modernist," according to an article on the Spanish Pavilion in an eighty-page insert on the fair in the *San Antonio Express-News*. "The discovery and civilization of the New World were, therefore, the necessary consequence of an historical situation in which Spain was the only nation capable of carrying out this task, from a technical, political and cultural point of view."[5] In this way, the Spanish conquest and the founding of San Antonio were depicted as necessary steps in the advancement of civilization as inherited from Europe. This version of history left out many intermediate steps between Spanish conquistadors and modern San Antonio. Most notably, Mexico was entirely absent. The commemorative insert included only one short article on Mexico, titled "Mariachi Music Will Lure You to Mexican Pavilion."[6] While Spain was depicted as integral to the heritage of San Antonio and Texas, Mexico was little more than a scenic and quaint neighbor with little historical or cultural connection to the dominant white civilization of Texas. Never mind Texas's fifteen years as a part of Mexico (and decade as a breakaway province still claimed by Mexico) or the fact that the majority of the population of South Texas was of Mexican origin—the Spanish heritage made a much more convenient linear historical narrative in which a civilized Spain gave way to the United States with no major complications in between.

HemisFair advertised Texas by supplementing older Texan mythological traditions with a limited type of multicultural tokenism that legitimized the contemporary political and social order. Gone were the overtly racist depictions of "Mexican cruelty" and "Indian blood" that had dominated the popular and academic history of the state.[7] These images were replaced by bland affirmations of frontier cultural interaction in San Antonio and South Texas. Rather than symbolizing a substantive change in which Mexican Americans were welcomed as equal partners in both the past and future of the region, these public pronouncements of cultural confluence veered toward the romantic image of the "noble savage," with Mexicans playing the part of savages. Anglos parading through old Spanish missions and helping themselves to healthy doses of Mexican food while listening to mariachi music saw no mention of the sprawling slum just west of the fairgrounds where the majority of the city's Mexican and Mexican American population lived. According to HemisFair's organizers, Mexicans and Mexican

Americans were little more than quaint remnants of a supposedly dying culture, picturesque but ultimately impotent and unimportant. This theme-park exoticism was the essence of the "confluence of civilizations" and cultures for HemisFair's organizers. The fair remained a self-contained fantasy universe that selectively depicted the history of the region as an exotic variant on the larger American pattern, with the Spanish mission standing in as a metonymic architectural and institutional presence that precluded any substantive examination of the continued Mexican and Mexican American presence in the region.

The historical narrative presented at HemisFair served as a reminder that the leadership of the city of San Antonio and the state of Texas was more than happy to overlook some of the present's uglier realities. The *San Antonio Express-News*, which had long ignored the existence of the city's West Side, did note in July 1968, however, that, "from west San Antonio, the Tower of the Americas [the fair's most prominent structure] looms in the far horizon like a remote and unreachable symbol of an affluence alien to the thousands who live in crowded housing projects and Mexican-American barrios. . . . Few, if any, feel the sense of pride and participation that other residents of San Antonio get from the fair."[8]

San Antonio may have represented a confluence of civilizations to the leaders of HemisFair, but it was a confluence that did more to legitimize their own social standing, as a sort of evolutionary certainty, than it did to expand the narrow narrative of Texas history or provide a truthful survey of cultural contact and contestation in the region north of the Rio Grande. Without a usable past to draw from, a fantasy heritage had to be created. HemisFair became the embodiment of this fantasy heritage, where the history of South Texas was commodified and repackaged as a cheerful justification for the political dominance of conservative elites.

This study seeks to look beyond this tendentious historical heritage of mythology and Lone Star bluster and examine the real "confluence of civilizations" that created South Texas. It analyzes the development of the system of labor and racial relations that came together in the fields and towns of South Texas from the late nineteenth century to the present, as Mexican and Anglo migrants fashioned an agro-empire out of the scrub and desert. In the past few decades a number of historical studies have directly challenged the traditional depiction of the history of the Texas-Mexico border region, drawing out the myriad problems in the HemisFair version of the past. My reconstruction of this history has attempted to integrate and build on the contributions of these historians. David Montejano, Neil Foley, and Emilio Zamora have written foundational texts on South Texas labor history. Although these authors do not agree on many topics, they have pointed toward the importance of racialization and proletarianization in the development of South Texas since the late nineteenth century.[9] Benjamin Johnson, Andrés Tijerina, and Elliott Young have illuminated the larger trends at work in the region in the late-nineteenth and early twentieth centuries.[10] David Gutiérrez, Kelly Lytle Hernández, Zaragoza Vargas, and Emilio Zamora, among others, have carried the story forward into the mid-twentieth century, focusing especially on the state's growing power and that power's effects on the region.[11] There is also a growing, vibrant historiography dealing with the politics of migration and mobility in the United States. Historians such as Cindy Hahamovitch, Mae Ngai, and Gunther Peck have examined the contingent and contested nature of mobility and its connection to questions of rights and notions of citizenship.[12] This study seeks to integrate these historiographical strands, disentangling the interrelated nature of migration flows, labor conditions, economic growth, and political change. It reveals the ways the Texas-Mexico border region emerged in the early twentieth century from geographic and economic isolation to become a laboratory for economic development and modern labor relations.

The primary focus of this study is South Texas, the region bounded by San Antonio to the north, Del Rio to the northwest, the Gulf Coast north of Corpus Christi to the east, and the Rio Grande to the west and south.[13] It is a vast region (more than 250 miles from its northern edge in San Antonio to its southern tip at Brownsville) but one that has long been drawn together by economic and cultural ties. Trade networks that connected San Antonio and the towns of the Lower Rio Grande Valley to the cities of northern Mexico and the Anglo settlements of East Texas, and the people who powered those networks as teamsters, ranch hands, and laborers, cemented the economic cohesion of South Texas. The area's Mexican-origin majority and deep ties to Mexico, even in a place as far removed from the border as San Antonio, produced a clear cultural cohesion. Local variations obviously exist in such a large area, and the nature of both the culture and the economy have changed since the late nineteenth century when this study begins, but the interconnectedness of the separate parts of the region has always been clear to residents and observers of South Texas.[14]

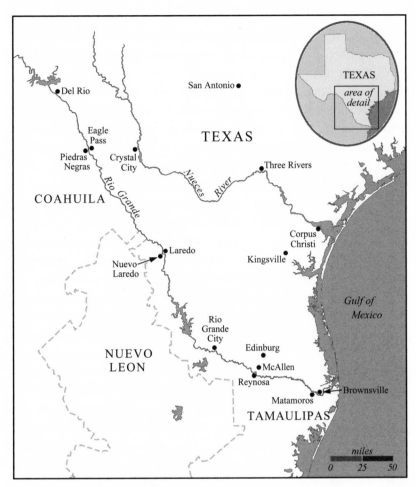

South Texas (Map prepared by Rebecca Wrenn)

The forces that shaped this history, the people who built the region, and the overall geographic scope of this study extend beyond this bounded space, however. Migration was the key to the making of South Texas. Despite its peripheral location and the seemingly unquenchable Texan desire to proclaim Lone Star exceptionalism, economic and social change entered the sprawling region between the Rio Grande and San Antonio from without.[15] Migrants leaving war-torn revolutionary Mexico and emergent capitalists leaving the crowded farming areas of the Midwest and Southeast transformed South Texas agriculture. This was the real "confluence of civilizations" that built South Texas. During the first half of the twentieth century, these migrants helped build a thriving agricultural economy that relied on the introduction of outside capital and the availability of migrant workers coming across the border from Mexico. Yet this was not a confluence based on harmony and equality, the imaginings of HemisFair's organizers notwithstanding. Employed by Anglo farmers, Mexicans and Mexican Americans found themselves relegated to the bottom of this emerging order, welcomed across the international boundary to be exploited for their labor but excluded politically and socially. What emerged was a social, political, and economic arrangement built on a cross-border caste system.

This new society emerged fully formed during the early decades of the twentieth century. Newcomer farm interests, eager to sweep away all vestiges of the ranching society that dominated the region, set about uprooting the older system of politics, landholding, and ethnic accommodation. In its place, they created a strictly segregated world that sought to preclude Mexican American autonomy and entry into the realm of the Anglo political and economic elites. Mexican American citizenship rights became abstractions to be ignored whenever necessary.

Just as important, and certainly related to the calculated disregard of any rights enjoyed by non-Anglos, was the focus of farming interests on maintaining control of mobility within their society. The multifaceted effort to achieve this control proved central to the South Texas model of labor relations. On the one hand, mobile workers built the new farm society. Growers had no interest in recreating the static land tenure patterns of the South, preferring temporary wage labor to sharecropping and tenancy. Workers constantly on the move, both within Texas and entering Texas from Mexico, provided farmers with necessary labor power without the reciprocal bonds that characterized older agricultural labor patterns. On the other hand, growers came to fear the mobility of their labor supply. While they preferred the freedom from responsibility during nonharvest times that came with migrant farmworkers, they worried that workers capable of moving when and where they wanted might abandon the fields of South Texas or use their mobility as a negotiating tool.

This seemingly ambiguous desire for both the mobility and immobility of the workforce shaped much of the South Texas farm society. And in many ways mobility and immobility acted as two sides of the same coin. A mobile farmworker was certainly welcome to farmers at the beginning of harvest season, though they expected this worker to remain for as long as needed and then leave when the work was done.

The politics of mobility in South Texas—determinations of who and what could cross internal and external boundaries, whether legally determined or arbitrarily imposed by force—emerged from the political takeover by farm interests and reflected their desire to shape the society to their needs. Their efforts to control mobility both mirrored and strengthened their construction of this caste-like social system.

South Texas was certainly not alone in creating an exploitative agricultural labor system. There is more than a passing resemblance to practices in other regions. South Texas segregation, for instance, was largely borrowed from the Jim Crow South, along with mechanisms of immobility like pass systems that had long operated in the southern cotton belt. Similarly, South Texas growers were not the first to rely on a mobile labor supply or foreign workers. Both of these practices occurred in California.[16] Texas growers, however, went further in their efforts to immobilize their labor even while the migrant stream that ran through South Texas remained larger than the more self-contained California migrant labor system.[17] When combined in South Texas, however, these practices often associated with the Southeast and Southwest created a potent form of labor relations built on mobile workers stripped of their rights. Unquestioned political control and continued migration from Mexico made these practices possible and helped launch an agricultural boom built on low wages during the 1910s and 1920s. This system became even more important in the following decades as, at every turn, the power of the state fell in behind employers. The exclusion of agricultural workers from labor protective legislation, the politics of immigration restriction that continually weakened the ability of Mexicans and Mexican Americans to claim rights, and the federal government's continued accession to demands for temporary foreign labor all strengthened agricultural employers' grip over their workers.

These developments have also affected the nation as a whole. The lessons learned by the growers of South Texas were not isolated to the border region. Employers elsewhere looked to draw out the labor pool and replicate the labor practices of South Texas. The effects of these practices migrated across the country just as Mexican and Mexican American farmworkers did in the decades after the Mexican Revolution. Rather than a social and political backwater, South Texas became an important model for agricultural interests throughout the nation. The migrant labor stream based in South Texas expanded as Mexicans and Mexican Americans sought better opportunities, which helped recreate the racially segmented workforce on farms far removed from the border. Ethnic Mexicans, regardless of their country of birth, were consistently depicted and treated as an alien presence within the United States that lacked the ability to join the dominant society. Their resulting lack of citizenship rights recommended them to employers across the nation.

The workers who moved through South Texas represented the ideal labor supply for agriculturalists. Highly mobile and available for seasonal employment, they were often stripped of basic rights because of their racially subordinate position and inability to exercise the privileges of citizenship. As such, the importance of the development of a South Texas model of labor relations extended beyond the fields of the Southwest. As the farms of South Texas continued to grow, they relied more and more on labor from Mexico. The growers in the rest of the United States followed suit and increasingly drew their labor from Mexico and other foreign sources as a means to ensure a surplus labor supply and low wages. In the race to the bottom among farming interests, the growers of South Texas led the way. The farm society that developed in South Texas has obviously not been the only example of a low-wage labor system, but one important strand of contemporary low-wage labor relations can be traced back to the practices developed in the fields and towns of South Texas. It is important to remember that this system did not harken back to older forms of labor relations. South Texas growers devised a thoroughly modern set of practices that relied on forced mobility, enforced immobility, and an activist state not present in earlier times. Their modernity, not their backwardness, is what makes these labor practices important.

THE BOOK IS divided into four parts. Part I, "Revolutions," examines the development of South Texas in the late nineteenth and early twentieth centuries. The first chapter, "The Wages of Development in South Texas and Northern Mexico," covers the demographic and economic changes that swept over South Texas and northern Mexico during the Porfiriato and the Mexican Revolution. Growing landlessness and reliance on wage labor created massive demographic upheaval and disturbed previously isolated regions and populations in both countries. These changes came even more rapidly after the outbreak of the Mexican Revolution as millions found themselves displaced by war. North of the Rio Grande, these tensions led to years of chaotic change and omnipresent violence that completely altered the economic and social reality of South Texas. Chapter 2, "The Revolution in Texas: International Migration, Capitalist Agriculture, and the Interstate Migrant Stream," focuses on the birth of commercial agriculture in South Texas during the 1910s and 1920s as improved transportation and irrigation facilities combined with the massive numbers of migrants leaving the violence and disorder of revolutionary Mexico to create an agricultural boom in the previously desolate ranching region.

Part II, "Securing the Revolution," details the ways the growers of South Texas sought to guarantee the continuation of their economic boom by attempting to control the mobility of labor into and out of their region. Chapter 3, "Breaking the Machines, Building the Color Line, and Immobilizing Mobile Labor," examines how the new farm elite sought to mold South Texas to their interests. Newcomer farmers dismantled older political structures and established a strictly segregated social and political environment, culminating in efforts to immobilize the surplus labor pool within South Texas. Through their combined efforts, agricultural and political interests created the South Texas model of labor relations, whereby farming interests guaranteed themselves cheap and plentiful labor through a varied regime of labor controls and a reliance on continuous influxes of workers from Mexico. Chapter 4, "Homing Pigeons, Cheap Labor, and Frustrated Nativists: Immigration Reform and Deportation," focuses on the ways the increased focus on border control and debates over immigration policies helped strengthen this form of labor relations during the 1910s and 1920s, even as farm interests feared that immigration restriction could jeopardize their ability to attract workers from Mexico.

Part III, "Challenging the Revolution," moves the analysis to the crisis years of the 1930s. Chapter 5, "The Politics of Depression," illustrates the conditions of the Great Depression in the region and the failure of local and state governments to deal with the worst consequences of the international economic crisis. Public aid remained almost nonexistent, but when it did come, local and state politicians wielded relief policies as the latest in a long line of laws meant to tilt the power in labor relations further away from workers. Despite the unsteady economic and social situation, however, Mexican and Mexican American workers in South Texas still launched a series of militant struggles to achieve their basic rights, the focus of chapter 6, "Organization and Rebellion."

Finally, part IV, "The Shadow of the Revolution," examines the long-term consequences of the South Texas model of development and labor relations. Chapter 7, "The Bracero Program and the Nationalization of South Texas Labor Relations," argues that the Bracero Program, begun as an international agreement between the United States and Mexico to fill agricultural labor shortages during World War II, served as a way for agricultural interests in the rest of the nation to recreate the labor supply conditions enjoyed by the growers of South Texas. As a result, the Bracero Program mobilized large numbers of foreign workers, stripped of their basic rights of choice and mobility, for use all over the country. The Bracero Program ended in 1964, but its importance and effects have endured. The epilogue examines the continued importance of this form of labor relations in the years since the 1960s, as South Texas has continued to serve as a model for employers elsewhere eager to avail themselves of poorly paid workers who lack the ability to claim the basic rights of citizenship. The lessons learned in the fields of South Texas, in other words, were not only borrowed by agricultural employers but also used as a model and applied to workers far removed from the fields. Industrial and service employers continue to try and emulate the enforced powerlessness of agricultural workers, even if they no longer point to South Texas as their explicit model.

This study examines the history of South Texas that remained unmentioned and intentionally ignored by HemisFair and its promoters. This history provides little justification for triumphalism, but it does illuminate a larger importance for South Texas and the social system that developed there during the first few decades of the twentieth century. By leading the charge toward a modern form of capitalism in which workers could be more easily stripped of their rights of choice and mobility, without the messy entanglements that come with older forms of peonage and bondage, the growers and economic elites of the region helped spread a thoroughly degrading form of economic and social planning that soon bred many imitators and analogs. The path leading from Mexican migrant farmworkers in the early twentieth century to workers in contemporary chicken processing plants or janitors in massive multinational retail corporations is not a straight one, but the similarities between the former and the latter are not accidental.[18] Today, as a result, Texas is everywhere.

PART I | *Revolutions*

In 1907 and 1908 the Laguna region of northern Mexico, straddling the states of Coahuila and Durango, resembled an armed camp. Unemployed workers filled towns such as Torreón and Gómez Palacio, camping in public places and erecting tent settlements on the outskirts. Migrant workers, once lured to the region's towns and farms by advertisements and contractors, were now threatened with arrest if they did not leave the area. Pitched battles between police and gangs of the unemployed—termed bandits by the upper and middle classes—violently punctuated increasingly monotonous stories of crime and general social menace. Reports of endemic banditry in the countryside and organized attacks on haciendas mixed in with this general cacophony of fear. Growers and factory owners armed tenants, overseers, and supervisors against an amorphous threat posed by the rootless population that flowed seasonally through the Laguna. The governor of Coahuila warned local officials throughout his state that an ill-defined but violent disturbance was imminent. Centrifugal forces seemed to tear at the fabric of social and economic life.[1]

Just a few years earlier, however, the Laguna had been the shining example of Mexican economic development and modernization, a booming agricultural, industrial, and mining region built out of the desert. The arrival of two major rail lines in the 1880s, connecting Mexico City to the Texas border, made the Laguna's primary city, Torreón, an important transportation hub. The arrival of the railroads spurred the growth of irrigation, which allowed for cultivation beyond the immediate vicinity of the Nazas River, the Laguna's only source of water.[2] Domestic and foreign capital flooded the region. The production of irrigated cotton and the rubber-bearing shrub guayule grew exponentially and led to the construction of textile mills and rubber-processing plants in Torreón and other towns. Improved transportation facilities allowed mines to ship more raw material than ever, but they also led to the construction of smelters in Torreón to process ore locally. The area of cultivated land quadrupled and cotton output quintupled between 1880 and 1890, then each doubled again from 1890 to 1910. Over the same period, silver, copper, and coal mining witnessed similar growth. By the turn of the century, the Laguna had become "the most highly capitalized and well-communicated area in Mexico."[3]

The wage laborers who came to the Laguna for work in the fields, mines, and factories made this economic growth possible. In the thirty years from 1880 to 1910 the population of the Laguna grew from 20,000 to 200,000, with an additional 40,000 annually living in the region during the harvest season, which lasted from July to October.[4] Those who came to the Laguna during the cotton harvest in 1910 received wages as high as six to eight pesos per day, compared to half a peso per day further south.[5] Decades of land consolidation in central Mexico, which only accelerated during the reign of Porfirio Díaz (1876–1911), created a massive population stripped of connection to the land and forced into wage labor.[6] These systemic changes in the nature of land tenure caused enormous demographic shifts, as many began to leave the crowded central rural regions for cities and the rapidly developing northern states. The steady flow of migrants leaving central Mexico and settling in the north, often as one step in a longer chain of migration, was the most important effect of this economic recentering.

These demographic changes signified a complete overturning of the normal agricultural and labor patterns of Mexico. Migrants to the Laguna came not for free land but for high wages and seasonal employment.[7] The developmental pattern of the Laguna signaled the creation in Mexico of a substantial pool of highly mobile wage laborers, attuned to seasonal labor demands and alienated from the land. By the beginning of the twentieth century, this meant that Laguna employers competed with agricultural, mining, and railroad interests in northern Mexico, Texas, Arizona, New Mexico, California, Colorado, and elsewhere for a growing but increasingly mobile workforce inured to seasonal wage relations.[8] In fact, many growers so feared the increased migration to the United States that they demanded that the Díaz government provide them with Chinese laborers to fill what they believed were imminent holes in the labor force.[9] Laguna growers hired *enganchistas* to scour central and northern Mexico for seasonal labor and passed antienticement laws to keep these same labor contractors from sending workers further north.[10] While this emerging economic system provided employment opportunities for many, the economic modernization of the late nineteenth and early twentieth centuries uprooted the population and propelled people into an unstable environment dependent on the vagaries of the world market economy and the decisions of foreign investors.

The global depression of 1907, which began with the collapse of several New York banks and expanded into a global credit crisis, occurred at the same time as a devastating drought in northern Mexico and the U.S. Southwest.[11] These combined pressures brought economic growth to a screeching halt.[12] The fragile labor peace disappeared with it.[13] Food prices in the Laguna skyrocketed throughout 1907 and 1908, while opportunities for wage labor disappeared. Even worse, the economic downturn led employers in the U.S. Southwest to send their workers back to Mexico, many of them into the worsening situation in the Laguna.[14] Employers in the region performed an about-face. They ignored their previous antienticement pleas and instead, joining with industrial and mining interests, forcibly demanded that migrant workers leave northern Mexico and go to the United States.[15] Thus the workers confronted a drastic reversal of the situation prior to the depression of 1907. They were not wanted by either the United States or the Laguna. As the economic and employment outlooks continued to deteriorate into the summer of 1908, tensions rose.

Reports of a group called the Mexican Cotton Pickers, supposedly militant unemployed workers ready to cross from Texas to Coahuila to begin an uprising, spread throughout the farms and towns of the Laguna in June 1908. While the Mexican Cotton Pickers never materialized, a band of armed men, likely drawn from the plentiful supply of hungry and unemployed that filled the region's towns, did attack the town of Viesca, near Torreón, at dawn on June 25.[16] The previous night rebels had seized the nearby Hacienda Los Hornos and used it as the base for their attack. Police put up little resistance as the armed band took over Viesca, cleaned out the local bank, released all prisoners from the jail, destroyed the *jefe político*'s home, and destroyed telegraph wires and railroad bridges. They maintained control of the town for a day and a half before they left one step ahead of federal troops from Torreón.[17] While this attack had little lasting significance, it served as the most violent proof yet that the social peace of previous decades in the Laguna had disappeared.[18]

The world that the Laguna's economic elites had built on the backs of a mobile labor force seemed to collapse in on them in 1907 and 1908, foreshadowing the implosion of the Porfirian state. More than simply a catalyst for the Mexican Revolution, however, the development and collapse of the Laguna and the Porfirian regime that it came to symbol-ize would have profound importance on both sides of the Rio Grande. As Friedrich Katz has argued, economic and infrastructural develop-ment in the Laguna and the rest of northern Mexico "illustrated in the most palpable way possible that what had once been a frontier was being transformed into 'the border' and what had once been largely beyond the reach of any country was now within the reach of two countries at once."[19] The same was true of the growing, mobile pop-ulation that made up the seasonal workforce of the Laguna. They not only found themselves pushed into annual labor migrations in Mexico and the United States by their alienation from the land and reliance on wage labor, but they also helped drag these previously peripheral regions into the international market and into the orbits of each federal government through their labor power. The paths of capital and devel-opment followed the migrant trail, just as migrant workers followed the paths of economic opportunity. Though the international bound-ary separated northern Mexico and South Texas politically, economic development and modernization in each flowed from the same general forces, as the effects of demographic shifts in Mexico and outside cap-ital drastically altered the border region. These paths for development and migration would only broaden with the outbreak of the Mexican Revolution. At the same time, the tensions created by the collapse of the Porfiriato would not remain bottled up within Mexico.

These workers would help inaugurate two very different revolutions in the coming years. The first, the Mexican Revolution, emerged from their demands for social justice amid the crumbling of the Porfirian regime. The violence and instability of the revolutionary years would send many of these workers, and many other Mexicans, into the United States. These workers then helped launch a second, economic revolu-tion in Texas through their labor power, dragging the desolate lands of South Texas through a rapid transition to a thoroughly modern and profitable, though deeply unjust and exploitative, agricultural econ-omy. The first two chapters—"The Wages of Development in South Texas and Northern Mexico" and "The Revolution in Texas: Interna-tional Migration, Capitalist Agriculture, and the Interstate Migrant Stream"—will explore the development and immediate effects of these two separate but related revolutions.

CHAPTER ONE

The Wages of Development in South Texas and Northern Mexico

The economic and demographic development of South Texas from 1876–1910 resembled Porfirian Mexico to a striking degree. As in Mexico, peace and relative stability in South Texas attracted outside capital in unprecedented amounts. In fact, one of Díaz's priorities on taking control in Mexico was the pacification of the northern border to end the frequent cross-border raids that plagued the region. The year before Díaz launched his Tuxtepec rebellion from Brownsville, Texas, an episode known as the Skinning War broke out in South Texas. In March 1875, a group of thirty armed Mexicans rode through the vicinity of Corpus Christi attacking stores and homes, killing five people in the process. This attack began a series of raids from Mexico, and an even greater number of counterattacks by vigilantes who swept through the Nueces Strip (the area between the Nueces River and the Rio Grande) attacking Mexican ranchers and stealing their land.[1] Díaz put an end to these attacks and counterattacks by cracking down on his side of the border, something military and law enforcement officials north of the border had been unable to do. Cross-border raids would not resume in any substantial way until the early years of the Mexican Revolution, when Díaz's grip on northern Mexico finally collapsed.[2]

Further, the burgeoning market of northern Mexico helped fuel much of the economic change in South Texas. San Antonio and Brownsville had long survived economically as transshipment points for goods (both legal and illegal) moving to and from northern Mexico. For example, in 1850, one-quarter of the labor force of Bexar County (of which San Antonio is the county seat) were *carreteros*, *arrieros*, or some other variety of teamster working in the extensive trade network that extended beyond the border into the interior of Mexico.[3] When Anglo newcomers began to drift into the region from the north in the late nineteenth century, they sought to take control of these important trade links to Mexico and expropriate lands belonging to Mexican Americans in the still underdeveloped region. Economic development in places like the Laguna and Monterey, in other words, was essential to development north of the Rio Grande.

This chapter will examine how these larger trends in Porfirian and revolutionary Mexico affected migration flows and economic modernization in South Texas, laying the groundwork for the creation of one of the most productive and prosperous agricultural regions in the United States. Driven by these events in Mexico and the untapped economic potential of desolate South Texas, two simultaneous migrations met in the region north of the Rio Grande. Land speculators and prospective farmers from the Southeast and Midwest United States arrived at the same time as migrants, exiles, and refugees from Mexico and in a few years completely altered the region's economic and social structure. These two simultaneous migrations not only recreated and expanded the scale of economic expansion previously seen in the Laguna but also pushed South Texas through years of intense change and near apocalyptic violence, creating a new society that would have been unthinkable just a few years earlier.

THE FIRST RAIL connection to South Texas was completed by the Southern Pacific at San Antonio in 1877, though this only served the far northern portion of the region. Although it eliminated the need for long trail drives to the Midwest for ranchers looking to send their livestock to market, it remained too distant to catalyze agricultural growth in the Rio Grande Valley. Nevertheless, the arrival of the railroad in San Antonio, and its spread through the rest of South Texas over the coming decades, resulted in widespread dispossession of landholders in the region.

This dispossession was uneven, occurring at different times in different parts of South Texas, but some aspects of the process remained constant regardless of when or where land transfers took place. A combination of economic pressure and physical compulsion, the invisible hand aided by the trigger finger, forced many off their land in ways that make differentiating legal and illegal methods almost impossible.[4] Threats of violence, armed confiscation, cold-blooded murder, and fraud coexisted and often intertwined with market pressures to gradually displace Mexican and Mexican American landowners in the region. The increased capitalization that came with the railroads, at the same time that the U.S. economy entered the tumultuous boom-and-bust cycle of the late nineteenth century, meant that poorly capitalized Mexican American landowners had to secure credit in order to keep their land. Many could not find banks willing to extend them credit, leading to sheriff's sales through county courts. These sales almost always resulted in the transfer of lands to Anglos.[5]

Newly arrived lawyers greased the skids for these changes. They descended on South Texas in the aftermath of annexation and the Mexican War, but they did not become central actors in the region's history until the Porfirian period brought a measure of stability to the border. The growth of the northern Mexican market attracted investors to South Texas from the East Coast and Europe (primarily Britain). Lawyers well-versed in Spanish, Mexican, and U.S. land laws became, according to David Montejano, "critical intermediaries between the land-based Mexican elite and the capital-based Anglo merchants."[6] The most successful of these lawyers worked both sides of the conflict, "defending the land rights of certain Mexican families" while "persuading others that they never really owned the land."[7] Not surprisingly, these land lawyers also became central figures in the political machines that came to dominate the region. In essence, then, those who had access to credit and the best lawyers were the ones who kept their land during these years.

The timing of the dispossession of Mexicans and Mexican Americans in different areas of South Texas can also be traced by the gradual expansion of the rail network into the rest of South Texas after 1877. From San Antonio, the Southern Pacific expanded to the border at Eagle Pass in 1878 (which then ran to the Laguna), while the International and Great Northern arrived in Laredo in 1883. At the same time, ranching impresarios Richard King and Mifflin Kenedy combined with Corpus Christi merchant Uriah Lott to build a railroad from Corpus Christi to Laredo that was completed in 1881. These rail links had a number of important effects. First, they brought wide swaths of South Texas closer to rail heads and therefore led to a new wave of land transfers as Anglo ranchers pressured their Mexican and Mexican American neighbors off of their lands. Second, and most important, by building the line between Corpus Christi and Laredo, the Lower Rio Grande Valley entered a period of isolation when Brownsville lost its status as the primary commercial center on the Texas-Mexico border. These effects were not accidental but instead were planned by the primary financiers of the Corpus Christi–Laredo railroad as a way to destroy the power of the Brownsville merchants, whose control of the border trade depended on a vast network of riverboats and wagons that reached deep into Mexico.[8]

The political structures that grew in South Texas in these years were both products of this gradual dispossession and bulwarks that blunted the worst features of land transfers. Political machines developed throughout South Texas based on a *patrón-peón* bond between the Anglo political bosses and the majority ethnic Mexican population. Thus, these machines maintained power, like the system of *jefaturas políticas* in Porfirian Mexico, through an uneasy system of overlapping mechanisms of coercion and accommodation.[9] This "peace structure," as David Montejano has described it, worked best in the more isolated portions of South Texas.[10] The entry of railroads, however, drained the strength of the machines, allowing traditional machine politicians to maintain their control only in areas that lacked rail linkages at the turn of the twentieth century, like Cameron, Hidalgo, Starr, and Duval counties. Thus, the border political machines were important aspects of the history of South Texas, but they had largely disappeared by 1920.

The best example of a South Texas political boss was Cameron County's James Wells, who parleyed his land law practice into a dominant position in the county's Democratic Party. By 1910 Wells's authority stretched into neighboring counties, where proxy machines practiced what historian Evan Anders has called "the peculiar brand of South Texas politics that combined graft, voter manipulation, and armed confrontation."[11] Fraudulent poll tax payments, payoffs, and intimidation of political opposition marked each election cycle as the machine balanced the need to woo Mexican American voters against the fear of Mexican and Mexican American numerical superiority in South Texas. When the *tamalada* (in South Texas the term meant not only preparation of tamales but also political officials' attempts to influence voters with food and alcohol) was not enough to maintain power, the machine turned to the Texas Rangers. As Evan Anders has argued, machine politicians were well aware of the tenuous nature of their control: "The past outbreaks of racial strife revealed the dangers of taking Mexican American subservience for granted, and the more perceptive politicians and ranchers understood the need to satisfy the popular expectations of paternalistic support and protection. Even as followers, the Hispanic majority strongly influenced the pattern of racial conduct."[12]

With the arrival of the railroad, however, the paternalistic politics of the late nineteenth century gave way to the appeals to white supremacy of the twentieth century.

The replacement of a ranching society by one based on farming had a number of inevitable consequences. The political economy of the two systems dictates very different forms of land and labor use. Ranching is a labor- and land-extensive undertaking that thrives in isolated, under-capitalized, underpopulated regions. Farming, in contrast, is labor- and land-intensive; it therefore sharply increases the value of land and requires the existence of a much larger labor pool than a ranch would. Market agriculture also requires a much more developed infrastructure, including irrigation works and railroad links, which necessitates the influx of outside capital. The rising land values that accompany any shift from ranching to farming often force the less-efficient, less-capitalized livestock operations (especially ranches owned by small producers) out of a transitioning region. These economic and demographic changes also have political consequences, as the previous political systems built on isolation, such as the political machines that dominated South Texas in the late nineteenth century, confront the changing reality of a new mode of ordering local societies. More than just a shift from one economic activity to another, in other words, the evolution of South Texas from a ranching society to a farming society altered almost every aspect of life in the region.

Stepping back and examining these changes, it is clear that the same mechanisms that created such momentous change throughout Mexico also catalyzed change in South Texas, with increased capitalization bringing political and economic modernization and the potential for instability and violence. As these larger structural changes occurred south of the border, land consolidation impelled migration among the rural population, pushing them out of central Mexico and toward the Texas-Mexico border. Once the railroads reached the border from Mexico they met up with the lines that stretched into the interior of the United States, as northward and southward waves of economic modernization came together along the Texas-Mexico border.

As a result, South Texas in the years after 1900 found itself in a situation similar to that of the Laguna twenty years earlier. The infrastructure of economic modernization had arrived, and with it floods of outside capital, but the region remained sparsely settled. As had occurred in Mexico, much of the rural population had been driven off their land by these changes, creating the beginnings of an agricultural labor force. Yet South Texas found itself at a crossroads. It possessed the transportation facilities and the capital to create a rich agricultural region but lacked sufficient labor. Meanwhile, skyrocketing land values triggered by this unrealized potential made traditional cattle ranching less economically viable.

The solution to these problems for the would-be planter elite of South Texas came with the collapse of the Díaz regime in 1910. Widespread violence would replace the enforced quiet of the Porfiriato and trigger a demographic shift more momentous than the gradual northward population drift of the previous three decades. The Mexican Revolution, in other words, would change the trajectory of both nations.

IN MAY 1911 disorder again descended on Torreón. Shortly after Francisco Madero, scion of the wealthiest family in the Laguna, declared from exile in San Antonio that his rebellion against Porfirio Díaz would begin November 20, 1910, armed bands appeared throughout northern Mexico. The so-called Maderista Revolution quickly spiraled out of the control of Madero and his mostly urban supporters. By April 1911 rebel bands had overrun the Laguna, with federal troops controlling only Torreón. Then on May 15, with no warning, the federal commander at Torreón retreated from the city under the cover of dark before revolutionary forces had a chance to attack. Just five days earlier the federal garrison at Ciudad Juárez had surrendered to revolutionary forces. These twin victories at two of the most important transportation centers in northern Mexico spelled the effective end of the Díaz regime. The dictator officially stepped down on May 25, 1911, but the Revolution had just begun.

Over the next decade, Mexico endured a constantly shifting civil war that saw massive conventional armies crisscrossing the nation in the midst of continual guerrilla fighting (as well as two separate invasions by the U.S. military). The early internecine warfare during Madero's presidency gave way to the united Constitutionalist effort against Victoriano Huerta after Madero's assassination. Huerta's defeat fractured the Constitutionalist alliance and led to the fiercest and most destructive fighting of the Revolution between the Conventionists (a loose alliance of the northern forces of Pancho Villa and the southern forces of Emiliano Zapata) and the reconstituted

Constitutionalists (under the leadership of Venustiano Carranza and Alvaro Obregón). By 1917 the Constitutionalists had isolated the armies of Villa and Zapata in their respective northern and southern bases and installed Carranza in a position of national dominance that he would maintain until his assassination in 1920, when Obregón assumed the presidency. Regardless, much of Mexico faced continued violence, often unattached or only nominally attached to the factional squabbles apparent on the national level, that was every bit as disruptive as the more traditional military campaigns of previous years. This general pattern would continue, in fact, into the late 1920s, as localized violence (or in the case of the Cristero Rebellion,[13] a full-scale regional rebellion) continued to plague much of the nation as the central government struggled to create a stable national state.[14]

The state of Chihuahua provided the best example of this continued instability as it endured almost constant upheaval throughout the 1920s. First, the specter of Villa continued to haunt the state, even after he laid down his arms after coming to terms with Obregón in 1920. After Villa's assassination in 1923, the remnants of the Villista military force maintained the capacity to wage guerrilla war in the rugged mountains of northern Mexico. In addition, hardly a year passed without some major uprising. In 1921 the state militia crushed a revolt by hundreds of indigenous villagers in southwestern Chihuahua. A number of rebel bands operated throughout the state in 1922, though they were eventually dispersed by federal troops. In December 1923 one of the largest rebellions of the 1920s began when Adolfo de la Huerta, who had been interim president after Carranza's overthrow in 1920, declared his opposition to Obregón and rallied much of the military to his side. Delahuertista forces continued fighting in Chihuahua through much of 1924. Nicolas Hernández, a leader of the Delahuertista rebellion, declared his own rebellion in mid-1925 and continued guerrilla operations until 1927. A coup against the state governor in 1927 led to another guerrilla outbreak that lasted until 1928. In addition, banditry remained endemic throughout the decade, sometimes melting into the organized violence of the other uprisings.[15] Thus, as Mark Wasserman has argued, "all Chihuahua earned for a decade of civil war was another decade of chaos."[16]

This continued violence forced more than a million Mexicans to migrate to the United States during the 1910s and 1920s. These exiles left behind the continued disorder and potential danger of the revolutionary process for a number of different reasons, though most embarked on their journey north of the border believing that their exile was temporary.

Politics and factionalism helped create a large body of emigrants. Former Porfiristas, Huertistas, and any number of other out-groups left for the United States throughout the 1910s and 1920s. San Antonio became the unofficial capital of exiled Mexico, though elite exile communities also developed in Los Angeles, El Paso, and New Orleans. Many of these émigrés hoped to eventually return to their homeland, but they remained on the sidelines while the Revolution continued. A noisy minority of the exiles sought to reenter the fray, hoping to retrace the steps of both Díaz and Madero in conquering Mexico from across the Rio Grande.

Another factor that fueled emigration was the threat of impressment into one of the countless armed groups that circulated throughout the country. Victoriano Huerta became notorious for his indiscriminate use of the *leva* to fill his Federal Army, but all military forces used the tactic at some point during the Revolution. Pablo Mares, a miner from a village near the western city of Guadalajara, Jalisco, "had to come to the United States, because it was impossible to live down there with so many revolutions. Once even I was at the point of being killed by some revolutionists. . . . The Villistas pressed me into service then, and took me with them as a soldier. But I didn't like that, because I never liked to go about fighting, especially about things that don't make any difference to one. So when we got to Torreón I ran away just as soon as I could. That was about 1915. . . . I went from there to Ciudad Juárez and from there to El Paso. There I put myself under contract to go work on the tracks."[17] For those who chose not to fight, then, exile often seemed the safest option.

Beyond direct threats to life and limb occasioned by military violence, the Revolution demolished the Mexican economy, leading many to emigrate to avoid starvation. Porfirian economic growth depended on the modern transportation and communication network. When this economic infrastructure collapsed under the pressure of years of civil war, the result was hyperinflation, decreased agricultural and industrial production, disrupted trade networks, and catastrophic food shortages. At the core of these problems was the deterioration of the national railroad network, which remained the linchpin of the Mexican economic system. Lack of investment capital in the disordered nation precluded any large-scale rebuilding efforts, but direct physical damage wrought the most devastation. The professional militaries ripped up tracks across the nation, especially in the North, to cut the supply lines of opposing armies. The Villista forces became notorious for their use of *máquinas locas*, train engines packed with explosives that would be sent careening toward opposing troop and supply trains.[18] Guerrilla forces often targeted tracks, bridges, and other railroad facilities, and would continue to do so well into the 1920s.[19] With Mexico's transportation network thus disrupted for years, mining and agricultural enterprises, where such activities were still possible in spite of the violence, had difficulty reaching secondary processing facilities in urban areas, which then had trouble finding access to international markets as rail lines to Veracruz, Tampico, and the U.S.-Mexico border had been reduced to scrap metal.

The consequences of this deterioration of primary production, processing, and trade were dire. The peso declined against the dollar, first slowly, then rapidly beginning in 1913. In January 1913 the peso was worth 49.5 cents (U.S.). It dropped to 7 cents by January 1915, stood at 2 cents in May 1916, and continued to drop.[20] Carranza and Villa only exacerbated these problems by printing massive amounts of paper money that continued to deteriorate in value from the moment the bills were printed.[21] Capital circulation collapsed, and much of the nation reverted to a barter economy wherever foreign currency was not available. In the North, dollars became the primary legal tender, though access to dollars was limited by the hyperinflation that made pesos almost worthless in relation to the dollar. These problems combined with the transportation situation to create a chronic shortage of circulating capital that rapidly became a crisis of subsistence for much of the nation.[22]

Disease also ravaged Mexico's population during the Revolution and its aftermath. Typhus, which often follows in the wake of war, devastated much of the nation, reaching its high point in 1916 and 1917. When that epidemic subsided, it was replaced in 1918 by the worldwide influenza pandemic, which hit northern Mexico's war-weary population especially hard.

Thus, there were many pressing reasons why the Revolution created large emigration waves during the 1910s and 1920s, even if some historians have ignored these factors.[23] Violence, economic collapse, food shortages, disease, and any number of other factors helped create a massive body of exiles and refugees, some of whom had previously been driven out of the central plateau by the changes wrought by Porfirian modernization, who moved across the largely unguarded border into the United States.[24] As scholar and activist Ernesto Galarza wrote in describing his own emigration away from the upheaval of the Revolution, "What brought me and my family to the United States from Mexico also brought hundreds of thousands of others like us."[25]

FOR THE FIRST two decades of the twentieth century migration across the U.S.-Mexico border was largely unregulated. Customs and immigration officials staffed "ports of entry" along the international boundary, but they were neither equipped nor trained to deal with immigrants who crossed into the United States at any point other than designated entry zones. The scant immigration legislation on the books in the early twentieth century was written with seaports in mind and limited only certain types of immigrants. Restrictions targeted the diseased, prostitutes, anarchists, those likely to become public charges, contract laborers, and Asians as threats to the general welfare.

Immigration officials largely ignored the entry of Mexicans into the United States for the first fifteen years of the century. An Immigration Service report from these years stated that "the policing of 2,000 miles of border line is practically impossible."[26] The problem for the Immigration Service was not immigrants from Mexico but instead "aliens who arrive in Mexico" who "do not enter that Republic with the intention of remaining permanently. The bulk of them are contract laborers, but whether they come under contract or not, they proceed to Mexico with the idea that they can reach the United States easier and escape the prescribed examination by simply evading the regular points of crossing, and entering surreptitiously."[27] Particularly distressing for immigration officials was the attempted entry of Japanese and Chinese workers via Mexico, though immigrants from Europe and the Middle East were also targeted as frequent violators of U.S. immigration law.[28]

In 1908 Secretary of Labor and Commerce Oscar Strauss (whose department then housed the Immigration Service) wrote to Secretary of State Elihu Root that "little if any difficulty is experienced in dealing with citizens of Mexico; the difficulties encountered relate almost wholly to foreigners of other nationalities."[29] Immigration officials' only concerns over Mexican immigration regarded those who came to the

United States on labor contracts, in violation of the 1885 Foran Act, which prohibited such arrangements between U.S. employers and foreign workers.[30]

Before the most violent phases of the Revolution, in other words, the Immigration Service viewed immigration from Mexico as expected and nonthreatening. Indeed, the commissioner-general of immigration wrote in 1913 that "Mexico is a natural supply of labor for the Southwest, and therefore the movement of laborers across the border is for the most part a natural one. Such laborers have been passing back and forth over the border for years, and in the great majority of cases the only apparent inducement to migrate is a knowledge that work at better wages than prevail in Mexico can be found here. Such immigration, of course, is not in violation of law."[31]

Still, refugees who reached the U.S.-Mexico border during the early years of the Revolution were hardly welcomed into the United States with open arms. The well-dressed walked across the border with little problem, but many who tried to cross at the designated border crossing stations, such as Brownsville and Laredo, often met with opposition from immigration agents and other officials in the United States who sought to limit the refugee flow. The immigration inspector at Laredo described the Revolution's effects on the type of immigrant who entered the United States:

> Before the revolution began and for some time after, we had each
> day from two to four Pullmans, most well filled; three to five
> first-class coaches and two to four second-class coaches. First
> the Pullman class disappeared, then the first-class traveler, until
> now we have only the second-class arrival; and even this class
> has deteriorated. In normal times we had many of the laboring
> class who were in the prime of life and fine specimens of physical
> manhood. This class has almost entirely disappeared, and only
> the ordinary laborer and a few women and children are now
> coming.[32]

An incident from October 1913 provides a good example of how U.S. border officials reacted to the growing number of Mexican immigrants. On October 1 and 2, thousands of refugees crossed from Piedras Negras to Eagle Pass, Texas, as the Constitutionalists seized the town from the Federals. Almost all returned south of the Rio Grande by October 5, but that night word spread that the Federals planned to retake the town. The next morning, October 6, the county commissioners in Eagle Pass declared a quarantine against Piedras Negras in an effort to keep the new influx of refugees from entering Eagle Pass. Since most of the population of Piedras Negras attempted to cross via the international bridge, the quarantine created a combustible situation where thousands of refugees crowded on the bridge, creating the very real possibility of trampling deaths. The Immigration Service inspector for Eagle Pass brought these concerns to the county commissioners, but they refused to allow refugees into Eagle Pass. The Immigration Service was then forced to provide temporary refuge outside of the city limits, and at 1:00 P.M. "such of the aliens as were admissible were permitted to enter during the afternoon, but the crowd, instead of lessening, seemed to steadily increase."[33] The crowds continued to congregate on the bridge for the next twenty-four hours, with the Immigration Service estimating that 8,000 crossed the bridge on the second day alone. When the Federals entered Piedras Negras that afternoon, the refugee waves ended as the troops stopped all traffic over the bridge.

On the next day, however, the Immigration Service decided that "if the aliens in detention were fed they would continue on our hand indefinitely. Therefore, it was decided to discontinue feeding them."[34] Since many of these refugees were Constitutionalists, they knew that return to Piedras Negras could be deadly, but officials in Eagle Pass were intent on sending the refugees back as soon as possible. Immigration inspectors "found that a considerable number belonged to the excluded classes," essentially those who immigration inspectors believed might become public charges in the United States, often based only on appearance. "Up to that time, very few had signified a willingness to return to their homes and, realizing that some immediate and positive action was necessary, it was decided to take a number, at least, of the excludable aliens out of camp and return them to Piedras Negras."[35] Over the next two weeks hundreds of refugees were sent back as excludable aliens. Some were given temporary admission, but not before undergoing a physical examination, a series of vaccinations, and fumigation of all belongings. The Immigration Service supervising inspector ended his report on this incident by stating that, while cooperation from officials in Eagle Pass would have alleviated some of the strains of the refugee situation, immigration officials should proceed along these same lines in future incidents, allowing refugees into the United States when necessary but maintaining a strict prohibition against the excludable classes that would force many of these migrants back to the revolutionary violence of their home country.[36]

Clearly, while no coherent legislation yet limited who could enter, the "likely to become a public charge" prohibition became a simple way for immigration officials to limit the number of entrants during the Revolution. While nothing like the Chinese Exclusion Act existed to keep Mexicans from entering the United States, the class and racial assumptions held by immigration officials and Anglos in the United States meant that a loosely enforced exclusionary spirit animated contact between border guards and Mexican immigrants. Thus, the years of the Revolution marked the beginning of a more conscious, if still largely unofficial, policy of limiting who could and should enter the United States from Mexico.[37]

THE WORLD THAT these immigrants walked into when they crossed the border, with or without authorization, was a rapidly changing one; here the railroads extended during the Porfirian years were creating an entirely new social and economic system. The one exception was the Lower Rio Grande Valley, which remained isolated from these changes for two decades, as the rail link from Corpus Christi to Laredo bypassed Brownsville and left Cameron and Hidalgo counties largely unchanged. When a railroad finally reached Brownsville in 1904, it brought profound consequences for the Lower Valley and all of South Texas.

All of the complications of increased capitalization that had occurred in the rest of South Texas during the last two decades of the nineteenth century now occurred rapidly in the deep South Texas counties of Cameron and Hidalgo, turning them seemingly overnight from sparsely settled, arid ranching lands into prime farm properties. The combination of the two-decade reprieve that the Lower Valley enjoyed while the rest of the region dealt with issues of displacement and landlessness, and the rapidity of these changes in the years after 1904, led to both a boom economy and a far more intense form of social tension that fell especially hard on the remaining Mexican American landowners.

One of the most important consequences of the railroads' arrival for this region was the impetus it gave to the development of irrigation works. Before 1904, some had tried to harness the Rio Grande as an irrigation source, but the region's geography did not allow for gravity irrigation and instead required expensive pumps and lifts to utilize the streamflow. Since the river often changed its channel and was prone to flooding, installing irrigation equipment without a reliable trade link to the U.S. market made little economic sense. Only with the construction of the St. Louis, Brownsville, and Mexico Railway did the possible profit begin to outweigh the risk. With the introduction of large-scale irrigation the Lower Rio Grande Valley made a rapid, chaotic transition from ranching to farming.

Large-scale irrigation only amplified the problems introduced by the railroad, though it also introduced a new series of issues that would have equally profound effects on both sides of the Rio Grande. As landowners and prospective farmers rushed to draw water from the river that connected South Texas to northern Mexico, they used up almost all of its dependable streamflow.[38] The timing of these developments was essential, because the fighting in Mexico meant that no central authority existed to deal with issues like water rights. According to the ill-defined international law on the subject, Mexico should have had the right to half the streamflow, but with no leverage during the development of these irrigation works, and with the U.S. government eventually declaring that "prior rights" of irrigators in Texas trumped all other concerns, the violations continued.[39] Thus, by 1920 the pattern was set, and most of the dependable streamflow of the Rio Grande was diverted into the fields of South Texas, helping to turn it into one of the most fertile agricultural areas in the nation. The adjacent state of Tamaulipas, which had the potential for similar development, had no means to secure irrigation water. The land under irrigation in South Texas increased from 54,000 acres in 1909 to 228,000 acres in 1919. In Tamaulipas 2,000 acres were under irrigation in 1910, which only increased to 20,000 acres by 1930.[40] Thus, as James Sandos has argued, "Mexico unwillingly paid with water" for the development of large-scale agriculture in the Lower Rio Grande Valley.[41]

With market access and a reliable water supply, the shift from ranching to farming in the Lower Valley began in earnest. Increased land values led to increased tax valuations, which meant that many ranchers had to sell their unimproved lands. Pasture land in the late nineteenth century cost between fifty cents and two dollars an acre. By the 1910s, unimproved land cost as much as $300 an acre, while land close to existing irrigation facilities sold for as much as $500 an acre.[42] For some, these land sales led to a profitable retirement. For others, the farm boom offered an opportunity to leave the sagging livestock market. For many ranchers, however, mounting debt and the loss of their land promised nothing more than economic uncertainty and a possible slide into wage labor. As in the late nineteenth century, these changes were especially damaging for Mexican American rancheros faced with a potent combination of market pressure and violence.

At the same time that these economic changes occurred in the Lower Rio Grande Valley, all of South Texas struggled to deal with the implications of the Revolution occurring just across the border. Throughout the 1910s and 1920s San Antonio served as the capital of exiled Mexico where "frustrated *políticos*, defeated generals and dispossessed landlords met, conspired, hoped and dreamed, churning out protests, plans and polemics, all under the watchful eye of Mexican and American intelligence."[43] Madero was just the first in a long line of exiled leaders to organize an opposition movement in the United States before returning to Mexico at the head of an armed force. Bernardo Reyes spoke openly in 1911 of organizing in San Antonio so that he could return to Mexico and overthrow Madero, and his organizing efforts were aided by politicians and power brokers in South Texas.[44] The adjutant general of Texas even complained that "federal, county, and city authorities seemed to be sympathetic to the Reyes movement, or at least apathetic."[45] Even more brazen, and even less successful, was the plot hatched by Victoriano Huerta and Pascual Orozco in 1915. The two plotted loudly in the El Paso area, and the press covered Orozco's travels to San Antonio and New Orleans to gather support, funds, and arms. Before they could launch their invasion during the summer of 1915, however, Huerta and many of his coconspirators were arrested by federal agents. Orozco managed to escape and remained at large for two months. In August, however, he was ambushed and killed by Texas Rangers. Huerta died in a Texas prison in January 1916. No major conspiracies came from South Texas after the deaths of Orozco and Huerta, but exile activity continued well beyond 1915.[46]

These conspiracies and plots did not go unnoticed in South Texas, adding to an atmosphere of concern and fear, especially among the Anglo minority. Uncertainty over what was happening in Mexico, who the refugees were, and whether the revolutionary violence would spread into Texas complicated already tense relations.[47] Indeed, throughout the early years of the Revolution small cross-border raids entered South Texas to seize supplies, arms, livestock, and any number of other goods in short supply in northern Mexico. President William Howard Taft responded in 1911 with a massive military buildup, creating the Maneuver Division, which brought one-fourth of the active-duty U.S. military to the Texas-Mexico border. The official explanation for this troop movement was to aid in the enforcement of neutrality laws, but it also appears to have been the first step toward possible U.S. intervention in Mexican affairs.[48] The buildup peaked in 1916, when the majority of the regular army and all of the National Guard were stationed in northern Mexico or along the border.[49]

Despite the federal mobilization, state and local officials in Texas sought increased defensive capacities while criticizing what they characterized as federal inaction.[50] Governor Oscar Colquitt was especially vocal in his criticism of the Taft administration, claiming that the federal government did nothing to protect U.S. citizens on either side of the Rio Grande. Colquitt claimed that "scores of women have been outraged by Mexicans," and that only by forcefully threatening the Mexican factions could the safety of U.S. citizens on either side of the border be guaranteed.[51] Reaction to Colquitt's statements varied. The *Chicago Record-Herald* denigrated the governor's efforts as "gassy patriotism," while the *Dallas News* attacked Colquitt's selective outrage: "The criminal record of Mexico moves him into insulting the President because he will not urge war to redress fewer outrages than are committed by Texans against Texans under the complacent eye of its Governor."[52] Colquitt also had his defenders, however, such as the *New Orleans Times-Democrat*, which applauded his declaration that "in the event Mexicans start any trouble we will protect our citizens and not wait for Washington to act."[53] Likewise, the *Houston Post* claimed that the "Texas Revolution had for its cause no greater outrages" than the supposed violence against U.S. citizens by Mexicans on both sides of the border, continuing the unfortunate Texan habit of relating everything back to the Alamo.[54]

The saber-rattling by Colquitt and others both reflected and influenced the increasingly tense relations between Anglos and Mexicans throughout South Texas. Politicians and officials were inundated with pleas for help from frightened landowners as rumors of conspiracies among Mexicans and Mexican Americans spread throughout the region. In June 1911 Ranger Captain John R. Hughes reported that "during the course of the revolution in Mexico we had more calls for assistance than we were able to answer. Lawless characters, both Americans and

Mexicans, took advantage of the unsettled conditions along the border to steal a great many horses and cattle, and commit other depredations, such as robbing small stores, remote from the railway and having no telephone or telegraph connections."[55] In reaction to these cross-border raids, Anglos clamored for protection, often demanding that the state protect their towns or property with a detachment of Texas Rangers.[56] The Rangers, founded as a frontier defense force in the mid-nineteenth century, acted in the early twentieth century as a highly politicized military force charged with eliminating any sign of political or social dissent.[57] And it was a military solution that many in South Texas sought as the specter of violence grew in the first years of the Revolution.

T. W. Dee, whose letterhead identified him as the "District Deputy Supreme Dictator for South Texas of the Loyal Order of the Moose," claimed that all Mexicans in the Kingsville area "spend every cent they can get buying up cartridges and storing them away. If they cannot buy a whole box, they buy a half box."[58] Another Anglo claimed that Mexicans "are holding meetings regularly, going, or on the move night and day and nearly all carrying guns." Because of these activities, "our people must be protected. Our women are very much troubled."[59] Likewise, the district attorney for San Antonio, W. C. Linden, warned that, "while I am not an alarmist in any sense of the word, there are too many evidences of a deep-seated intention of a large and powerful organization, composed largely of the criminal classes, who openly say that they hurl defiance at all law and at all authority, to do some atrocious and lawless act in connection with this matter."[60] Similarly, Dudley Lansing, a Texas National Guard officer in San Antonio, reported that "there were in this city, several thousand armed Mexicans, under an acknowledged leader, who were ready to fire the oil tanks east of the city, so as to attract police and fire protection, when they intended to raid the hardware stores."[61] There were also related stories of the anarchist International Workers of the World rallying and organizing Mexicans in the Crystal City area, adding to the fears that some sort of outside agitation would lead to violence in South Texas.[62] Whether these stories were fabricated became immaterial as centrifugal forces threatened to pull apart the fragile social institutions that had only partially preserved peace.

By 1915 South Texas thus had all of the prerequisites for the outbreak of widespread violence. The two-headed monster of racial animosity and the workings of the market drove economic and political changes that threatened to strip autonomy from the Mexican and Mexican

American majority. The Mexican Revolution then pushed hundreds of thousands of refugees into South Texas. Among these refugees were revolutionaries, political exiles, spies, arms dealers, and others who heightened the region's already tense atmosphere. Finally, the feeling of many Anglos that Mexicans were willing and able to become a fifth column within the United States added an ugly, conspiratorial edge.

WHEN BASILIO RAMOS walked from Matamoros, Tamaulipas, to Brownsville, Texas, in January 1915, he brought the spark that would ignite this powder keg and start an all-out race war.[63] Ramos had grown up in Nuevo Laredo but had lived a number of years in the United States, graduating from high school in Norman, Oklahoma.[64] He had been a secretary at the customhouse in Nuevo Laredo from 1910 to 1914, but the Constitutionalists arrested and imprisoned him when they captured the state of Tamaulipas from the Huertistas. Upon his release, Ramos went to San Diego, Texas, and remained there until December 1914, when he returned to Mexico despite his Huertista ties. Not surprisingly, the Constitutionalists arrested him again. Into the prison where he was held in Monterrey, someone smuggled a document known as the Plan de San Diego, which Ramos and some of his associates signed. The person who smuggled the document into the prison remains unknown, as does the plan's author, but the document called for an uprising to begin on February 20, 1915, at two o'clock in the morning. Its goal was to achieve the "independence and segregation of the States bordering on the Mexican nation, which are: Texas, New Mexico, Arizona, Colorado, and Upper California, of which States the Republic of Mexico was robbed in a most perfidious manner by North American imperialism." The "Liberating Army for Races and Peoples" would welcome those who belonged "to the Latin, the Negro, or the Japanese race," and would execute all Anglos over the age of sixteen. In addition to breaking off the five southwestern states, the plan also called for the seizure of six neighboring states to serve as a homeland for African Americans.[65] The conspiracy would begin in South Texas.

The Constitutionalists released Ramos from prison in January, and he left for Texas to spread word of the uprising and form local juntas. He carried with him a copy of the Plan de San Diego, letters of introduction to individuals believed to be sympathetic to the plan in a number of South Texas towns, and a pass of safe conduct through the Constitutionalist lines signed by General Emiliano Nafarrate,

Carranza's commander along the Texas-Tamaulipas frontier.[66] Ramos went west to McAllen to try and enlist Dr. Andrés Villarreal in the plan, but Villarreal immediately informed local authorities, who arrested Ramos and discovered the papers he carried with him.[67]

Ramos's arrest gave Texas authorities their first knowledge of the Plan de San Diego, which many Anglos viewed as proof that Mexicans formed a dangerous element within their nascent farming empire that needed to be controlled by any means possible. Anxiety intensified with South Texans' worst fears now confirmed. In the context of World War I, moreover, fears of German intrigues within the United States became entangled in rumors of Mexican conspiracies.[68] When the date of the proposed uprising came and went without violence, however, tensions abated and talk of the plan changed from terror to mockery.[69] When Ramos stood trial in May on charges of sedition at the Brownsville federal court, the judge ridiculed the prospects of such an uprising and declared that the defendant "ought to be tried for lunacy, not [for] conspiring against the United States."[70] Ramos posted bail, went back to Mexico, and disappeared from the historical record.

The fragile peace continued until July 4, 1915, when the Border War began in earnest.[71] On that day, a band of approximately forty armed, mounted Mexicans raided Los Indios Ranch in Cameron County, beginning two weeks of periodic attacks by this single group of raiders. The first confirmed death occurred on July 9, when a foreman of the Norias Division of the King Ranch killed one raider.[72] Three days later, two Mexican American police officers were shot at a dance near Brownsville: one was killed and the other badly wounded. Federal investigators argued that "the Mexican officers knew of the plans of their fellows before the real beginning of the operations and that this was the cause of the several efforts to assassinate them."[73] Over the next two weeks, reports of attacks on police officers, raids on ranches and stores, and attempted assassinations of landowners cropped up every few days throughout Cameron and Hidalgo counties.

The raids entered a more daring phase toward the end of July, and they inspired a more thorough and random counterattack from law enforcement and vigilantes.[74] On July 25 a band of mounted raiders burned a bridge of the St. Louis, Brownsville, and Mexico Railway and cut telegraph wires near Harlingen. The raiders not only sought to isolate the Lower Valley by cutting its transportation and communication links to the rest of the state, but they also attacked a clear symbol of the new order that came to South Texas with the entry of the railroad. A few days earlier, Governor Ferguson sent Ranger Harry Ransom to the Lower Valley to lead a pacification campaign. Ransom was in his third tour of duty with the Rangers (the first two in 1905 and 1909), but he rejoined the force after stints as a guard on a state prison farm and chief of police of Houston.[75] He left his position in Houston after killing a defense attorney. Ferguson hired him after he successfully appealed his conviction in the murder case. Ransom stocked his Ranger company with other former prison guards, and they went to the Lower Valley as an officially sanctioned assassination squad that turned the limited violence of the first few weeks of the Border War into a scorched-earth campaign of annihilation.[76] Ransom declared that a "bad disease calls for bitter medicine. The Governor sent me down here to stop this trouble, and I am going to carry out his orders. There is only one way to do it. President Díaz proved that."[77] While Ransom and his men did not commit all of the atrocities that occurred over the next few months in the Lower Valley, they instigated this type of violence and reflected the willingness of much of the Anglo minority to use extreme methods to ensure domination at all costs. Some Anglos in the region even went so far as to justify this violence as a reckoning for past "crimes." "Somehow," wrote one South Texan in a letter to the adjutant general applauding the Rangers' actions, "I have never been satisfied with the Alamo and Goliad events, and always have felt that there was something yet due the Mexicans from us, and if there is a second call for a war, the Mexicans will certainly get what is due them from the Texans."[78]

Coming on the heels of the events of the previous week, the lynching of Adolfo Muñoz on July 29 took on enormous significance. Farmers in San Benito accused Muñoz of scheming to rob a local bank and having connections with the armed raiders who had been active in the area since the beginning of that month.[79] Cameron County deputy sheriff Frank Carr and Ranger Daniel Hinojosa arrested Muñoz and loaded him in a car to drive from San Benito to Brownsville. The officers alleged that two miles outside of San Benito eight armed, masked men stopped their car and forced them to turn over Muñoz. The next day, Muñoz's corpse, riddled with bullets, hung from a tree along the road between San Benito and Brownsville.[80] Whether he had been killed by vigilantes or the Rangers had created the story to divert attention from their extralegal murder, Muñoz's death marked a turning point. This very public murder seemed to embolden vigilantes and law enforcement, while it had a chilling effect on Mexicans and Mexican Americans. According to J. T. Canales, a prominent Mexican American political leader, "every person who was charged with a crime refused to be arrested, because they did not believe that the officers of the law would give them the protection guaranteed them by the Constitution and the laws of this State."[81] While this sort of extralegal killing had long been known as "rangering" or a "rinchada," the specter of these random murders grew to a scale beyond anything ever seen in South Texas. William G. B. Morrison, a lawyer in San Benito, described the lynching as "the spark that fired the flame among the white people."[82] A federal investigator saw the lynching as "an expression of the indignation of the people against the repeated failure to enforce the laws."[83] Regardless, all saw Muñoz's murder as an important intensification of the violence. Anglo law enforcement and vigilantes continued to kill with impunity while more Mexicans and Mexican Americans refused to cooperate with people they now viewed as potential, even probable, executioners.

Personal conflicts fueled some of this violence. The most important, though by no means the only, example of personal conflicts taking on added significance during the Border War began on August 3, 1915, at Los Tulitos Ranch in Cameron County. Aniceto Pizaña owned Los Tulitos. His neighbor, Jeff Scrivener, had long coveted Pizaña's land.[84] No evidence connected Pizaña to the first month of raiding, but Scrivener informed military and law enforcement officials that Pizaña harbored an armed band. In response, a posse of about thirty Rangers, sheriff's deputies, and others attacked Pizaña's home. In the firefight that ensued, Pizaña escaped, Pizaña's son was shot in the leg, his brother was arrested, one soldier was killed, and two sheriff's deputies were injured.[85]

In the aftermath of this attack, Pizaña followed his friend Luis de la Rosa into active participation in the Plan de San Diego. De la Rosa had owned a small general store in Rio Hondo, north of Brownsville, but when police arrested him in early 1915 for slaughtering stolen cattle, he decided to leave South Texas after years of abuse at the hands of Anglo law enforcement. He moved his family to Matamoros and joined the Plan de San Diego conspiracy. A few days before the attack on Los Tulitos, he had written Pizaña, asking that he join the conspiracy, too.[86] Before the attack, however, Pizaña had too much to lose in aiding the raiders. That changed on August 3, and thereafter Pizaña and de la Rosa would be the plan's primary military leaders.[87]

The Muñoz lynching and Los Tulitos attack transformed the Plan de San Diego from a cross-border conspiracy into a South Texas rebellion. The first conspirators and raiders, such as Ramos and his associates, had been Mexican, but as the violence continued more and more Tejanos appear to have joined in the raiding. The nature of these bands makes any definitive conclusion about their composition difficult, but the wanton violence of Anglo vigilantes and law enforcement seems to have pushed many into league with the borderland revolutionaries who launched the conspiracy. An escalating cycle of reprisal killings resulted.

Revenge killings occurred just three days after the attack on Pizaña's ranch, on August 6. De la Rosa led a band that murdered A. L. Austin and his son Charles in the town of Sebastian. Austin had recently moved with his son to Sebastian, a new town established in the wake of the entry of the railroad, to participate in the burgeoning agricultural empire. He served as president of the Law and Order League, which, according to federal investigators, "had driven several bad men out of that section."[88] Austin gained a reputation as a brutal racist, making him an obvious target for raiders. There is no evidence that he participated in any of the vigilante violence that preceded his murder, but groups like the Sebastian Law and Order League formed an important component of the private forces, so his murder served as a symbolic attack on these groups.

Not surprisingly, the reaction to the Austin killings was swift. By the next day posses had killed several Mexicans unlucky enough to be in the vicinity. A party led by Adjutant General Hutchings and Captain Ransom alone killed three Mexicans, while a number of vigilante bands took advantage of the open season created by the Austin killings to massacre others.[89] These reprisals occurred at the same time that raiders stepped up attacks on railroad and irrigation facilities throughout the Valley. They tore up tracks, burned railroad bridges, and attacked repair crews, ratcheting up the fear of some Anglos that the raiders would be able to isolate the Valley from the rest of the state and then carry out the genocide promised by the Plan de San Diego.

On August 9 the most daring attack yet occurred when sixty or seventy raiders descended on the Norias Division of the King Ranch.[90] The symbolic importance of this attack was clear: the King Ranch had long been a hated symbol of Anglo land thievery. Three raiders died in the ensuing battle. Texas Rangers arrived at the ranch after the fighting finished. The next morning, however, two Rangers tied the corpses of the raiders to their horses, dragged them through the brush, and deposited them in a clearing. They then posed with the corpses for a photograph, which was widely reproduced as a picture postcard throughout South Texas and northern Mexico. In fact, Immigration Inspector J. W. Berkshire wrote that the increased ferocity of attacks by raiders in August came from anger over the wide distribution of the postcards.[91] Within the context of the times, as Richard Ribb has argued, this photo evoked the same lessons of racially motivated violence as spectacle lynchings.[92] The Rangers sought to document and publicize their violent solution for banditry, in spite of the fact that they had not been at Norias during the gun battle.

Violence continued to accelerate during August and September, with almost daily killings and systematic attacks on railroad facilities, irrigation works, and even army detachments posted near the Rio Grande. Probably the most frightening attack of all occurred on October 19, when a band of raiders derailed a passenger train six miles north of Brownsville. "The Bandits went through the train shooting all Americans," according to a federal investigator.[93] They did not attack Mexicans and Mexican Americans, which many took as incontrovertible proof that non-Anglos were all in on the Plan de San Diego. Again, the counterattack was swift and deadly, with unknown numbers caught up in the blind vengeance of law enforcement and vigilantes. In the immediate vicinity of the crash, Rangers captured four Mexicans. Captain Ransom walked them into the brush and shot them in the back, after asking Cameron County sheriff W. T. Vann if he wanted to join him in what Ransom clearly considered a joy killing.[94] Additionally, according to R. B. Creager, a lawyer in Brownsville, blacklists circulated throughout the Anglo communities of the Valley, "and the name of any Mexican who was suspicioned [sic] by any men of standing in the valley or even half way standing who would report the fact that a certain Mexican was a bad Mexican would be placed upon one of those lists and it was a common rumor and report, and it was true, that in most instances that Mexican would disappear."[95] The adjutant general's office received a flood of letters and telegrams from would-be vigilantes volunteering to join the fight against the raiders, with swaggering claims that "we will have them planting dead Mexicans for weeks."[96]

The cross-border raids slowed by December 1915, then revived during the summer of 1916 in the vicinity of Laredo.[97] But these raids were overshadowed by the ferocity of the counterattacks that followed. These counterattacks inspired many Mexicans and Mexican Americans to flee south to Mexico, in spite of the Revolution. A writer for the *San Antonio Light* reported that "2000 have left Texas through fear of sudden death."[98] The author went on to state, "In outlying sections away from towns, suspicion is still so great that Mexicans found out alone at night might as well be dead, and a Mexican seen on horseback with a gun or rifle at any time of the day is in danger of death."[99] A few days later, the *Light* also reported that "some authorities have allowed Mexicans' bodies to lie where they were shot so that their friends might find them and profit by this warning."[100] The next day, the same paper reported that a "strong force in restoring quiet appears to be the stoppage of indiscriminate killing of Mexicans which has been charged against some peace officers. No violent deaths of Mexicans without the semblance of legal formalities have been reported for several days."[101]

The counterattack, then, sought nothing less than ethnic cleansing. One Valley resident later recalled that during "those troubles, one good citizen—a lawyer who held high places in the judiciary of Texas—suggested to me that we ought to compel all Mexicans resident on the Border to go across the river until the troubles were over, and then go out and shoot all that were left."[102] While this proposal was never put into practice, the Texas Rangers led what appeared to be a systematic effort to rid large portions of South Texas of Mexicans through wholesale, anonymous murder.

Peace began to return to South Texas by the end of 1915. War fatigue on all sides probably helped diminish the violence. The most powerful force opposing the indiscriminate killing of Mexicans and Mexican Americans, however, appears to have been the large number of landholders who needed labor for their farms. Commerce came to a screeching halt in mid-1915, and for the newcomer farmers the lack of a labor pool soon trumped concerns over the Plan de San Diego raids. By putting pressure on state officials, land barons were able to tame the savagery of the Texas Rangers and local law enforcement, putting an end to the worst of the slaughter by December 1915, but not before thousands had been killed in a matter of months and untold thousands more had been driven from their homes. Despite the cessation of violence, however, the hopes for Anglo-Mexican accommodation, even on the skewed terms that had existed in previous decades, disappeared. As Benjamin Johnson has noted in his study of the Plan de San Diego, "Texas Rangers and vigilantes not on the state payroll accomplished in months what it might have taken years of economic pressure and more sporadic violence to wrest from Tejanos."[103] South Texas reemerged from the Border War vastly different than before.

THE PLAN DE SAN DIEGO and the Border War have always elicited the same question from historians: How could the adherents of the plan possibly hope to accomplish their goals? For most, it looks like the "most bizarre irredentist conspiracy in American history" or a suicidal attempt to foment a race war in the United States.[104] When placed within the context of the Mexican Revolution and the momentous changes wrought by the entry of the railroad into the Lower Rio Grande Valley, however, these events take on a new meaning and importance. The plan may still seem quixotic, but the motivating forces behind it begin to emerge when we tease out the tangled strands of the society that straddled the Rio Grande. The complexity of this situation can be maddening and difficult to fit within the strictures of nationalist history or to boil down to the pervasive simplistic mythology that serves as Texas history, but it points toward the essential linkages between the histories of the United States and Mexico at the same time that it provides an alternative vision of a past drowned in blood.

The Plan de San Diego and the Border War occurred because Mexican and Mexican American rebels, who had seen their own society displaced and marginalized by the rapidly changing economic order on both sides of the border, sought to extend into Texas the revolutionary changes taking place just across the river in Mexico. Conversely, the Anglo migrants coming to Texas from the north brought their own ideas of revolutionary change with them. They sought to seize political and economic control from the tottering old regime of South Texas. These two clashing visions were both introduced into the region after 1905. All of the changes that occurred in South Texas during the Revolution and in the coming decades flowed out of this clash. The victory of the Anglo vision was far from assured, but the overwhelming force of law enforcement and Anglo vigilantes crushed hopes that an alternative society would develop in South Texas.

The violence of the Mexican Revolution, the wave of refugees that it created, the economic changes in South Texas, and the Border War cannot be understood independently. Together, they provide an explanation for the momentous changes that turned South Texas on its head in the first twenty years of the twentieth century. Gone was the gradual change of the late nineteenth century, replaced by sweeping, violent upheaval that grafted capitalist agriculture firmly onto South Texas and dissolved what was left of interethnic accommodation in the region.

The revolution in Texas could now begin.

CHAPTER TWO

The Revolution in Texas

International Migration, Capitalist Agriculture,
and the Interstate Migrant Stream

Trainloads of prospective buyers and home seekers, derisively referred to as "home suckers" by those in South Texas, headed south for the Rio Grande Valley in search of land that had been too desolate and unproductive for large-scale agricultural production only a few years earlier. Drawn by speculators' and irrigation companies' claims of open land and fabulous wealth, these caravans left regularly from the cities of the East and Midwest during winter. Beckoning for visitors to "brush the icicles off your whiskers and come on down to this land of sunshine," many a snake-oil salesman and huckster found employment enticing farmers south to the burgeoning agricultural region.[1]

While the organizers of these journeys counted on rising temperatures to tempt winter-weary farmers to invest in the Rio Grande Valley, they also realized that the sparse and forbidding landscape of much of Texas, especially the brush country north of the Valley through which all of these trains had to pass, posed a potential problem. The organizers of these trips developed a few ways to distract potential buyers. The Southwestern Land Company, one of the largest and most important land companies in the Lower Rio Grande Valley, distributed a song book at the beginning of each trip and led group sing-alongs. The organizers hoped to distract travelers from their arid surroundings by having them focus on the words to songs like "All Hail the Power of Jesus's Name," "The Battle Hymn of the Republic," "The Eyes of Texas are Upon You," "Carry Me Back to Ole Virginny," "Jingle Bells," and "Till We Meet Again."[2] Other companies developed a variation of the sing-along ruse by leading travelers in prayer meetings at opportune times. They closed window shades and led group prayers and the singing of hymns. The meetings ended and the shades came off the windows when the worst views had passed.[3]

Once the trains arrived in the Rio Grande Valley, the land parties began. The prospective buyers would travel to land company holdings, and local teenagers would drive them around to view the different properties. One of these makeshift chauffeurs recalled, "It was not difficult to sell these people land. . . . You'd go and let 'em pick an orange or two off of a tree; let 'em look at the palm trees. You'd take 'em across the river and feed 'em in Mexico. Show 'em the onions growin',' the cabbages, and all the vegetables growin.' They'd fall over themselves buying land."[4] The results of these land parties and aggressive marketing of South Texas land was a massive migration of people and capital from the north that met the growing Mexican immigrant population in the region south of San Antonio. As a result, the populations of agricultural areas like Cameron, Hidalgo, Zavala, and Dimmit counties grew rapidly from 1910 until the outbreak of the Great Depression, while towns appeared almost overnight throughout South Texas to provide population and transportation centers in the new farm belt.

This chapter will examine the demographic and economic effects of these two migrations, one pushed north by the Mexican Revolution and the other drawn south by the promise of future agricultural wealth, on the border region and the United States as a whole during the 1910s and 1920s. The entry of hundreds of thousands of Mexicans during and after the Revolution introduced an enormous, exploitable labor pool to South Texas and the rest of the Southwest. These migrants entered the region at the same time that newcomer farm interests descended on South Texas from the Midwest and Southeast. These simultaneous population shifts allowed for the explosive growth of the agricultural economy that began in the mid-1910s and continued, despite depressed conditions elsewhere, into the 1930s. Agricultural (and some industrial) interests in the rest of the United States watched this spectacular growth fueled by labor surpluses and low wages and sought to draw much of this labor force away from the border region, helping to create a nationwide migrant labor stream. In the aftermath of the Mexican Revolution and the cataclysmic violence of the Plan de San Diego, a farming empire developed in South Texas that was fed by continued immigration from Mexico. The mobile workers who passed out of and through South Texas built this agricultural empire from the ground up and unwittingly helped shape a form of modern agribusiness wholly

dependent on temporary labor. Able to ignore the agricultural patterns of the past (such as sharecropping and tenant farming with their
year-round reciprocal obligations) and make up the rules as they went,
farming interests in South Texas looked to the temporary wage worker,
mobile but always restrained by the overwhelming economic and political power of their employers, as the sole source of labor in their rush to
create a modernized form of capitalist agriculture. This labor diaspora
not only fueled the revolution in Texas but also formed an essential
building block for the growth of agribusiness throughout the nation.

WHILE THE PLAN de San Diego and the Border War that followed it
were the most extreme manifestations of the Mexican Revolution in
South Texas, equally important was the rapid economic development
made possible by the refugees from war-torn Mexico. The refugee
population entered into a fledgling farm economy, and these migrants
helped build the agricultural empires of South Texas, changing the endless stretches of scrub brush that covered the semiarid vastness of the
region south of San Antonio into an irrigated boom area. Early farming successes attracted outside investment into the previously isolated,
near worthless land north of the Rio Grande. While this growth was
partially dependent on the railroad's entry into the Lower Rio Grande
Valley in 1904 and the impetus it gave to the construction of irrigation
facilities throughout the region, the arrival of the new labor pool from
Mexico was every bit as important. The combination of railroad access,
capital growth, and the availability of a migrant labor force happened
roughly simultaneously in the Lower Rio Grande Valley and the Winter
Garden. Other agricultural areas in South Texas, such as the Laredo
and Corpus Christi regions, possessed rail links decades earlier but
lacked the necessary surplus labor pool. Workers were the final necessary ingredient for the creation of a thriving agricultural economy.

Labor migration from Mexico was not a new phenomenon of the
revolutionary era. Immigration officials, border residents, and agriculturalists already viewed Mexican labor as "a natural supply of labor for
the Southwest."[5] The difference lay in the scale of this population movement during the two decades following the outbreak of the Revolution,
and the uses to which these immigrants could be put now that the other
prerequisites for large-scale agriculture existed in the border region.
A customs inspector in the Lower Rio Grande Valley clearly understood the relationship between Mexican immigration and South Texas

agriculture when he reported on conditions in the fall of 1913: "Practically the entire population of Northern Tamaulipas, opposite the counties of Cameron, Starr, and Hidalgo, in the State of Texas . . . are and have been sojourning in the United States since about the first of June, on account of conditions existing in that part of Mexico at the present time." He continued, "It is true that in the lower Rio Grande valley of Texas, on account of the immense irrigation projects and agricultural interests, there has been a great deal of work." He worried, however, that the same pressures for migration existed further west along the Texas-Mexico border without the same opportunities for farm labor employment, creating the potential for a large number of idle refugees. "There is very little of farming interests along the Rio Grande, except in the lower valley, consequently the Western part of the State has no opportunity for using cheap labor."[6] As the inspector observed, the refugee population was spreading beyond the Lower Valley and into the region west of Laredo along the Texas-Mexico border. He worried that lack of employment opportunities would only exacerbate the destitution of these immigrants, but he failed to recognize that these potential laborers would build the agricultural economy in the Winter Garden region beyond Laredo from the ground up.[7]

In fact, by 1913, agricultural growth was already in its early stages in the Winter Garden. Only one year earlier, in the vicinity of Asherton, ethnic Mexican onion clippers called a strike for higher wages. The *Carrizo Springs Javelin*, a newspaper overflowing with angry sarcasm and poorly conceived puns, reported that some "Asherton Mexicans got the idea that onion clipping was skilled labor, and that they ought to be fashionable and strike. Likewise they thought they had the onion growers where they couldn't kick. The onion raisers couldn't see the raise. They offered to come through with half the extra money, but the clippers said it was a whole loaf or no crust, and they were pretty crusty about it too. The onion men simply sent out for more Mexicans, and now the former clippers are in the soup, no money, no job, and no strike fund in the treasury."[8] Even if the customs inspector did not realize it, the farmers of South Texas had already begun to tap into the new group of immigrants as a source of cheap labor and, in this case, as potential strikebreakers.

Determining the total number of migrants that entered the area is problematic, however. The total population growth of Mexicans and Mexican Americans in South Texas can only be shown impressionistically, as census data from the first half of the twentieth century are so flawed as to be almost useless. The first problem was the socially marginal position of many Mexicans and Mexican Americans within the United States, which made accurate census enumerations difficult if not impossible. The second problem lies in the fact that Mexican/Mexican American did not become a separate category until 1930. The censuses of 1910 and 1920, which still maintained strict biracial enumerations, counted Mexicans and Mexican Americans as "foreign born whites whose country of birth was Mexico."[9] This distinction meant, at least in theory, that all immigrants and their children fell under this distinction, while all others were classified as native-born whites. These classifications changed in 1930, when a separate ethnic category of Mexican appeared, defined as "all persons born in Mexico, or having parents born in Mexico, who are not definitely white, Negro, Indian, Chinese, or Japanese."[10] But again, this system of classification differentiated between first- and second-generation populations and those who had been in the United States longer, divided haphazardly according to ill-defined distinctions and the racial notions of individual census takers, who very well could have applied whiteness to individuals and families according to notions of class or acculturation rather than the stated vague criteria.

The numbers for these years, as a result, are more useful for determining patterns than as definitive data. The 1910 Census recorded 135,232 Mexicans and Mexican Americans in South Texas, or 37 percent of the population.[11] According to the 1930 Census, the Mexican population in South Texas had more than doubled since 1910, with 371,486 Mexicans and Mexican Americans making up 46 percent of the population.[12] Just as important, the Mexican American population in South Texas had spread out from the border counties, especially into the San Antonio area and the Winter Garden district of Dimmit and Zavala counties.[13] In 1910 only the eleven counties along the border contained majority Mexican and Mexican American populations. By 1930, however, several additional counties away from the border contained majority Mexican and Mexican American populations, while no county in the region had a Mexican-origin population that made up less than a quarter of the total population. Again, these numbers are certainly undercounts, but they do provide insight into the broad outlines of demographic trends during the first two decades after the outbreak of the Mexican Revolution.

The majority of immigrants entering the United States from Mexico came to Texas. Not until the 1930s would more Mexicans enter the United States along California's border, and not until the second half of the twentieth century would the majority of Mexicans and Mexican Americans in the United States live outside of Texas.[14] While the growth of a resident Mexican and Mexican American population and the birth of intensive agricultural enterprises occurred at roughly the same time in Texas and California, the sheer numbers entering Texas created different dynamics than in California. While California agriculture did depend on migrant workers (many of them recruited in Texas), South Texas relied wholly on the floating agricultural workforce that emerged from Mexico and formed an interstate migrant stream that began and ended in the region south of San Antonio.[15] South Texas, in other words, remained the geographic center of the Mexican-origin population in the United States.

These immigrants entering Texas were not preindustrial blank slates, however.[16] Even though the vast majority of Mexico's population remained in rural areas throughout the Porfiriato and early years of the Revolution, the demographic changes during those decades introduced much of the rural population to the vagaries of capitalist development, wage labor, and seasonal migration to places like the Laguna and the U.S. Southwest. Many arrived in Texas during the Revolution as experienced wage laborers, despite employers' depictions of these recent arrivals as passive, inefficient, unintelligent peasants. The repetition of these tropes had more to do with justification for poor wages and poor treatment of workers than with any reflection of reality.[17] Like the Mexican migrant workers in California studied by Devra Weber, the immigrants arriving in South Texas "were veterans of the expansion of industrial and agricultural capitalism both on haciendas and the mines, fields, and industries of Mexico and the United States. The majority came originally from Mexico, but it was a Mexico in which the transformation to a capitalist economy, well underway by the 1890s, had become an essential part of their work, lives, and migrations."[18]

SOUTH TEXAS HAD been a tall-grass land before the cattle industry reached its peak in the 1880s. Overgrazing thinned the grass and allowed mesquite and other shrubs to dominate the landscape.[19] By 1910 much of South Texas was brushland dominated by mesquite, huisache, and cactus that had to be grubbed out by hand.[20] Thus, as ranching gave way to farming and immigrants from Mexico sought labor north of the Rio Grande, many went to work clearing vast tracts of troublesome vegetation.[21] Using flamethrowers and grub hoes to uproot and destroy the shrubs, these workers performed the grueling necessary first steps in preparing the land for intensive agriculture.[22] According to Colonel Sam Robertson, a railroad and irrigation impresario in San Benito in Cameron County much given to hyperbole, "I do not know of any other race that could have stood the tick-infested jungles that covered the land when I built the railroad into it."[23] For their troubles, these workers received wages even lower than contemporary railroad and farm laborers, stuck as they were in what was unquestionably the bottom rung of the occupational ladder.[24]

With the vegetation gone, the land had to be leveled for irrigation. This leveling was also performed by contract labor at extraordinarily low wages. And like the process of clearing the land, leveling drastically increased land values. Once the land had been leveled, it could be provided with the irrigation water controlled by the irrigation companies that multiplied throughout South Texas.[25] In 1909 irrigation reached 54,000 acres of farmland in Hidalgo and Cameron counties. By 1919, 228,000 acres received water from irrigation companies, while the area of coverage spread beyond the immediate vicinity of the Rio Grande. Irrigation reached 338,000 acres of South Texas land by 1929, now even further north and west from the Lower Rio Grande Valley.[26] The rapid increase in the amount of land suited to intensive agriculture was made possible by the continual clearing and leveling done almost entirely by laborers recently arrived from Mexico, with mechanization not providing a replacement until the 1920s.[27]

Cleared land and irrigation pumps were of little intrinsic value without a labor force capable of transforming the theoretical wealth of prepared land into marketable crops. Migrants from Mexico arrived at a fortuitous moment for those looking to make the transition to farming. Increased migration from Mexico strengthened the pull on prospective farmers who came to South Texas seeking cheap land, more plentiful cheap labor, and the chance to make more money than was believed possible in the older farm areas they left. Land companies and railroads distributed pamphlets throughout the nation advertising the fabulous wealth lying just beneath the surface in South Texas. One company melodramatically offered to fulfill a collective longing: "There is hardly a person who has not had at some time or another a more or less defined longing either to own or operate an orange or grape fruit grove. There is a romance about the thing that can be compared only to the quest for gold."[28] Another went even further in declaring that the land of the Rio Grande Valley was "as rich and fertile as the COM- MANDING GENERAL OF THE UNIVERSE knows how to make—It Is His Masterpiece—fit dwelling for the favored sons of men."[29]

The availability of cheap, exploitable labor was one of the primary selling points for farmlands in South Texas. Many companies advertised that Mexican workers would work for one dollar a day or less and gave growers a competitive advantage over farmers elsewhere. But low wages were only one aspect of the labor situation used by the land companies to sell South Texas real estate to newcomers. John Shary, the founder of the Southwestern Land Company and one of the most important boosters of Rio Grande Valley farm development, mentioned low wage rates but quickly moved on to another key element of his sales pitch. "The entire family works and are very handy," he reported, "especially in picking cotton and corn, transplanting vegetables and in harvesting and packing time. . . . The women soon become fair domestic servants and the men will work day and night, rain or shine, in their own steady way and can plow a furrow much straighter than the average farmer." Not only would entire Mexican families work ceaselessly for new land- owners, Shary promised, but Mexicans possessed an innate expertise in all aspects of farmwork.[30] Shary also ensured prospective buyers that "the 'labor problem' does not exist in the Valley; and the labor supply is apparently sufficient to meet the needs of all future development."[31] Not only were Mexican workers cheap, in other words, but they could also be counted on to obey employers, avoid organized labor, and continue arriving in almost limitless numbers. Similarly, the Houston Chamber of Commerce tried to take advantage of proximity to the labor pool of South Texas by sending pamphlets to New England textile companies claiming that "unorganizable Mexican labor in inexhaustible numbers can be secured in Texas for new textile mills."[32]

One important variation on the theme of cheap labor also appeared frequently in this literature. The editor of a farm journal wrote, "I doubt if it's a good place for a very poor man, because Americans don't work much down here, nearly all the labor being done by Mexican peons."[33] Similarly, the Carrizo Springs Chamber of Commerce advertised the opportunities for farming in South Texas while also making it clear that not everybody was welcome: "This is not a community for a man without money. That is due to the great supply of Mexican labor that we have. A man depending on common labor for the upkeep of his family cannot compete with them. . . . But to the man with $5,000 or more, Carrizo Springs offers a better opportunity than any other section in the country."[34] While this line of advertising sought to keep out the poverty of the rest of the nation and to exclude many who might have hoped to move to South Texas (the indebted most obviously), it also made clear the centrality of race and racial difference in the development of the region. The racial line would be both stark and utilitarian, allowing anyone to determine at a glance an individual's place in the local hierarchy. Mexicans and Mexican Americans would do the work and Anglos would own the land. Further, Mexicans would remain laborers and would never emerge as competition to farm owners. They were nothing more than a cost of business. In other words, these promoters sought to convince newcomers that they need not fear either the unfamiliar Mexican population or the arrival of problems like poverty and class conflict. A strict color line would take care of it.

Despite the vaguely populist nature of much of the promotional literature, South Texas farm society was tightly controlled from the top. The farmers associations and irrigation companies, which often operated as offshoots of the major land companies, enjoyed almost complete power. The farmers associations handled much of the preparation of new lands and recruited much of the labor used by individual farmers, while the irrigation companies provided the water that made agriculture in the region possible. With their control of the land, labor, and water, it should come as no surprise that the leaders of these organizations also controlled the politics of the evolving region.[35] They stripped power from the old political machines and strove to eliminate Mexican Americans entirely from the political realm.[36]

This growing political power emerged along with a mythology that justified the way these changes occurred. Promotional literature for the Southwestern Land Company, for instance, proclaimed, "The past ten years have wrought a miracle in the Valley. From a few thousand people, mostly Mexicans, living in a cluster of 'jacals' the section has now a population of about 200,000 persons—the progressive, liberal, enterprising and thrifty people of a dozen middle western states, with a sprinkling from practically every state in the Union."[37] This depiction of the recent past not only laid bare the racial assumptions that only Anglo migrants could make use of a region allowed to lay dormant by the native ethnic Mexican population, but it also offered a modern take on the notion of manifest destiny. By their own description, these land and irrigation impresarios were pioneers, even miracle workers, wresting wealth from the desert. Importantly, though, they viewed themselves as thoroughly modern pioneers. The Southwestern Land Company promotional literature proclaimed that the company's owner, John Shary, "has been to the citrus industry of the Valley what Henry Ford has been to the automotive industry."[38] Shary was thus not a throwback to the genteel southern plantation owner but a forward-looking agricultural industrialist. Whether this pervasive, self-serving mythology had any basis in fact, the agricultural economy of South Texas that justified it entered into a period of unprecedented growth by the mid-1910s.

The outbreak of World War I provided additional momentum for the farm boom and its surrounding mythos. The war in Europe increased the demand for agricultural goods. Land values soared, more land was put under the plow, and total output grew. Importantly for the farmers of South Texas, this wartime economic boom did not extend to Mexico, which continued to suffer under severe economic conditions brought by the continued instability of the Revolution, so the waves of immigration did not slow down. All of these factors led to profits thought impossible before the war. According to scholar-activist Carey McWilliams, this led growers to seek even greater power and wealth: "Reading over the transactions of the farm organizations during this period, one is impressed with the obscenity of the large growers' greed, the brutality of their demands. They were literally wild with a frenzy of profit-patriotism."[39]

The years after the end of World War I witnessed a worldwide agricultural depression, as the artificially high prices of the war years plummeted, dragging credit-dependent farmers (and even entire nations) into bankruptcy. Such was not the case in South Texas, however. A number of small operations went out of business as market prices dropped, but the region's economy as a whole continued to grow throughout the postwar years as outside capital poured into the farm regions, the amount of cultivated land increased, and output increased. The Winter Garden, especially, grew rapidly in the years after the war, becoming one of the primary off-season sources of produce at the same time that similar operations developed in California and Florida. After 1919, as the nation as a whole entered a long agricultural depression, the Winter Garden became one of the most important farming regions in the country.

Spinach and onions were the primary crops, but appreciable amounts of cabbage and tomatoes also came from the Winter Garden. What began as an experiment—four acres of spinach grown near Crystal City (Zavala County) in the winter of 1917–18, yielding three carlots (enough to fill three train shipping containers)—rapidly grew. By 1920, 200 acres of spinach had been planted in Dimmit and Zavala counties combined, shipping 148 carlots. By 1929 Zavala County had more than 8,000 acres of spinach under cultivation, making it the largest spinach-producing area in the world. More than 3,000 carlots shipped from Crystal City alone in 1929, while similar growth occurred in the nearby counties of Dimmit and Webb. These three counties combined produced more than half of the national spinach crop during the boom years of the 1920s. Similarly, the Winter Garden became one of the largest producers of Bermuda onions in the United States, shipping three-quarters of the state's carlots in 1929, when Texas led the nation in Bermuda onion production.[40] Not surprisingly, the area irrigated grew just as rapidly during these years. In 1919 Zavala County had 1,642 acres irrigated and Dimmit County 5,397 acres. A decade later Zavala increased to 13,126 acres, while Dimmit had 13,694 acres under irrigation.[41]

This spinach boom brought even more outside investment and led to the consolidation of the spinach holdings into the hands of the large shippers who controlled the irrigation companies and the national marketing of Winter Garden spinach.[42] One example of this consolidation was Fred Vahlsing, a New York grocer. Seeking a way to provide fresh produce year-round, and witnessing the enormous production coming out of the Winter Garden, Vahlsing purchased land in the area. By the end of the 1930s, long after the bottom had fallen out of the spinach market because of the Great Depression, Vahlsing controlled 10,000 acres, had 3,000 employees, operated packing sheds and an ice plant, and shipped produce to 127 cities in the United States.[43] While Vahlsing was surely more successful than the vast majority of newcomer farmers who appeared in the Winter Garden and the rest of South Texas during these years, he provides a perfect illustration of how outside influence shaped the region and of the enormous growth and consolidation that this new capital introduced in the agricultural economy.

While the rest of South Texas did not witness growth as rapid as the Winter Garden's, the scale of growth was impressive throughout the region during the 1910s and 1920s. As a whole, the total value of farms in Texas rose from $1,843,208,395 in 1910 to $3,700,173,319 in 1920 (during the tail end of the war agricultural bubble) then dropped to $3,045,270,798 in 1925.[44] Only California matched the level of statewide growth in farm values. Crop values, however, outpaced any other state in the nation, rising to $900,472,787 in 1919 before falling back to $756,105,985 in 1924. During the same years California peaked at $282,579,083.[45] Some of the growth came from the cotton fields of central and east Texas, but moving down to the county level shows that much of this growth occurred in South Texas. Cameron County witnessed an increase in total farm value from $7,894,738 in 1910 to $29,430,868 in 1925, multiplying fourfold in only fifteen years. Immediately adjacent to Cameron, Hidalgo County underwent equally explosive growth, increasing from $9,926,121 in 1910 to $36,930,822 in 1925.[46]

Crop values in South Texas did not rise quite as dramatically as total farm value, but the growth still dwarfed what was happening in the rest of the nation. Cameron County crop values rose from $1,773,036 in 1919 to $4,908,117 in 1924, while Hidalgo increased from $2,424,467 in 1919 to $6,440,219 in 1924. Nueces County (Corpus Christi) grew from $4,142,022 to $8,189,511 between 1919 and 1924, while Willacy County, located just north of Cameron, saw its crop value rise from $34,771 in 1919 to $785,235 in 1924.[47] Total carlot shipments also increased sharply as a number of new crops flourished throughout South Texas. The spinach boom in the Winter Garden was matched by a citrus boom in the Lower Rio Grande Valley and a cotton boom in the Coastal Bend area near Corpus Christi.[48]

Clearly, then, South Texas rapidly became one of the most productive farming areas in the nation in the 1910s and 1920s. Like similar changes in the same years in California and Florida, this growth flowed not only out of the increased capital and transportation facilities that came with the expansion of the national railroad network and the growth of national and international markets for agricultural goods but also out of the construction of a system of industrialized agriculture that took advantage of the seemingly endless supply of cheap labor to create massive agribusiness complexes. The result was what Carey McWilliams called "factories in the field."[49]

South Texas became one of the most important centers for the growth of modern agribusiness. At the heart of industrial farming was the creation of a racial/ethnic division of labor that mandated limited job opportunities. In the context of South Texas, that meant that white and ethnic Mexican (as well as the much less numerous African American) workers had prescribed positions within the workforce. Ethnic Mexicans could not advance above the status of sharecropper or wage laborer. There also existed a sort of glass floor that effectively barred many Anglos from these lower status sharecropper and wage labor positions, creating a flip side of the "wages of whiteness" that priced them out of any positions below tenant farmer.[50] Farmers throughout South Texas refused to lease to Anglos on halves, offering them only the terms of thirds and fourths, which required the capital to fund most of the crop. Employers described wage labor as "Mexican work" beneath whites.[51] Soon, even those tenant and sharecropper positions disappeared as South Texas farmers transitioned fully to migrant wage labor. These strictures helped create a rigidly segmented job market similar to the Jim Crow South. Unlike their brethren in the South, however, South Texas growers could rely on continued migration from Mexico to replenish and expand their labor supply. This segmented, ever-expanding labor supply helped to maintain a wage scale in South Texas lower than anywhere else in the nation.

The importance of this difference between the farms of South Texas and those of the Southeast cannot be overstated. While both relied on racial segmentation and coercion, the farms of the Southeast relied on static forms of labor, while agribusiness in South Texas and the West had shifted to a reliance on mobile labor fed by continued immigration to the United States. Corporate farms' ability to attract an overabundance of workers allowed them to keep wages down through the constant threat of hiring replacements. When the harvest ended, workers disappeared from the farms' immediate vicinity, erasing the yearlong reciprocal duties that came with tenant farming and sharecropping in the older agricultural areas of the Southeast.[52]

The methods by which agricultural interests recruited their armies of labor differed little from the recruitment procedures of northern factories; these techniques were more Detroit than Mississippi. Emilio Flores, an official with the Mexican Protective Association in San Antonio, described the normal operation of this system to a congressional investigating commission:

> There are so called employment agencies in Laredo and other
> border cities who get "orders" from farmers throughout Texas,

specially north and east as well as central Texas, and it is these agents of the said employment concerns that get these Mexicans just as they cross the Rio Grande and ship them off to [their] destination, many times misrepresenting things to them and causing great hardships to these Mexicans and their families. The employment agencies at the border generally work under an agreed combine with others of the same class in San Antonio, Tex., and the concerns at San Antonio see to it that the "consignment" goes through to destination without leaving the cars if possible. When they have to be transferred from the I. & G.N. to other railroad stations they are marched straight across the city of San Antonio up Commerce or Houston Street, and it is no uncommon sight to see as many as a hundred or more marching together. These employment agencies are generally paid by the farmer $1 a head when delivered at destination and provide transportation for the men and their families. When put to work at destination or upon their first pay day they are informed that so much has been charged to each and every one of them for transportation and employment fees, which said amounts are deducted from their earnings. When they sometimes refuse to comply, because of the promises of the employment agency at the border or at San Antonio, they are guarded until they work out what they owe. I have known of a number of Mexicans to be chained in Gonzalez County and guarded by armed men with shotguns and made to work these moneys out.[53]

Even as agriculturalists banded together into growers associations, they continued to rely on labor contractors to draw workers from throughout South Texas and across the border in Mexico. Others, however, relied on less formal means to draw labor. Onion growers in the Winter Garden, for instance, attracted some of their harvest workers by distributing advertisements among migrant cotton workers as they moved from the Lower Rio Grande Valley to West Texas, a method not as reliable as contractors but one that cut out the need to pay recruitment fees to a middleman.[54]

Growers in South Texas recruited workers from two primary areas. First, they looked to the cities and towns of the region, which, as Paul Taylor argued, acted as "fluid reservoirs of agricultural labor" from which residents could quickly move to and from farming regions on short notice, "stimulated by the character of the labor demand, which not only fluctuates seasonally but shifts every few days from field to field."[55] Even in the larger towns and cities such as San Antonio, Laredo, Corpus Christi, and Brownsville, an important segment of the population survived on irregular, seasonal agricultural labor. Importantly, there was no recruitment from other states into Texas, which enjoyed a labor surplus that made outside recruitment from anywhere but Mexico unnecessary.

The second important area of recruitment, then, was Mexico. While border enforcement and the laws governing who could cross the border for what purposes changed during the decades from 1910 to the Great Depression, the methods of procuring labor from Mexico remained remarkably unchanged. Contractors sent representatives to the border towns and transported workers north. According to Taylor, "Some farmers of Nueces County and other parts of Texas have been accustomed to send dependable Mexicans to Mexico to recruit others, even if necessary giving them money to pay immigration fees. . . . In Nueces County, for example, one farmer was describing the practice to me, when another, aware of its illegality, interrupted him."[56]

For many farmers, however, this system left too much power in the hands of the labor contractors. In 1923 growers and farmers' associations forced the state to create the Texas Labor Bureau as a free employment agency in order to, in the words of the bureau itself, "protect the poor people against these unscrupulous" contractors.[57] The labor commissioner declared two years after the establishment of the bureau, "Before the establishment of this service many pickers picked in South Texas and there remained, many in Central Texas moved no further, but now many start in the South and wind up in West Texas."[58] While the Labor Bureau did little more than direct workers during the cotton harvests throughout the state, it pointed toward a more active role for the state in the structuring of the agricultural labor market that would become increasingly important in the coming decades as the growers became more politically powerful and more insistent that the government bend to their whims.

These methods of labor contracting, both public and private, helped create an intrastate migrant labor stream that served two primary purposes. First, it acted as a necessary method of achieving subsistence for farm laborers who could not survive on the wages from a single harvest. Second, it maintained low wages by keeping workers constantly in motion and unable to bargain for higher pay before a new harvest began and they had to move. For the workers, their continual migration provided both agency and exploitation. For the growers, this system provided the cornerstone for everything they did.

The largest and best organized migrant stream moved north and west following the cotton harvests from the Lower Rio Grande Valley through the Corpus Christi area, then up into Central and East Texas, with some moving as far as West Texas and the Panhandle in the late fall. At its beginning each year, approximately 25,000 migrant workers picked cotton in the Valley in the early summer, to be joined by another 25,000 in Nueces and San Patricio counties, helping Nueces produce more cotton than any other county in the nation by 1930.[59] In the fields of Central Texas the army of migrant pickers grew to approximately 200,000, with some then traveling as far as Amarillo in the Panhandle before returning south at the end of the season.[60]

Cotton picking only lasted through the summer and fall, and since the wages earned during cotton season were often not enough for the year, almost all of these migrants also had to work in the fields for the rest of the year. For those from the Lower Rio Grande Valley, that often meant working in citrus or produce. For those from San Antonio, it could mean seasonal labor in the pecan shelling industry or one of the other semi-industrial enterprises that shut down during harvest season. A typical year for a farmworker from the Winter Garden involved the following, as described by a rancher and farm owner from Carrizo Springs: "They plant onions here beginning in November. Then they work in spinach, onions, cauliflower. That runs to about May. Then after a month or two, they start to pick cotton around Brownsville and work north with the cotton until about November when they return home."[61]

The increased availability of farm machinery in the 1910s and 1920s also affected the ways industrial agriculture evolved, but not always in the expected fashion. The decision to introduce machinery into the production process depended on factors far more complex than a simple linear progression of technological improvement and modernization for the sake of modernization. On the one hand, the increased availability of tractors for plowing lessened the necessity for labor during the early stages of each season, which helped kill sharecropping and create a greater reliance on short-term migratory harvest labor. On the other hand, mechanization also became a contingent aspect of the emerging labor system. Louis Bailey, a cotton farmer in Agua Dulce, near Corpus Christi, claimed that the "Bolshevik ideas of the Mexicans that the white can pay them anything are going to ruin them. We are going to substitute machinery for them. The country is full of labor now." He later added that the "cotton pickers are bringing the machine on themselves."[62] Likewise, a large landowner in Nueces County told Taylor, "I keep a plow going to keep Mexicans in a frame of mind to do it at a reasonable price," before making clear the reason for wielding the threat of mechanization: "Not that we want to beat the Mexicans out—but if we have machines, the pickers would be satisfied with $1 instead of $1.25 a hundred pounds."[63] Some even cast their decision not to employ machinery as a sort of charity: if machines operated in the cotton fields of Nueces County or if mechanical onion transplanters operated in the Winter Garden or Willacy County, farmers would no longer be able to "make work" for Mexicans.[64] To be sure, mechanization was not used solely to undercut the bargaining power of labor, but it was an essential part of the calculations made in determining whether or not to introduce machinery.

The Taft Ranch near Corpus Christi became the archetype of the modern southwestern agricultural enterprise. Taft land was divided into six 1,000-acre farms. Each "operated as a self-contained unit that consisted of a white superintendent, Anglo or Mexican foremen, and Mexican laborers."[65] According to historian Neil Foley, on the Taft Ranch and the farms that followed its lead, "King Cotton was subject to a board of directors and his retainers were now mostly Mexican wage laborers."[66] Similar to the mining companies of the Mountain West and the railroad company towns of the Midwest and Northeast, the Taft Ranch established a sort of closed society where all monetary circulation went through the corporation. Company stores, company housing, company gins, and other facilities tied workers (both migrant and nonmigrant) to the Taft Ranch by refusing to allow them to do their business elsewhere.[67]

While the Taft Ranch might be one of the largest examples of this new form of agribusiness, it was just one of many that helped define the shape of modern agribusiness. Here we see not only the intersection of seemingly backward forms of peonage with the modern corporate system in the creation of this closed system but, more important, a vertically and horizontally integrating corporation that looked very similar to the steel companies of the late nineteenth century or the automobile manufacturers of the twentieth century both in complexity and sheer size. Texas had more of these large-scale farms (as the Bureau of Agricultural Economics termed them) than any other state in 1930.[68] Thus a thoroughly modern agribusiness regime was born in South Texas that relied on a racial division of labor, the creation of a reserve army of labor, and the use of mechanization as a contingent aspect of the production process. These factors spurred the massive growth of agribusiness throughout the Southwest during the first half of the twentieth century as the trans-Mississippi West outpaced the more traditional agricultural areas of the Southeast and the Midwest.

IT WAS NOT long before agricultural and industrial interests in other parts of the nation took notice of the spectacular growth in South Texas, especially the region's seemingly endless pool of Mexican and Mexican American workers. By 1912 Arizona cotton growers began advertising for labor in South Texas newspapers. When cotton prices skyrocketed during World War I, these same cotton growers sent labor agents to El Paso and San Antonio to recruit larger numbers of pickers, reserving special trains to transport workers free of charge to Arizona.[69] Likewise, railroad companies had long looked to South Texas and the U.S.-Mexico border region for much of their workforce.[70] By the eruption of World War I, however, northern and midwestern business interests looked jealously at the labor supply built up in South Texas. Throughout the last years of the 1910s and the 1920s, these agricultural and industrial interests successfully drew many Mexican and Mexican American migrants out of South Texas, while also copying the often-illegal recruitment practices of Lone Star farmers by recruiting workers in northern Mexico, bypassing South Texas altogether.

Private labor contractors and labor agencies dominated the procurement process, serving as middlemen between the workers of South Texas and northern Mexico and prospective employers far from the border. Some recruitment occurred in informal settings such as Milam Park (also known as La Plaza del Zacate), which served as a gathering spot on the western edge of downtown San Antonio. Labor agents walked through the crowds offering jobs, cash advances, and a number of other enticements for agricultural, industrial, and railroad interests around the nation who viewed San Antonio as "a virtual Ellis Island for the tens of thousands of newcomers from Mexico in search of work and new opportunities," according to historian Zaragoza Vargas.[71]

Frank Cortez operated the largest employment agency in the area out of a funeral parlor on El Paso Street on San Antonio's West Side. Between March and May of each year he would recruit thousands of workers to go north to the sugar beet fields operated by the Michigan Beet Growers' Employment Committee, for which he received a recruitment fee of one dollar per head. While some of these workers came from San Antonio, as many as two-thirds paid their way from places like Brownsville, Corpus Christi, Crystal City, and south of the border, hoping to be sent north toward greater opportunity and away from a South Texas agricultural boom that refused to trickle down to the workers. San Antonio became, in the words of Carey McWilliams, "the hunting ground of labor contractors; the capitol of Mexico that lies within the United States."[72]

When recruiting season began, workers would begin to gather outside Cortez's funeral home as early as four o'clock in the morning. The line quickly wrapped around the block and often entailed a wait of several hours. Once applicants finally entered the office, they were interviewed and given physical examinations. Those rejected for medical causes (usually either tuberculosis or venereal disease) would seek employment through another labor agency or become "freewheelers" who traveled north independently. Those accepted for transport by Cortez had to wait around the El Paso Street area until they left for Michigan, which could be as long as a few months after they first walked into the funeral parlor.[73]

Once the day came to proceed out of San Antonio, the workers were loaded onto flatbed pickup trucks. Often forty or more packed the backs of these trucks as they roared north, forced to stand for the entire trip because there was no room to sit or lie down. Employment agencies and the employers who contracted the labor paid the truck drivers to make the trips as quickly and inconspicuously as possible. Not only did the drivers often refuse to stop for any reason, but they also drove at unsafe speeds (especially given their cargo loads) and took more hazardous, secondary routes to avoid attention from law enforcement. According to Carey McWilliams, the drivers, "as a rule," were "a domineering and dictatorial lot; as arrogant as ship captains on a slave galley."[74] Their passengers surely agreed. Telésforo Mandujano, who traveled on one of these trucks from San Antonio to Ohio, recalled that the truck stopped only once or twice en route, forcing the passengers to use coffee cans as urinals. One man even tied himself to a stake on the bed of the truck so he would not fall out of the truck if he fell asleep.[75] Salomé Ravago, who endured a trip from San Antonio to Michigan, remembered a journey that required five days and four nights in a truck with only partially functional brakes. "The workers finally forced the driver, at the point of a gun, to stop and buy brake fluid with money which they lent him," recalled Ravago.[76] Workers took these risks, Carey McWilliams argued, because "employment in sugar beets in Michigan" was "preferable to field work in Texas."[77]

During the 1920s, growers from a number of different parts of the United States experimented with labor recruited from South Texas. In 1925 cotton growers in the Mississippi Delta imported hundreds of Mexicans and Mexican Americans in an attempt to replicate the Taft Ranch model of cotton culture. Within a few weeks more than one-fifth had contracted malaria, abruptly ending the experiment (though it is worth mentioning these same growers tried again in the 1930s with more success).[78] Despite a number of similar experiments, however, the Upper Midwest was, far and away, the primary destination for workers recruited in South Texas. More specifically, the massive sugar beet combines in Michigan and nearby states remained the most prominent importers of labor.

Before looking at the specifics of what these migrant laborers did once they reached the beet fields, it is worth examining the structure of the sugar beet industry.[79] Carey McWilliams argued that "the sugar-beet industry has been created out of public funds and today is being subsidized to the extent of $350,000,000 a year by the American public. It is this subsidy which, in part, makes possible the perpetuation of rural sweatshops and what has been aptly characterized as industrialized slavery."[80] Born out of tariff protections against Caribbean sugar beginning in the late nineteenth century, sugar beet corporations emerged as massive, vertically integrated agricultural enterprises little different from the other industrial corporations of the time. In the Midwest the Michigan Sugar Company and the American Beet Sugar Company dominated the production and processing of beets, while the Great Western Sugar Company held a virtual monopoly over the industry in Colorado. These corporations owned the processing factories but little if any land. Instead they used their financial muscle to control every aspect of production through a complex, multilayered system of contracting that left every aspect of the process under the control of the corporation. They sold seed to the landowners, who had

A family of migrant sugar beet workers in the fields in East Grand Forks, Minnesota. The workers hold a sugar beet in their left hand and a topping knife in their right hand. (Photograph by Russell Lee, October 1937. Library of Congress, Prints and Photographs Division, Farm Security Administration/Office of War Information Collection [LC-USF3301-011331-M1].)

little choice but to grow sugar beets, and contracted to purchase the entire crop back at predetermined prices. In Colorado, the Great Western Sugar Company even loaned money to banks that was then used to finance growers, while in the Midwest the corporations tended to finance growers directly. The companies also handled all recruitment for nonlocal labor, which was the vast majority of the sugar beet workforce throughout the boom years of the 1920s.[81]

It was the corporations, not the growers, then, that contracted through Frank Cortez and others like him. And like a mirror image of the campaigns advertising opportunities for wealth in South Texas that appeared throughout the Midwest in the 1910s and 1920s, the sugar beet companies placed advertisements in a number of Spanish-language publications advertising the opportunities available in the sugar beet fields. The Columbia Sugar Company of Michigan ran ads in San Antonio's *La Prensa*, arguably the most important Spanish-language newspaper in the United States during those years, promising ample opportunity for work and, most important, a respectful atmosphere free of the anti-Mexican prejudice of Texas. As Kathleen

Mapes has argued, "the recruiters depicted work in Michigan's sugar beet fields not simply as a way to make money but as a different kind of life than most Mexicans could expect in a Jim Crow Texas."[82]

Prior to the 1920s sugar beet growers had relied on European immigrants as their primary labor force. In both Colorado and the Midwest, German-Russians made up the majority of the workforce during the first fifteen years of the century. The sugar beet companies, which had announced plans in some areas to build homes for these Eastern European workers, clearly viewed them as a stable and presumably permanent part of the production process during the 1910s.[83] During World War I, however, immigration from Europe halted at the same time that the market for beet sugar expanded. As a result, the sugar corporations increased production while searching for a new source of laborers. As one sugar company official told a Michigan newspaper, "unable to get a sufficient number of Russians [we] were compelled to resort to the dark skin fellows."[84] By 1918 Mexicans and Mexican Americans had become the primary labor force in the beet fields, and by 1927 they made up at least three-quarters of the migrant workforce.[85] This shift in labor force also extinguished the companies' eagerness to build housing for their workers. In securing workers from South Texas, the sugar beet companies seem also to have borrowed the preference of South Texas growers for mobile workers who disappeared when the season finished.[86]

At the same time, the beet fields became one of the most important economic opportunities for Mexicans and Mexican Americans trapped in the self-reinforcing cycle of migrant farmwork in Texas. A study of migratory farmworkers from Crystal City, Texas, in the 1930s showed that 60 percent of surveyed families worked seasonally in the sugar beet fields before returning south at the end of the season. Even though beet labor only lasted a few months each year, it was the most important source of income for farmworkers in the Winter Garden, even more important than the local spinach harvests.[87]

Beet wages, however, could be considered high only by the standards of field work in Texas. In 1923 the Beet Growers Association, which worked with the Great Western Sugar Company in Colorado, admitted as much in a letter to its members. It reported that Colorado beet growers required 7,700 field workers from Texas for the upcoming harvest. The association warned that beet growers in Michigan would recruit more than 6,000 from Texas. More threatening, however, was steel company interest in South Texas Mexicans and Mexican Americans:

Sign of an employment agency in Corpus Christi, Texas, advertising for migrant workers to harvest sugar beets in Michigan. (Photograph by Russell Lee, 1949. Russell Lee Photograph Collection, Study of the Spanish-Speaking People of Texas, Identification No. rwL13943iief_0002. The Dolph Briscoe Center for American History, University of Texas at Austin.)

"They pay 40c to 50c per hour, offer steady work for a year, free transportation, if labor works 90 days, opportunity for promotion, etc. This is an especially hard line of competition for agents recruiting field laborers. . . . *Employers from all states are looking to Texas to supply additional common labor that they need.*"[88] Clearly, the sugar beet growers and corporations understood the condition of farm laborers in Texas, and they knew their own position in the national economy and wage structure. Their profits depended on the continued existence of workers in South Texas willing to work for low wages, and competition from industrial employers threatened this labor supply.

When the migrant workers finally arrived in the beet zones they often found that they had to deal with a different set of problems than those they had encountered in the fields and towns of Texas. First, the sugar corporations instructed labor contractors to transport recruits north before the work began so that there was a guaranteed force available

Agricultural Worker Migrant Stream from Crystal City, Texas, 1938
(*Source*: Menefee, *Mexican Migratory Workers of South Texas*; map
prepared by Rebecca Wrenn)

at the start of the season. Workers who arrived in April or May had to
wait without pay until late May or early June before the first operations
began. The first of the season's three pay days did not come until July,
so the workers had to rely on advances or credit from local stores while
they waited.[89] Later in the 1920s payments declined to twice per season, pushing workers even further into debt. In addition, many of the
sugar companies withheld a few dollars from each pay period until the
end of the season in order to ensure that workers did not leave in search
of higher wages before the harvest ended. They did not pay workers
these earnings until the harvest had already ended and many of the
workers had to leave for employment elsewhere.[90] Many contracts
also contained clauses that shielded the company or landowner from
any responsibilities if the crop failed, leaving the contracted workers
stranded in remote beet fields more than 1,000 miles from the point
of recruitment.[91] George Edson, a Labor Department investigator,
reported that, because of these policies, "at the end of the beet growing
season, they find that through charges of transportation, commission,
supplies and accommodation and certain other deductions, they have
no pay left."[92] Still, workers returned to these sugar beet fields year after

year because they offered the possibility of a bare subsistence that did not exist in the fields of Texas.

Wages were, in fact, even lower than they appeared because employers and contractors paid male heads of household for labor done by entire families. Corporations determined acreage allotments according to the number of workers in each unit, including children, but they avoided leaving proof of child labor in the actual contracts. In the fields, however, the corporations and the landowners welcomed child labor. A study in Michigan in 1920 determined that among beet worker families, 20 percent of six-year-olds, 60 percent of eight-year-olds, and roughly 100 percent of ten-year-olds worked in the fields with the rest of their family. A study taken in the Wisconsin beet fields four years later found that 52 percent of field workers were under the age of fifteen, while only 21 percent were older then twenty-one. Thus, although this fact was purposefully hidden by the contracts, children actually performed the majority of beet labor.[93]

Once they entered the fields, migrant workers faced an arduous series of tasks that lasted from late May until the end of the harvest in November. First came blocking and thinning during May and June. Workers removed unneeded plants from each row with a hoe. Long-handled hoes had been used before the arrival of Mexican and Mexican American workers. During the 1920s, however, bolstered by declarations from agricultural experts at nearby land grant colleges, the corporations instituted the short-handled hoe. While more accurate and less likely to damage the crops than the long-handled variety, it required workers to stoop in order to reach the plants. As Dennis Valdés noted, "The simultaneous introduction of the short-handled hoe and Mexicano workers linked the two in the popular and academic mind."[94] The short-handled hoe remained the standard implement until blocking by machine became possible in the late 1920s. In the meantime, however, these stumpy implements caused ruptured discs, torn back ligaments, and arthritis of the spine.[95]

The preharvest operations finished by early August, so workers faced another period without work before the harvest began in late September or October, again falling back on advances and credit to subsist. Some were able to find temporary work elsewhere, in fields or railroads, as they waited for the harvest to begin. By the time the arduous task of topping came around, the season changed and much of the work had to be done in the rain and cold. Walking through the fields with large knives used to slice the top off of the beets, workers frequently cut themselves, with missing fingers and accidental gashes on arms and legs commonplace.[96]

At the end of the six-month season, male adults earned, on average, $160 in the midwestern beet fields in the late 1920s. While that represented a substantial improvement over the wages available in the fields of Texas, these wages had declined from those earned by the European workers a decade earlier. In 1920 European adult males had averaged $280 for the season. Clearly, then, the spectacular growth of the sugar beet industry, like that of agriculture in South Texas, depended on a depressed wage scale made possible by the miniscule pay available in the region south of San Antonio, as well as the practices of family recruitment and child labor. According to Carey McWilliams, beet migrants returned to Texas "as they left, with scarcely any money."[97]

Not all of these recruited workers returned to Texas at the end of the beet season, however. Labor Department investigator George Edson found that 90 percent of Mexicans who had been in the United States for less than a year returned to Mexico or Texas at the end of the beet harvest, beginning the annual agricultural cycle all over again with the winter harvests in South Texas. After two or three years in the United States, however, only 35 percent did so. Fifteen percent remained in the countryside near the beet fields, while fully 50 percent moved to nearby urban areas.[98] While Edson's numbers seem rather high considering the thousands of migrant farmworkers who returned to South Texas every winter, they point to the growth of a permanent Mexican and Mexican American population, especially in the Midwest, as some migrant workers shifted away from the border states.

The ultimate goal for those who remained in the Upper Midwest, especially those who moved to urban centers like Chicago and Detroit, was to secure some form of industrial labor. Eventually, according to Zaragoza Vargas, "farm work was viewed as a last resort, casual labor performed only by greenhorns or by Mexicans who constituted the permanent labor migration force from Texas."[99] Beet work, it was hoped, would serve as a lower rung on a ladder leading to better-paying and more stable employment in the steel mills of Chicago or the automotive plants of Detroit. And as had been the case with the sugar beet corporations, northern industrial interests welcomed Mexican and Mexican American workers as a valued supplement to the reserve army of labor collecting in the cities of the Upper Midwest.

Some industrial corporations recruited workers directly from South Texas, following the same general operating procedures as the sugar beet growers. Labor agents from steel mills competed with all of the other contractors circulating among the prospective migrants gathered in Milam Park in San Antonio, while Buick recruited some workers directly from Texas for its Flint assembly plant.[100] Bethlehem Steel also recruited a number of workers directly from Texas, but under an unusual arrangement. The postwar depression slowed operations across the nation, but when the steel industry resumed its predepression levels in 1923, Bethlehem Steel looked to South Texas as a logical source for labor. Between April 6 and May 30, 1923, 912 men, 29 women, and 7 children, all Mexican nationals, traveled to Pennsylvania under contract. The Mexican consul-general in San Antonio signed the contract, providing the migrants with the implicit protection of the Mexican government. Both the company and the imported workers seemed to sour on the arrangement in the next few years, however. By 1929, only six years after the first thousand recruits arrived from Mexico, less than 400 Mexicans remained in Bethlehem, and they eventually left during the Great Depression. Like the efforts to recruit ethnic Mexican field workers to the Mississippi Delta, this attempt to bring workers out of the U.S.-Mexico border region and into northeastern steel mills failed, though this did little to diminish the hopes of some that this malleable labor pool could be successfully exploited by northern industry.[101]

More often, however, Mexicans and Mexican Americans sought employment in northern industry on their own initiative, traveling away from the border region in search of more opportunity and less discrimination, the same hopeful path followed by African Americans leaving the South during the same years.[102] Whether they entered the cities after working in the beet fields or traveled there solely for urban employment, all saw the industrial cities as a substantial improvement over their lives in Mexico or South Texas. One migrant to Chicago described Mexicans' broadening geographical range:

> In the early days before Díaz was deposed and there was work
> enough in Mexico for all, one heard only of the states of Texas
> and California. The few Mexicans who left Mexico went there and
> wrote back from there. After a while we heard of New Mexico and
> Arizona, but beyond that there was no more United States to us. I
> remember distinctly with what great surprise we received a letter

in our pueblo from a Mexican who had gone to Pennsylvania. "Oh, where can that be! That must be very, very far away. It must be farther than New York, close to England." It was not until years after the war that we heard of St. Louis, then of Chicago and Illinois. Things were very good, I heard, so I came here direct from Laredo.[103]

Many migrants to Chicago and Detroit followed the same path, bypassing employment in the border states and traveling directly to the industrial North. The result, according to labor economist Paul Taylor, was that "Mexicans have entered the heart of industrial America. They are now the latest and lowliest newcomers in the long succession of migrating nationalities that have furnished the labor to build and maintain the basic industries of the United States."[104] When George Edson studied the presence of Mexicans and Mexican Americans in the North in 1927, he found that 30,827 held industrial employment in the industrial belt stretching from St. Paul, Minnesota, to the steel mills of Pennsylvania.[105]

Despite improved wages, however, insecurity was still a primary reality in the lives of ethnic Mexican industrial workers. Many Mexicans and Mexican Americans found themselves confronted by the same obstacles to advancement as African Americans entering industrial employment. Relegated to the most dangerous jobs, laid off at the first sign of market instability, and often victims of the seasonal nature of most industrial production, many of these newly arrived migrants found themselves pushed back into a life of transiency. As they shifted between cities like Chicago, Gary, and Detroit, they found themselves secluded in crowded, dirty neighborhoods between industrial districts.[106] When industrial labor could not be found, some had to return to the fields for the relative security of sugar beet harvesting. As Kathleen Mapes argues, "for many the path from rural fields to urban centers proved to be more circular than linear."[107] Industrial migration thus frequently created a parallel migration stream more compact geographically and slightly more stable than its interstate agricultural counterpart but one still characterized by instability and insecurity.[108]

The Montano family followed this unstable path between agricultural and industrial labor. All fifteen members of the family entered the United States at Laredo in 1920, and exhausted much of their money in paying the head tax required for entry. They first went to San

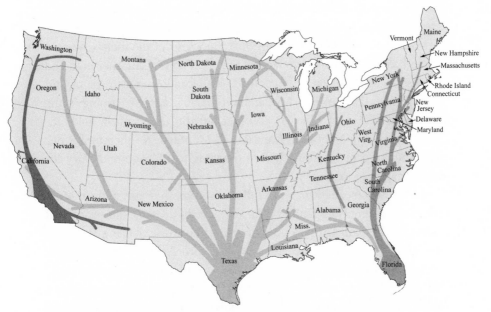

National Agricultural Migrant Streams (*Source*: Shostack, *Hired Farm Workers in the United States*; map prepared by Rebecca Wrenn)

Antonio, where four men in the family secured jobs at a dairy farm outside the city. After seeing a billboard advertising sugar beet employment in Michigan, the family went to a farm near Saginaw, where every member of the family participated in planting and harvesting. During the late stages of hoeing, four family members went to Saginaw and secured employment in the General Motors Central Foundry. As the steel industry slid into recession in 1921, however, three of the four lost their jobs. The family remained in the beet fields until 1924, when Venturo, his wife Maria, and their daughter went to Detroit, where Venturo worked in the massive Ford River Rouge plant. His job lasted until 1928, when a layoff forced the Montanos to return to the beet fields, no more financially stable than they had been when they first trekked north.[109]

Taylor uncovered a number of similar stories among Mexicans and Mexican Americans in Chicago. One man recalled leaving Mexico in 1918 and traveling first to San Antonio, where he became a cement worker. As the cotton harvest approached, work slowed down in San Antonio, so he entered the cotton migrant stream, hoping to earn more money there than in the city. He left Texas in 1920, arriving in Chicago during the winter. A month and a half after arriving he found work in a steel mill. But, he complained, "it was not steady and they took advantage of the hard times to bring down the wages of the men. I worked about half the time and was laid off the other half."[110] Another man had worked in Texas cotton, the beet fields of Colorado and Minnesota, and steel mills in Erie, Pennsylvania, and St. Louis, before arriving in the stockyard district of Chicago. Another left the Texas cotton fields for railroad labor in Nebraska, Kansas, and Montana. He then took work as a shepherd in Montana before traveling to Chicago and Gary for industrial employment.[111]

Taylor also recalled the path followed by another family from Mexico. They entered the United States at Laredo in 1920 and proceeded north to the San Antonio area, first finding work clearing land and grubbing brush near the city. Next they proceeded north to Belton (between Austin and Waco) to work in a cottonseed-oil factory where an uncle had previously worked. With insufficient work available there, the entire family continued north to Fort Worth, where they contracted to work in sugar beets near Billings, Montana. The next year they worked in the beet fields near Casper, Wyoming, stayed in Denver for the winter, and then worked the beet fields in Colorado. By 1927 the family had a total of fifteen dollars and an old car, which they took to Raton, New Mexico, where they stayed for a year working the coal mines. They left for the Texas cotton harvest in the fall of 1928, then went south to the Winter Garden to transplant onions, where they remained after the outbreak of the Great Depression. "The wanderings of individual Mexicans over a period of years may thus appear more or less erratic," wrote Taylor, "but they usually follow one or another of the seasonal swirls."[112]

These agricultural and industrial migrations greatly altered the demographic reality of the Mexican and Mexican American populations in the United States. While the vast majority still resided in the border states, large communities emerged far beyond the traditional Mexican American homeland. The Mexican population in Michigan was ten times larger in 1920 than it had been in 1910. During the same years, the Mexican population increased by a factor of ten in Wyoming; nine in both Nebraska and Idaho; five in New York, Pennsylvania, and Illinois; and four in Iowa.[113] In addition to this increasing migration to the Midwest, there was also an important movement from Texas toward California and the rest of the Southwest.[114]

Looked at together, these permanent and seasonal migrations created a Tejano and Mexicano Diaspora that spread the Tejano and Mexican population throughout the nation. At the same time these migrations created linkages between these disparate communities that helped nurture and stabilize an increasingly unstable population. They were not, in the words of anthropologist Roger Rouse, "spatially demarcated communities," nor were those who traveled between these places "capable of maintaining an involvement in only one of them."[115] Instead, they represented the construction of a complex, if haphazard, culture and community that stretched from northern Mexico to the Upper Midwest and, in the insecure migrant stream, provided a measure of stability that helped shape much of Mexican and Mexican American life in the United States during the two decades before the Great Depression.[116]

DESCRIBING THE AGRICULTURAL growth that began in the 1910s and 1920s, Carey McWilliams wrote, "Texas is currently in the midst of a revolution in its agricultural economy of such magnitude as to be, in the words of one qualified observer, 'beyond the imagination and comprehension of the average man.'"[117] In South Texas, this meant that a region previously deemed too arid and isolated for large-scale agriculture became one of the wealthiest farming areas in the nation. While this growth occurred at the same time that the expanded railroad network, refrigerated rail cars, and other technological and infrastructural improvements helped create a national market for agricultural goods, such developments could not have occurred in South Texas without the availability of large numbers of Mexican and Mexican American workers to prepare the land and harvest the crops.

While the changes wrought by the revolution in Texas agriculture occurred more slowly and seemed more mundane than the violence and disorder of the revolution in Mexico discussed in the previous chapter, their long-term effects were no less important. The economic, political, and social consequences of these changes would spread well beyond the border region, as the geographic impact of South Texas growers spread with the migrant labor stream that passed through the Texas-Mexico border region. The outcomes of these revolutions cannot be considered as wholly separate matters. The Mexican Revolution helped drive the revolutionary shift in Texas, while the massive changes in South Texas would remain one aspect of the ongoing legacy of the Mexican Revolution on both sides of the Rio Grande.

PART II | *Securing the Revolution*

In May 1930 John Willson, the president of the Cotulla Chamber of Commerce, sent a letter to fellow South Texan and U.S. House minority leader John Nance Garner. He hoped that Garner would lobby the commissioner-general of the Immigration Service to return immigration officials to Cotulla. "Our county officers and our citizens would very much appreciate anything you can do that will bring to the attention of the department, the necessity of having these immigration officials stationed back at Cotulla," Willson wrote. He explained that "Cotulla is sixty seven miles from the border and is a strategic point for the location of these men for the reason that many times, aliens who have got by the border patrol and have relaxed their cunning and precaution, are picked up at this point." He reiterated again and again how the immigration inspectors had been "high-class men" who were "efficient and honorable and upright in the discharge of their duties" while in Cotulla.[1]

At first glance, this correspondence seems unremarkable. Garner was one of the most powerful men in Washington (in the next four years he would ascend to the House speakership and the vice presidency under Franklin Delano Roosevelt), so he received many letters asking for favors. Nor is the request from the Cotulla Chamber of Commerce unusual. Towns in South Texas frequently requested state and federal law enforcement personnel to protect against any number of threats, both perceived and real. But for a town and region that relied on migrant labor as the basis of the economy, this request does seem odd. The South Texas Chambers of Commerce opposed any restrictions on immigration from Mexico and often protested mass deportations as direct attacks on the rights of farmers and, with much less emphasis, workers. Many of the Chambers of Commerce joined in protesting the deportation of large numbers of Mexicans from South Texas in the late 1920s by the Immigration Service. So why did they seek to bring immigration inspectors back to Cotulla in 1930? Was this a case of Depression-era anti-Mexican sentiment or something else entirely?

Willson's effort to justify this request makes clear the rationale for the appeal and sets this letter off as illustrative of a number of important aspects of South Texas farm society. He explained to Garner that the immigration officials at Cotulla had targeted immigrants "who were getting by to go to points in the north" such as "Arkansas, Missouri, Illinois, and Michigan." In providing this service, the federal agents were "men of good judgment and with a sense of justice and our county officials found that they were good men to cooperate with in the discharge of their duties." In closing, he reiterated, "We would like very much to have these men stationed back at Cotulla, and if it is possible for you to use your good office to that end, we will appreciate it."[2]

The motive for this request, then, had little to do with concerns over unauthorized immigration into the United States. Willson and the Cotulla Chamber of Commerce were happy to have unauthorized immigrants in South Texas, so long as they did not leave. The cooperation and good judgment they praised in the inspectors had little to do with scrupulous efforts to uphold the law and everything to do with willingness to selectively enforce laws that would aid the growers of Cotulla and the rest of South Texas. Unauthorized immigration was only a problem for Willson and the farm interests of South Texas if those immigrants went further north in search of more rewarding work.[3]

Willson's letter thus points to the contested and ambivalent nature of mobility in the emerging farm society, especially for the Mexican and Mexican American migrants who did the heavy lifting in constructing the region. The Chamber of Commerce and the farmers it represented consistently argued that they needed all obstacles to recruiting labor removed so their local economy could expand; at the same time they sought to immobilize any workers who tried to leave South Texas for employment elsewhere. The politics of mobility—determinations of who and what could cross internal and external boundaries, whether legally determined or arbitrarily imposed by force—helped growers ensure the profitability of farming in the region, but it also proved essential in shaping the labor relations and, more generally, the caste-like social structure of South Texas.[4]

Although mobile labor built this farming region, growers also feared that mobility could destroy them. Despite their rapid ascent since the beginning of the twentieth century, the growers of South Texas feared that their economic success could disappear just as suddenly if they could not maintain a steady oversupply of Mexican and Mexican

American labor. They could not ignore the expansion of the interstate migrant stream that they had unintentionally helped create. Even as their own production and profits grew, the growers of South Texas feared that the increased northward migration of Mexicans and Mexican Americans threatened to end the agricultural boom. Accordingly, farming interests worked throughout the 1910s and 1920s to limit the mobility of migrant farmworkers and thereby secure the ongoing agricultural revolution.

At the same time, however, these same growers demanded unfettered access to workers from Mexico. Many supported efforts throughout the 1910s and 1920s to restrict immigration from Asia and Eastern and Southern Europe, but they proclaimed time and again that they had an inherent right to bring in labor from across the Rio Grande. They feared, with good reason, that any disruption in the flow of Mexican labor into Texas could bring their newly built empire crashing down even faster than the interstate migrant stream. South Texas growers realized better than anyone that their primary advantage lay in their proximity and access to Mexico.

Willson's letter, and the almost countless other efforts like it to simultaneously inhibit and encourage mobility, point to the importance of the politics of mobility in the quest to assure continuing growth. The following two chapters deal with both aspects of this contradictory legacy. Chapter 3, "Breaking the Machines, Building the Color Line, and Immobilizing Mobile Labor," examines the effort to immobilize Mexican and Mexican American workers, as Willson hoped immigration officials could do at Cotulla. Through a complete overhaul of the political system and the establishment of rigid segregation, farming interests sought to impose labor controls on the working population that would guarantee an eternal oversupply of available labor. Chapter 4, "Homing Pigeons, Cheap Labor, and Frustrated Nativists: Immigration Reform and Deportation," then deals with the effort to head off immigration restriction at the U.S.-Mexico border and the effects of those efforts on the region's Mexican and Mexican American populations. While neither of these efforts to shape the politics of mobility was entirely successful, both proved enormously important in determining the broad outlines of this society and in defining who could and could not freely exercise their right to mobility.

CHAPTER THREE

Breaking the Machines, Building the Color Line, and Immobilizing Mobile Labor

Elias Garza, a native of Cuernavaca, Morelos, entered the United States at Laredo in 1912 with his Texas-born wife and children. This was his third trip north of the border seeking employment. In the decade before this entry at Laredo, Garza had worked on the railroads in Kansas and at various jobs in California: he had handled dynamite in a stone quarry, skinned hogs in a packing plant, and performed maintenance work at a railroad station. He returned to Mexico after his second trip to the United States, but "things were bad there, for that was in 1912, and the disorders of the revolution had already started."[1] Thus, Garza crossed the border a third time with his family. In San Antonio, they contracted to pick cotton in the Rio Grande Valley along with several other Mexican immigrants. When they arrived at the farm, the planter pointed Elias and his family toward a shack that had previously housed chickens. Garza demanded better accommodations, but the farmer refused and told them to leave. As they began to depart, the sheriff arrested Garza and his wife and took them to the county jail. There the farmer claimed that Garza had skipped out on him without reimbursing his transportation costs from San Antonio. "He charged me twice the cost of the transportation," recalled Garza, "and though I tried first not to pay him, and then to pay him what it cost, I couldn't do anything. The authorities would only pay attention to him, and as they were in league with him they told me that if I didn't pay him they would take my wife and my little children to work. Then I paid them."[2] After this legally sanctioned shakedown, Garza and his family continued to Dallas, El Paso, Arizona, and eventually Los Angeles, tracing a path similar to that of hundreds of thousands of other Mexicans who entered the United States during these years and unwittingly became vital elements in the growth of the southwestern economy and the formation of a distinct South Texas model of labor relations.

That model of labor relations, the cornerstone of economic growth in South Texas agriculture, depended on exactly these sorts of temporary hindrances to labor mobility. While growers built their agribusiness operations through the use of migrant labor, they also understood that mobility could cut both ways—it could provide cheap labor but it could also allow that labor to move elsewhere in search of higher wages or better treatment. As a result, during the boom years of the 1910s and 1920s they often sought to restrain mobility during harvest time and other periods when labor shortages loomed, while also allowing that labor to leave during slack periods when migrant workers were not wanted or needed. In order to achieve these goals, however, they had to reshape the political and social environments around them to suit their labor supply needs.

This chapter examines the ways growers and politicians in South Texas attempted to guarantee the continuation of their farm boom. By constructing overlapping systems of political, spatial, and economic domination, the political and economic elites of South Texas fashioned a system, however imperfect, that assured the persistence of a low-paid surplus labor force and a growing agricultural economy. The political takeover of the farming interests, the strengthening of social segregation, and the construction of a more systematic web of labor controls combined with large-scale immigration from Mexico and the growth of irrigation capacity and railroad facilities to spur on the farm boom throughout the 1910s and 1920s.

AS AGRICULTURAL PROFITS grew and land consolidation continued apace in South Texas, local political change followed.[3] The paternalistic political machines that had faded during the late nineteenth century in other parts of South Texas remained in control in the ranching areas after the turn of the century. Jim Wells, the archetype of the South Texas political boss, maintained his hold on the Lower Valley into the twentieth century. The newcomer farmers, however, viewed the operations of the machines as insidiously antirepublican and dangerously apathetic to the desires of farmers. They wanted local government to promote the interests of growers. Throughout the 1910s, political battles raged between old-timers and newcomers over Mexican voting. The newcomers claimed that the machines bought Mexican votes and that only by eliminating this corruption could republican government come to the Lower Valley. Alba Heywood, a land speculator in the San

Benito area of Cameron County, described this antimachine feeling: "I do not think that the Mexican ignorance and the Mexican corruption that they talk so much about is our menace. I think our menace is the intelligence and shrewdness and corruption of the American men who lead them." But, he continued, "I don't believe in spraying the leaves to cure citrus canker and don't believe in cutting off the limb. . . . I think citrus canker, and we have political citrus canker, should be gone after as they go after citrus canker, and cut the tap root. Mine is the tap root theory."[4] The machine politicians, eager to maintain their control, did what they could to proceed as they always had, offering paternalistic protection to Mexicans and Mexican Americans while trying to hold off the political insurgencies erupting around them.

These battles were fought in two different ways. The first method, borrowed by the newcomers from the tactics of the Jim Crow South, was the white primary. Maverick and Dimmit counties, both located in the Winter Garden region southwest of San Antonio, instituted these exclusionary tactics in 1913 and 1914, respectively. The *Carrizo Springs Javelin* (Dimmit County) editorialized that "in times past the handling of the Mexican vote has not been such as would reflect any credit upon the people of the county," before asking rhetorically, "Are you a white man standing with white men, or are you—well, something else?"[5] After the White Man's Primary Association succeeded in disenfranchising Mexicans Americans in Dimmit, the *Javelin* waxed poetic: "The White Men's Primary, by eliminating one of the most unscrupulous elements of local politics, will do much to give Dimmit County civic righteousness, and the people want it."[6] By denying the vote to Mexican Americans, attacking the weakest link in the structure of political control created by the machines, these newcomers forced the machines into a defensive position from which they could not recover. Mexican American voting rights were sacrificed at the altar of "progressive" political reform that put the control of county government in the hands of a new farming elite who viewed ethnic Mexicans as nothing more than a labor supply that should have no voice in governing the region.

The second method, used by both sides, was the creation of new counties. From 1911 to 1921, the seven counties of the Rio Grande Valley underwent a form of political mitosis to create a total of thirteen counties. Population growth had nothing to do with this subdivision—instead, new counties were created as enclaves for either farming or ranching elites. The first two counties carved out of the original seven were Brooks and Jim Hogg, both established in 1911. Brooks broke away from Starr County, a border ranching county firmly under the control of Jim Wells's ally, Manuel Guerra. Likewise, Jim Hogg was created out of Zapata County, a machine stronghold and ranching county. White farmers controlled the politics of both new counties from the beginning.[7]

A second wave of county subdivisions began almost immediately. Different from Brooks and Jim Hogg, however, these new counties were defensive bulwarks created by ranching interests to maintain some control and leave counties that had become increasingly farmer dominated. Willacy (1911), Jim Wells (1911), Kleberg (1913), and Kenedy (1921) counties emerged out of old ranching areas of Cameron, Hidalgo, and Nueces counties.[8] In these new counties, the old machine practices continued, creating what were essentially isolated enclaves within a rapidly changing economic, social, and political environment.

In statewide politics, William Hobby's entry into the governor's mansion in 1917 as a midterm replacement for the impeached James Ferguson gave the farm interests a strong ally in Austin. Hobby was a late convert to the Progressive wing of the state Democratic Party, but he emerged as a fervent opponent of the old political machines and a staunch ally of prohibitionists. Both sides prepared for a clash in the 1918 elections, as Hobby ran against Ferguson for control of the state's Democratic Party. Ferguson's electoral hopes depended on the South Texas machines and the strongly anti-Prohibition Germans in the Hill Country north of San Antonio. Emerging in the midst of World War I and the continued violence spawned by the Mexican Revolution, the Progressive forces united behind Hobby attacked their opponents as lackeys of the Kaiser and Mexican bandit leaders who sought to destroy republican government in Texas through liquor-dealing and vote-buying. In this context, the interests of the state Progressive establishment coincided perfectly with farming elements in South Texas. Hand in hand, they launched a campaign of intimidation during the 1918 elections that sought to eliminate voting by Mexican Americans and thus destroy any remaining strongholds of machine power.

The Texas Rangers took a prominent role in these events. When Hobby took office in 1917 he appointed James Harley, a former state representative firmly within the Progressive camp, as his adjutant general. In January 1918 Harley created the Loyalty Ranger Force under the command of Captain W. M. Hanson.[9] Three men appointed from

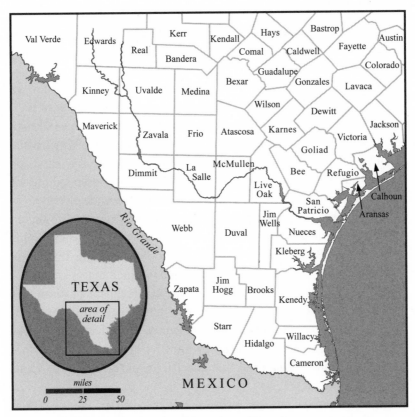

South Texas Counties (Map prepared by Rebecca Wrenn)

each county in Texas made up the Loyalty Rangers, whose purpose, according to Harley, was to "act as a Secret Service Department for the State, County, and Municipal officers in the execution of all State laws, especially House Bill No. 15, better known as the 'Hobby Loyalty Act.' Through the assistance of the Loyalty Secret Service Department this office has been advised as to Mexican revolutionary activities carried on, principally outside of San Antonio, and in the border counties in Mexico and this State."[10] In fact, Loyalty Rangers served as a political bludgeon against enemies of Hobby and his wing of the state Democratic Party, especially in the Rangers' traditional stomping grounds of South Texas. At the same time, Harley revoked all Special Ranger commissions granted by James Ferguson and replaced the entire force with his own appointees. By the time of the 1918 elections more than 500 Hobby supporters received patronage positions in the Ranger Force, making any notion that the Rangers were an apolitical law enforcement body laughable. The group had merely switched patrons. Rather than the political bosses and their machines, the Rangers bowed to new masters: the farmers of South Texas and their elite allies in the rest of the state.[11]

On primary day, July 27, 1918, Loyalty, Special, and regular Rangers swarmed polling places across South Texas, making no secret of their efforts to dissuade Mexican Americans from voting. In Corpus Christi, Rangers threatened Mexican Americans with prison if they voted, while in Duval County they functioned as menacing observers to dissuade voters from supporting local boss Archie Parr in his reelection bid for the state senate. Their strategy worked in the statewide elections, as Hobby won the nomination easily, outpolling Ferguson two-to-one in South Texas (which Ferguson won two-to-one two years earlier). In his local election, Parr thwarted these efforts in typical South Texas style and managed to win the nomination in spite of the Rangers and opposition from Hobby, who rightly viewed Parr as a Ferguson partisan. His opponent, D. W. Glasscock, held a lead of 1,200 votes with returns in from all precincts but those in Duval County. Since Duval had fewer than 1,000 registered voters, Hobby and the Progressives cried foul when Duval officials reported that had Parr won the county by 1,280 votes (1,303 to 23).[12]

Legal wrangling ensued, but the courts ruled in favor of Parr, undoubtedly bending to pressure from Jim Wells. Glasscock responded during the general election with a write-in campaign, which had more of a chance of victory than running as a Republican in South Texas. Openly working for Parr's opponent, Harley sent the Rangers to interrogate "all questionable voters." Seven days before the general election Hobby ordered his adjutant general to position Rangers throughout South Texas as a warning to dissuade the usual vote-getting practices of Parr and the machines. Rangers openly threatened Mexican American voters. In Alice, very near Parr's home in San Diego, the number of votes dropped from 300 in the primary to 65 in the general election.[13] But it was all to no avail. Despite the show of force and ham-handed attempts to block voting, Parr defeated Glasscock and retained his senate seat.[14]

Despite this setback for the machines' enemies, the 1918 elections marked an important turning point. Not only did Hobby and the Progressives maintain control of the governor's mansion, but they further damaged the machines through their blatantly partisan use of the

Rangers. While Hobby remained nominally allied with Jim Wells in Cameron County and the Guerra family in Starr County, he and his allies made no secret of their desire to change the nature of politics in South Texas toward a system more responsive to farmers' interests. Parr may have been their primary enemy, but all of the political bosses remained vulnerable as long as their political longevity relied on buying votes from the Mexican American majority. With the Rangers now firmly on the side of the farming interests, the machines found themselves caught between the new political ascendancy and their former constituents, whose memories of the genocidal violence of 1915–16 had yet to fade, and who remained angry that nothing had been done to protect their voting rights. While the machines had already been on the decline, their deterioration accelerated in the aftermath of the 1918 elections and the conspicuous silence from the likes of Jim Wells and his associates.[15] Only in isolated areas, such as Duval and Starr counties, did the machines maintain this support during the agricultural boom of the 1920s.[16]

As the machines faded, most overt sentiment in favor of Mexican American voting rights disappeared. Interviewed several years later, Asherton farmer Littleton Richardson explained that the political bosses "used to give the Mexicans whiskey and free meals for thirty days before election. As a result they got no work done during that time. So to put a stop to the whole thing they organized the white man's primary."[17] Since these newcomers hated Mexican American voting and interruptions in their workforce with equal ferocity, they responded in what they deemed the only way to make sure that neither happened again. In 1923 the state legislature, bowing to pressure from East Texas interests looking to shore up protections against African American voters and South Texas interests eager to do the same with Mexican Americans, mandated a statewide white primary. Mexican American voters were not entirely eliminated by this legislation, since local voting registrars and Democratic Party officials were able to determine who was white, but when combined in the years to come with poll taxes and other similar efforts, the measure crippled voting strength throughout the region for decades to come, even as Mexican American majorities expanded.

There were exceptions, of course. The Taft Ranch, for instance, continued to operate in the same manner as the disgraced machines had. Managers and foremen instructed their workers not to "make up their minds on politics until they had heard from the management."[18] The company paid all poll taxes for its employees, then recovered the money by garnishing wages. They herded workers to the polls on Election Day and dictated their votes. Thus Mexican American voting aroused little anger when it benefited agribusiness interests, especially in areas where farmers still sought to wrest control from opposing political factions. As farming interests took unquestioned control, however, they simply phased out the tactics they learned from the machines and pushed Mexicans and Mexican Americans out of the political realm while still relying on them in the economic realm.

In many counties, good government leagues created a new form of political machine, built wholly on the principle of exclusion rather than on the delicate parasitic relationships that underlay the power of the older political bosses. Clothing disenfranchisement in the rhetoric of progressivism, these new machines depicted themselves as redeemers of the political system who would return control to the rightful leaders. Beneath these empty exaltations of civic righteousness, however, lay the same threats of violence that had always remained just below the surface in South Texas, made especially resonant by the memories of genocidal war less than a generation earlier. Many South Texas Anglos seemed to agree with a resident of Dimmit County interviewed by Paul Taylor: "There isn't much probability of the Mexicans taking enough interest to vote. If they did, first some plan would be devised by law to keep them from voting. Second, if that could not be done there might be calamity from a physical standpoint and there might be some dead Mexicans."[19] Relying on legal maneuvering and the specter of violence, these new political elites constructed local and regional political dynasties that remained in control for decades.[20]

Along with these changes in the political order came an even more important restructuring of the social system that mirrored the enforced political powerlessness of the ethnic Mexican majority. When farming interests captured political control of an area, they immediately set about implementing a system of segregation that went beyond the residential segregation that had long been a fact of life in the region. This segregation, according to historian David Montejano, "was not merely a natural unfolding of previous foundations or legacies—not just an immigration of more prejudiced Anglos or an assimilation of the old. This was a new society, with new class groups and class relations, with the capacity to generate an 'indigenous' rationale for the ordering of people."[21] The adoption of widespread segregation, in other words, replicated the racial divisions of the labor force and applied them to all aspects of South Texas society. "Outside the social order but a necessary part of it," wrote Montejano, "Mexicans were attached to the new agricultural society through the construction of separate and subordinate institutions that rigidly defined their position as farm laborers."[22]

A seemingly unquestioned tautology justified this social separation. The powerlessness of Mexicans and Mexican Americans, though often achieved through violence, became the justification for their banishment from full citizenship in the farm society. Conversely, their supposed unfitness for full citizenship validated their political and economic powerlessness. Clearly, economic considerations, manifested in racialist feeling as a further subconscious rationalization, determined the hierarchical structure of this new agricultural society. Beyond simple racism, then, the farmers of South Texas created a system they deemed utilitarian in its stark simplicity that guaranteed a reliable, cheap workforce whose basic rights remained an abstraction to be ignored whenever convenient.

The general attitudes expressed by Anglo residents of South Texas during these years exhibited just this kind of earnest belief in the rationality of their system, with some even going so far as to celebrate the perfection of this recently constructed arrangement. G. A. Tallmadge, a farmer near Corpus Christi originally from Milwaukee, scolded labor economist Paul Taylor for the scholar's lack of enthusiasm for what he observed in South Texas: "Don't come down here from the north and describe the poverty of the Mexicans at the back door of the white man's high civilization. Don't forget that he's an independent individual. There never lived a person in such freedom." Tallmadge continued his admonishment, complaining that Taylor and others should not "get to pitying the Mexican and depreciating the white people holding him in subjection. He wouldn't have it any other way. The white man will cuss the Mexican, and then in the evening, on the cattle ranches, he's down by the fire with him, with the frying pan, and eating tortillas with his coffee. There never was a grander companionship between men."[23]

Likewise, John Stone, an onion grower in Carrizo Springs, viewed the wages he offered as charitable: "We have to have the Mexicans as cheap labor. We carry them when things are tight; they won't save. They owe me about $500 now, and I will lose about half of it. I can't afford to pay them high wages, and then carry them when times are tight. I wish they would save for themselves, but it isn't in their nature to do it." Any more money, claimed Stone, would ruin the workers. Not willing to leave it at that, however, Stone continued:

> The Mexican is getting paid two bits too much; he gets from $1.50 to $2.00 a day. He should get about $1. When he has a dollar in his pocket he won't work. You get more onions transplanted at 5 cents a row than you do at 10 cents. It's just the nature of the Mexican. He needs about $8 a week if he has a family, for clothes, shoes, and food. What a Mexican should be paid is just enough to live on, with maybe a dollar or two to spend. That's all he deserves. If he is paid any more he won't work so much; or when we need him, he's able to wait around until we have to raise the price above what's legitimate.[24]

Stone's attitude was typical of the newcomer farmers who viewed interethnic relations through the lens of economics, deciding that what was best for their bottom line necessarily had to be best for everyone. Not so typical was another statement by Stone, in which he seemed to revel in coercing Mexican and African American women into sex, further revealing the dehumanization necessary to rationalize this kind of social system:

> We favor a Mexican more than we do a negro. You can get more work out of a negro, but a Mexican is a better citizen. You never heard of a case of rape by a Mexican; it happens all the time with the negroes. And a Mexican respects a white man; you can do anything you want with their women; their men won't attack you; of course some of the better educated Texas-Mexicans would just as soon go after you. With the negro women you can do anything you want if you just get them off from the rest; the Mexican women will never say yes; you just have to go ahead or you'll get left. Some of the Mexican men seem to feel it an honor that a white man will pay that much attention to their women.[25]

In such an atmosphere, it is no surprise that a Nueces County tenant farmer proudly declared, "I have only hit three Mexicans in eight years and I consider that a pretty good record."[26] Nor that a Dimmit County farmer stated, "We feel toward the Mexicans just like toward the nigger, but not so much."[27]

As farm towns were founded throughout the region in the late 1910s and 1920s, segregation followed in the immediate aftermath. While most public accommodations practiced some form of segregation, school segregation was most telling of the nature of this society.[28] Some towns built schools solely for use by Mexicans and Mexican Americans, while others secluded students in different classrooms within the same building, but the basic pattern remained the same throughout the region.[29] Segregation's defenders supported school separation in the same terms as they did labor relations. They claimed that separation was good for Mexicans because it kept them from directly competing with Anglos, while also stressing that it protected Anglo children from intimate contact with Mexican children.

John Stone summarized these general feelings in his interview with Paul Taylor: "Reasons for separation? They're low morally, and many of their children aren't clean; either they would be left behind by the faster progress of the white children, or the white children would be held back. The Mexicans could go to the white schools if they knew enough and insisted; they're Caucasians. But they are satisfied; they know that the white children would make it pretty hard for the Mexican children and would probably get the best of them."[30] Similarly, when Paul Taylor asked an Anglo tenant farmer why the nearest school refused to admit Mexicans, he roared back, "Because a damned greaser is not fit to sit side of a white girl. Anybody who wants to get in trouble around here can just try to put them in the same school. A man would rather his daughter was dead than that she should marry a Mexican. The Mexicans are too dirty and filthy. If they separate in school the children learn the difference and they won't mix with the Mexicans. Of course, if they contend for it, we will either have to take them into the school or else build them another."[31]

In addition to these predictable defenses of segregation, however, some supporters made no pretense of hiding the fact that they used separation as a way to further subsidize Anglo schools. As happened with African American schools in the Southeast, funds received from the state for Mexican schools went almost entirely into the white educational system. A school superintendent in Nueces County stated unapologetically that "Mexicans in this district draw about $6,000 state aid, and we spend on them about $2,000. This is true everywhere in Texas. We also have an $18,000 property tax and that all goes to the white school."[32] A Winter Garden farmer likewise readily admitted that the "school board uses the money it gets from the state for the Mexican scholastics on the white school. If they didn't have to they wouldn't have any school for the Mexicans. When you say anything to them about it, their attitude is 'oh well, they're Mexicans.'"[33]

Another important aspect of the educational system in these farming towns was the lack of any attempt to enforce compulsory attendance laws. While this could be seen as a result of the general apathy toward the educational needs of the Mexican American population, it had much more to do with issues of labor availability.[34] Paul Taylor estimated that at no time during the year did more than 25 percent of ethnic Mexican children between the ages of seven and seventeen attend school in Dimmit County, while the average attendance rate was much lower than that.[35] Children who did attend school regularly often found themselves on vacation weeks earlier than white students so that they could work in the fields. The "Mexican schools" in Nueces County, for instance, finished their school year a month early so that students could be put to work chopping cotton.[36] These segregated schools thus acted as little more than places to warehouse potential field laborers during the off-season. When added to the fact that many of these children had to travel with the rest of their families on the migrant trail for months, it can hardly be surprising that most Mexican and Mexican American children did not make it as far as the fifth grade. Far from accidental, this system developed as an intentional aspect of the ethnic and labor relations regime established by farmers who felt that "education they get in the schools here spoils them, and makes them trifling; they become peddlers, or bootleggers, or seek some easy way of making a living."[37] Freedom from hard work, apparently, was a right earned only by the employers of Mexican and Mexican American labor.

The larger towns and cities of South Texas did not have a system of segregation quite as rigid as the farm towns, but conditions in places like San Antonio, Laredo, Eagle Pass, Corpus Christi, and Brownsville largely mirrored what was happening in the small towns of the Winter Garden, the Lower Rio Grande Valley, and the other farming areas. Still, many in these farm towns pointed to San Antonio and the other large towns as places where Mexicans and Anglos associated too freely, such as the farmer in Carrizo Springs who stated disapprovingly that "in San Antonio and Laredo and some other places they do vote and go to the same schools. But not here."[38] Likewise, a school board member in Dimmit County explained, "Politics is the reason for mixing of Americans and Mexicans in San Antonio and Laredo. There they can't offend the Mexicans."[39] Despite these estimations of an overly egalitarian atmosphere in San Antonio, however, a rigid pattern of residential segregation accomplished the same kind of social separation. Restrictive covenants and other similar measures forced most Mexicans and Mexican Americans into the city's increasingly overcrowded West Side. With residential segregation accomplished, city leaders merely had to draw school district lines in such a way that created de facto, if not de jure, educational segregation.[40]

The results of this residential segregation in San Antonio, however, could be dire. The lack of proper sanitation facilities such as running water and sewage lines in much of San Antonio's West Side created an acute public health crisis that continued to fester under the noses of the city's Anglo leadership. Tuberculosis rates among Mexicans and Mexican Americans in the city dwarfed those among Anglos and African Americans, which themselves were high by national standards. A local publication described the neighborhoods of the West Side as mired in "primitive conditions that beggar description. . . . Living conditions actually below those of the cattle in some of San Antonio's modern dairies are used as human habitations in many instances, and whole sections are so lacking in sanitary provisions as to form an actual health menace."[41] As the population grew throughout these years, the newcomers found themselves stacked on top of new neighbors, trapped in a corner of a city that refused to allow their physical expansion into the North or South Side. Ramshackle, dilapidated housing littered this bounded section of town, leaving the population susceptible to natural disaster. In the midst of the farm boom to the south, the residents of the West Side found themselves victims of a massive flood that swept through the central and western portions of the city in September 1921.

Not surprisingly, the West Side of San Antonio was the area of the city most prone to flooding (though much of the city lies in a flood basin). When exacerbated by the lack of sturdy housing or reliable sewage and water services, the potential for catastrophe was constant, even if ignored. While the San Antonio River and its many tributaries usually maintained low flow levels, when floods did occur they could become raging torrents that, before partial flood control came during the 1930s, ripped through districts adjacent to the river and its network of creeks.[42]

Photograph of corral housing commonly found on the West Side of San Antonio, Texas. (Photograph by Russell Lee, March 1939. Library of Congress, Prints and Photographs Division, Farm Security Administration/Office of War Information Collection [LC-USF33-012095-M2].)

Beginning on Wednesday, September 9, 1921, heavy rain pounded the Hill Country north of San Antonio, dramatically raising the water level in Olmos Creek and the San Antonio River. The rain continued unabated until Friday night, when in a matter of a few hours almost eight inches of rain fell on the city and the area to its immediate north. This torrent of water roared into the San Antonio River, bursting its banks that night. Water from the river and swollen creeks combined with the water already running in the streets of downtown and the West Side to create a fast-moving, twenty-foot-high, half-mile-wide surge of water that destroyed hundreds of homes and killed an unknown number of people.[43] When the water finally receded, a zone two miles long and a half-mile wide had been destroyed, with buildings swept away and human and animal corpses buried in massive piles of debris.[44] According to the *New York Times*, the path of destruction included the "heart of the business section . . . as well as the thickly populated west side, where today thousands of Mexicans are homeless and the dead not yet counted."[45] Poorly constructed hovels and rickety tenements had no chance of holding up against the flood waters, turning the segregated barrio of the West Side into a temporary flood basin that assured heavy loss of life.[46] Like the Ninth Ward of New Orleans or the hillside slums surrounding Caracas, Rio de Janeiro, and Mexico City, San Antonio's West Side remained under the constant threat of natural disaster.[47] Political elites ignored these hazards, however, because the area's population was deemed racially and politically inconsequential.[48]

These same rains left trails of death behind them outside of San Antonio as well. In Williamson and Milam counties, north of Austin, more than 100 were killed when the San Gabriel River burst its banks and flooded surrounding low-lying areas. Almost all of the dead were ethnic Mexican migrant farmworkers forced to live in temporary housing in the lowlands along the rivers and tributaries in the region. In the crossroads town of Thorndale sixty-five bodies were recovered, all of them Mexican or Mexican American. On a single farm near Elm Grove twenty-nine Mexican farmworkers died. Only two Anglos died in these Central Texas floods.[49] Similar to their brethren in San Antonio, these Mexican and Mexican American farmworkers had, in the words of Mike Davis, "little choice but to live with disaster" given the effects of social segregation.[50]

Efforts to deal with these flooding issues in San Antonio revealed similar unwillingness to provide the same protections and services to the West Side as to the rest of the city. "Concerned ultimately (and only) with the reconstruction of the commercial core," wrote historian Char Miller, "the urban elite ignored the legendary drainage, housing, and sanitation problems confronting those who lived on the city's west and south sides; their plight was theirs alone. Nothing captures these disparities more perfectly than the paired announcements coming from city council in August 1924: at the same time it released millions of dollars to fund the Olmos Dam [meant to keep flood waters from the downtown area], the council voted to spend a meager $6,000 to cut brush along the San Pedro and Alazán Creeks. This remarkable discrepancy in financial investment and flood prevention technology would continue for the next fifty years. The management of San Antonio's floodwaters, as with so much else, was channeled along sharply etched ethnic divisions and class lines."[51] Such was the logical conclusion of the practice of segregation in South Texas.

THE POLITICAL DOMINATION wielded by farm interests allowed them to institute and enforce the residential and educational segregation that both reflected and maintained the caste-like social separation between Mexicans and Anglos in South Texas. But their financial and political success bred anxiety. As farmworkers became more mobile and extended their seasonal migrations well beyond the state borders of Texas, farm owners and their allies in South Texas worried that their low-wage surplus labor pool could disappear, drawn away by promises of higher wages elsewhere. In the midst of spectacular growth in their own farm profits, they worried that sugar beet corporations, northern manufacturing concerns, the enhanced availability of cheap automobiles, and a number of other factors had begun to sow the seeds of the collapse of agriculture in South Texas. Whether these concerns were the result of paranoia, greed, or legitimate concerns over the sustainability of the growth of the boom years, South Texas agriculturalists looked to immobilize these workers to make sure that harvest surpluses never disappeared and wages stayed low. Throughout the 1910s and 1920s, farmers and politicians experimented with a number of methods to achieve these goals, leading them to create a wide array of measures designed to undercut and erase the free labor rights of Mexican and Mexican American farmworkers.

Farmers devised labor controls that sought to undercut the migratory reality of agricultural labor while maintaining by any means necessary the low wages that made agriculture in South Texas so profitable. Geographer Don Mitchell referred to this as "the history, on one side, of finding ways to control the movement of labor, and, on the other, of finding the means to make that mobility subversive."[52] Despite the coercive nature of these efforts, however, farm interests maintained a notable consistency in arguing that they could not compete with industrial employers and therefore needed to protect themselves from outside enticement of their workers by doing whatever the situation required to maintain an oversupply of labor. South Texas farmers, like agribusiness interests elsewhere, justified these controls by constructing an ideology that appeared to evolve out of the paternalism of the Old South but that was stripped of any notions of mutual obligation and then extruded through the atomized social thought of corporate capitalism.[53] What emerged from this atmosphere, according to historian David Montejano, was an "inchoate web of labor controls in rural Texas."[54]

The level of sophistication of these measures varied, with methods reminiscent of slavery existing side-by-side with much more subtle, legally sanctioned schemes of guaranteeing seasonal labor surpluses without the messy problems that came along with bondage. Peonage remained the most basic method of controlling labor, and its use continued throughout the farm boom of the 1910s and 1920s. It obviously carried a number of liabilities, but with unquestioned political and economic dominance in their home counties, many farmers viewed forms of bondage as a simple way to guarantee overabundant labor, even if this lacked the elegance of the schemes used elsewhere.

Many employers enticed workers with stories of high wages, then sought to force them to work when their actual wages turned out to be much lower. One man who worked in Nueces County recalled, "We were supposed to be paid $1.50 a hundred pounds for picking cotton, but we received only $4 or $5 a week in cash. We were paid partly in money and partly in credit at the ranch store, and the prices at the store were high." When several workers predictably left, "they gathered the rest of us in the garage and posted the mayordomo at the door with a rifle. Then the owner came with a pistol and threatened to kill any man who left."[55] More subtle than these methods, but seemingly also less successful, were the practices described by a former labor scout for farmers near Laredo: "We used to take their shoes and hats and put them in another house, but they got away from us anyway in 1919, and we used to even guard each door of the houses they slept in on a big farm. We used to put wives separate from the husbands, but the men left their wives to come north."[56]

In many areas, however, a more subtle, if no less coercive, system of labor controls emerged that drew on the connivance of political and law enforcement officials ignoring blatant violations of a number of laws. One early example of this occurred with the construction of a dam on the Medina River, forty miles west of San Antonio, for irrigation purposes at the very beginning of the farm boom in 1911 and 1912. The Alamo Cement Company of San Antonio recruited workers from Mexico in direct violation of the alien contract labor law for both the production of cement and the construction of the dam for the Medina Dam and Irrigation Company. According to a labor contractor who later contacted the Department of Justice to report illegal activities by his competitors, the labor agent hired by Alamo Cement and the Medina Company "had no difficulty getting the men across, because he tipped the guards who were named 'Frenchy' and Benavides" at Laredo.[57] Despite this testimony, there was no prosecution for violation of contract labor law.[58]

In addition, however, the Mexican consul general at San Antonio, Manuel Esteva, reported instances of peonage at the Medina Dam to the Department of Justice shortly after the alien contract labor investigations.[59] These reports from the consul general went to the assistant U.S. attorney in San Antonio, Charles Cresson, who ignored the case and reported to Justice Department special agents that there was no merit in the peonage cases.[60] In addition to his position as assistant U.S. attorney, Cresson was the second vice president of, chief counsel for, and stockholder in the Medina Dam and Irrigation Company.[61] By the time the Justice Department discovered these conflicts of interest, the construction of the dam ended and Cresson was free to enjoy the profits flowing out of the irrigation works made possible by his shielding of the company from possible prosecution. In such a situation, it was hard, if not impossible, to determine where farm enterprises ended and the supposed guarantors of political order began.

A related method of labor control relied on timely and racially determined enforcement of vagrancy laws, again reminiscent of labor practices in the cotton belt of the Southeast.[62] The best example of this system operated in Willacy County, just north of Cameron County in the Lower Rio Grande Valley. In what came to be known as the "Raymondville Peonage Cases," the outlines of a plan emerged in which farmers and the top officials of the county government conspired to immobilize farmworkers. The farmers contracted laborers from San Antonio and nearby towns under terms that changed once they arrived in Willacy County. As in the case of Elias Garza that began this chapter, those who refused to work were arrested for vagrancy and charged twice the cost of their transportation. Those arrested were then forced to work off their debt by picking cotton, under armed guard, for the farmer who originally recruited them. Willacy County officials also operated a "pass system" during the harvest that forbade any farmworker from passing through or leaving the county without the permission of the farm owners. Not surprisingly, vagrancy charges and convict labor followed violation of the pass law for anyone caught up within this machinery of peonage. Thus, the cotton farmers of Willacy County had a virtually unpaid workforce that was legally sanctioned through the connivance of county law enforcement. Almost all of these "vagrants" were Mexicans or Mexican Americans, but a few Anglos found themselves caught in this web. In fact, the prosecutions that eventually ended this system arose out of the arrest of two Anglos for vagrancy.[63]

The prosecutions of the Willacy County peonage cases sent chills throughout South Texas. Reactions often echoed the feeling that growers "have to watch out for the peonage law now, so it almost requires a lawyer to keep out of the laws."[64] Another respondent, quick to forget the nature of the prosecutions, complained, "We feel we need some sort of law to protect us. The Mexican ought to have to live up to his contract; it wouldn't hurt labor."[65] Another man complained that farmers "ought to be able to make them work out their debt. The peonage cases were extreme. There was a labor shortage in 1926. They don't generally do that."[66] Beyond this collective hand-wringing, however, angry farmers found the time to brutally assault one of the primary witnesses for the prosecution outside his home in Raymondville, and then throw a party to celebrate the release from prison of the sheriff of Willacy County.[67]

Taken together, these methods of immobilizing labor certainly inconvenienced and probably intimidated many workers, but they did little to stop worker mobility. As the Willacy County system hummed along during the boom years of the 1920s, tens of thousands of Mexicans and Mexican Americans left Texas for employment elsewhere. For those unfortunate enough to find themselves caught in the web of labor control, however, the system probably did not seem as porous as it does in hindsight. Even if it failed in some respects the system accomplished the ultimate goal of maintaining a region-wide surplus labor pool without allowing wages to rise.

In addition to measures that targeted the workers themselves, a parallel set of strictures sought to protect farmers in South Texas from contractors and labor agents seeking to entice workers away with promises of higher wages. Like the methods for stripping workers of their rights to free labor, antienticement schemes varied from simple to complex, from covering single farms to operating statewide. At the local level, antienticement efforts often resulted in simple threats to labor contractors.[68] These measures were informal just as often as not, enforced by individual farmers or farmers' associations rather than by law enforcement (though we have already seen how difficult it can be to differentiate between the two).

By the mid-1920s, however, the increased attention paid to South Texas labor by northern agricultural and manufacturing interests, combined with demands to maintain the growth in the agricultural economy, created intense pressures to protect farmers against the poaching of labor agents. One example of these conflicts unfolded between 1926 and 1929 in the Winter Garden. Farming developed later around the town of Catarina than in the rest of the region. Catarina's late settlement and development meant that its population was almost entirely made up of recent arrivals from the North. When production around Catarina reached substantial levels in 1926, these farmers drew much of their labor from nearby towns, primarily Asherton and its longer-settled population, through Mexican American labor contractors. One Asherton farmer complained, "Part of the trouble is due to the northern people with money and big acreages who don't know how to handle the Mexicans like the southerners. They offer them too high wages. The Mexicans are not cheap labor any more."[69] Another complained that the "northerners who settled here were somewhat shocked at the $1 and $1.25 a day wages. The Mexicans are worth only about $1.25, but the Mexican contractors are shrewd, and they steam them up to pay more."[70] To stop the exodus of their workers to the fields twelve miles away in Catarina, the Asherton growers turned to the state judiciary. "We got an injunction from Judge Mullally in Laredo against Mexican contractors of Catarina who were paid big bonuses to come and get our labor," explained an Asherton resident, before incorrectly asserting, "There's a law in Texas against taking labor out of a community where there's a shortage there."[71] Examining this episode, Paul Taylor noted, "This reliance on some device hampering to one's competitor and to the movement of labor is characteristic in south Texas."[72]

While northerners in their midst certainly alarmed the farmers of South Texas, much more frightening for them were the northern agricultural and industrial concerns that transported their workers far beyond the state's borders.[73] Growers and politicians in Texas argued unanimously and loudly that the increased poaching of labor by northern interests and their labor contractors threatened the continued expansion, even the very existence, of the agricultural economy of South Texas. The Texas Farm Placement Service, looking back on these years, declared that blame for this situation lay with labor contractors: "[The contractor] had no regard for seasonal needs of Texas farmers. If he could persuade the migrants to start for the Michigan beet fields or elsewhere, so much the worse for Texas farmers if the labor supply was short. The emigrant agent very soon became one of the most serious problems in Texas labor."[74] Others, such as a Texas farmer who testified before the House Committee on Immigration and Naturalization in 1926, blamed the northern interests that employed both the contractors and the workers: "Whenever the beet growers of the various States of the Union come to south Texas for laborers to harvest their crops, they are taking them away from us, leaving us in an even worse condition than before, when they could find a supply of labor in eastern cities for their beet fields."[75]

In the 1920s these fears of contractors run amok combined with strong efforts to limit immigration into the United States (discussed in the next chapter), raising fears that the workers sent north could no longer be replaced by new immigrants if outside political forces decided to close the border. The Texas labor commissioner pointed to Mexico as the only source of relief for Texas farmers, arguing, "The tendency on the part of farm labor to leave agricultural pursuits for wage opportunities afforded in commercial and industrial centers is fast approaching a tragedy and farmers complain they are unable to meet competitive wage scales offered in the urban labor markets. This can only be remedied and is being remedied by hiring Mexican labor whose standard of living is far below the American worker."[76] Therefore, with their immigrant workforce now threatened, Texas farmers and politicians looked to outlaw the contracting of labor for employment in other states.[77]

These efforts culminated in the Emigrant Labor Agency Law of 1929.[78] Supported by the American Federation of Labor, the South Texas Chamber of Commerce, the Winter Garden Chamber of Commerce, and a number of other groups interested in keeping Mexican and Mexican American workers in Texas, the law was introduced by A. P. Johnson, the state representative from Carrizo Springs.[79] The original version of the law charged a $7,500 occupation tax to any contractor wishing to send workers out of Texas, thereby criminalizing all nonlicensed contracting. In addition, county taxes and the required posting of a $5,000 return bond for each worker in the counties of recruitment added additional financial obstacles for contractors.[80] A federal court soon struck down the $7,500 fee after Michigan sugar beet corporations petitioned, but the legislature quickly replaced it with a $1,000 occupation tax.[81]

The proponents of this law believed that Texas and its farmers had a natural right to Mexican workers that superseded the needs or rights of the rest of the nation. In an illuminating statement, the Emigrant Labor Agency Law's chief sponsor, A. P. Johnson, justified the bill on the grounds of these supposed rights, while also clearly pointing to the threat of the eventual end of immigration from Mexico: "It is the same situation as where you have had a stream of water running through your ranch. If someone turns its source off you want to put up a dam to hold what you have got."[82] Similarly, a Nueces County farmer declared, "We got a law passed to keep the Mexicans in Texas and out of the beets. The border states need a temporary passport from Mexicans; put a boundary on Texas."[83] In theory, then, Texas farmers had insulated themselves for the time being from both out-of-state labor migrations and the looming threat of immigration restrictions on Mexicans.

In practice, however, the Emigrant Labor Agency Law was not the insurmountable obstacle hoped for by its proponents. According to J. R. Steelman, the director of mediation for the U.S. Department of Labor under Franklin Roosevelt, the Emigrant Labor Agency Law was "circumvented in several ways, chiefly by the '*grapevine.*' In this the *labor agents* merely stop in at gas stations and pool rooms and spread the word that much work at fine wages is to be had in such and such a place. It is amazingly effective. *Agents* are also *posted* at *highway junctions* to 'direct the flow' to the cotton areas needing labor. *Signs* are put up along the highways. *Newspaper advertisements* are extensively used, and bring some results."[84] In addition, the law included a loophole that exempted from its provisions "private" contractors, meaning those who worked for only one client. Thus labor agents avoided paying occupational taxes and return bonds because they only worked for a single employer, even though that corporation might provide thousands of workers to dozens of growers.[85] Finally, in the words of Carey McWilliams, the "principal consequence of this law was to make of out-of-state recruitment a kind of illegal, underground conspiracy."[86] The already harrowing passage north became even more dangerous for the workers, as contractors now sought more than ever to hide their activities from state authorities. In the end, the law was "harassing, but it presents no insuperable barrier to sugar beet or other companies' shipping thousands of laborers out of Texas," according to Paul Taylor.[87] The best indication of the short-term ineffectiveness of the law came in 1940, however, when T. Y. Collins, an official of the Texas Bureau of Labor, announced that the state had yet to collect any occupational taxes from labor contractors.[88]

Not until 1943 would the sugar beet corporations of the Upper Midwest finally apply for an emigrant labor agency license and set up official recruitment centers in San Antonio and other towns.[89] This substantial investment in Texas labor recruitment occurred for two primary reasons. First, the outbreak of World War II caused agricultural interests throughout the nation to fear that they might lose their labor supply to military service and increased opportunities in higher-paying industrial jobs. Second, as Emilio Zamora has argued, the web of labor controls that emerged in the 1910s and 1920s was greatly strengthened during the war by the concerted efforts of the U.S. and Texas governments to "freeze" agricultural labor on the farms of Texas. In 1942 the Texas Railroad Commission, in tandem with Farm Bureaus throughout the state, sent "motor transportation inspectors" to stop contractors and individual truckers from sending workers out of the state.[90] At the same time, the U.S. Employment Service, the War Manpower Commission, the Farm Security Administration, and other federal agencies sought to guarantee sufficient labor for the farmers of Texas. Both state and federal officials declared that their interference in the labor market had helped guarantee employment for migrant laborers who otherwise might have been exploited by labor contractors. Their true intentions were to appease growers afraid that their surplus labor supply might move elsewhere.[91]

More important, however, the Emigrant Labor Agency Law made clear the racial assumptions underlying Texas labor law. As David Montejano has argued, "The political situation for the Mexicans in Texas . . . appeared quite ominous. With 85% of the State's migratory labor force composed of Mexicans, the thrust of these labor laws was unequivocally clear; they were in essence a set of racial labor controls."[92]

The Emigrant Labor Agency Law, despite its sieve-like enforcement capacity, was the logical conclusion of the political and agricultural developments of the 1910s and 1920s. It served as both a reflection of and integral element in the construction of the caste system of South Texas. The self-reinforcing collusion of farmer and politician placed the state firmly behind growers' interests in every regard, and the well-being of both groups depended on the construction of a system that stripped political power from ethnic Mexicans as a means to immobilize and exploit them. The Emigrant Labor Agency Law serves as the ultimate symbol of the dominance of farming interests in the political, social, and economic realms.

More important, it symbolized the political ascendance of a South Texas model of labor relations that combined a racially segmented job market with a clear denial of the basic rights of choice and mobility for Mexicans and Mexican Americans. While the rural South featured many of the same strictures—antienticement laws and racial job market segmentation most obviously—the constant flow of migrants from Mexico set South Texas apart. Not only could South Texas growers replenish their labor supplies almost at will, but they were able to erase the need for tenants and sharecroppers. Their workforce came from the migrant stream of Mexicans and Mexican Americans that stretched from northern Mexico to the U.S. Midwest. Despite the shortcomings of the web of labor controls, its ability to immobilize workers seasonally even as new migrants continued to come from Mexico helped create a unique model of labor relations dependent on foreign workers and the denial of basic rights.

BY THE EARLY 1930s the growers and political elites of South Texas had managed, to a shocking degree, to reshape their society to fit their needs. They achieved this feat through three simultaneous, related efforts: the replacement of the political machines with organizations firmly under grower control, the establishment of a rigid pattern of social segregation that would reflect the color line that already defined the labor force, and efforts to limit worker mobility whenever growers feared that mobility might hurt their ability to recruit labor. Farmers were not universally successful in their efforts, but they did manage to bend the region's institutions and many of its people to their benefit.

The seizure of political power, on both the local and statewide levels, required little more than the adoption of "progressive" white primaries that effectively disenfranchised nonwhite voters and therefore removed the core constituency of the fading political machines. With the levers of political power firmly in their hands, farming interests then moved to consolidate their control over the region and assure its continued economic success. The new farm towns that emerged throughout South Texas were born segregated, while residential and school segregation spread throughout the region, highlighting further the race-based divisions already enshrined in agribusiness labor practices. Finally, always afraid that their reliance on temporary labor alienated from the land could come back hurt to them, South Texas elites looked to all manner of schemes to limit the mobility rights of their workers. While this web of labor controls proved eminently surmountable for most migrant laborers, its greatest importance lies in the effort to construct and maintain it. In the Emigrant Labor Agency Law and efforts like it, growers presented their view of the farm society in its purest form: a world in which nonwhite workers remained voiceless and powerless, simultaneously mobile and immobile, but always dependent on the whims of the agribusiness elite. These immobilizations, in other words, not only helped artificially enlarge the labor pool and lower wage rates but also simultaneously reflected and upheld growers' view of a rigidly hierarchical world where they pulled the strings that animated the people beneath them. Antienticement laws, however, only dealt with interstate migration of Mexicans and Mexican Americans. South Texas growers also feared losing their access to workers coming from Mexico. This threat proved to be much more complicated and forced the growers and politicians of Texas to side with their mortal enemies in the sugar beet industry as both groups took to the hustings to denounce immigration restriction.

CHAPTER FOUR

Homing Pigeons, Cheap Labor, and Frustrated Nativists

Immigration Reform and Deportation

Espiridión de León came to the United States from Mexico in 1916 and settled in the town of Mercedes in Hidalgo County, Texas. He married a Texas-born woman in 1927. By 1931 he and his wife had three children, all of whom were U.S. citizens. Although de León had worked for a local landowner for years and had never run afoul of the law, he became concerned once U.S. Immigration Service deportation drives began in the Lower Rio Grande Valley in the late 1920s. The Immigration Act of 1924 granted immunity from prosecution or deportation to unauthorized migrants who had entered the United States before passage of the law and stayed there continuously, so de León obtained a notarized statement in August 1929 stating that he had been in the United States for twelve years without returning to Mexico, to protect him from the threat of expulsion. Despite this document, however, immigration agents seized de León in March 1931 while he was walking down a Mercedes street. One officer grabbed him by the collar and shook him, while the other pointed a gun at his head and forced de León to state that he had entered the United States after 1925, in violation of the 1924 immigration act. This coerced confession led to an immediate deportation decision. A few days later de León found himself in Río Rico, Tamaulipas, unable to return to his family or find a job in Mexico. He was reduced to writing a letter to the governor of Texas begging for help.[1]

Despite de León's precautions, he found himself caught up in the machinery of immigration control. His deportation was not simply the result of a short-lived wave of nativist mania caused by the Great Depression. If that had been the case, why would he have obtained a notarized document to protect himself from Immigration Service deportation parties in August 1929, almost two months before the stock market crash that signaled the beginning of the Great Depression? He clearly reacted to a law enforcement campaign that began earlier. While the Great Depression and economic nativism have long served as the simple explanations for the deportation of thousands of Mexicans during the late 1920s and early 1930s, the case of Espiridión de León and the thousands of other deportees sent back to Mexico from South Texas point to something different. These deportations were the result of decades of nativist agitation and arguments over the proper place of Mexicans in the hierarchy of racial desirability that shaped immigration law in the United States.

Agricultural interests dependent on these workers who flowed through the Texas-Mexico border region perceived a very real threat in efforts to limit immigration through the introduction of higher head taxes, literacy tests, and national-origins quotas. They watched as nativists successfully pushed the federal government to pass restrictionist legislation in the 1910s and 1920s that began to systematize and limit who could and should enter the United States.

Between 1917 and the beginning of the Great Depression, when political nativism and the South Texas farm boom both reached their respective high-water marks, each side waged unrelenting battle to ensure that its conception of proper immigration controls would regulate who could and should enter the United States. Nativists were successful in passing a series of restrictive immigration laws, but immigrants from the Western Hemisphere remained outside of the restrictive quotas. As a result, the Southwest, which had been peripheral in the earlier formulations of restrictionist legislation, became the primary point of contention as these immigration debates continued. Nativists turned their attention to this hole in their regime of restriction in the years after the passage of the Immigration Act of 1924, focusing especially on the Texas-Mexico border region. This area had become a primary source of surplus labor for agricultural interests as far away as the Upper Midwest, so growers fought just as hard to maintain their access to Mexican workers. The focus of both restrictionists and antirestrictionists on this region meant that the U.S.-Mexico border, and South Texas in particular, remained the geographic center of this debate into the 1930s.

Congressional nativists tried in both 1926 and 1928 to push through legislation that would have placed Mexico under the restrictive quotas,

but they were unable to overcome the political clout of the antirestrictionists. Rather than give up after repeated legislative defeats, however,
nativists instead looked to bureaucratic means to their goal. Beginning
in 1928, they turned to large-scale deportation as the solution to their
problem, allowing them to simultaneously limit the number of Mexican
citizens in the United States and claim that this law enforcement campaign proved that Mexicans were likely to commit crimes and therefore were not desirable immigrants. This campaign of deportation
swept across South Texas throughout 1928 and 1929, before the Great
Depression had begun. These were not simply random sweeps but
arose directly from nativist desire to cut off immigration from Mexico.
Since they had been thwarted in their attempts to have Mexico included
in the quota laws, officials devised large-scale deportations in the Rio
Grande Valley as an end run around the repeated legislative failures of
restrictionists in Congress. Instead of viewing deportation as an alternative to quota restrictions, however, the Immigration Service saw the
two strategies as complementary. Only after the economic collapse of
1929 did deportation efforts replace the efforts for quota restrictions
and spread to the rest of the country. By focusing almost entirely on
deportations in California and the urban Upper Midwest, historians
have neglected the earlier deportation drives in Texas. Since large-scale
deportations did not start in California until 1930, an exclusive focus
there makes the deportation campaigns seem like a simple reaction to
the Depression, ignoring the more complex reality.

Rather than being a departure from previous practice, as most historians have assumed, the deportation drives normally associated with
the Great Depression instead represent a clear continuity of immigration restriction as it was practiced in the early decades of the twentieth
century.[2] For growers, this apparent setback in their efforts to maintain
access to Mexican workers instead solidified their position atop farm
society by attaching more firmly the taint of illegality and illegitimacy
to Mexicans and Mexican Americans. Farmers might have lost some of
their control over the politics of mobility, but they gained the sanction
of the federal government in ignoring the rights of their labor force.

THE FIRST STEP toward a new, systematic immigration code came
with the Immigration Act of 1917. Previously, the Chinese Exclusion
Act of 1882, the Foran Act of 1885, and a series of additional laws
in the early 1900s had deemed Asians, foreign contract laborers,

anarchists, prostitutes, the diseased, and anyone "likely to become a public charge" unfit for entry. The new law doubled the head tax for entry to eight dollars per person and added a literacy test (in their native language) for heads of household, while maintaining all of the older restrictions.[3] Along the U.S.-Mexico border, many applicants immediately withdrew their applications. Presumably, many simply entered as undocumented migrants across the largely unguarded southern border.[4] Not surprisingly, the growers of South Texas, in the process of building their agricultural empires in 1917, angrily decried the legislation. Picking up their refrain that they had an inherent right to Mexican labor, the growers fretted that the immigration restrictions would ruin them. The Department of Labor, the Immigration Service, congressmen, and senators received an almost endless stream of letters and telegrams from farmers and others in Texas who demanded an end to immigration restrictions. A mine manager in Central Texas, for instance, wrote to Senator Charles Culberson of Texas that it was "the 'hewers of wood and carriers of water' class of Mexicans that we are after." In other words, he and other employers wanted precisely the sort of immigrants the head tax and literacy test were meant to exclude. "Lots of these Mexicans are in Mexico today and want to return to Texas but can not," he complained. "All labor in every line is very short, and scarce, high prices are being paid, and you cannot get the labor because the labor is just simply not there."[5] Similar urgent pleas for help came from all over Texas, as Chambers of Commerce, often rechristened as Councils of Defense during World War I, begged for more labor from Mexico.[6]

This pressure quickly had its intended result. Eighteen days after the immigration act went into effect on May 5, Secretary of Labor William B. Wilson bowed to these insistent calls for increased immigration. On May 23, 1917, he issued a departmental order that suspended the literacy test, head tax, and contract labor exclusion for Mexican agricultural workers on the grounds of "an emergent condition, caused by the war."[7] By July 1918 these exemptions to the immigration law also covered workers leaving Mexico for work on the railroads, in any mining enterprise, or construction work in any of the four border states, despite the concerns of the commissioner-general of the Immigration Service that the decision "to permit industries other than agricultural to avail themselves of such supply of common labor as can be obtained in Mexico (the even approximate amount of which is altogether problematical) is

quite likely so to deplete the supply available to the agricultural interests as to interfere materially in the direct production of the foodstuffs."[8]

A few months later Secretary Wilson gave further reason for these
exemptions in a letter to Samuel Gompers, head of the American Federation of Labor. Explaining the necessity of his actions, he wrote: "You
are aware of the strong pressure that has been brought to bear upon the
Government to reverse its settled policy as regards Asiatic labor, and
to let down the barriers raised by legislation, for the purpose of per-
mitting the wholesale importation of such labor under the plea of wartime necessity. The Department is of the belief that the action taken by
it to meet the real emergency that existed, through the utilization of
the labor of Mexico, the Bahamas and Jamaica (as well as that of our
own possession, Porto Rico), has been to a large extent the means of
relieving the pressure mentioned."[9] In other words, Wilson justified his
decision to the ardently restrictionist Gompers as the lesser evil that
would placate agriculturalists without allowing the reintroduction of
Chinese immigration, the old bogeyman of craft unionists. Mexicans,
in other words, would not remain in the United States as long as the
hated Chinese.

Employers hoping to take advantage of these exceptions filed
an application with either the Immigration Service or the U.S.
Employment Service stating the number of workers needed, the "class
of work," wages offered, and place of employment. Upon acceptance
of the application, the U.S. Employment Service admitted the laborers
from Mexico, photographed each of them for identification purposes,
and turned them over to the employer. The Labor Department made
it clear that these exemptions, and the workers admitted under them,
were only temporary. As a means of ensuring that these immigrants did
not remain in the United States permanently under these exemptions,
the department administered a hold-back scheme whereby employers
withheld 25 cents for each day of employment up to a maximum of
$100, after which the employer withheld $1 each month for the dura-
tion of the immigrant's time in the United States. Employers then sent
this money via postal money orders to the inspector in charge at the
immigrant's place of entry, who deposited the money in a postal savings
bank in the name of the immigrant. Exempted laborers received these
withheld wages from the bank when they left the country. Any worker
who did not return to Mexico at the end of this employment forfeited
these earned wages. These holdbacks also allowed the Immigration

Service to maintain approximate knowledge of the location of each contracted worker through the money orders.[10]

During the first year of this program of exemptions, 9,401 Mexicans entered the United States to work, but farmers complained that this system still damaged their interests. They sought the removal of all restrictions on immigration from Mexico, complaining that the temporary admission system established by the Department of Labor was too time-consuming and bureaucratic. At the head of the forces seeking to compel the Department of Labor to drop all regulations was Herbert Hoover, then head of the U.S. Food Administration, who waged a persistent campaign to convince President Woodrow Wilson and the Department of Labor to ignore the Immigration Act of 1917 when it came to the entry of Mexicans. In June 1918 he complained to Felix Frankfurter, then assistant to the secretary of labor, "There are several restrictions in force which are handicapping the movement of Mexican labor north across the border." He called for an end to the hold-back scheme, because it "is bad, as it is deducted from his wage and further, we do not want him to return." Expanding on this point, Hoover grumbled, "There also exists a clause providing that he must return in six months and, although this period is possible of extension, the restriction should be waived so that there is no limit on his stay in the states." Finally, he called for an end to the requirement that "farmers must meet and contract with the laborer at the border. We hope to overcome this by having special representatives make these contacts at Brownsville, Eagle Pass, Laredo, and El Paso." In conclusion, Hoover declared, "We need every bit of this labor that we can get and we need it badly and . . . we will need it for years to come."[11]

One week later the secretary of labor replied to Hoover's entreaty. Referring to Hoover's complaint that the entry of Mexican workers should be permanent, Secretary Wilson reminded Hoover that "this Department is confronted with provisions of law which absolutely exclude from permanent entry to the United States a vast majority of the ordinary laborers that live in the Republic of Mexico." While he assured Hoover that his department would "do everything within its power and its authority under the law to further the production and conservation of foodstuffs," Secretary Wilson closed his letter with a subtle rebuke to Hoover and his agricultural allies: "The Mexican border, it is the consensus of opinion of the Departments, is the weakest point in our line of defense so far as espionage, the carrying and securing of military information, and similar patterns are concerned." In other words, even though he declared exemptions to the Immigration Act of 1917 within a few days of its enactment as a wartime emergency measure, he clearly agreed with the nativist contention that the government needed to impede permanent migration to the United States.[12]

A chorus of other voices joined Hoover's, however, and increased the pressure on the Department of Labor and the Immigration Service to completely ignore the Immigration Act of 1917. Many of these supplicants demurred that their calls for Mexican labor were "written with as much, or more patriotism, as . . . personal interests," asking only that the government remove "an obstacle which hampers one of the greatest needs of our Country today."[13] Telegrams from across Texas poured in, pleading "as a 'win the war' measure that all restrictions against Mexican labor be lifted except health regulations."[14]

When World War I ended in November 1918, however, the reason for the Mexican exemptions disappeared. The next month, on December 15, 1918, Secretary Wilson ended the exemptions. Importations continued until January 15, 1919, while all agricultural workers already in the United States were permitted to stay until the end of the next growing season.[15] Not surprisingly, the looming reinstitution of the head tax and literacy test prompted a storm of protest from agricultural interests around the nation. Sugar beet corporations claimed that they had expanded their operations during the war years at the "urgent request of the Food Administration," and they demanded that the secretary of labor continue the exemptions.[16] Texas growers echoed the same sentiments. Fred Roberts, the president of the South Texas Cotton Growers' Association, declared, "We are short of labor. The real fact is we have not any labor. . . . We have always had free access to the Mexicans on the other side of the border, and we have always been going there for our labor." He estimated that 250,000 Mexican workers would be necessary to gather the coming cotton crop, which could only be secured if the immigration law was ignored.[17] Roy Miller, a South Texas cotton grower, even argued that farm interests sought the resumption of unrestricted immigration of workers from Mexico for humanitarian reasons: "I think one of the greatest services the people of this country could render the people of Mexico today would be some arrangement whereby they could come across and help us and get paid for it. That would do more than anything else to tranquilize conditions on the border."[18] Despite these protests, however, the Department of Labor allowed the exemptions to lapse in early 1919. Thus, beginning in 1919, Mexicans and their prospective employers either had to abide by the letter of recent immigration law or ignore it and assume that enforcement would be lax.

WHILE THE END of World War I led agriculturalists across the nation to plead for an end to the specific immigration regulations that they found inconvenient, the aftermath of the war also witnessed a dramatic increase in aggressive nativism, culminating in the passage of far more restrictive legislation in the 1920s that drastically expanded the federal government's ability to exclude new immigrants. The momentum that allowed for the passage of the literacy test in the Immigration Act of 1917 only grew, as both political parties clamored to appease the nativists. While Mexico and the rest of the Western Hemisphere remained exempt from the most exclusionary elements of these new laws, the Immigration Acts of 1921 and 1924 did have profound effects on Mexican immigration.

The devastation of World War I, and the massive refugee populations it created, brought a worldwide trend toward exclusion.[19] As historian Mae Ngai has argued, "the international system that emerged with World War I gave primacy to the territorial integrity of the nation-state, which raised the borders between nations." As a result, claims of inherent rights became cemented more firmly and ineluctably to citizenship status granted by nation-states.[20] Stricter exclusionary immigration measures severely limited the rights that any noncitizen could claim within any nation-state. For Mexicans and Mexican Americans in the United States, whose rights and citizenship had long been ignored, these trends did not bode well.

As congressional nativists formulated legislation to realize these exclusionary ideals, the tenuous nature of Mexican existence in the United States was again illustrated as the economic downturn of 1920–21 led to a deportation drive that sought to expel immigrants who overstayed their exemptions as well as any others deemed "a menace to the peace of the community." Especially vulnerable were Mexicans in places like Chicago and Detroit, as the Immigration Bureau launched a nationwide sweep of urban areas in 1921, deporting any Mexicans who could not provide proof of permanent residence in the United States. This deportation campaign not only foreshadowed the massive repatriation campaigns that began later in the decade, but it also served as proof for some that Mexican immigration differed substantively from immigration from other nations because it could be easily reversed and pushed back south of the border. The belief that Mexicans were both economically necessary and easily discarded had much to do with Mexico's exclusion from the immigration quotas in 1921, 1924, and after.[21]

Individuals and groups who wanted Mexico and the rest of the Western Hemisphere placed under quota restrictions often found themselves on the defensive against powerful agribusiness interests that vigorously lobbied to limit the severity of proposed legislation. Sugar beet corporations, southwestern growers, and others dependent on the labor of Mexicans argued that quotas not only would decimate their workforce but were entirely unnecessary in the context of Mexican immigration. On many counts, the restrictionists and antirestrictionists shared the same beliefs in the racial degeneracy of Mexicans, but their conclusions as to its meaning differed. Antirestrictionists continually argued that Mexicans possessed an innate homing instinct that impelled them to return to Mexico after time spent in the United States. According to this belief, Mexicans were little more than laboring tourists who would inevitably leave of their own accord. John Nance Garner, congressman from South Texas, became one of the primary spokesmen for this viewpoint.[22] He constantly reiterated the notion that Mexicans rarely stayed after their work was done: "The whole family comes over and works and all the children will get out there and pick up the onions and set out the onions, and they will put up a little shack—they do not even put up a house. They throw a little brush around the place and that is their camping place, and when they get through with it, and if they have as much as $25, which is 50 pesos in Mexico, and they go back to Mexico."[23]

The antirestrictionist argument rested on the assumption that Mexicans were not really immigrants at all but rather were temporary sojourners who lacked the desire or the capacity to enter U.S. society. Antirestrictionists ridiculed the restrictionist fears that Mexicans would degrade the nation's racial stock and instead argued that Mexicans represented the only foreign labor force that did not represent a social threat. George Clements of the Los Angeles Chamber of Commerce, for instance, argued, "If we cannot get the Mexican to supply . . . casual labor, we have but one place to turn—the Porto Rican negro or as he is commonly known, 'the Portuguese nigger.'" Appropriating the language of the nativists, Clements continued, "I do not think I need to stress the biological problem, particularly in California and the border states where so many of our people are dark skinned. [The Puerto Rican] is an American citizen, and once coming to us becomes a real social problem as well as adding to our American negro problem which is all ready [*sic*] sufficiently serious enough to have become a national question." Finally, he asked rhetorically, "Is there any wonder we want to keep our Mexican labor?" Mexican immigration, according to Clements, kept the Southwest from repeating the racial problems of the Southeast by carefully seeking a workforce that supposedly left as suddenly as it had appeared.[24]

The antirestrictionists sought a labor policy rather than an immigration policy with regards to Mexico. Despite the rising tide of nativism, then, they shielded their economic needs from the looming threat of quota restrictions by turning the nativists' arguments against them, depicting Mexicans as an inferior group but one that would remain eternally peripheral to the social and economic life of the United States. While the argument was far from over in the early 1920s, for the time being Mexicans remained exempted from quota restrictions. Their legal status became that of "permanently marginal laborers," whose continued tolerance by Anglos in the United States required endless work without any efforts at social improvement. Were these Mexicans to test the limits of their marginality, the antirestrictionists explained, rapid deportation would solve the problem. For proof they pointed to the deportation campaigns of 1920–21.[25]

As a result, the 1921 and 1924 laws did not specifically limit immigration from Mexico. Instead, lawmakers focused on Asia and the sources of the "new immigration" from Europe. They devised quota systems that drastically reduced the number of admissible immigrants from Eastern and Southern Europe and outlawed further immigration from Asia (with the temporary exception of the Philippines, still a possession of the United States). The literacy test remained in place and the head tax and visa fee increased to eighteen dollars, so the obstacles constructed across the U.S.-Mexico border by the Immigration Act of 1917 only grew with the 1921 and 1924 laws. Thus, while Mexico and the rest of the Western Hemisphere avoided the nativists' numerical wrath in the early 1920s, these laws exacerbated unauthorized immigration along the nation's southern boundary, already introduced by the Immigration Act of 1917.

The 1924 law proved especially important in encouraging unauthorized entry, particularizing the image of the illegal alien as Mexican, and fashioning the law enforcement reaction to these supposed threats to national sovereignty. The new arrivals faced a new set of obstacles to entry that were often easier avoided than overcome. As demand for laborers in agriculture and industry grew in the 1920s, the number of illegal entries from Mexico increased apace. The vagaries of immigration legislation, then, made the Mexican immigrant the "prototypical illegal alien."[26]

Within these formulations of illegal entry, agents of the newly formed Border Patrol emerged as the nation's symbolic protectors from a lawless border region. They acted as both the enforcement mechanism for these laws and the specter of violence and deportation that hovered over unauthorized entrants as they crossed the border, sought employment, and attempted to bargain for the improvement of any aspect of their employment or living conditions.[27]

The increase in deportations to Mexico during the 1920s created by these changing laws became proof for many that Mexicans were the most flagrant and potentially dangerous violators of the law. The unintended consequences of these laws and their effects on population movements across the U.S.-Mexico border created the image of a typical unauthorized alien that shrouded the Mexican and Mexican American populations with the stigma of illegality and illegitimacy. Thus, as Mae Ngai argued, "walking (or wading) across the border emerged as the quintessential act of illegal immigration, the outermost point in a relativist ordering of illegal immigration."[28]

THE IMMIGRATION ACT of 1924 was far from the end of the fight over quota restrictions, however. Nativists realized that their system still excluded the Western Hemisphere from the quota system. They worked tirelessly throughout the remainder of the 1920s to complete their regime of restriction. The same basic outlines of the debates over the original quota laws continued during the second half of the 1920s. Restrictionists increased their attack on the racial suitability of Mexicans, while antirestrictionists pleaded economic necessity as they also continued their argument that Mexicans possessed an innate homing instinct that made their eventual expulsion possible. Now that immigration policy for Europe and Asia had been decided, however, the intensity of the argument only grew as one side sought to patch the largest hole in the quota laws, while the other fought to maintain the labor source it deemed necessary for continued growth and low wages.[29]

The leader of the restrictionist forces in Congress was John Box of East Texas. Box's district was located in an old cotton-raising region struggling to compete with the cotton growers of South Texas and their Mexican workforce, so restrictionist sentiment was more politically powerful in that region than elsewhere in the state. Restricting immigration from the Western Hemisphere, especially Mexico, obsessed Box during his tenure in the House of Representatives from 1919 to 1931.[30] From his seat on the Immigration and Naturalization Committee, Box tried to secure the passage of a bill that would extend quotas to the entire Western Hemisphere, first submitting a bill to the committee shortly after the passage of the 1924 quota law. In 1926, at Box's urging, the committee held hearings on the matter, and both sides arrived in Washington ready for battle.

Growers came to the hearings claiming to have already suffered labor shortages because of the 1924 law. They declared that any further tightening of the regulations would ruin the nation's agricultural economy. The majority of their arguments rested on the same basis as they had a few years earlier. A *Los Angeles Times* writer nicely captured these arguments when he wrote, "Mexican labor ebbs and flows over the border as it is needed here," bringing with it a "minimum of social complexities."[31] The same logic emerged from other antirestrictionists. Congressman Edward Taylor of Colorado proclaimed, "There is not a member of this committee, not even Brother Box himself, who is more of an immigration exclusionist than I am. I would like to put up the bars higher than they are and give the melting pot a chance to melt for a few years, and assimilate Americanism." Still, he pleaded with his fellow congressmen to allow his state's sugar beet interests to draw labor out of Mexico because it was an issue of short-term economic necessity, not "a matter of immigration at all."[32]

The antirestrictionists also attempted to assuage some of the restrictionists' fears by calling for the creation of a guest worker program that would only admit Mexican workers on a temporary basis. Though they had complained incessantly throughout the World War I exemption program, growers clearly feared that the growth in political nativism threatened immigration from Mexico. Arizona congressman Carl Hayden, for instance, pointed to German guest worker programs that brought in farmworkers from Poland and Lithuania to fill labor shortages. "There is no country in the world which desires more to preserve the racial integrity of its people than Germany," he argued. "The plan apparently worked well, and I do not see why the American Government, under similar circumstances, could not adopt the same idea for the benefit of our farmers" by exempting Mexicans farmworkers from immigration restrictions.[33]

Congressman Box and the rest of the restrictionist forces challenged both the usefulness and the legality of such a guest worker program. In addition to not believing that these temporary migrations would be as benign as their supporters claimed, Box also argued that guest worker programs violated the spirit of free labor, creating a system no different from peonage. He thus vehemently rejected the logic of the antirestrictionists' proposal. If the system operated as it should, it would have created a situation that Box deemed unconstitutional, and if temporary entry became permanent settlement then all of the restrictionists' efforts would have come to naught.[34]

Countering these arguments based on economic necessity, the restrictionists focused on the racial status of Mexicans. In a study partially funded by the Department of Labor and published by the House Immigration and Naturalization Committee, Princeton University economist Robert Foerster laid out the case for exclusion on eugenic grounds. He argued that "no effective democracy resting on universal suffrage can come quickly in a country whose population is still so retrograde as the Mexican in the essential prerequisites of democracy."[35] The core of Foerster's contention lay in his belief that "our control over the future race stock of the United States will apparently never be greater than it is today," and only through careful legislative action could the nation avoid the potential damage done by continued immigration from Latin America.[36] He complained that the 1924 immigration law gave preference "emphatically to immigration from the brown and black stocks."[37] Further, he continued, "If hereafter every immigrant from countries and islands lying to the south of the United States were to be replaced by an immigrant from approved parts of Europe, nothing but gain would result for the United States."[38] If, in contrast, "Latin American stocks have a race value for our civilization substantially above what has been indicated in this report and that mixture of our stocks with those other stocks, contrary to the present stage of knowledge, should result in good, there would still be ample time and opportunity to admit those stocks."[39] Until such usefulness and capacity could be proven, however, Foerster called unequivocally for the restriction of immigration from Mexico and the rest of Latin America and the Caribbean.

Adding to the racial arguments, Congressman Box also tried to depict Mexicans as inherently criminal and therefore unfit for entry into the United States. During the testimony of a South Texas grower, Box interrupted and attempted to read off a list of narcotics, liquor, and smuggling indictments against Mexicans in Texas. He claimed, "Eighty per cent of the names are those of Mexicans."[40] Box, however, had trouble reading the names, leading S. Maston Nixon, the South Texas farmer, to reply derisively, "The Congressman can not pronounce the Mexican names, yet he claims to be an authority on the Mexican. That sounds quite peculiar to a Texan." Hoping to hurry Box along, Nixon drily remarked, "You might state the number of Mexicans—it will save a lot of time in your attempt to pronounce their names."[41] While this effort by Box to cast Mexicans as dangerous criminals proved comically unsuccessful, it would remain one of the key aspects of restrictionist arguments.

While the restrictionists certainly enjoyed a wide audience, the pressure from growers' interests remained too strong for Box's bill to make it out of committee. Chairman Albert Johnson shared Box's qualms about a guest worker program, which he believed was "a sort of peonage system," but he also believed that some sort of seasonal admissions system had to accompany any quota arrangement for the Western Hemisphere.[42] Caught in the middle of these conflicting interests and proposals, the Box bill quietly died in 1926, but not without drawing more attention to the issue and making John Box the poster boy for Mexican immigration restriction.

Over the next two years mail flooded into Box's office.[43] Some of these writers opposed the restriction efforts, such as the president of the Navasota Cooperage Company (in East Texas, north of Houston), who wrote that "you are very badly in error and evidently are being urged by labor Unions and those that have not the interest of the farmers and industries at heart. . . . The people in general, especially the farming class which constitutes a large majority of the voters have their eyes on their congressmen and senators more than ever before and when election time comes around they are going to be remembered. And it will be well for you and your colleagues to look after the interests of Texans instead of so many lobbyists."[44] Letters opposing restriction efforts were a tiny minority of the mail received by Box, however.

The vast majority supported Box's efforts, though the reasons for supporting restriction varied widely. Some echoed the arguments made by Samuel Gompers and the American Federation of Labor.

W. F. Cottingham, the business manager of the Kleberg and Nueces County District Council of Carpenters and Joiners of America, wrote that "a great majority of Mexican Aliens that are allowed to come into Texas to work on the farm soon find their way into cities and towns where they can get shorter hours and better wages and soon forget there is a farm in Texas." He also claimed that urban business interests were the real culprits, not agriculturalists, because they sought more Mexican immigrants as a way to rid themselves of unions and "maintain themselves as overlords of this vast domain."[45]

Many more writers supported Box's efforts for racial reasons. Morrison Swift, radical turned eugenicist, enthusiastically supported the Box bill. "If every alien were shut out the American population would naturally increase to supply the labor demand," he wrote. "Manual labor would become as worthy and dignified as teaching, clerking, and banking, and the impossible problem of assimilating furnace-baked fossil foreigners who cannot be changed would disappear. Thereafter we should breed brains in strong physiques instead of brainlessness in bulk."[46] C. M. Goethe, ardent eugenicist and president of the California-based Immigration Study Commission, claimed that the "high power Mexican white" did not immigrate to the United States. Immigrants came only from what he termed "low Amerind stocks," and they represented a severe threat to the United States because "Mexican Amerind fecundity under American sanitation would speed the exhaustion of our food supply."[47]

A similar avalanche of letters arrived at the offices of Chairman Albert Johnson and the other congressmen on the Immigration and Naturalization Committee as pressure continued to build to apply quota restrictions to Mexico and the rest of the Western Hemisphere. As a result, in 1928 the House Immigration and Naturalization Committee and the Senate Immigration Committee held a new series of hearings on the Box bill and its Senate counterpart, introduced by William Harris of Georgia. These bills called for the quotas enacted in 1924 to apply to the entire Western Hemisphere. Under that formula, which calculated annual limits as 2 percent of the foreign-born population in the United States in 1890, Mexico would have received 1,500 quota slots.[48] As in 1926, both sides came to Washington ready for a fight.

The arguments remained roughly the same as two years earlier, with the restrictionists relying on eugenics and the antirestrictionists claiming economic necessity. The antirestrictionists also claimed time and again that they were pioneers in the process of constructing an economic empire out of the desolate environment of the West, and that the federal government owed them access to Mexican labor. C. B. Moore, a representative of southern California growers' interests, argued that "25 years ago when the industrial East was building up the enormous industries they have, there was not very much question about immigration; and I doubt very much if any immigration laws regarding European immigration at that time could have been enacted. Likewise, we are a new country in the West; we are pioneers out there. This valley I represent has been built out of a desert in 25 years."[49] The restrictionists' efforts appeared to be gaining momentum, however, with the Department of Labor firmly supporting their position under the leadership of Secretary James Davis, described by the journal *Eugenics* as "an exponent of restriction along scientific lines."[50] On the other side, the Departments of Agriculture and Interior supported the antirestrictionists. George C. Kreutzer, the director of reclamation economics in the Department of the Interior, testified that his department had invested $38 million in irrigation projects in regions dependent on Mexican labor. He warned the restrictionists that the "return of the government's investment in these projects and the prosperity of related industries are dependent on favorable economic conditions continuing. They have withstood the period of depression and deflation following the war. If the labor conditions are seriously disturbed it would greatly affect the earning power of these enterprises."[51]

The most powerful and influential assistance for the antirestrictionists, however, came from the Department of State. Secretary Frank Kellogg complained, "This Government has questions of a most important and acute nature pending with Mexico and certain other countries of Latin America."[52] He argued that immigration restriction unnecessarily jeopardized negotiations over things like land claims of U.S. citizens left over from the Mexican Revolution, trade relations, and many other issues brought to the fore in the 1920s, and threatened to derail a number of international agreements.[53] In an appearance before the Senate Immigration Committee he explained that Mexico was the only Western Hemisphere nation that presented immigration problems, and that these were overstated by restrictionists. He contended that Mexicans only came to the United States seasonally, then returned to Mexico, echoing the homing-pigeon analogy long used by antirestrictionists.[54]

On the strength of Kellogg's testimony and the considerable remaining clout of agricultural interests, the quota bills again died in committee. In order to appease the defeated nativists, however, the State Department quickly tightened visa controls to limit legal migration from Mexico through administrative means. Beginning in April 1928, Kellogg ordered consuls in Mexico "to exercise greater care in issuing immigration visas and to refuse visas to all applicants not entitled to them under the law."[55] According to the chief of the Visa Office, "it became apparent that many of the aliens entering on our southern border became public charges after their arrival here; moreover, many of them appeared to be subject to exclusion because of the practice which has grown up along the southern border of importing large numbers of aliens after solicitation and promises of employment."[56] Rather than wait for a quota bill to reemerge, the State Department informed its officials in Mexico to restrict the number of visas by more rigorously enforcing the contract labor and "likely to become a public charge" exclusions. These administrative changes resulted in a sharp decline in visas, and therefore in legal entries from Mexico. In essence, the State Department sought to stop Box and his supporters from pushing for legislation by achieving similar results administratively.[57] This step produced the results desired by nativists, but without complicating diplomatic relations with Mexico.[58] Similar to the 1924 law, this action did not restrict the number of Mexicans who could enter the United States, but it did complicate legal entry and drove many more to avoid the bureaucratic hoops altogether and simply enter without legal sanction.[59]

But the tightening of visa restrictions was only one part of the federal government's reaction. The Department of Labor and the Immigration Service reacted to the legislative failures of 1928 with large-scale deportations of Mexicans from South Texas. The deportation of Mexicans accomplished two goals for the Immigration Service: it removed unwanted immigrants and it built up a numerical case that Mexicans were inherently criminal and therefore should not be allowed to escape quota restrictions. In essence, the Immigration Service began large-scale deportations as a way to fabricate a crime wave that would help build the case for future legislation, and it chose South Texas as the site of this campaign because the region had the largest Mexican-origin population. Every annual report of the Immigration Service after the passage of the Immigration Act of 1924 called for the inclusion of the Western Hemisphere under the quota restrictions. For instance, the commissioner-general of immigration stated in 1927 that he could not "reconcile the unlimited flow of immigrants from the Western Hemisphere with the sharp curtailment of immigrants from Europe."[60] More important, in each annual report from 1929 to 1932, when deportations reached their peak, the commissioner-general went out of his way to detail the percentage of immigration crimes committed by Mexicans, using the same tactic as John Box had in the 1926 hearings. Similar numbers were not provided for natives of any other nation. For example, in 1929 the commissioner-general reported that during the previous fiscal year, "the total deportees of the criminal and immoral classes for the past year was 1,856, the Mexicans alone numbering 1,000 or 53.9 per cent."[61] The Immigration Service hoped to build a stronger numerical case for quota restrictions on Mexican immigration even as the State Department tried to undercut that possibility.

One of the earliest deportation drives occurred in May 1928, one month after the secretary of state called for visa restrictions, in the vicinity of the Rio Grande Valley town of Donna. Near the end of the month the San Antonio district director of the Immigration Service stated that "our records as to the number that have been actually deported from this station, Donna, which includes Weslaco, during the month of May to the present time, is 72; that this number included several that were not laborers, some prostitutes, some criminals."[62] Not surprisingly, a great cry of indignation rose up in response to these deportations because, as one local complained, "I had been told that the laboring conditions were being unfavorably hampered through the activity of the Border Patrol."[63] Congressman John Garner, one of the most forceful voices opposing quotas for Mexican immigration, jumped into the fray to protect the Valley's labor supply, but the deportations continued anyway.[64]

In April 1929 the district director of the Brownsville immigration office reported that more than 2,600 had been deported to Mexico from the district, while hundreds more remained in custody awaiting deportation. Almost 20,000 were deported from the Rio Grande Valley in 1929 alone.[65] These raids sowed fear in the Mexican and Mexican American communities of South Texas, with many refusing to leave their homes lest they be arrested and sent to Mexico. An article in the *San Antonio Express* on October 20, 1929 (nine days before the Black Tuesday stock market crash), complained, "Families are being torn apart, husbands and wives separated, parents taken from young children, homes and farms abandoned, as thousands and thousands of Mexican people are deported from the American borderland, into Mexico—into their native land, but one which has become practically a foreign country to them." Even worse, the author claimed, "The fact that there are about 30,000 Mexicans in this section alone who are subject to deportation, for having crossed the Rio Grande on a short visit, or for inability to read, or for some other reason, has made it possible for a sort of terrorism to flourish among the Mexicans themselves." Colonel Sam Robertson, a South Texas land speculator and prominent political figure, explained, "The Mexican people were in this land long before the Americans owned it, and before they were here in any numbers. We are now doing what the English did to the French in Acadia. We are deporting these people from land which we took from them, and it is contrary to the principles of American justice." Rather than actual justice, however, Robertson sought labor, and he saw the deportation drives as a clear extension of the efforts for legislative restrictionism. He referenced the Immigration Act of 1917 when he complained, "Corns on their hands are a better recommendation than ability to do a little reading." But the immediate impetus for the deportation drives was clear: "With the beginning of agitation for the Box Bill, which would limit Mexican immigration, but would not limit immigration from Canada, the application of more strict immigration regulations was started along the border. . . . The Valley and all the border states are conducting an unceasing campaign against the Box Bill, declaring it would cut off their supply of labor, which is being sadly depleted now by deportations."[66] Robertson and his fellow agribusiness barons complained about deportations as an issue of injustice that threatened the integrity of Mexican and Mexican American communities, but they clearly cared more about the implications for their own surplus labor supply.[67]

The raids that took place in 1928 and 1929 primarily targeted Mexican neighborhoods and workplaces. One exception occurred in Brownsville in 1929 when Border Patrol agents arrested and deported a number of Mexicans waiting for documents outside of the Mexican consulate.[68] Tactics changed, however, after the stock market crash and the Depression that followed. With stronger economic justification added to the restrictionist logic of the first deportations, raids shifted to places like hospitals and health clinics, while immigration officials launched raids on El Paso public schools in March 1931, resulting in the detention of more than 500 schoolchildren. Whole communities were uprooted as deportation rates continued to accelerate. These arrests almost always occurred without warrants and often came through coerced confessions and guilty pleas.[69] By the end of 1931, however, deportations from the Rio Grande Valley declined as the Border Patrol and immigration service shifted their focus to other parts of the state and the country. Only after the stock market crash, however, did these campaigns begin in areas other than South Texas.[70]

The momentum of deportation, in other words, accelerated after the stock market crash signaled the severity of the coming crisis. The economics of the Depression and increased unemployment throughout the nation amplified nativism, leading many to call for the expulsion of immigrants rather than limits to their entry. The anti-Mexican sentiment of the 1920s was quickly redirected into efforts to strip Mexicans and Mexican Americans of their rights of citizenship and the physical right to remain in the United States. Fears that illegal (or simply non-Anglo) immigrants might drain public coffers through relief payments led federal, state, and local officials to carry out well-publicized deportation campaigns throughout the nation after two years of trial-and-error provided by operations in South Texas.

In many ways, the proimmigration forces of the 1910s and 1920s introduced the argument that allowed many to rationalize the necessity and even the righteousness of deportation during the 1930s. Their contention that Mexicans, often defined as a racial group rather than a nationality, possessed an innate homing instinct that always drew them back to Mexico after time traveling and working in the United States became the self-fulfilling justification for removal. Restrictionists and antirestrictionists came to the same conclusions during the Depression. The workers who had been so sought-after during the farm boom in the Southwest and in sugar beet regions came to be seen as a potentially catastrophic economic drain after the market collapsed and unemployment skyrocketed. Mexican Americans also fell under this scrutiny. The overly simplified notion that "Mexican" connoted an unchanging racial categorization meant that many U.S. citizens of Mexican descent found themselves adrift on this tide of cranky nativism and oppressive state activism.

AS A NUMBER of historians have pointed out in recent years, the Immigration Acts of 1917, 1921, and 1924 did not apply quotas to Mexican immigration, but they did create the issue of unauthorized entry from Mexico. In fact, all of the nations of the Western Hemisphere escaped strict numerical limitations to immigration, but the obstacles to legal entry grew regardless. Head taxes, visa fees, and literacy tests were added to older exclusions against Asians, contract laborers, prostitutes, and the catchall designation of "likely to become a public charge." For many immigrants, and for many longtime residents of the borderlands, these new immigration restrictions were more easily avoided than obeyed. As enforcement of these laws increased, however, especially after the creation of the Border Patrol in 1924, Mexicans increasingly came to be seen by both law enforcement and the general public as the archetypal illegal immigrants.

This image of Mexicans (and Mexican Americans) as potential, even probable, unauthorized entrants fueled debates over policy and the very nature of Mexican immigration and Mexican immigrants. Restrictionists claimed that Mexicans represented a racial threat to the United States that could weaken its democratic institutions and degrade its Anglo-Protestant culture. Antirestrictionists, for their part, did not necessarily think that Mexicans were capable of democratic self-governance but instead argued that Mexicans would remain eternally separate from the dominant culture. They were not really immigrants at all, antirestrictionists argued, but instead a cost of business. Neither side truly desired an immigration policy regarding Mexico. Antirestrictionists wanted a labor policy that masqueraded as an immigration policy, while the restrictionists just wanted to throw up a wall while they searched for the next group of threatening immigrants. Both sides in this debate also prepared the ground for the deportation campaigns by continually declaring that Mexicans were not really immigrants, making their expulsion seem less an issue of inherent rights than a logical act of political expediency. Both sides also ignored entirely the voices of the Mexican-origin population, who were presented as little more than caricatures or straw men throughout these debates: pliant beasts of burden or a future race problem, without any option in between.[71]

The debates that ensued after 1924 focused essentially on whether it was possible or desirable to allow for the rights and citizenship of Mexican-origin people, though always through the lens of economic calculation justified by the idea that they remained in the United States as the "hewers of wood and carriers of water." By the time of the Great Depression, these changes helped solidify a distinctly separate-but-unequal social sphere for Mexicans and Mexican Americans in the United States. Calls for immigration restriction and the looming threat of deportation augmented the already formidable power wielded by farmers and politicians in maintaining a de facto system of segregation and labor market segmentation that created a distinct caste system that endured for decades to come. Fixating on the Great Depression as the short-term cause of these problems, however, ignores the much longer trajectory of anti-Mexican nativism and the way Mexican immigration has always lain outside the normal workings of U.S. immigration law.

Just as important, both Mexicans and Mexican Americans found that their ability to claim rights steadily diminished as a result of these changes in immigration law. While these laws and regulations obviously applied more directly to citizens of Mexico than to citizens of the United States, both groups felt their effects. Mexicans and Mexican Americans often viewed themselves as distinct groups with distinct interests rather than as a monolithic group brought together by notions of common race or ethnicity.[72] For policymakers, employers, restrictionists, and others viewing the Mexican-origin population from afar, however, the notion that "Mexican" identity defined people as a race erased these distinctions. With each successive restrictionist action, whether a new law or a deportation campaign, the difference between Mexicans and Mexican Americans blurred for those who viewed them as a racially and culturally distinct population. As Mae Ngai has argued, the effects of this regime of restriction, which increasingly cast Mexicans as the primary violators of U.S. immigration law, was to make Mexican Americans "alien citizens"—people "born in the United States with formal U.S. citizenship but who remained alien in the eyes of the nation."[73]

In other words, at the beginning of the Great Depression, the balance of power in South Texas had shifted even further toward the growers. Their efforts to construct a system of absolute mobility controls bent to their economic needs had failed, but it was an auspicious failure. They may have lacked the power to determine when and where their workers moved, and they could not completely push aside the nativist campaign to restrict Mexican entry into the United States, but their workforce now enjoyed even fewer legal protections than before. In the fight over the politics of mobility in South Texas, defeats often became victories.

PART III | *Challenging the Revolution*

A mob of approximately 5,000 people surrounded Municipal Auditorium, located on the northern edge of downtown San Antonio, on the night of August 25, 1939. They had come to protest the state convention of the Texas Communist Party and the city's mayor, Maury Maverick, who had given the Communists a permit to use the auditorium. Emma Tenayuca, a native San Antonian labor activist and Communist Party member, received permission to hold the meeting in a wing of the city building that seated little more than 100 people. Maverick agreed to grant the permit, in spite of his distaste for the Communists, because of his greater belief in the right of free speech. In San Antonio, however, protecting the First Amendment was grounds for mob violence.[1]

The first protests against the issuance of the permit came almost immediately from Archbishop Arthur Drossaerts of the San Antonio diocese, who was soon joined by the American Legion, the Knights of Columbus, the Texas Pioneers Association, members of the local Ku Klux Klan, and more than a dozen additional civic groups outraged by Maverick's decision. These groups decided to hold what they called an "Americanism" rally outside of Municipal Auditorium as the Communists met inside. Maverick realized that such a gathering could easily turn violent, especially since the Nazi-Soviet nonaggression pact had become public in the days leading up to the convention. More than 200 police would surround the auditorium, while firemen would stand atop the building with fire hoses to thwart any attempts to storm it. Maverick and his chief of police assumed that this show of force would discourage violence.

The hopes for a peaceful convention and counter-rally soon vanished. Many protestors arrived at the auditorium carrying rocks and bricks, which they brandished at police officers. A mix of teenagers, military veterans, and curious onlookers, many in various stages of intoxication, waited impatiently as the crowd continued to grow. Inside the auditorium, barely 100 people watched a mob fifty times larger form just outside. The vast majority of the convention-goers were of Mexican origin, with the rest evenly split between African Americans and Anglos. Party officials made a point of telling attendees that they could sit wherever and with whomever they wanted.

Amid the growing crowd of protestors outside, someone began an impromptu rendition of "The Eyes of Texas Are upon You." The crowd picked it up and followed with "The Star-Spangled Banner," "America," "Dixie," and "The Battle Hymn of the Republic." The mood of the crowd turned minutes after they finished singing, however, when they heard voices inside the auditorium begin to sing "The Star-Spangled Banner." Incensed that Communists would sing the national anthem, the mob surged toward the entrance, ignoring the lines of police stationed there. The firemen atop the building blasted the crowd with water, but did little to slow the forward advance. One of the rioters counseled the crowd to wait for Emma Tenayuca to "open her damn mouth and if we don't like it, then rush her."[2] Nearby, one angry rioter drove his car onto the plaza and tried to run over one of the policemen. He failed, but the crowd cheered and encouraged him with cries of "Run over him! Kill him!"[3] Inside the building, those attending the convention huddled in corners as rocks came flying through the windows and enraged rioters began to climb inside. The police managed to guide the attendees out a back door unharmed, but rumors that Maury Maverick was inside drove even more rioters into the auditorium. Once inside, they set about demolishing everything left behind by the Communists. As one participant lamented, "We might as well tear it to pieces now. It's been contaminated by communists anyway."[4]

As this first spasm of violence wound down, Rev. M. A. Valenta of the nearby San Francisco de Paola Catholic Church announced a parade that would proceed immediately from Municipal Auditorium into downtown San Antonio. An American flag taken from the Communist meeting room became the standard behind which the "parading vandals" marched.[5] It is not clear if this parade was supposed to be as circuitous as it became, but marchers ended up passing through much of downtown as they swept south and west toward City Hall, then lurched back east and slightly north to hold another rally in front of the Alamo. During the march the head of a local American Legion post, Clem Smith, cheerfully told a newspaper reporter, "We have a Catholic, a Jew and Ku Kluxer leading us. . . . I am the Jew."[6] Along the meandering path of their march, rioters assaulted a few passersby. They attacked one man who failed to remove his hat as the stolen flag passed. A volley of rocks bounced off a car that contained a man, two women, and a baby when somebody decided that it was Maury Maverick's car. It was not. Shortly thereafter, a lone policeman tried to stop the crowd in its march toward the Alamo. An unnamed woman tackled the policeman before the rest of the crowd surrounded him and stole his gun and cap. When the marchers finally reached the Alamo, they stopped briefly to recite the Lord's Prayer with Valenta before breaking up into several roving bands that wandered through the downtown area for several more hours. One of these groups ended their night by burning the mayor in effigy at City Hall.[7]

By the next day the leaders of the riot pointed to Maverick and the police as the instigators of violence at the auditorium. Alexander Boynton, defeated Republican candidate for governor of Texas in 1938, told the press that the police effort to keep the crowd from destroying Municipal Auditorium "was a perpetration of insult and shame exceeded only by the butchery of Texas heroes by the hordes of Santa Anna."[8] Of course, one night earlier Boynton had described the riot to a reporter as "the most outstanding event that has happened in San Antonio since the fall of the Alamo."[9] Boynton's limited capacity for historical comparison notwithstanding, his seemingly contradictory depictions of the riot point toward the simultaneous anger and delight that drove the crowd into committing what one reporter called "the greatest exhibition of mob violence and vandalism in the city's history."[10]

While the presence of Communists at a city-owned facility dedicated to the memory of soldiers killed in World War I might have created controversy regardless, this riot grew out of issues more complex than simple ideological anger. The violence that ensued, almost cartoonish in its gleeful destructiveness, illustrated a number of the fault lines in South Texas society during the Great Depression. For the rioters, the Communists served as a handy stand-in for the serious challenges to the economic and political system of South Texas that seemed to emerge from every direction during the Great Depression. The Communist Party never had a substantial following in the area, but that mattered little under the circumstances. By 1939 a series of unionization efforts and strikes had taken place throughout South Texas, momentarily threatening the region's labor regime. Emma Tenayuca, who had received the city permit for the convention, became the individual most associated with these efforts to shift the balance of power away from the region's employers. Her presence inside Municipal Auditorium surely goaded many of the rioters to their reactionary violence. Likewise, it had only been a few months since Maury Maverick, a former Democratic congressman and ardent New Dealer, had won election as San Antonio's mayor and defeated the deeply corrupt political machine that had controlled the city's government for decades. Allies of the old machine, suddenly stripped of the graft that had flowed into their pockets for years, seized on the Communist convention as an event that could embarrass the Maverick administration—the more violently the better.

These rioters were not driven by hunger or poverty, in other words, but by a reactionary desire to halt efforts to change the nature of economic and political control in South Texas. Catholic priests, members of the Ku Klux Klan, and Jewish members of the American Legion rarely agreed on anything, but in San Antonio in the waning years of the Great Depression they combined to try to silence any effort to push South Texas down a more progressive path. They were joined by dozens of other religious and civic organizations who feared that the conditions of the Great Depression could provide fertile ground for a thoroughgoing reform of the region's status quo. Of course, the economic decline of the Great Depression could have different political implications, both inspiring calls for change and solidifying control by elites who had the political and economic means to withstand the worsening conditions around them.

The next two chapters will deal with these cross-currents in South Texas during the Great Depression. Chapter 5, "The Politics of Depression," examines the objective conditions of life during the 1930s. Continued deportation campaigns, higher unemployment rates, and lower wages exacerbated the problems already present in previous decades. Political solutions to these problems, even during the height of New Deal reformism, proved rare and fleeting as agribusiness interests and conservative politicians maintained control of much of the state despite countervailing pressures. Chapter 6, "Organization and Rebellion," focuses on the efforts to force change in South Texas. While these protests rarely ended in victory, they did reveal the depths of the problems confronted by the majority of South Texans. Farmworkers and factory operatives tried to drag the region's political and economic elite toward constructing a more just society, and their efforts reveal much about the reality of life in Depression-era Texas.

CHAPTER FIVE

The Politics of Depression

In May 1938 Manuel Juárez left San Antonio's largest and lowest paid industry. He abandoned his seasonal job as a pecan sheller on the West Side of San Antonio to travel to the cotton fields near Corpus Christi after hearing rumors that the coming harvest would be a substantial one. A widower, he packed his six children into his 1926 Ford Model T and arrived in Nueces County along with thousands of other families who had heard the same claims of plentiful work. Juárez and his family were sorely disappointed when they were unable to secure daily employment. In the forty-five days that they remained in the Corpus Christi area, they found only periodic work in the fields and earned only ten dollars. They decided to leave in mid-July when they heard that the harvests in Lamesa in West Texas offered more regular employment. After a 650-mile, eight-day trip, they found conditions at Lamesa just as bad as in Corpus Christi, and in their sixty-five days there the Juárez family earned only eighteen dollars. They were able to eat only by pooling money with other families in the same situation. Finally, in October, Manuel borrowed money for gasoline to return home, but his car died fifteen miles short of San Antonio. He hitchhiked into the city and persuaded a friend to tow his car into town, where he sold it for five dollars in cash and five dollars in credit from a local grocery store. He used the money to rent a tiny shack in the heart of San Antonio's West Side barrio. When he tried to go back to work at the pecan shelling plant he had left in May, he discovered that all shelling operations had shut down because of a strike by the Mexican and Mexican American pecan shellers he had left behind months before.[1] Juárez and his family disappear from the historical record at this point and vanish into the overcrowded barrio of San Antonio's West Side.

The Great Depression did not create these problems, but it deepened hardships and intensified conflicts that people like the Juárez family had long suffered. Agricultural prices, unstable but high in South

Texas during the boom years of the 1920s, went into free fall. Farmers responded by cutting already miniscule wages. The interstate migrant stream grew, as more and more of the unemployed turned to farm-work for survival and as New Deal crop reduction programs and the Dust Bowl sent former farm owners and sharecroppers from Arkansas, Oklahoma, and East Texas into the circuit of agricultural migration. Manuel Juárez found himself competing for lower-paying jobs as he tried to follow the well-worn path of agricultural migration that in earlier times had supported many of his neighbors in San Antonio's West Side (as in similar barrios throughout South Texas). South Texas jobs did not dry up during the Great Depression; rather, local growers benefited from the influx of poverty-stricken migrants. Unlike much of the rest of the country, however, the city of San Antonio and the state of Texas made little if any effort to alleviate these problems through direct relief or work relief programs, even after the New Deal brought federal money pouring into local governments around the nation. In addition, the continuation and expansion of anti-Mexican deportation efforts during the early years of the Great Depression only added to the pressures placed on the Mexican and Mexican American populations in South Texas, placing them on the defensive against the visible forces of law enforcement and the invisible forces of the market.

This chapter examines the stresses that the Great Depression placed on the system of agricultural and semi-industrial growth that had developed in South Texas in the previous decades. The seem-ingly endless influx of new immigrants from Mexico stopped, but the economic crisis of the 1930s helped maintain the labor market seg-mentation and web of labor controls that had developed earlier. The advent of the New Deal did little to alleviate these problems, as relief money and attempted legislative regulation either did not apply to the working conditions of South Texas or were fashioned into policies that aided farm owners and business interests. By the end of the Great Depression, even more asymmetrical power relations had developed in South Texas as the loose strictures employed during the 1920s closed in more tightly around the citizenship and labor rights of Mexicans and Mexican Americans.

FOR MANY IN San Antonio and South Texas, the early days of the Great Depression looked very similar to the conditions they had endured for years.[2] Residents of San Antonio's West Side, for instance, may not have noticed any immediate change in the months and even years after the stock market crash of October 1929 signaled the severity of the coming economic crisis. They had long lived with inhumane levels of poverty and disease, and that did not change in the 1930s. A change did come, however, in the amount of outside attention afforded these long-term problems. For a number of progressive journalists, public health advocates, and other like-minded individuals, the living and health conditions of the slums of San Antonio's West Side served as one of the clearest object lessons of the nation's failure to deal with the consequences of the crumbling of the capitalist order. In San Antonio they found the seedy underbelly of the laissez-faire economic system. Journalist Tad Eckam described the city's slums as a "blighted *demimonde*."[3] Father Carmelo Tranchese, an Italian Jesuit who assumed the helm of the Guadalupe Parish in the heart of the West Side in 1932, claimed, "I am familiar with the slums of San Francisco, New York, London, Paris, and Naples, but those of San Antonio are the worst of all."[4] "The West Side is one of the foulest slum districts in the world," wrote Audrey Granneberg in *Survey Graphic*. "Floorless shacks renting at $2 to $8 per month are crowded together in crazy fashion on nearly every lot. They are mostly without plumbing, sewage connections or electric lights. Open, shallow wells are often situated only a few feet away from unsanitary privies. Streets and sidewalks are unpaved and become slimy mudholes in rainy weather."[5] These conditions had plagued the West Side of San Antonio for years, but only with the arrival of the economic crisis did outsiders pay attention.

The Chicago-based American Public Welfare Association conducted a public welfare survey of San Antonio in 1939 and 1940 that revealed the seemingly intractable problems facing the residents of the West Side. It reported that "there has been mass unemployment, between 15,000 and 20,000 unemployed persons, for over a decade in San Antonio."[6] Especially hard-hit were the Mexican and Mexican American populations.[7] In 1931 Mexico's Secretariat of Foreign Relations estimated that 19 percent of San Antonio's Mexican residents were unemployed, while other towns in South Texas faced even worse conditions: 20 percent unemployment among Mexicans in Brownsville, 28 percent in McAllen, and 30 percent in Corpus Christi.[8] In addition, according to the authors of the public welfare survey, "The migrant laborer who has residence in San Antonio plays no small part in the unemployment picture, for his itinerant work at low wages means a period of complete unemployment at no wages. San Antonio has for years been a reservoir for a migratory labor supply which is used in many different sections of Texas, both south and north of the city, as well as northern states."[9]

Chronic unemployment and low wages in combination with residential segregation created "low standards of living, and ultimately ill health, poor housing . . . and their related social problems."[10] The infant mortality rate in San Antonio was 96.3 per 100,000, more than twice the national average. San Antonio also had the highest tuberculosis death rate in the nation, at 159 per 100,000 population.[11] That was more than double the state rate of 76 per 100,000. More revealing, however, is the disease rate in San Antonio by ethnicity. The Anglo tuberculosis death rate was 52.8 per 100,000—less than the state as a whole. Mexicans and Mexican Americans, in contrast, died from tuberculosis at a rate of 302.7 per 100,000.[12] The crowded and unsanitary living conditions also aided the spread of diseases like measles and whooping cough, leading the American Public Welfare Association to declare, "The teaching of isolation procedures is futile where isolation cannot be achieved in any way. Here again the need for more adequate relief and higher economic standards is only too apparent."[13]

John Caulfield, an official with the Farm Security Administration, described the migrant farmworkers of South Texas in a similar manner. "This ragged multitude on the march which is making such a dramatic pageant along the highways of South Texas is but one more chapter in the continuous parade of migrants across the face of the nation," he explained. "But it is a disquieting, sinister migration without a goal and with little hope, expect for that whisper of faint hope which it is said the human soul never loses." Like the public health advocates and progressive reformists who expressed shock at the long-standing conditions they found on the West Side of San Antonio, Caulfield seemed to believe that the "sinister migration" he witnessed was new. "Other migrations evidence a building-up," he argued. "Each family on the march meant a new farm to be opened. This newest migration evidences a tearing down, a disintegration. It is the drifting homeless wreck of the small farms which our previous migrations created." In other words, Caulfield saw the migrant labor stream as a pathological creation of the Great Depression rather than a long-standing problem. Had the Depression not occurred, Caulfield seemed to presume, these farmworkers would have remained farm owners. "The plight of the 350,000 migratory farm laborers of Texas may not be in itself a major problem," he continued. "But it is a significant rash upon the surface. It is indicative of a deep-seated and baffling disease, which, if not effectively treated, threatens every fundamental of our national life."[14] For the migrant farmworkers he sought to describe, however, these long-standing problems certainly represented more than just a "significant rash" created by the recent economic downturn.

As Manuel Juárez and his family found, living on migrant agricultural labor wages became even more difficult as agricultural prices plummeted, causing farmers to lower the already depressed wages for seasonal farm labor.[15] With a seemingly bottomless pool of surplus labor guaranteed by soaring unemployment rates, farmers found that wage rates could fall as low as their conscience or their imagination would allow. Rates for cotton pickers in the Corpus Christi area, the most productive cotton region in the country at the beginning of the Depression, dropped precipitously during the early years of the Depression. Picking rates in 1930 ranged from seventy-five cents to a dollar per hundred pounds of cotton. By 1931 workers could only expect sixty to eighty cents per hundred pounds. Rates bottomed out at thirty to thirty-five cents per hundred pounds in 1932.[16] Likewise, onion harvesters in Dimmitt County in the Winter Garden earned about sixty cents a day in November 1938, while spinach work near Laredo paid a relatively princely sum of $2.50 to $4.00 per week in December 1938.[17] A very different perception of reality, however, emerged from those who employed these migrant farmworkers. Walter Ellis, who owned land in the Lower Rio Grande Valley, reported to officials of John Shary's Southwestern Land Company at the depths of the economic crisis in 1932, "Even now when people are talking depression and waiting for something to happen we are going right along planting and gathering good crops, and receiving fair returns considering the conditions elsewhere. I was driving out for an hour this morning and saw three new houses under construction."[18] He evinced no awareness of whose labor allowed those "fair returns" to flow into his pockets.

A Works Progress Administration (WPA) study of migrant workers from Crystal City in the Winter Garden revealed many of the continuities of migrant agricultural labor of previous decades that persisted into the 1930s. The 300 families studied throughout 1938 followed a path similar to the migrant laborers of the 1920s, beginning each harvest season in South Texas, moving north for cotton picking, then leaving the state for sugar beet work. The vast majority of Crystal City migrants worked the local spinach harvest from November to March, though they earned a tiny fraction of their yearly income from the winter-long spinach work. Ninety-five percent of these families then left the Winter Garden for work elsewhere. One-third worked briefly in the onion fields of Willacy and Webb counties, while the rest proceeded straight to the cotton harvests in Nueces County. Beet work then finished the agricultural year, after which the families returned to their home bases in Crystal City. Most of these migrants' earnings came from the sugar beet work. The vegetable and cotton harvests provided little more than money to cover the trips to and from the beet fields. According to the WPA researcher, "These four crops dovetailed with one another so neatly that in only one month of the year, April, did total family unemployment rise above 4 percent."[19] Almost as an aside, however, the researcher noted, "In spite of this regularity of employment, however, wages were so low that many of the Crystal City families were in need at the time of the survey."[20]

The industrial work centered in the West Side of San Antonio often offered wages even lower than agricultural work. Cigar and garment factories paid no more than four to six cents an hour to their predominantly Mexican and Mexican American female workforce throughout the Depression.[21] Pecan shelling, the largest industry in San Antonio, paid even less. "Wages plummeted to one cent per pound for pieces and one and one-half cents for halves at the depth of the depression," reported the former secretary of one of the pecan shellers' unions. "On that basis even the 'champions' could earn no more than $1.50 per week; some of the less skilled received only sixteen cents for a week's labor."[22] The WPA study of Crystal City migrant laborers, performed during the same year as a study of pecan shellers in San Antonio, found that the "average annual income of the Crystal City Mexicans was about twice that of the urban Mexican group studied in San Antonio."[23] In addition, much of the urban employment was seasonal, which meant that many pecan shellers and garment workers also spent part of each year pursuing agricultural labor along the migrant trail. In most cases, the line dividing agricultural and nonagricultural labor was hazy, and the exploitative relationships developed in agricultural employment were replicated in the temporary labor opportunities available to migrant workers in San Antonio and the other towns of South Texas.

For those Mexicans and Mexican Americans in South Texas who had been able to save money during the years before the Great Depression, bank failures added additional difficulties. While most workers earned wages too miniscule to deposit anything in a bank, some had been able to build up savings during the boom years of the 1920s. The Mexican consular service noted that throughout the Depression "the accumulated savings by Mexican workers during long years of arduous labor have been almost totally lost" because of bank failures.[24] The San Antonio consulate, for instance, reported that most of the affected Mexican nationals in that city were laborers.[25] The situation became so dire that the consul general in San Antonio, Enrique Santibáñez, asked the mayor of San Antonio to declare a moratorium on evictions of Mexican tenants unable to pay their rent. The mayor refused the request, however, because such an action "would be bad publicity . . . [for] San Antonio[, which] ranked as [one of the two] American cities holding their own in these strenuous times."[26] It is not clear what the mayor meant by this statement, but he was apparently unaware of or unconcerned about the national notoriety already attached to living conditions in the shacks whose rent payments he refused to postpone.

Complicating the lives of many in South Texas even further was the continuation and expansion of deportations that began in the region in 1928. Unlike the pre-Depression deportation drives, these growing campaigns of removal met with little of the feigned outrage so common in the late 1920s. John Garner, Sam Robertson, and the farming interests that relied on Mexican labor had protested throughout 1928 and 1929 that deportations threatened their labor supply and, secondarily for their purposes, trampled on the rights of the resident Mexican population. By 1931 few such voices could be heard, as the volume of nativism rose and farming interests realized that the conditions of the Great Depression alleviated any potential for labor shortages.[27]

Complaints of stolen jobs and a sort of economic populism that depicted Mexicans as the stooges of the wealthy and powerful were the most common manifestations of anti-Mexican sentiment in Depression-era Texas. For instance, the Bricklayers and Masons International Union, an all-white union with locals in San Antonio and the Lower Rio Grande Valley, complained vociferously to the Department of Labor and the War Department that construction jobs on military bases throughout the region went to Mexicans. In December 1930 the secretary of the San Antonio local wrote to the international about work at Fort Sam Houston: "On December twenty second there were thirteen Mexicans and four white mechanics employed at six dollars a day. The wages were then reduced to four dollars per day. Consequently the white men refused this cut, leaving the aliens to complete present masonry work. . . . Will the government employ a contractor who discriminates not only against organized labor but the white race as well?"[28] The secretary of the international then wrote to the Department of War, complaining that the union saw no reason why the military "preferred Mexicans to Americans, especially during the present unemployment crisis."[29] Around the same time the international secretary also received a letter from Rio Grande City (Starr County) complaining that all masons and carpenters on jobs at Fort Ringgold were Mexican. "It seems a pity in the face of this depression that our own government would do this when American citizens of these two crafts are walking the streets without employment and in need of work to support their families and pay the heavy taxes and such expenses as it takes to keep their homes," wrote the local union officer.[30] These complaints never mentioned nationality or citizenship. Instead, their arguments were based on notions of racial difference and the presumed illegitimacy of Mexican American citizenship and labor rights.

Along the same lines, a man from Wharton, Texas, complained to the immigration commissioner, "Mexicans are a curse upon Texas, pest in our white schools, and burden on relief and pension rolls. They come across to work on the farms, soon drift north to towns and cities, forcing more negroes out of employment and onto relief rolls." He continued by demanding that the immigration service not allow more Mexicans into Texas. "I imagine Rep. Cleberg [*sic*] [owner of the King Ranch] will be asking you to lift ban on Mexicans as he (rather his wife) owns perhaps over a million acres down in the vicinity of the valley. It would be good if such estates as that would have went under during this depression."[31]

These same nativist pressures came to bear throughout the nation. "When it became apparent last year [1932] that the program for the relief of the unemployed would assume huge proportions in the Mexican quarter, the community swung to a determination to oust the Mexican," reported scholar and activist Carey McWilliams in Los Angeles in 1933. "Thanks to the rapacity of his overlords, he had not been able to accumulate any savings. He was in default in his rent. He was a burden to the taxpayer. At this juncture," wrote McWilliams with as much sarcasm as he could muster, "an ingenious social worker suggested the desirability of a wholesale deportation."[32] While the roots of the deportations go back further than McWilliams noted, his description nicely captures the simple arithmetic of the 1930s that justified these actions.

These deportation campaigns did change in important ways in the early 1930s, however, as the Great Depression deepened and calls for Mexican removal became more insistent. From 1928 to 1931 most deportees were sent to Mexico for either illegal entry or for lack of documentation, in keeping with the immigration-restriction focus of the late 1920s. After 1931, however, more deportees were caught for vagrancy violations and sent back to Mexico as individuals "likely to become a public charge," signaling a shift to a tactic more in line with the economic crisis of the 1930s. In other words, the deportations that occurred after 1931 reacted less to immigration violations as such and more to the nativist desire to rid the nation of Mexicans.[33]

For those caught in the machinery of deportation there was little if any recourse against the growing nativism that swept through every level of the law enforcement establishment. Once detainees appeared in court they often faced judges who had predetermined their guilt. One federal judge in particular, F. M. Kennerly, compiled an astonishing sentencing record in South Texas. He heard seventy illegal immigration cases in a six-hour session in July 1931, at the peak of the deportation drive in the Valley, and found all seventy guilty. Eleven went to prison and fifty-nine were deported. A three-hour court session in Laredo that same year yielded ninety-eight convictions in ninety-eight cases, leading to seventy-two deportations.[34]

Many arrested for immigration violations did not go to trial, however, as officials allowed them to choose voluntary deportation. This method meant that deportees returned to Mexico without a misdemeanor conviction and therefore maintained, theoretically, the option of returning to the United States legally.[35] Many of the deportees never made it as far as a hearing before a judge, instead simply relinquishing any claim to remain in the United States for the possibility of returning at a later date when more auspicious economic conditions returned. While the coercive nature of these "voluntary" deportations is obvious, they did allow some hope for eventual legal return to the deportees and reduced the bureaucratic workload of immigration officials and the federal court system.

More important numerically than deportees, however, were repatriates who left for Mexico for reasons other than legal entanglements. There were any number of reasons why Mexicans, and even some Mexican Americans, chose to leave the United States during the Great Depression. Some left because they wanted to return to their homeland rather than remain in a country that clearly sought to get rid of them. Others left because chronic unemployment did not allow them to keep up with the higher cost of living in the United States, made worse by the fact that noncitizens were ineligible for public works employment. Fears of deportation led many to depart. This variety of repatriate became much more common during the peak of deportations in the early 1930s and was the desired result of the deportation raids that sought to frighten Mexican communities as much as remove illegal entrants. Others left with help from local charities that sought to rid their communities of Mexicans, while a number of municipal relief boards chartered trains to transport Mexicans on relief rolls out of the country. The large number of repatriates who accepted these offers of transportation only strengthened the notion held by both nativists and their opponents that Mexicans remained little more than temporary sojourners who would all eventually return south of the border.[36] In all, hundreds of thousands of Mexicans and Mexican Americans traveled south to Mexico during the Great Depression, temporarily reversing the migration patterns along the U.S.-Mexico border. Not surprisingly, the peak years for repatriation came during the peak years of deportations, 1929–32.[37]

During these same years, the Mexican government emerged as a driving force in bringing Mexicans back south of the Rio Grande. With the political turmoil of the 1920s behind it, the government energetically sought to draw the substantial pool of emigrants back to Mexico both for humanitarian reasons and to aid in the nation's modernization.[38] An early example of these attempts to integrate repatriates back into the nation came with the establishment of the Don Martín Colony that straddled the states of Coahuila and Nuevo León, about fifty miles from Laredo, Texas.[39] The construction of a dam on the Río Salado was meant to create a massive irrigation network across the previously arid region, opening up an enormous expanse of cultivable land, in individual plots, that would attract repatriates. Throughout 1930 and 1931 prospective colonists left for the Don Martín Colony, and by mid-1931 almost all of the land had been distributed. Almost all of the colonists had returned to Mexico from Texas and found initially that they could actually make more money there than north of the border where cotton prices remained low.[40] Despite an auspicious beginning, however, the Don Martín Colony soon ran into a number of problems, from insufficient federal funding to severe drought. Foremost among these was a basic conceptual flaw. The dam could hold sufficient water to irrigate 65,000 hectares, but the amount of water that flowed into the Río Salado could only irrigate 30,000 hectares. As a result, the lake behind the dam had gone dry within a few years, dooming the project.[41] By the end of 1931 the Mexican government had already begun to transport colonists elsewhere to alleviate worsening conditions. Much of the colony was deserted by the end of the decade.[42]

As deportation numbers dropped and the flow of repatriates slowed, the Mexican government's efforts to entice emigrants back diminished. One last effort was made, however, in the last years of the Great Depression to achieve the goals of the Don Martín Colony. In the spring of 1939 work began on the construction of an agricultural colony meant entirely for repatriates near Matamoros, Tamaulipas, named the "18 de marzo." This new project was meant to ameliorate some of the problems of landlessness and poverty among repatriates and migrants, but it also sought to increase Mexico's agricultural exports with the help of farmworkers experienced in U.S. agriculture.[43]

Undersecretary of Foreign Relations Ramón Beteta launched a campaign to publicize the undertaking and gauge interest throughout the United States, but it received little response outside of Texas. In South Texas, however, Beteta was met with enthusiasm at each stop.[44] Importantly, Beteta wrote to President Lázaro Cárdenas that most of the prospective repatriates were U.S. citizens.[45] Whether this meant that these potential colonists simply wanted to leave the United States or that they responded to the revolutionary nationalism of the Cárdenas regime, clearly a substantial number of Mexican Americans were despondent enough over their condition in Texas that they sought expatriation. A little more than 7,500 had come from throughout South Texas to the "18 de marzo" colony by the beginning of 1940, taking up newly irrigated land on the site of an expropriated hacienda.[46] Like the Don Martín Colony, however, lack of funds and drought doomed this effort. The end of the Depression and renewed demand for labor in the United States in the early 1940s sounded the death knell of colonization efforts.

The "18 de marzo" colony, however, helps bring into focus the pressures on Mexican and Mexican American communities in the United States. Expatriation could not have been a decision that Mexican Americans made lightly. They risked the loss of U.S. citizenship and the uncertainty of a fledgling agricultural colony in a desolate corner of

Tamaulipas. Nevertheless, thousands flocked to "18 de marzo" and hundreds of thousands of others embraced similar uncertainty as repatriates. Confronted by a worsening economic situation and an aggressive campaign to rid the nation of Mexican-origin people, many simply left, their actions both chosen and forced.

By the time of the "18 de marzo" colony, however, the migration trends that have come to define the economic collapse had already come to an end. By the late 1930s there was at least a trickle of return migration to the United States by repatriates who found conditions in Mexico even worse than those they had left north of the border. While the official immigration statistics provide little help in uncovering this northward migration during the Depression, it is clear that many had begun to return north in large numbers by 1936 and 1937, but not without difficulty.[47] Most of those who tried to reenter the United States found their way blocked by more stringent application of immigration laws and more liberal usage of the "likely to become a public charge" exclusion. Those who had received assistance from charities to pay for their transportation to Mexico were especially targeted as unfit to reenter the country.[48] Thus many repatriates found themselves stranded between two nations struggling to reemerge from the depths of the Depression, with neither government willing or able to help them. Many simply entered illegally rather than deal with the red tape and probable rejection that came with applying for legal entry.

They returned north of the Rio Grande during the late 1930s because agricultural interests still welcomed them. In fact, growers continued to call for more Mexicans to come and harvest their crops even at the height of deportations and repatriations to Mexico. The voices calling for renewed immigration from Mexico were often drowned out in the early years of the Depression, but by the late 1930s the familiar refrains of farmers declaring acute labor shortages could be heard loud and clear. This renewed demand for labor from Mexico reached its peak in 1936 and 1937, when growers throughout South Texas bombarded the federal government with dire predictions of economic ruin if a surplus labor supply could not be found.[49] Beginning in the summer of 1936, growers in the Lower Rio Grande Valley complained that they did not have sufficient labor for what promised to be one of the largest cotton harvests in years. Additionally, weather conditions during the spring and summer delayed the harvest by about three weeks, so Valley cotton growers had to compete with harvests in the cotton fields near Corpus Christi. According to the Immigration and Naturalization Service (INS) inspector in charge at Brownsville, the farmers of the Valley "started paying from 40 cents to 50 cents for their cotton picking at the beginning of the season. A great many farmers from up state, where cotton was also opening at the same time although ordinarily it opens from three to four weeks later than the Valley cotton, came here, offered more money to available pickers and hundreds of Valley residents left for up state to pick the cotton there at better prices."[50] According to the *Valley Morning Star*, with the labor situation "rapidly reaching a crisis, protest has been filed with the U.S. Labor Bureau office at Fort Worth, against alleged practice of growers of the Corpus Christi–Robstown area in trucking laborers from this section with the promise of higher pay."[51] The McAllen Chamber of Commerce even went so far as to demand a law that prevented truckers from taking workers out of the Valley during harvest time, hoping to create an intrastate version of the Emigrant Labor Agency Law.[52]

Growers called for the end of labor poaching (by *other* growers), the complete suspension of all public works projects, and the institution of a guest worker program similar to that established during World War I.[53] Despite these requests, according to the state administrator of the WPA, "District Immigration Director Whalen stated in telephone conversation he opposes this because there will be only about thirty days of this work and experience has taught that cost of importing labor and then returning it to Mexico, particularly latter, is not justified by results obtained. He stated this service is still trying to find and expel some Mexicans who were imported for this purpose during the war."[54] Despite repeated refusals by the federal government to accede to a renewed foreign contract labor program, growers continued to agitate for workers during the 1937 and 1938 harvests.[55] Growers did not get their wish for a government-operated foreign contract labor program in the waning years of the Great Depression, but their demands do exhibit how completely the situation had changed from a few years earlier when migration trends seemed only to point south.

WHILE THE NEGATIVE state activism of the deportation campaigns was the clearest sign of government activity in South Texas in the early years of the Great Depression, the New Deal did bring more constructive forms of state activism. The number of deportations and repatriations declined dramatically, while tentative efforts to use public funds and governmental power to deal with the worst aspects of the economic situation increased.

While relief programs alone could not have solved the problems faced by many in South Texas, their presence presumably would have ameliorated the worst features of unemployment, low wages, and the difficulties that flowed out of chronic poverty and overcrowding. During the years before Franklin Roosevelt assumed the presidency in March 1933, the Hoover administration did little to provide federal relief funds. The creation of the Reconstruction Finance Corporation (RFC) allowed for some distribution of relief funds to states and localities, but little of this money ever made it to individuals. The Roosevelt administration, in contrast, opened the possibility of large amounts of federal relief money for states and municipalities through the Federal Emergency Relief Administration (FERA), the Works Progress Administration (WPA), and a number of other programs that distributed direct and work relief. The New Deal also offered the first official federal labor protections through the National Industrial Recovery Act (NIRA) in 1933 (the right to organize), the National Labor Relations (Wagner) Act in 1935 (which banned unfair labor practices and established a federally mandated process of collective bargaining), and the Fair Labor Standards Act in 1938 (which created the forty-hour week, the minimum wage, and the ban on child labor for most nonfamily employment). While these laws and programs held out the promise of a rudimentary social welfare net and basic employment rights where none had previously existed, legislators excluded all agricultural workers from these protections in order to pass these laws over objections from southeastern and southwestern conservatives.

There was some ambiguity in how these exemptions were put into practice, however. For instance, the vegetable and fruit packing industries claimed that they should be exempted because they worked with agricultural products and because they employed agricultural workers. This line of argument pointed to one of the clearest weaknesses in the labor protective legislation of the New Deal. Agricultural workers remained vaguely defined as people who worked in "the area of production" of agricultural products, a decidedly unclear designation that employers expanded to suit their own needs. The National Labor Relations Board (NLRB) clarified the distinction slightly in 1935 when it separated the legal rights of field workers and processing workers, giving only the processing workers the right to collective bargaining and NLRB supervision. As Cindy Hahamovitch has argued, this clarification of status for field and processing workers "was certainly more easily implemented" than the previous vague distinction between the two, "but it was just as arbitrary."[56] Just as important, it solidified the exclusion of basic labor rights for those who worked in the fields. In the end, "agricultural worker" became an accusation as much as a description: such workers were those too poor and powerless to be recognized as anything else.[57]

The migrant farmworkers of South Texas, therefore, fell outside of these workers' rights reforms. Adding insult to injury, they also had a difficult time receiving federal relief funds. The WPA distributed surplus commodities and clothing to those in need, but it required anyone receiving these goods to have lived for at least a year in the state and for at least six months in the county where he or she applied for relief.[58] In order to survive, migrant workers in Texas had to leave the state each year and had to move frequently from county to county, so they fell between the cracks of basic federal relief efforts.

Just as damaging to these migrant workers was the passage and implementation of the Agricultural Adjustment Act (AAA) and its plow-up scheme to raise agricultural prices by removing surplus product, especially cotton, from a glutted market.[59] Farmers were supposed to distribute a portion of their compensation for reducing their crop to tenants and sharecroppers, though most simply rid themselves of the suddenly superfluous farm hands.[60] Farm laborers lacked even that unenforced protection, and now found themselves part of a swollen migrant stream competing for even fewer jobs in the fields. The nature of this problem makes it impossible to quantify the losses suffered by farm laborers as a result of AAA, but the fate of Manuel Juárez and his attempts to gain employment in the cotton fields sheds some light on the difficulties created by the New Deal for farmworkers in South Texas.

Another problem arose from the refusal of authorities in charge of distributing federal relief work to allow women to perform tasks they perceived as "nontraditional." Though women made up the majority of San Antonio's industrial workforce and the women of South Texas had long endured the migrant labor stream, the administrators of the WPA and other agencies rarely gave women relief work outside of sewing, food processing, domestic service, or nursing.[61]

In addition, many of these federal relief programs distributed funds to the states, not directly to the intended recipients. The

Line of people waiting for free surplus clothing at the Works Progress
Administration Clothing Department office in San Antonio. (Photograph
by Russell Lee, March 1939. Library of Congress, Prints and Photographs
Division, Farm Security Administration/Office of War Information Collection
[LC-USF33-012058-M1].)

small-government, conservative ideology that dominated the Texas
state government guaranteed an almost complete lack of cooperation
with the federal government in allocating New Deal funds. The small
amount of federal money that ever made it through Austin and filtered
down to the local level was often consumed by graft. As a result, after
a number of New Deal programs had proven disruptive to the agricultural laborers of South Texas, those due relief from other New Deal
programs had a difficult time collecting any.

Individuals or families seeking direct relief or work relief fared
no better in their dealings with the state government than they had
with federal relief programs. The state of Texas, for example, spent
only three and a half cents per person per year on public health, or
roughly the same spent on the health of livestock.[62] The Texas constitution, then and now the outdated constitution written shortly after
Reconstruction, forbade the establishment of a statewide system of
relief.[63] Since much federal relief to the states required the state to put
up matching funds, a series of standoffs ensued between the Roosevelt
administration and the government in Austin over federal money. The

federal government often sent the funds anyway after trying to force the state to use some of its own money, but only after long delays in which relief payments stopped for those who relied on them.[64]

The state government typically did little more than report on the problems arising around Texas. For instance, in December 1932 Governor Ross Sterling wrote to relief boards across the state about the dire situation in San Antonio. He explained that "San Antonio pays less for income taxes than any city in the United States in proportion to its population. The amount of wealth production, the amount of income is probably lower than any other city of its size. . . . In other words the necessities of San Antonio are much greater in reference to the population than other cities of its size." Rather than suggest aid from the state, Sterling then listed all of the major charitable organizations attempting to deal with the mammoth relief load. The Catholic Women's Organization operated multiple health clinics and soup kitchens, the Veterans of Foreign Wars gave relief to hundreds, the city's Milk and Ice Fund (set up to distribute private charitable donations) provided milk for children under the age of five, and several fraternal organizations chipped in whatever aid they could. The state government's role, however, went no further than describing this desperate situation.[65]

Municipal governments throughout South Texas did even less. San Antonio provided the best example of how city and county officials remained either unable or unwilling to match federal efforts to provide relief in the face of almost complete abdication of these duties by the state government in Austin. For instance, from January to September 1931, Detroit spent $6.59 per capita for relief, Los Angeles spent $3.40, Chicago spent $2.41, Denver spent $0.79, El Paso spent $0.29, and San Antonio spent $0.15 per capita.[66] Among cities of similar size, only Memphis spent less on relief per capita than San Antonio.[67]

When the Great Depression began, a political machine that had maintained control of the city almost continuously since the late nineteenth century gave no sign that it would change its habits of graft and apathetic leadership.[68] While the machine had never provided any semblance of credible governance, the massive population increase during the 1910s and 1920s, especially on the West Side, caught the city government completely unaware. Rather than using public funds to improve the sanitation or infrastructure in an already overburdened city, the increased tax base that came with a growing population merely provided more opportunities for graft.[69] The city Health Department served as the ultimate symbol of San Antonio's machine rule. A writer for *Collier's* magazine asked two "prominent men" what was the most shameful aspect of the machine-run municipal government. Both pointed to the Health Department. "Generally," according to the author, "a health department is designed to promote the public welfare. In San Antonio it is used as an agency through which collectors shake down that poor, miserable class of females who make their livings as members of the world's oldest profession."[70] As San Antonio's population descended further into economic ruin during the Great Depression, all other aspects of the city government reflected the same level of callous disregard and calculated greed.

Machine politicians simply appointed their successors during these years. Mayor John Tobin died in 1928 but supposedly made a death-bed request that District Attorney C. M. Chambers succeed him. Three years later Chambers died and another deathbed request made City Attorney C. K. Quin the heir apparent; Quin remained in office until 1939.[71] While the mayor's seat stayed within this tight circle of machine loyalists, a key cog in the power structure was Charlie Bellinger, political boss of the African American East Side.[72] Despite Jim Crow segregation in public accommodations, San Antonio's nonpartisan municipal elections eliminated the white primary that had excluded African Americans from voting in much of the rest of Texas. While African Americans made up less than 10 percent of the city's population, they accounted for a large percentage of poll-tax payments and made up a quarter of the voters in all county and municipal elections.[73] Although this system did not provide the African American community with any real authority in city and county governance, it did lead the city to provide basic services to the East Side that it denied to the West Side barrio: paved streets, electricity, water and sewage connections, and a number of other public facilities.[74]

In addition to the thousands of votes regularly in Bellinger's pocket, the machine also turned to old-fashioned vote-buying outside of its East Side stronghold. In 1938 the nature of this corruption became even clearer when a reformist newspaper, the *Bexar Facts*, printed a series of affidavits of ineligible voters who admitted to receiving poll tax receipts from machine officials.[75] A few months later a grand jury indicted Mayor Quin and two of his top aides for spending city money on bribes to 400 individuals for "working around the polls."[76] Not surprisingly, such a city government demonstrated little concern for establishing a system of local relief, preferring to spend municipal funds to maintain its grasp on power.

Despite having the largest relief load in the state, Quin and other machine officials continued to argue that private charities should handle all relief activities.[77] Throughout the Depression, the federal government remained the primary, if not the only, source of relief funds for the city and county. The WPA and the National Youth Administration (NYA) employed thousands, while the FERA supplied surplus farm products to the poor. According to the public welfare survey in 1940, "The federal government with only minor assistance provided relief and service for 94.6 percent of the total number of cases assisted in Bexar County. Private agencies cared in some manner for 4.9 percent of the remainder, and the county government for one-half of one percent."[78]

Often, however, local officials distributed this federal aid, leading to a familiar pattern of graft and strong-arm tactics through which relief became a means of bludgeoning the poor as much as aiding them. A *San Antonio Express* article from August 7, 1937, announced, "Approximately 1,000 Bexar County families formerly on relief here will head for the Rio Grande Valley to pick cotton or find other means of sustenance Monday, H. K. McBath, district administrator of the Texas Relief Commission, declared Friday."[79] McBath also added, "I see no reason for the Federal Government to feed people able to work when work is available. We are not only cutting them off the rolls, but we have cut WPA 'referrals' to virtually nothing."[80] In addition, farmers hiring workers from federal projects did not have to match WPA wages. They simply had to pay "prevailing agricultural wages," a vague guideline that allowed employers to set wage rates wherever they pleased.[81] In spite of the federal money meant to provide relief funds for the San Antonio area, then, public relief agencies remained more concerned about funneling potential farm laborers to the fields of the Rio Grande Valley and guaranteeing a plentiful labor force for local manufacturing concerns. Labor shortages did not exist, but farmers and business interests feared that employment on federal work projects could provide workers leverage to demand higher wages. In the hands of local administrators, however, public works programs became little more than updated versions of tried-and-true labor practices in South Texas, with the shotgun-wielding overseer now replaced by the bureaucrat as the guarantor of surplus labor in the cotton and vegetable fields. What the New Deal variant of this tradition lacked in potential for violence it made up for with economic leverage.

A clue to where this federal money actually ended up can be found in an investigation launched by the Texas Senate into the operations of the Bexar County Board of Welfare and Employment. The number of salaried employees on the county board fluctuated between 250 and 450 depending on time of the year, and it clearly served as a patronage agency that did little more than provide do-nothing jobs for friends of the city machine and allies of the administration in Austin. The board secretary testified that $140,000 had been spent on relief during September 1933, but $35,000 of this went for administrative salaries. By comparison, Tarrant County (Fort Worth) spent $1,300 per month for relief administration. Bexar County's relief load was certainly larger than Tarrant County's, but not twenty-five times larger. The secretary also admitted that salaried workers bought food from the relief commissaries at wholesale prices, while immediate family members of city and county officials received relief payments. The total number on relief was 50,000, or approximately one-fourth to one-fifth of the total population, though it is impossible to know how many of these received relief thanks to political ties rather than need.[82]

The investigation that discovered this financial malfeasance had not been launched to provide better service for relief recipients, however. It was part of a patronage battle between different factions in the state Democratic Party maneuvering for advantage in the upcoming 1934 gubernatorial election. County relief boards provided one of the easiest sources of political patronage, so enemies of the Miriam Ferguson administration sought to discredit Bexar County relief officials so that they could insert their own operatives. Once installed in the relief offices, they could then strong-arm relief recipients into voting for selected candidates.[83]

Despite the continual flow of federal money into machine coffers, however, the seemingly constant revelations of corruption led to the creation of strong countervailing pressures during the Depression to end machine rule in San Antonio. A number of reform movements had emerged since machine government first latched onto the city in the nineteenth century, but one of the most thoroughgoing and successful, if only briefly, arose in reaction to the conditions perpetuated by the machine during the Depression years. This reform movement was led by Maury Maverick, the scion of an old San Antonio family whose name became shorthand for nonconformist rebelliousness in the nineteenth century, and who was briefly able to bring a form of modern municipal government to San Antonio.

Maverick won a seat in Congress in 1934 by defeating the mayor of San Antonio, machine stalwart C. K. Quin, in the Democratic primary.[84] A number of factors contributed to Maverick's victory over the machine, but the most important seems to have been his ability to attract large numbers of West Side residents away from the machine.[85] From his seat in Congress, Maverick rapidly became one of the most ardent advocates of the New Deal, emerging as the central figure in a group of liberal congressmen, predictably dubbed the "Mavericks," who routinely agitated to expand social welfare legislation beyond the timid measures taken during FDR's first term.[86] While Maverick's attention remained focused on national issues (a fact which his enemies would use against him), he did succeed in steering a number of public works projects to San Antonio, primarily through the WPA and NYA. He also worked to secure money for slum clearance and public housing construction to remedy some of the worst public health problems, especially on the West Side.

Maverick retained his seat in the 1936 election but faced a determined challenge from the city machine in 1938.[87] Paul Kilday, the brother of Police Chief Owen Kilday, ran a fierce campaign to "eliminate from Congress one who has overwhelmingly shown himself to be the friend and ally of Communism."[88] An official of the Department of Labor, surveying the San Antonio scene in 1938, wrote, "Unfortunately this city is ruled by the most corrupt ring in the country. It has marked for slaughter at the next election Congressman Maury Maverick, a man I do not know, but he must be on the right side."[89] In July 1938, Kilday won the primary by a vote of 24,929 to 24,383 for Maverick. Kilday won the Anglo North Side and the African American East Side decisively, while Maverick carried the Latino West Side and the working-class-Anglo South Side. Amid evidence of vote-buying and other illegal electoral maneuvers by the machine, Kilday replaced Maverick in Washington.[90]

After the election, Maverick determined that he had been defeated because of the machine's grip over the city. The only way to make sure that this did not happen again was to destroy the machine at the local level. Maverick thus decided to run for mayor in 1939. He challenged Quin, the man he had defeated five years earlier in his congressional campaign. Quin and the machine appeared more susceptible to electoral challenge than they had in years. Not only had Maverick proved that the West Side could be stripped away from the machine during his years in Congress, but grand jury indictments against Quin and his top aides for bribery came down in December 1938 and produced a split between Quin loyalists and those who sought to jettison the troubled mayor.[91] As a result, two machine candidates ran for mayor against Maverick.[92]

The San Antonio establishment made no secret of its disdain for Maverick, with the *Express* publishing a front-page editorial that accused the former congressman of "defaming" San Antonio, which they claimed was the cleanest city in Texas.[93] The local AFL, through its *Weekly Dispatch*, endorsed Quin because Maverick openly supported the CIO. Quin also found strong allies in many of the leaders of the Mexican American middle class within the League of United Latin American Citizens (LULAC).[94] While the organization remained nonpartisan, a number of its leaders were conspicuous at a Quin rally held at Sidney Lanier High School on the West Side.[95] Despite the opposition of many of the city's most powerful political players, however, Maverick won the 1939 election with 18,375 votes, while Quin received 14,874 and a second machine candidate received 11,503.

Less than a month after this election, local labor leader and Communist Party official Emma Tenayuca spoke before the Communist Party's city convention. Her speech focused almost entirely on Maverick's victory. She suggested to the attendees that "the results of the election can be interpreted as being a revolt of the masses of San Antonians against machine rule, against corruption and graft, against violations of civil liberties, the exposure of which was made primarily by the struggles of the Mexican people. Further, it expresses the rapidly growing progressive sentiment of the people of Texas in behalf of all measures that tend to better the conditions of the masses." The ouster of the machine, she argued, gave progressives the chance to consolidate their control, with organized labor and the Mexican-origin population in the vanguard. More than just an effort to maintain control in San Antonio, however, she also viewed Maverick's victory as the first step in pushing the state and the nation further to the political left.[96] In many ways, Tenayuca's speech announced all of the worst fears of Maverick's opponents.

For the next two years Maverick set about dismantling the structures of machine control and replacing them with a progressive municipal government. Even the often antagonistic local newspapers had to admit that Maverick brought positive change. He transformed the Health Department from a national disgrace into an agency whose achievements were recognized by the U.S. Health Service. The deeply corrupt police force was reformed and handed over to a new chief brought in from Evanston, Illinois.[97] Enormous improvements were made in sewage facilities and mosquito control on the West Side, eliminating some of the most hazardous public health conditions in the barrio.[98] Maverick was also the driving force behind a campaign to change the city charter to allow for relief expenditures.[99] He moved to uproot the thriving red light district west of downtown, which had long served as a source of revenue for machine officials. Finally, actual civil servants, rather than cronies and machine loyalists, took over much of the machinery of city government.[100]

Maverick also continued the push for public housing in San Antonio that he had begun during his years in Congress. The newly created U.S. Housing Authority emerged from the New Deal to provide a Keynesian financial spark to the moribund housing industry. One aspect of this effort involved the replacement of slum areas controlled by absentee landlords with federally subsidized housing projects. These new projects would not only eliminate the public health problems that came with unsanitary slums, but they would also create construction jobs that could help alleviate unemployment. Maverick's ties with the Roosevelt administration helped achieve slum clearance and the construction of five public housing projects in San Antonio. The U.S. Housing Authority approved contracts for Alazán and Apache Courts on the West Side, Wheatley and Lincoln Heights Courts on the East Side, and Victoria Courts on the South Side between 1938 and 1940.[101]

The first, largest, and most important of these was Alazán Courts, in the heart of the West Side. As the time came to begin construction, however, one large problem arose. In order to build the new housing, old structures had to be removed. The owners of these houses, all absentee slumlords responsible for the appalling living conditions on the West Side, stalled in an attempt to force the federal government to pay more for their properties. Nathan Straus, the administrator of the U.S. Housing Authority, personally stepped in and refused to pay the inflated prices demanded by the owners, writing to Eleanor Roosevelt that the "San Antonio project has been held up by the selfishness and greed of individual landowners."[102] The delay was brief, however: local officials pleaded with Eleanor Roosevelt to speak to the president on their behalf, leading the U.S. Housing Authority reluctantly to accept the prices demanded by the homeowners.[103] Alazán Courts opened in 1941, followed shortly thereafter by the adjacent Apache Courts.[104]

While these projects did not eliminate the West Side's problems, they did alleviate them. Of course, Maverick's outspoken efforts to take these properties away from the absentee landlords as the first step in slum clearance earned him even more opponents.

The reformism inaugurated by Maverick did not win over his numerous enemies, and the machine began to regroup immediately after its defeat in 1939, searching for issues and events it could use to discredit the administration in the 1941 election. Their first and biggest opportunity came on August 25, 1939, when the Communist Party held its state convention at the Municipal Auditorium. The enemies of Maverick, Tenayuca, and the progressive shift in city governance used the mayor's refusal to ignore the First Amendment as an excuse to riot and try to reinstall the machine in City Hall. The mayor's son, Maury Maverick Jr., later recalled that the family had to hide at a friend's house the night of the riot after receiving a series of death threats. "Parts of the mob came to our home looking for us; others went out to intimidate my grandparents," he wrote. "I saw my father's career come to an end [that] night."[105] Before the burning effigy of Maverick was cut down from City Hall, hundreds of enraged locals demanded the mayor's recall. Hundreds more signed a petition calling for his ouster and blaming him for the riot.[106]

The machine used the events of that night to paint Maverick as a communist sympathizer in the 1941 mayoral election. With only one machine candidate in this election, Quin won and ended the two-year experiment in progressive government. A journalist for the *San Antonio Light* reported that the machine was "determined to wipe out every vestige of the preceding administration."[107] Even the archconservative *Dallas News* concluded that Quin's victory meant that San Antonians voted to rid themselves of responsible government.[108]

In retrospect, the Maverick interregnum brings into greater relief how little the politics of the Depression at the federal, state, and local levels did to alleviate South Texas's problems in the 1930s. Before 1939 state and local officials evinced little interest in cooperating with federal reformers and instead attempted to use the New Deal programs as either sources of graft or as new tools to enforce control over workers. Only during the two years of Maverick's reign, in addition to his four years in Congress, did any benefit accrue to San Antonio. The New Deal's decentralization was its undoing in South Texas. As a result, the Mexican and Mexican American majority in South Texas found itself fighting to maintain even the unstable existence of previous decades.

THE POLITICS OF Depression in South Texas evinced subtle changes from previous patterns, even as many things remained essentially unaltered. For the Mexican and Mexican American majority of the region, the Great Depression represented a slight worsening of the existing difficulties—fear of deportation, high unemployment, low wages—even while the solutions presented by the New Deal did little to solve the problems in South Texas. The exclusion of agricultural workers from labor protective legislation, residency requirements for public works employment, and crop destruction programs either did nothing to help the poor or worsened their situation. Local and state governments typically ignored the poor altogether. The exceptions, such as Maury Maverick's brief time in office, tend to prove the rule.

The effort that brought Maverick to office, however, points to the other side of the legacy of the Great Depression in South Texas. While the 1930s were marked by worsening poverty and frequent exposés of the inhumane conditions faced by residents of areas like San Antonio's West Side, these years also saw aggressive efforts to change the reality of life for the majority of people in the region. Rather than succumb to the growing pressures of the Depression, the Mexicans and Mexican Americans of South Texas launched a series of challenges to the political and economic system that had been built on their backs. Voluntary repatriation and participation in the agricultural colonies in Mexico served as one method of resisting these worsening conditions. Those who remained in the region, however, launched a different sort of resistance through workplace struggles that proposed basic but thoroughgoing reforms in the political economy of South Texas.

CHAPTER SIX

Organization and Rebellion

Standing before a group of journalists, San Antonio police chief Owen Kilday bellowed, "It is my duty to interfere with revolution, and communism is revolution."[1] As he spoke on Friday, February 25, 1938, 240 men found themselves crowded into the Bexar County Jail, which had a normal capacity of sixty. Police had arrested roughly 200 of them in the previous week in cracking down on what city leaders characterized as a revolution. Almost all of the inmates were charged with illegal picketing or blocking a sidewalk, crimes they committed in an effort to improve wages and working conditions in the pecan shelling industry. Despite their crowded conditions, and the fact that many of the prisoners nursed wounds from street battles with police, the jail soon echoed with songs and jeering exhortations. The most popular song, soon heard throughout the jail, declared, "Kilday está loco." Others sang mockingly of the "Pecan Czar," against whom the prisoners had been striking when arrested. After a few hours of this raucous behavior, interspersed with complaints against overcrowded conditions, the city jailer declared that he could not control the prisoners. Chief Kilday arrived shortly thereafter and directed police officers to turn fire hoses on the singing inmates. In addition to violating the most basic rights of those arrested for activities protected by the First Amendment, Kilday also provided a perfect symbol of official reactions to working-class protest movements in South Texas: rather than allow these efforts to expand into a full-fledged social movement, Kilday tried to drown them in the county jail.[2]

The chief of police, like many political and economic leaders in South Texas, feared that these signs of worker activism could prove disruptive and potentially transformative. In one sense, the leaders had little reason for concern. During the Great Depression, the ad hoc system of labor controls developed in earlier decades combined neatly with the possibility of expulsion from the United States and mass unemployment to create an even more potent system of employer control over labor. In spite of these conditions, however, the agricultural and semi-industrial workers of South Texas waged a sustained, if largely unsuccessful, campaign of labor organization during the 1930s. The efforts by ethnic Mexican workers to organize themselves revealed many of the same broad outlines as labor clashes in more industrialized areas. New Deal labor legislation heightened workers' expectations and drove them to confront their employers in South Texas as they did throughout the nation. Further, many of these organizational efforts grew out of wildcat strikes and walkouts in reaction to the steadily worsening working conditions of the Great Depression. But these unionization efforts in South Texas contended with a series of complications not present in the CIO and AFL organization drives in the Midwest, Northeast, or even the Southeast. Employment segregation and falling wages combined with the growing fear of deportation to create a volatile situation in South Texas when the violently antiunion businessmen of the region confronted the largely Mexican and Mexican American workforce. This confrontation yielded few victories for the workers. But as Paul Taylor wrote in describing the San Joaquin Valley cotton strike in 1933, "As the faulting of the earth exposes its strata and reveals its structure, so a social disturbance throws into bold relief the structure of society, the attitudes, reactions, and interests of its groups."[3] The strikers' efforts made visible the violence of South Texas labor relations that had remained largely hidden in the years since the Plan de San Diego as police, vigilante groups, and the Texas Rangers reprised their familiar roles.

SOUTH TEXAS'S FIRST Great Depression–era labor action occurred in November 1930 during the spinach harvest in Crystal City.[4] The Catholic Workers Union of Crystal City, presided over by Rev. Charles Taylor of the Crystal City parish, demanded wages determined "not simply by what [employers] can get out of [the workers], but what [the] laborers need to live," as well as an end to outside labor recruitment when a sufficient supply of workers lived within the immediate vicinity of the spinach fields.[5] Less than a week after workers formed the union and went on strike, twenty-five growers agreed to most of their demands. Wages increased, outside labor recruitment diminished, and general working conditions improved. One result of this settlement, according to Taylor, was that higher wages allowed more children to return to school during the spinach harvest than in previous years. After the settlement, however, the Catholic Workers Union disappeared, little more than an anomalous successful effort that held no real importance for the future. A few more years would pass before another agricultural union emerged in South Texas.[6]

In August 1933 another organizational effort began in Laredo with the formation of an independent union, the Asociación de Jornaleros, which welcomed agricultural laborers as well as miners, construction workers, and other laborers.[7] According to one of the leaders of the Asociación, "We formed our organization when the [National Relief Administration, which guaranteed the right to join a union] was inaugurated."[8] The militantly antiunion county machine harassed the Asociación throughout 1934, almost crushing the organization through the use of blacklisting, agents provocateurs, and deportation threats.[9] The onion harvest in March 1935, however, revived the Asociación as it took over a walkout among onion cutters demanding higher wages and better working conditions.

Before the strike, onion workers in the Laredo area earned about sixty cents for a twelve-hour day throughout the one-and-a-half- to two-month harvest season.[10] These wages would have been low even if work was guaranteed, but surplus labor made it difficult to guarantee employment throughout the season for individual work-ers. Many laborers drove to the fields at their own expense to find that they could secure only a few hours' work at best. The strike in March 1935 began as a spontaneous protest by 1,200 onion work-ers against these conditions, and the Asociación soon moved in to lead the strike effort.[11] In a petition sent to growers and the Webb County Chamber of Commerce, the union demanded $1.25 for a ten-hour day, more than a 100 percent raise, with twenty cents per hour overtime pay. They also asked that drinking water be placed in the fields near the workers, that employers pay for transportation to and from the fields, and that growers pay for the treatment of any inju-ries suffered on the job.[12] "We represented the workers of the onion fields and approached the growers for collective bargaining regarding wages, etc.," José Jacobs of the Asociación wrote. "The growers disre-garded us completely and the result was our first and only strike."[13] The union refused to negotiate with individual growers, demanding instead a uniform agreement covering all Laredo-area onion grow-ers.[14] According to the *Laredo Times*, "strikers timed their actions just as growers in this section were ready to start the movement to market of some 1,000 carloads of onions."[15]

For four days (April 12–15, 1935) strikers lined U.S. Highway 83, leading from Laredo to the onion farms, and attempted to block all traffic to and from the fields. Estimates of total numbers of strikers blocking the roadway varied from 300 to 2,000.[16] Accusations of communist infiltration soon swept the city. Rumors floated through the area that angry workers planned to dynamite bridges leading out of Laredo.[17] Fears of violence escalated even further when, on the night of April 14, growers were able to send three truckloads of strikebreakers through the picket lines after mounting a machine gun on the top of the lead truck, though the workers from two of the three trucks left the fields and joined the strikers.[18] Deputy sheriffs acted as escorts for this armed convoy under the orders of District Attorney John Valls, the head of the county political machine.[19] After this incident, District Judge J. F. Mullally, another important figure in the county machine, sent an urgent request to Austin for Texas Rangers, writing, "Peace officers and onion growers request me to apply to you for sufficient men to control the onion strike situation which is beyond the control of local officers."[20]

Meanwhile, a prominent grower, H. G. Samuels, agreed to accept the union wage of $1.25 a day for ten hours on April 13, but the union rank-and-file refused to sign the individual agreement, afraid that signing a partial agreement would bring the strike to a halt as workers left for the fields. Department of Labor conciliator J. R. Steelman, who had been called into the area by the Webb County Chamber of Commerce, tried to get the workers to sign the contract with Samuels, afraid that the strike could turn violent if an agreement was not reached. Few doubted that the situation would change once Texas Rangers appeared.

The Rangers arrived on April 15 and immediately cleared the highway of strikers, breaking the blockade.[21] Fifty-nine strikers had been arrested by noon on April 16.[22] J. R. Steelman wrote that the "Texas Rangers and the operators thought the proper way to handle the situation was to drive the workers back to the field."[23] Still, Steelman was able to elicit an agreement from a few growers in the Laredo area for wages of $1.25 for a ten-hour day. On the night of April 16 the workers agreed to the contract, and the strike ended. While the union and its rank-and-file still doubted that the agreement guaranteed that things would not return to status quo ante as soon as the federal conciliator left, threats of violence and deportation from local law enforcement, the Rangers, and growers led them to end the strike.[24] The union declared a victory, but Steelman remained more circumspect in his immediate reaction to the settlement, telling the *Laredo Times* that "it was only a compromise. The growers missed a good opportunity to make another strike this season impossible had they come in and mutually signed the agreement. . . . The growers must change their attitude. They must learn that times have changed and that workmen do have the right of collective bargaining."[25] Even though Steelman overstated the protections provided to agricultural workers by New Deal labor legislation, his predictions soon came true as most growers maintained wages around sixty cents a day. When the union made noises about renewing the strike, all growers repudiated the $1.25-a-day wage level. No strike followed as most of the workers feared violence and seemed to have lost confidence in the union's ability to accomplish anything.[26] In the end, the growers probably benefited from the delay in harvesting. Market prices for onions increased during the strike.[27]

While these setbacks muted unionization efforts in the Laredo area for much of the rest of the decade, a little less than a year after the onion strike another attempt to organize workers occurred. A pair of meetings took place in San Antonio and Laredo in March 1936 to announce the founding of a new labor organization called the Confederation of Mexican and Mexican-American Laborers, an offshoot of the Mexican Federation of Workers (Confederación de Trabajadores de México, or CTM).[28] While the Laredo meeting featured many of the workers who had been active in the Asociación de Jornaleros, this new union had the backing of the Mexican consul in Laredo, Juan Richer, and the consul-general in San Antonio, Benjamin Hill.[29] A *Laredo Times* reporter kept shorthand notes of the Laredo meeting. Richer reportedly stated that he was aiding the Asociación "by instruction of my government." The reporter also recorded speeches by a number of union leaders, including the statement of Emilio Martínez that "we are always intimidated on the fact that we are Mexican citizens and that we have no rights in this country, but we do have rights, and this gentleman here (pointing to the Consul) is the one who is going to demand those rights."[30] While the willingness of Mexican consular officials to aid Mexican workers would surely never have extended very far, foreign aid offered more hope for agricultural workers than the U.S. government, which continually treated farmworkers as an untouchable caste that existed beneath labor protective legislation or governmental concern. It is also worth noting that the citizenship of individual workers seems not to have been a salient division in this case. Within the context of agricultural labor in

South Texas, neither Mexican nor U.S. citizens wielded much authority with Texas officials or employers. Consular offers of help, no matter how vague, were clearly meant for citizens of both nations.

Cries of foreign subversion soon followed, with Congressman Martin Dies turning to accusations of communist infiltration.[31] The Texas state deputy of the Knights of Columbus wrote to Secretary of State Cordell Hull to complain that Richer "presided at meeting of radical element here in Laredo." He further claimed that Richer acted under orders from President Lázaro Cárdenas "to organize labor groups in the United States," which represented "unwarranted interference with American affairs" by a foreign government.[32] After the State Department registered complaints with the Mexican government, the Secretariat of Foreign Relations replaced Richer as consul and recalled him to Mexico City.[33] But an anonymous informer, writing to J. R. Steelman, claimed that the Richer episode was actually an abortive attempt to revive the onion strike from a year earlier: "Indeed, it did look as if we were going to have the same old trouble this year, the only difference this time was the Mexican Government seemed to have taken upon its shoulders to agitate the trouble and organize the Mexicans and Mexican-American citizens. However, the publicity which has resulted from the meeting in San Antonio and the one here and the resultant investigations by various departments of our government has completely broken the back of this Mexican government interference in our affairs, and we do not look for any further trouble when the onion shipments start."[34] The author's predictions proved correct, as organizing in the border counties continued to decline throughout the rest of the 1930s. More important, though, the brief furor over Mexican consular interference in agricultural labor relations allowed the more fundamental issues of labor rights to be pushed aside. Onion growers could ignore their unilateral abrogation of the contracts signed just a year earlier by pointing to the activities of two consular officials and a handful of unionists.

While the labor movement unraveled in Laredo, CIO unions, primarily the United Cannery, Agricultural, Packing, and Allied Workers of America (UCAPAWA), began to move into other parts of South Texas in 1937 and 1938.[35] These efforts were part of the larger push by the CIO to organize the South, including Texas, during the late 1930s and into the 1940s. Union leaders argued, "As long as the south remains unorganized, it constitutes the nation's Number One economic problem and is also a menace to our organized movement in the north and likewise to northern industries."[36] Few places had a smaller union presence than South Texas or offered lower wages, so the efforts to organize the region's workers fell in line with the CIO's larger strategy, while they also encountered the concerted opposition of local employers, politicians, and law enforcement.[37]

One UCAPAWA organizational effort occurred among shrimp hullers in Aransas Pass. Located along the Gulf Coast just north of Corpus Christi, the town was the home of the Rice Brothers Cannery. Shrimp shelling occurred almost entirely during the fall, with only a few workers remaining throughout the year. The seasonal workers often had to turn to agricultural labor during the off-season. Even during the peak of the season the average worker made only about $1.50 per day.[38] In other words, these processing workers dealt with the same low wages and seasonal unemployment as their farmworker brethren. The only real difference was their ability to appeal to the federal government for protection under labor protective laws.

A spontaneous walkout of 350 workers after Rice slashed hulling wages led to a strike near the end of October 1937. According to A. J. Holmes of the shrimp hullers' union, "The shrimp peelers have been peeling a small bucket of shrimp which holds about 6 lbs of shrimp for 5 cents and they happen to be small shrimp. So when they began to get larger shrimp which Mr. Rice gets more for, Mr. Rice proceeds to swap out a large bucket which holds 2 times as much shrimp and tells them that is all he is going to pay."[39] The UCAPAWA moved in and took over the strike effort while trying to broaden the union's base beyond just the hullers, the lowest paid workers at Rice. Cannery workers and employees from the boat division, however, ignored the union's entreaties. The strike fell apart after seven weeks when a union representative took all of the strike funds and disappeared. Disgusted, the hullers went back to work.[40]

To protect against another strike, Rice Brothers tried to establish a compulsory union under the company's control, but the National Labor Relations Board (NLRB) declared it an illegal company-dominated union in December 1937. Because of the NLRB ruling against Rice's union, the CIO decided to try its luck again among the shrimp shellers the next year. An organizer arrived in July and began to piece the local back together. Throughout August the UCAPAWA representative met with Rice management, but Rice refused to consider any contract because, it claimed, Mexican workers "have no idea what a contract is made for and have no conscientious scruples about breaking a contract at will."[41] The union decided to strike at the peak of the season, starting September 14, 1938.

That morning, as the union set up a picket line around the plant, a group of armed men assaulted the pickets. It is not clear who these people were, but the scant evidence points to white Rice employees from the boat and cannery divisions. One of the attackers died, another was shot (probably a case of friendly fire), and several more were injured. The president of the local, Christopher Clarich, was beaten into a coma and remained in critical condition for days, during which time he was indicted for the murder of the vigilante.[42] A few more days passed before negotiations restarted, but after several days of fruitless meetings the NLRB commissioner convinced Rice to accept a contract that allowed for collective bargaining and provided a pledge of nondiscrimination but ignored issues of wages. Rice finally accepted on the night of September 26, 1938.[43] The next day the agreement went before the union, where it passed by only two votes. The NLRB commissioner reported that "all of the white members and the intelligent Mexicans who understood English [voted] to accept and all the other Mexicans [voted] against it."[44] Those who voted against the agreement threatened not to return to work, but they came around the next day when Christopher Clarich approved the agreement from behind bars.[45] The strike thus ended with union recognition but no improvement in the wage scheme that had caused the first outbreak a year earlier.[46]

It is worth noting that very little union activity of note occurred in the Lower Rio Grande Valley during the Great Depression, despite the Lower Valley's importance to the development of the South Texas agricultural boom. UCAPAWA efforts to organize field workers in 1937 and 1938 were abandoned by the union as hopeless, while the union struggled slightly longer to organize workers in the packing sheds. Each of these efforts disappeared without much notice.[47] While it is inherently difficult to explain why something does not happen, a combination of factors created this situation. The lack of federal protection for agricultural unions would certainly seem to be the primary explanation, since this helped tighten the grip on economic and political power enjoyed by the agribusiness interests who would have been the targets of these unionization efforts. The seasonal nature of the work also made successful organizing more difficult as unions had little chance to take root in an area that the workers had to leave. Finally, as would become apparent decades later during the failed United Farm

Worker organizational efforts in the Lower Valley, the ready availability of replacement workers in border towns just across the Rio Grande
made any effort to emulate workers elsewhere in protesting their treatment seem foolhardy and doomed to failure.

TO THE NORTH of these events in the border counties and along
the Gulf Coast, the largest and most sustained unionization efforts
in South Texas took place in San Antonio, where a series of strikes
erupted among Mexican and Mexican American factory workers during the years from 1933 to 1938.[48] The industries that had come to San
Antonio to take advantage of its low wages and exploitable workforce
suddenly confronted a thoroughgoing, sustained effort for improved
working and living conditions. The organizational efforts in San Antonio not only demanded improved wages, safer working conditions, and
the basic rights of free labor, but they also called for a complete redefi-
nition of the place of the predominantly Mexican-origin working class
within the city and the larger polity. They became an essential catalyst
for the effort to bring democracy to San Antonio that briefly flourished
late in the decade. It was the workers of the West Side, in particular,
who both served as object lessons of the consequences of municipal
government incompetence and carried the city into its brief interregnum of responsible government under Maverick.

The lack of any real municipal efforts to deal with issues like working conditions or public health meant that the potential for abuse by
employers remained a constant threat, beyond the well-established
history of low wage rates in San Antonio. These conditions allowed for
two parallel developments. The first was the establishment of factories that housed pecan, garment, and cigar workers. The necessity of
a surplus labor pool for this sort of low-wage work meant that these
factories were all located in the West Side barrio, which not only provided a local workforce but also assured that Mexicans and Mexican
Americans filled all of these jobs. The second development in the 1930s
was the explosion of homework in each of these industries, a phenomenon much more prevalent on the West Side than in any other part
of the city.[49] Even the negligible public health protections provided by
the rudimentary factories disappeared for homeworkers, with whole
families crowded around a kitchen table sewing children's clothing or
shelling pecans in order to provide a bare subsistence. The Roosevelt
administration and the National Relief Administration (NRA)

attempted to regulate homework, but federal guidelines that called for health inspections and other protections for workers remained unenforced on the local level while the machine held political control of the city.[50] Because these operations all occurred on the West Side, these two strands of economic development remained hidden from view until the workers themselves began to pull back the veil in the mid-1930s.

In both the factories and the homework sites on the West Side, women did the vast majority of the work. This situation had not come about accidentally but was a conscious policy of San Antonio's primary industrial employers. By situating their facilities and targeting their homework output in the West Side, the cigar, garment, and pecan shelling industries narrowed their labor pool to include primarily Mexican and Mexican American women. While this theoretically should have shrunk their available supply, the massive surplus labor pool in San Antonio made this strategy workable. Further, these employers clearly viewed women in general, and ethnic Mexican women in particular, as more exploitable and less capable of fighting their exploitation than other employees. These practices had clear antecedents in the early New England textile mills, but they were now strengthened by a few other complementary ideas. The notion of the "family wage" that was championed by both employers and unions, however irrelevant it might be in the midst of chronic unemployment, served to justify shrinking wage levels for women.[51] When combined with the notion that Mexicans and Mexican Americans enjoyed no inherent rights in the United States, employers' preference for this workforce becomes clear.

The San Antonio Trades Council (AFL), through its newspaper the *Weekly Standard*, occasionally commented on working conditions on the West Side. In January 1934 the paper reprinted a speech by the chairman of the Regional Labor Relations Board, Rev. Peter Wynhoven, in which he stated that San Antonio was the "most deplorable spot for the workingman in the United States." He fumed that if "one-half of the cities in the United States had such deplorable working conditions, there would be a revolution. It is a great surprise that San Antonio people are so long suffering and patient."[52] A few months later a writer in the *Dispatch* argued, "The selfish few that would profit from this low paid labor employment, are not of the citizenship that cherish great pride in the city's history and progress, but are newcomers from other cities suffering from a congested population that has been exploited by them, or their predecessors, until education and a desire for higher citizenship has drained their reservoir of low paid labor. . . . San Antonio is the last frontier for this class of exploiters."[53] The only mention made of homework came in January 1937, when the paper noted with some surprise, "We are told that an authentic survey has revealed between 15,000 and 20,000 families who eke out a precarious existence from employment in their homes, such as shelling pecans, garment and handkerchief making, which, sad to state, are ofttimes mere hovels for which words can scarcely be found to portray the squalor existing in them."[54]

Cigar making, garment assembly, and pecan shelling dominated the job market on the West Side and served as employers of first and last resort for the thousands of Mexicans and Mexican Americans crammed into the barrio. While pecan shelling remained the least desirable and lowest paid work throughout the 1930s, the other two industries also maintained miniscule wages and appalling health and safety conditions in their facilities, adding to the already acute public health crisis on the West Side. Because of these conditions and the refusal of employers or the city government to deal with them, the West Side witnessed one organization campaign and strike effort after another from 1933 to 1938, culminating in the massive pecan shellers' strike that the city machine decried as an attempted revolution.

The cigar industry was the first to undergo this turmoil. The Finck Cigar Company, founded in the late nineteenth century, dominated the industry in San Antonio, employing about 800 women in 1933. Wages hovered around twenty cents an hour, but workers also faced a series of penalties that often drove their actual wages even lower. One of the most galling of these penalties was a fine of three good cigars for every poorly rolled one, though Finck still sold the supposedly ruined cigars.[55] But this was just one of the cigar workers' many grievances. Any workers who did not produce their quota of cigars from the material given to them had to pay the difference back to Finck. For each minute that workers were late, they were docked one cent from their already meager wages. There was no punch clock to determine when they arrived at work, however. Instead, one woman's job was to remember who was late to work and by how much. The opportunities for abuse in this system are obvious. Workers were also only allowed five minutes to use the restroom each day. Edward Finck, the son of the company's founder, would often enter the women's restroom to remove workers he thought had spent too much time away from their work. The company also placed a daily quota of 500 cigars on each worker, but it did not allow them to go over the quota. If workers finished a few hours before the workday ended, they had to stay in the factory until a supervisor allowed them to leave.[56] Finally, Finck refused to abide by the newly created NRA Cigar Code, which set wage minimums at thirty cents an hour.[57]

While anger over these issues had simmered for years, the workers finally acted in August 1933 when 400 women, under the leadership of Mrs. W. H. Ernst, walked out in the first major strike in Depression-era San Antonio. This first strike lasted for a month before the mayor, C. K. Quin, intervened and had each side send representatives to try and negotiate an end to the strike. Edward Finck agreed to improve conditions, though he never made clear what that entailed, and hire back the strikers on the condition that Ernst could not return to work. The workers reluctantly accepted the agreement, though Finck refused to sign anything. In the end, some of the strikers were hired back while about 100 remained blacklisted. The company also reduced penalties for poorly rolled cigars from three to two well-rolled cigars. Wage rates remained below the NRA-mandated thirty cents an hour, with strippers earning $0.175 per hour and rollers earning $0.225 per hour. Inexplicably, the NRA accepted Finck's refusal to abide by industry standards and awarded the company a Blue Eagle.[58]

The 1933 strike was just the first of several staged against Finck during the mid-1930s. The initial strike effort, waged entirely by the workers themselves, gained the attention of the Cigar Makers' International Union of the American Federation of Labor, which provided limited support for Finck workers for the next few years. Conditions failed to improve after the first strike, however, as Finck refused to rehire some of the initial strikers, and the bizarre, often dictatorial, practices that had inspired the workers' anger continued unabated.[59] The next walkout came in August 1934 after Finck ignored agreements made with the workers and the NRA and again cut wages and increased penalties for work deemed substandard. Unlike during the first strike, however, the union attempted to keep strikebreakers from entering the cigar factory. A number of violent confrontations resulted between strikers and replacement workers. As a result, the San Antonio Police and Bexar County Sheriff's Department involved themselves in this second strike, after remaining on the sidelines in 1933. Chief of Police Kilday and Sheriff Albert West threatened to arrest and deport all picketers who refused to return to work, and on a few occasions sheriff's deputies threatened strikers in their own homes.[60] Mayor Quin remained conspicuous by his absence in dealing with this strike, instead allowing Kilday to crush it as he saw fit. When it became clear that Finck and the city government were determined to defeat their efforts, the workers called off the 1934 strike after a few months.[61]

A new strike broke out in March 1935, however, over these same issues of low pay, substandard working conditions, and dictatorial management, with the final outrage coming when Finck raised the penalty for poorly rolled cigars once again.[62] The police and sheriff's deputies resumed their determined efforts to crush the strike, especially after a number of violent outbreaks between strikers and strikebreakers during the first few days of picketing. A number of these instances of violence were at least partially instigated by the police, who escorted strikebreakers past the picket line. There were also instances of police trying to force strikers into the factory to work.[63] A writer for the *Weekly Dispatch* noted, "Evidently the management had arranged for the protection of the law, and Chief of Police Kilday, and Sheriff A. West, with their assistants, were on hand to protect the sanctity of property against the personal rights of the workers."[64] The Cigar Makers' Union tried to force Finck into arbitration through the new protections in the Wagner Act, but the company refused, intent on continuing to use the police to maintain operations during the strike. After eight months, the strike ended with Finck employing a completely nonunion workforce after the striking workers succumbed to the constant harassment. As a final insult, all strikers found themselves blacklisted throughout the city after the strike ended.[65]

While the 1935 strike ended in failure, it set the tone for the strikes that followed in other industries, as increasingly militant workers confronted more aggressive and overt police interference and increased intransigence by San Antonio's employers. It was against this background of growing tensions that the garment workers' and pecan shellers' strikes occurred. Kilday and city officials remained the chief backers of the city's employers, while a number of future activists emerged from the Finck strikes as militant organizers determined to create some change in the economic and social relations of San Antonio.[66]

Shortly after the organizational efforts began in the cigar factories, women in the city's garment factories also sought to use the opportunities accorded them by the creation of the NRA to increase wage rates and improve working conditions. Unlike the cigar industry, which had a long history in San Antonio, the garment industry was a relative newcomer to the city. Protective legislation passed in the Northeast, especially New York, led many clothing manufacturers to establish assembly factories in places like San Antonio. As a result, the industry grew rapidly in the late 1920s and early 1930s.[67] Like the pecan shelling industry, these factories were almost completely nonmechanized, relying instead on hand work provided by workers earning wages far below those in the more mechanized eastern garment assembly plants. The strikes that occurred from 1934 to 1938 emerged out of conditions similar to those at Finck Cigar.

The International Ladies Garment Workers Union (ILGWU) began operations in San Antonio in 1933 in an effort to raise wages in the industry's cheapest labor outpost.[68] The union's early activities sought not only to organize as many of the Mexican and Mexican American female workers as possible but also to force the companies to submit to the voluntary NRA standards. The NRA code for the garment industry required a wage of thirty cents an hour for southern states (two cents below the wage level for the rest of the country). The U.S. attorney for San Antonio even filed an injunction against one of the garment manufacturers for violating the NRA code.[69] Complaints by union and federal officials, however, fell on deaf ears, according to a writer for the *Weekly Dispatch*. The employers of the city sought "to make San Antonio a cesspool for low paid workers" by contending that "southwestern garment manufacturers could not compete under the code with garment workers of Puerto Rico."[70]

Recruiting workers into the ILGWU proved difficult, however, as employers launched a propaganda campaign to dissuade their employees from joining the union, while the conditions of widespread homework complicated organizational efforts by decentralizing the workforce. Still, through the efforts of ILGWU organizers and local activists, the union had recruited a number of workers from a few of the garment manufacturers by 1936.[71] The first strike occurred in 1936 against the Dorothy Frocks Company for higher wages and union recognition. The San Antonio police quickly returned to the pattern of behavior developed during the cigar strikes, acting as armed escorts for strikebreakers while continually harassing strikers and threatening to deport those who did not return to work.[72] In an effort to continue production, the company shifted its operations to another factory. The strikers set up a picket around this new location, leading to a memorable confrontation in which fifty strikers surrounded and disrobed strikebreakers attempting to enter the facility.[73] When that did not work, Dorothy Frocks simply shut down its San Antonio operations and moved to Dallas. The company returned to San Antonio a few months later and signed a union contract, but employment never reached prestrike levels. A year later the ILGWU won another victory when the Shirlee Frocks Company agreed to raise wages to twenty cents an hour, which almost doubled previous wages but still lagged well behind NRA regulations.[74]

These qualified victories brought newfound respect and notoriety to the ILGWU, with more workers seeking membership while other garment manufacturers sought to formulate plans to keep the union out of their factories. A typical response to these events came from the Texas Infant Manufacturing Company. It summarily fired any workers suspected of ILGWU membership or sympathies, while also establishing a company-run union, the Council of Garment Workers, which all employees had to join. In response to these clear violations of the Wagner Act, the ILGWU lodged a complaint with the National Labor Relations Board in early 1938, demanding that the fired workers be rehired and that the Council of Garment Workers be dissolved. The NLRB ruled in favor of the union, but Texas Infant refused to abide by the ruling. As a result, the ILGWU declared a strike in March 1938. As with previous strikes, the company attempted to hold out through the use of strikebreakers, while the police harassed and arrested strikers when they were not acting as armed guards for Texas Infant. The company finally gave in under the pressure of the strike and a boycott effort. The difference between this effort and the cigar strike seems to have been the steady support provided by the ILGWU in the face of police and employer harassment, support the cigar workers never received. On the strength of this string of victories, the ILGWU continued to grow in San Antonio into the early 1940s, the only example of such sustained union success in the region.[75]

While the cigar and garment workers called attention to the brewing discontent among the workers of the West Side, the activities of the Workers Alliance were the most militant reaction to the conditions in San Antonio. The Workers Alliance was a national organization that sought to organize public works employees and the unemployed, but its activities in San Antonio focused largely on issues of local concern, especially those facing the workers of the West Side. The San Antonio council burst onto the scene during 1935 in the aftermath of the early cigar and garment strikes. "One of the very first issues at the Workers Alliance here was the right of workers to organize without fear of deportation," according to local activist Emma Tenayuca. "But the pressure of economic conditions moved faster in the direction of poverty. . . . The Workers Alliance gathered a tremendous momentum when the workers returned from the fields, not having worked, without money and without food."[76] In the Workers Alliance, then, we see an effort to deal with the combined problems of migrant farmwork and urban poverty that were everyday issues for residents of San Antonio's West Side. City officials responded fiercely to the alliance's activities. According to Tenayuca, "Scores . . . were herded before the United States Immigration office and threatened with deportation merely for membership in the Workers Alliance," including many U.S. citizens.[77]

By 1937 the alliance focused primarily on efforts by local officials to cut WPA jobs so that workers could be routed to field work in other parts of South Texas. Tenayuca and other activists in the alliance had conducted a number of letter-writing campaigns to WPA officials in Washington demanding expanded employment opportunities in San Antonio and an end to wage discrimination that allowed Anglos to earn more on public works projects than Mexican Americans.[78] On June 29, 1937, the Workers Alliance staged a protest at the city's WPA office after employment rolls had been slashed at the request of Texas farm interests. According to a Workers Alliance sympathizer, "Realizing the need of large numbers of petitioners in order to command the attention of local officials, through them indicating to Federal authorities the necessity for further continuance of the WPA program, the San Antonio Workers Alliance, on June 29, 1937, sent a complaint committee of about one hundred men and women to the district WPA office to protest the discharge of over one thousand WPA workers in San Antonio."[79] The local WPA director returned from lunch to find the delegation waiting for him. Rather than speak to them, however, he immediately called the police to remove them from the building. The police arrived and, using their oversized nightsticks, drove the protestors out of the building. For his part, Mayor Quin immediately released a statement declaring that the Workers Alliance had engaged in a sit-down strike and that he approved of the police's violent removal of protestors.[80]

A few hours later a squad of police appeared at the Workers Alliance headquarters on the West Side. Armed with axes and clubs, they forced everyone out of the building, clubbing "everyone within reach."[81] After everyone had been forced out, the police then proceeded to systematically demolish everything in the office. A reporter for the *San Antonio Light* wrote, "Banners, flags, pictures, charters were ripped from the walls, torn into shreds and stomped on. . . . Benches and chairs were hammered to pieces. One officer of the law placed a typewriter on the floor and tromped on it. . . . A duplicating machine was demolished. The stove was kicked over and broken. A drawerful of dishes was found and officers broke them piece by piece."[82] The *San Antonio News* reported that "officers pounded out a tune on the piano, then turned it over and broke it."[83] Meanwhile, on the street outside police randomly attacked passersby: "Out in the street one man was struck in the legs with a nightstick, then arrested as he hobbled off because it was alleged he was not moving away fast enough. A woman was also arrested because she did not move fast enough."[84] Such an overwhelming show of force could only have been meant as a warning to the Workers Alliance and any prospective agitators that the San Antonio Police would not hesitate to resort to violence (either systematic or random) when possible. It also provides a strange counterpoint to the mob violence that some of these same policemen would face a few years later during the Municipal Auditorium riot.

In the aftermath of this savage attack, Police Chief Kilday declared that he had found a large amount of literature, written in a foreign language (if Spanish can be considered a foreign language in San Antonio), that appeared, to his trained eye, to be "Communistic."[85] These pamphlets provided all the proof Kilday and the machine needed to assert that the protests breaking out on the West Side were led by outside agitators, despite the fact that Tenayuca and the other leaders were San Antonio natives. Still, when Tenayuca's lawyer tried to secure her release from jail on a writ of habeas corpus, the judge bellowed back, "She belongs in jail. Let her stay there!" Since she was a "damned Communist," the judge declared that he did not care what the police did to her.[86]

Despite the ferocity of this police attack, Tenayuca and the Workers Alliance continued to agitate on the West Side, especially among the workers of the city's largest employers: the pecan shelling companies. In many ways, pecan shelling served as a perfect symbol of employment in San Antonio's West Side. Its workers suffered under horrific working conditions and earned the lowest factory wages in the nation. These low wages and the plentiful labor supply allowed the pecan companies to maintain completely nonmechanized operations, while also providing massive profits for the operators. With strikes breaking out in the other industries of the West Side, the pecan workers also launched a series of strikes between 1934 and the early 1940s.

Because of its location, San Antonio had been the center of pecan shelling for fifty years by the time of the Great Depression. Almost half of the national pecan crop was produced within a few hundred miles of the city. During the nineteenth century pecan gathering had served as a means of supplementing meager incomes for the poor, who would scavenge the countryside for pecans and sell them in San Antonio for five to six cents a pound.[87]

The commercial pecan industry, however, did not develop until the late nineteenth century. The first major figure in the San Antonio pecan industry was Gustave Duerler, the owner of a candy manufacturing company. Hoping to take advantage of the surplus of pecans in San Antonio, he sent twenty barrels of pecans to markets on the East Coast in 1882. The success of this speculative venture prompted Duerler to expand his pecan shelling operation. Since pecan shells make up more than half of the total weight of each pecan, it was cheaper to shell them in San Antonio than to ship them elsewhere to be processed. He "hired local Mexicans, whom he paid to crack the nuts with railroad spikes, then pick out the kernels with tow-sack needles."[88] Shelling was done by hand for the next several years, but by the early 1920s the industry had begun to mechanize most of its operations. These machines graded and cracked the pecans. Workers then picked out the shells. San Antonio firms and their primary competition in St. Louis utilized these machines during the early 1920s.[89]

The industry changed drastically in 1926, however, with the formation of the Southern Pecan Shelling Company. Begun by Julius Seligmann and Joe Freeman with a $50,000 investment, Southern Pecan rapidly came to dominate the industry.[90] Rather than trying to keep up with the mechanized operations of the other pecan firms, Seligmann and Freeman, in the words of social scientist Harold Shapiro, "inverted the technological process."[91] Realizing the potential of the massive surplus labor pool available on the West Side, Southern employed only hand labor from the beginning of operations in 1926, slashing its overhead costs.

It also instituted a contractor system. Through this arrangement, Southern Pecan sold unshelled pecans to contractors who hired the labor and provided work space. The contractor then sold the shelled pecans back to the company at a predetermined price. Since it held a virtual monopoly, Southern Pecan was able to dictate every aspect of the production process to these contractors.[92] It set the prices and wages, and anyone who deviated from Southern Pecan dictates risked blacklisting. By the early 1930s, Southern Pecan operations stretched out over more than 400 shelling sheds throughout the West Side as well as an unknown number of homes where families shelled pecans.

The contractor system gave Southern a number of advantages over its competitors. It did not need a large central factory, which limited overhead. Most important, however, by passing off issues of hiring and workplace management to contractors, the company rid itself of any worry about the consequences of low pay, long hours, and unhealthy working conditions. Even though the contractors remained little more than impoverished employees of Southern Pecan, the company could continually pass blame for the consequences of their business practices down the line to those who operated the shelling sheds. As a result, Southern Pecan outcompeted its local and national competitors and held an almost complete monopoly over San Antonio pecan shelling by the mid-1930s.[93]

At the onset of the Great Depression, Southern Pecan, through its network of contractors, was the largest employer on the West Side, employing between 10,000 and 20,000 shellers during the peak season each year.[94] Only a fraction of this number worked during non-peak seasons. The seasonality of pecan shelling was not dictated by the perishability of pecans, however.[95] Instead, labor needs determined the peak operating season for pecan shelling. During the winter months, when migrant farmworkers returned to their off-season homes on the West Side, an enormous number of the seasonally unemployed resided near the pecan sheds, providing Southern Pecan with the largest possible pool of surplus labor at the lowest possible wages.

Pecan shelling and migrant farmwork fed off each other. Pecan shelling wages acted as a subsidy for agricultural interests in other parts of the state and country, providing employment for migrant farmworkers between seasons. Conversely, sugar beet or cotton employment served as a subsidy to the pecan shelling industry, allowing it to continue paying minuscule wages. This linkage became especially important as the Depression deepened and agricultural jobs became harder to find. In turn, the infinitesimal wages afforded by both pecan shelling and migrant farmwork forced many workers to seek out what little relief, public or private, could be found in San Antonio.[96] As a result, pecan shelling and migrant labor acted as a two-headed parasite that fed off of both local relief and the workers of San Antonio's West Side, creating a self-sustaining cycle of falling wages and intensifying poverty.

Regardless, pecan shelling provided necessary winter employment during the worst years of the Great Depression for most of these workers.[97] As CIO organizer George Lambert recalled, "The pecan shelling industry wasn't that important economically or any other way to San Antonio except that it provided the barest subsistence living to the migratory farmworkers, who came in and shelled the pecans for Seligmann in the winter months."[98] The 10,000 to 20,000 workers in the shelling sheds at the peak of each season during the Great Depression was a product of nothing more than the abject economic desperation of many on the West Side. The pecan sheds offered the worst wages in the city, with most workers unable to earn more than two dollars per week. Between September 1 and December 31, 1937, according to Social Security returns from Southern Pecan, regular employees received between $10.18 and $47.11. The single highest-earning employee, in other words, averaged less than three dollars per week over that four-month period.[99] Thus, many pecan workers actually made less money in their urban jobs than they did as migrant farmworkers. Cotton pickers, for example, tended to make a dollar more per week than pecan shellers.[100] Still, the owner of a small pecan-shelling operation claimed that pecan wages were sufficient for Mexican workers: "The Mexicans don't want much money. . . . Compared to those shanties they live in, the pecan shelleries are fine. They are glad to have a warm place to sit in the winter. They can be warm while they're shelling pecans, they can talk to their friends while they're working, their kids can come in after school and play because it's better than going home. If they get hungry they can eat pecans."[101] Workers did not need subsistence wages, according to this shed owner, because they could stuff themselves with pecans while chatting with their friends.

One former sheller, who began working alongside her parents as a young girl, recalled that "conditions were very, very poor. When you get fifty, sixty persons all in one place, you know, sitting side by side, sitting on wooden benches . . . and being there for eight hours, maybe nine [or] ten hours a day, that's a bad situation. Of course, we had no sanitary conditions at all. . . . The majority were women. Later on as the depression progressed, men had to come in and sit next to the family to do the work.

You take, for example, my father—I think that as a last resort he had to go in and shell pecans. He was a very proud man, but he had to leave his pride behind him and to go in there and sit next to us to earn a living because there was nothing else."[102] Once they found themselves within the contractors' sheds and began shelling, workers had to deal with a constant cloud of pecan dust that caused respiratory problems for many elderly workers. Their fingers often became swollen and infected after hours of handling broken shells each day. Even worse, basic standards of public health were impossible to maintain in these structures with poor ventilation and a complete lack of lighting or running water.[103]

This long list of dangers and grievances continued to grow during the 1930s as Seligmann and Southern Pecan refused to raise wages. Throughout the Depression Seligmann pronounced that he and the rest of the pecan industry wanted to pay higher wages, but competition and low profits made this impossible.[104] He also carried this message into his dealings with the federal government. In August 1933 the National Pecan Shellers' Association, an industry group of which Southern Pecan was a member, agreed to abide by NRA regulations to raise weekly wages for workers to around $6.50, with an absolute ceiling at $12.00. The NRA code committee drew up regulations for a minimum wage of $11 per week for men and $7 for women. Furious at this agreement, Seligmann withdrew from the National Pecan Shellers' Association and formed the Southwestern Pecan Shellers Association, which demanded a separate code for southern pecan companies, similar to the garment industry. At a meeting before the code committee, Seligmann testified that "Mexican Pecan Shellers eat a good many pecans, and five cents a day is enough to support them in addition to what they eat while they work."[105] He also argued that his nonmechanized operation needed a completely different wage scale than the mechanized operations elsewhere or his company would collapse. He needed many more workers than his competitors in St. Louis, so he felt that he should be allowed to pay them much less. The NRA code committee bowed to the pressure for lower wages (though not as low as Seligmann wanted) and created a new code with a minimum wage of fifteen cents per hour or six dollars per week, which would have tripled pay in San Antonio. When the code became effective in October 1934, however, Seligmann simply ignored it.[106]

The first attempts to organize pecan workers predated Southern's refusal to abide by the NRA code, however. Two separate unions were formed in 1933. The first, El Nogal, was an independent union that claimed almost 4,000 members but did little during these years.[107] The second, the Pecan Shelling Workers Union, was led by Magdaleno Rodríguez and bankrolled by Julius Seligmann in an effort to keep smaller pecan operations from undercutting Southern's wage scale. Rodríguez carried on a strange campaign of threatening to strike any employer that cut wages, while also demanding that employers not adopt the NRA code. He argued that NRA wages would force thousands of pecan shellers out of business, but he simply acted as a bludgeon against any employer who dared offer wages different than those mandated by Southern Pecan.[108]

Nevertheless, Rodríguez led the first pecan strike in July 1934 against shelling sheds not operated by Seligmann. These sheds had recently cut wages from six cents a pound for pecan halves and four cents for pieces down to four and a half and three and a half cents a pound. The strike lasted a few weeks before collapsing. The same union attempted a number of similar strikes the next year against a few small pecan operators who sought to cut wages but again failed to achieve anything.[109] Rodríguez claimed to represent more than 10,000 workers, but his union was little more than a one-man affair, and it faded away during the next few years, only to reemerge when Seligmann required Rodríguez's obstructionist activities to check the growth of a more legitimate union in 1938.[110]

The industry remained quiet for the next few years until January 31, 1938, when Southern Pecan told its contractors to lower wages from six cents per pound for pieces and seven cents for halves down to five and six cents. This wage cut caused a spontaneous walkout by more than 6,000 shellers.[111] Magdaleno Rodríguez's old union, now rechristened the Unión de Nueceros Unidos, was briefly revived by Seligmann to try and end the strike, but it failed to draw the strikers back to work. Rodríguez's union remained on the scene, however, as a goon squad sent out by the pecan company to threaten strikers.[112] The early leadership of this strike came from the veteran activists of the previous West Side strikes and the Workers Alliance, primarily women like Emma Tenayuca, María Solis Sager, and other local community leaders.[113] A Department of Labor conciliator later stated, "At the time of the strike there were no real union leaders present so 3 Communists took charge."[114] Within a few days, however, Donald Henderson (also a Communist) and the UCAPAWA arrived in San Antonio and took control of the strike as part of that union's brief efforts to expand into Texas.[115] They formed Pecan Workers Local No. 172 and demanded union recognition, collective bargaining rights, and the restoration of the pay cut until arbitrators could determine proper wage rates.[116] While these were hardly revolutionary demands, Southern Pecan and the city machine treated them as such.

The importance of this strike soon grew far beyond the efforts of previous years in the cigar and garment industries. What began as a spontaneous walkout over slashed pay rates soon morphed into a full-fledged social movement on the West Side with repercussions that went far beyond considerations of wage levels in a single industry, even one so central to the community as pecan shelling. As CIO organizer George Lambert recalled, "It had at its inception taken on the aspect of a mass uprising among the Mexican-Americans in the entire West Side of San Antonio, and was being participated in actively by hundreds and perhaps thousands who didn't themselves make a living in the pecan industry."[117] Sugar beet migrants and WPA workers, who formed a "middle class" among laborers on the West Side, worked as organizers and bodyguards throughout the strike.[118] This community-wide support only grew over the course of the strike, as support committees, mass meetings, and picket lines multiplied throughout the barrio.

On the other side of this struggle, the city machine and Southern Pecan maintained a grim determination to use any measures necessary to crush the strike. Joseph Myers, chief Labor Department conciliator during the strike, noted, "The ring feels that if the pecan shellers are allowed to remain organized they would help to re-elect Maverick [to Congress]. . . . This will explain why the Chief of Police is determined to break up the union, and to publicly proclaim that there shall be no peaceful settlement of the strike. They have, apparently, enlisted the support of Immigration Inspector W. W. Knopp, who has declared his intention to deport all Mexicans not regularly admitted to this country, some 63 found and arrested on the picket lines."[119] Chief of Police Kilday declared that he was attempting to stop a revolution, and under those circumstances any means were justified.

The pecan operators and the police could count on two additional allies in this struggle: elements in the Mexican American middle class and the archbishop of San Antonio. The Mexican Chamber of Commerce and LULAC were conspicuous in their opposition to the strike, just as they were a few years later in supporting the city machine against Maury Maverick. According to historian Richard Garcia, "It seems that the middle class did not want to be disturbed. During the 1934–38 period, when different sectors of the Mexican laboring class were striking, the life of the ricos and the upper middle class continued as usual. Labor strikes thus did not unify the Mexican community, they separated it."[120] Likewise, Archbishop Arthur Drossaerts was an early opponent of the strike effort (just as he would be an early instigator of the Municipal Auditorium riot). In a congratulatory letter to Chief Kilday during the strike, he wrote, "Our police force has had a hard task of it these past three weeks. They fought, not the downtrodden sufferers of an egotistic capitalistic system, but the dangerous leadership trying to make hay while the communistic sun was apparently appearing above our San Antonio horizon."[121]

Given the gulf between these forces, it is no surprise that the ensuing strike became quite contentious and violent. From the very beginning, Chief Kilday circumvented labor law and the First Amendment when he declared that there was no strike and therefore the city did not have to allow any form of picketing. A few days after the first walkout, he announced, "I am going to break up the picket lines this morning or any other morning the same situation arises, on the grounds that there is no strike."[122] Thus, the police and the city machine declared that all unrest came, not from any legitimate grievances or legitimate organization, but from outside agitators seeking chaos as a means to their ultimate end of a communist takeover. Police arrested picketers surrounding the few shelling sheds attempting to continue operations during the strike, while also announcing that the pecan industry continued to operate as before. In all, more than 1,000 were arrested and thrown into the Bexar County Jail.

The violence that occurred was almost entirely instigated by San Antonio's law enforcement establishment. Special police were deputized and sent into the West Side to enter strikers' homes and threaten them with arrest and deportation if they did not return to work.[123] Mass meetings, or even small crowds of people with no relation to the strike efforts, were tear-gassed. The city health department even rose from its long slumber to close down a soup kitchen frequented by strikers for health code violations. A riot then ensued when an angry crowd protesting the closure was dispersed with teargas and randomly beaten by club-wielding police.[124] Two days later (two weeks into the strike), the *San Antonio Light*, which tended to be the most moderate of San

Antonio's daily newspapers, printed a front-page picture of an officer holding new, larger nightsticks, in what was clearly meant as a warning to the strikers, under the headline, "Police Get Clubby."[125]

Department of Labor conciliator Joseph Myers remained in San Antonio throughout the strike and recorded the reign of terror as it occurred. As one of the only people in contact with both the strike leaders and city officials, he witnessed both sides of this struggle. On February 11, 1938, he reported that Kilday's claims of communist agitation were "only a subterfuge." In addition, he declared, "Brutality of police beggars description" and "will ever remain a disgrace to this city."[126] Four days later he reported, "The Chief of Police very curtly informed" officials looking into the case "that any attempt to picket he would have his police use tear gas and clubs and break up any kind of picketing. City firemen have also been armed with clubs and made to aid the police."[127] The campaign launched by Kilday and the police to crush the strike, or any other signs of dissent on the West Side, seemed to indicate that they truly believed they were fighting against an uprising that threatened to bring more than higher wages and unionization. Still, the police counterattacks did not derail the protest movement among the Mexicans and Mexican Americans of San Antonio but instead seem to have imbued it with a radical determination to force change, which only became more determined with each nightstick and tear gas attack.

During the second week of the strike, Governor James Allred attempted to force the two sides together to resolve the issue. He sent the State Industrial Commission to San Antonio to investigate the situation and report back to him. When the commission tried to convene on February 14, however, Mayor Quin refused to give the group any accommodations for its meeting. County officials, however, allowed the group to meet in a room in the Bexar County Courthouse. For the next two days the commissioners heard testimony from a number of individuals on both sides of the strike. At the end of these hearings the commission reported back to Allred that "wages are abnormally low, that living conditions are insupportable, and that no evidence has been adduced to justify police interference with picketing."[128] Despite the clear condemnation of the actions of Southern Pecan and the city government, however, strike efforts and police counterattacks continued through the end of February.

Finally, on March 9, both sides came together and agreed to submit the case to a board of arbitration, which ended picketing and the violence that came along with it. Southern Pecan would appoint one arbitrator, Local No. 172 would appoint a second, and the third would be an impartial arbitrator agreed to by both sides. Each side appointed their arbitrator, but Seligmann refused to agree to a third person, in what seems to have been an attempt to hold up the proceedings and allow police harassment to force the union's hand.[129] After almost a month of stalling, however, Seligmann agreed to the final arbitrator and the board finally sat down on April 1 to investigate. While the board collected information and prepared its decision, Seligmann, through Mayor Quin and Congressman Lyndon Johnson, agitated for relief subsidies from the Department of Agriculture for pecan companies, especially Southern Pecan, claiming that the strike and increased foreign competition threatened to destroy the industry.[130] On April 13 the arbitrators released their report, stating that "the Pecan Industry in San Antonio is in a perilous plight, conditions are very bad, not only for the workers, but for the Operators and contractors."[131] They further decided that an immediate restoration of the wage cut would threaten the industry, so the board decided that wages would increase to 6.5 cents per pound for halves and 5.5 cents for pieces, effective for six months.[132] Both sides accepted the decision, and Southern Pecan and the minor operators agreed to closed-shop contracts effective until November 1, 1938.[133] For the time being, it appeared that the union had won a small victory.

The controversy was far from over, however. The passage of the Fair Labor Standards Act (FLSA) in 1938 complicated the situation by mandating a national minimum wage of twenty-five cents. The pecan operators first tried to get around this law by claiming that pecan shelling was agricultural employment and therefore exempt from federal labor law. Individual contractors under Southern Pecan tried to claim that their business was entirely intrastate, and therefore did not fall under federal jurisdiction. When these tactics did not work, Southern Pecan simply shut down the industry in late October 1938, while Seligmann went to Washington to lobby for exemption from the wage and hour provisions of the FLSA.[134] When pecan shelling began again a few weeks later, most of the shelling sheds never reopened and the operators instituted a "stretch-out" that forced workers to shell an amount well beyond the ability of most employed in the sheds.[135] As this slow process of weeding out workers continued, Southern Pecan persisted in its efforts to gain an exemption from the minimum wage while planning to remechanize the industry more than a decade after it had reverted to hand shelling.[136] By 1940 the pecan workforce had shrunk to a fraction of its peak in the 1930s even as the union maintained a hold on the newly mechanized facilities of Southern Pecan.

In the end, then, the pecan shellers had little time to savor their victory. A few years later, economist Frederic Meyers noted that the catastrophic effects on business that some had predicted would result from the Fair Labor Standards Act had not occurred. He wrote that "some 'straggler' enterprises are forced out of existence, and some employees find themselves without jobs, although, actually, few cases of reduced employment in industries affected most by the act have been found."[137] In a footnote below this statement, however, Meyers wrote, "The only major case of unemployment that has come to the attention of this author was the pecan-shelling industry, in which the increased wage from prevailing levels of under $0.10 per hour resulted in the utilization of already existing mechanical techniques for shelling pecans and the displacement of a very large part of the labor force."[138] Once again, the Mexican and Mexican American workers of South Texas found themselves victims, if unintentionally, of New Deal legislation meant to ameliorate their situation. With their union now a hollow shell, especially for those no longer employed in pecan shelling, and the emergent social movement on the West Side dissolved, little seemed to have changed by the early 1940s. The reformist tendencies that emerged around the strike effort helped defeat the city machine in the 1939 mayoral election, but two years later that victory also disappeared. For those who had previously depended on pecan shelling for subsistence, some could find employment at Finck Cigar, which claimed no interstate business and therefore did not have to pay the minimum wage, while others had no choice but to return to the migrant stream.[139]

These changes in pecan shelling, like the other commercial activities in South Texas that depended on cheap labor and low overhead costs, point to a few important conclusions. One is the lack of a clear line dividing these urban processing operations from agricultural field work. While a clear delineation between agricultural and nonagricultural employment runs through labor law, the actual conditions of pecan shelling, shrimp hulling, and vegetable canning differ little from the conditions of agricultural labor. Seasonal unemployment, low wages, and a dependence on agricultural wages during part of the year by many of the industrial workers in South Texas belied the simplistic dichotomy of agricultural and nonagricultural labor. But this reality points to a more important point. The failed unionization efforts in South Texas during the Great Depression help illuminate more clearly the most glaring failures of the New Deal reform efforts. The effects of the political calculations that stripped agricultural workers of the labor rights enjoyed by other workers and the continued inability or unwillingness of the federal government to rein in the most violent tendencies of the South Texas political and economic elites could be seen all too clearly in the collapse of the working-class efforts to force change in the region. Broken by police harassment, intense poverty, threats of deportation, and a lack of basic enforced rights, the condition of the workers of South Texas stands as one of the clearest, most shameful failures of the New Deal.[140]

IN MANY WAYS, the Municipal Auditorium riot signaled the end of the reformist hopes of the Great Depression social movements in South Texas. Wrapping themselves in a stolen flag, the mob's leaders unleashed their revenge (and many drunken teenagers) on those who hoped to change the trajectory of the region. Many of these same people, enraged that the police would try to stop them from tearing apart an auditorium emptied of Communists, had sat back and cheered the police who clubbed picketers and tear-gassed bystanders just a year earlier during the pecan sheller strike. In both situations, the economic and political elites of the region remained largely undisturbed. Their power may have been challenged briefly, but they never really lost control.

Standing at the beginning of the 1940s, the situation of the workers in San Antonio and South Texas must have looked very similar to the way they began the era of the Great Depression. Segregation still held sway in labor and social relations. Migrant agricultural labor remained the economic mainstay of ethnic Mexican communities. Violence lurked just below the surface of these relations, though primarily as an unspoken threat rather than a regularly practiced mode of coercion. Beyond these surface similarities, however, the events of the late 1920s and 1930s had substantially altered the realities of life for many in South Texas.

Deportation and repatriation campaigns that targeted Mexican and Mexican American communities made a mockery of the rights of citizenship, while the intensification of the web of labor controls did the same for workers' rights. When Mexicans and Mexican Americans attempted to overcome these handicaps through organization and unionization, they confronted the overwhelming power of employers, law enforcement, and vigilantes united to crush anything that smacked of pleas for improved wages or working conditions. Thus, if at the end of the Depression conditions looked the same as before the economic collapse, these similarities hid a number of scars that had developed over the previous decade. While strikers and activists attempted to change the rigid political and racial structures of South Texas during the Depression, their failures resonated for decades to come. Unionization efforts disappeared in much of South Texas until the farmworker strikes of the 1960s, while efforts for political reform and civil rights protection moved into the more genteel arena of middle-class protest movements led by LULAC and the G.I. Forum.[141]

If the nation as a whole crawled out of the depths of the Depression with the beginning of World War II, the Mexicans and Mexican Americans of South Texas had a more difficult path to recovery. While the struggle for full citizenship continued through World War II, it would be many years before it would bear fruit. In the meantime, they watched as the war effort helped spread the labor relations of South Texas to the rest of the nation in a way that went well beyond the efforts of northern agricultural and industrial interests in the 1920s to recruit Mexicans and Mexican Americans.

PART IV | *The Shadow of the Revolution*

More than three decades in the House of Representatives had done little to blunt the famously combative nature of Henry B. Gonzalez. The congressman from San Antonio had engaged in many fierce legislative battles during his time in office, but in 1996 he found himself revisiting a policy he thought had gone away years earlier. A proposed immigration reform bill emerged from committee in March 1996 that called for the creation of an enlarged guest worker program that would streamline existing regulations and provide additional temporary labor for agricultural employers.

Two California Republican congressmen, Elton Gallegly and Richard Pombo, authored this proposal, which would, in their words, "provide a less bureaucratic alternative for the admission of temporary agricultural workers."[1] The amendment to the immigration reform bill that emerged from the House Agriculture Committee in March 1996 called for the new guest worker program to grant 250,000 temporary visas to agricultural workers in the program's first year. This massive new program was meant to exist alongside (and dwarf) the long-running H-2A temporary foreign worker program, which brought 11,400 farmworkers (almost all from Mexico and Jamaica) into the country in 1995.[2]

The idea for this new, less-regulated guest worker program came directly from the National Council of Agricultural Employers and was attached as an amendment to the immigration reform bill. More than just a massive expansion of the existing agricultural guest worker program, the Gallegly-Pombo scheme would have stripped away one of the primary safeguards in H-2A. Employers would only need to "attest" that their hiring of foreign guest workers would have no adverse effect on domestic workers. H-2A employers, in contrast, had to prove that there was no available domestic labor supply. Since the federal government already had a spotty record of enforcing the protections against adverse effect written into the more stringent H-2A program, Gallegly-Pombo seems to have been designed primarily as a program that would shift the power in agricultural labor relations even further toward employers by creating a massive new unregulated labor pool whose members had no rights as citizens.[3]

Congressman Gonzalez wrote a scathing letter to fellow Texas Democrat John Bryant, the ranking Democrat on the House Judiciary Subcommittee on Immigration, shortly after the immigration reform bill emerged from committee. With a mixture of anger and confusion, Gonzalez wrote, "I strongly oppose the new guest worker proposal and, to be honest, I am flabbergasted that this is even being considered." He then proceeded to give Bryant a history lesson. "I helped lead the fight to end the bracero program over thirty years ago. . . . The current protestations of agricultural producers that they face shortages of labor is the same argument they used three decades ago, but obviously the U.S. agricultural sector didn't collapse with the end of the old guest workers regime," he explained. "If the growers want to ensure an adequate labor supply, then they should offer decent wages and adequate living conditions, which is something they should do anyway." He closed the letter by explaining the stakes as he saw them: "This just makes no sense (although it will make many dollars for some big agricultural producers) and it is a recipe for a return to the bad old days of abuse and squalor for farm workers, conditions from which they are still struggling to fully extricate themselves."[4]

Gonzalez's argument against guest workers had changed little in thirty years. In September 1963 he declared before the House of Representatives, "Within the last month on Capitol Hill there has been a swarming literally of lobbyists representing groups all the way from the Campbell Soup Company to phony ersatz farmers from California who have been inundating this Capitol and the members of the House with information that would lead anybody to think there was an absolute emergency need for this type of labor."[5] The long-standing Bracero Program, which brought Mexican seasonal agricultural workers to the United States, was grinding to a halt after more than two decades. Gonzalez hoped to drive one of the final nails into its coffin, while agricultural interests sought to extend the life of a program they had shaped to their needs since the beginning of World War II.

His reasons for opposing the Bracero Program were simple, and consistent with his feelings thirty years later. "If there is a gap between the affluent and the poor in this land," he argued, "there is a chasm for the migrant worker, and he is at the bottom. . . . Texas, and specifically South Texas, is the locus of that chasm, for it is here that we have the greatest concentration of migrant workers in the nation." Guest workers exacerbated this problem because they created an unavoidable adverse effect on the conditions of agricultural labor. A guest worker "came exactly when he was needed, ordered just like a machine. He worked hard, he was easy to control. If he didn't satisfy he could be shipped off. It was all very neat," argued Gonzalez. "The community could get all the labor it wanted, at a cheap price, and with none of the inconveniences of dealing with human beings. American migrants were not wanted; they were free men, and they had families, and they had rights, and they had problems that could not always be ignored."[6]

Guest worker programs, in other words, were only a symptom of a much larger problem. They were the logical extension of a worldview that saw labor as nothing more than a line on a ledger, a cost of business rather than a messy issue involving rights or people. Gonzalez saw the consequences of that belief system in the intense poverty of South Texas, which both predated and helped configure the employer's ideal of the guest worker. The South Texas model of labor relations that developed in the early twentieth century did not simply disappear. It expanded and continued to mutate as it moved around the country, but its core concepts remained remarkably consistent. Gonzalez, in other words, recognized the link between the historical roots of migrant poverty in Texas and the intense desire of employers for foreign guest workers. In these demands for cheaper, more easily managed labor, Gonzalez saw the shadow of the agricultural revolution in Texas.

The final two chapters deal with the lasting importance of the South Texas model of labor relations as it has prospered and expanded in the years since the outbreak of World War II. Chapter 7, "The Bracero Program and the Nationalization of South Texas Labor Relations," deals with the largest guest worker program in U.S. history and the overwhelming importance of Texas as both a model and an obstacle to the smooth running of the system throughout its existence. From its inauguration in 1942 as a temporary wartime emergency measure until its quiet demise in 1964, the Bracero Program took the spirit of the deeply unequal labor relations of South Texas and spread them to the rest of the nation as a supposedly rational, necessary response to the exigencies of the agricultural labor market. The epilogue examines the continued resonance and importance of this model of labor relations as it has moved beyond the agricultural realm and into service and industrial employment.

CHAPTER SEVEN

The Bracero Program and the Nationalization of South Texas Labor Relations

In February 1952 Clifford Parliman, a farm owner and self-described "industrial engineer" from Edinburg (Hidalgo County), wrote to Texas governor Allan Shivers with a simple request: "It would seem the time has come where we people of this great State of Texas should begin to seek ways and means to get out from under the yoke of the United States, so that we may operate independently." What great injustice had caused Parliman to make this radical suggestion? "The U.S. Congress and Senate enacted a law controlling our migratory Mexican labor," wrote Parliman, "which law perpetrated a terrible injustice upon the border farmers." He continued, "We have had a belief that Texas came into the union under terms wherein we could again take up our independence if it were un-economical for us to remain as a State of the Union." He concluded his letter to the governor by arguing, "Texas could, as an independent territory, place an export tax upon gas and oil and other products that should give revenue for operating and maintaining a standing Army. With this independence we could make our own laws as to how we wish to handle Mexican labor and you and I know Texans could make laws with Mexicans that would not be unfair but which could and would be closely observed. In other words we understand the Mexicans and they understand us, hence could draw better laws by far than the Yankees who do not understand the Mexicans, could draw for us."[1]

Despite this complaint that the labor agreement between the United States and Mexico known as the Bracero Program justified secession from the union, Parliman proceeded to contract eight braceros for his Hidalgo County cotton farm in March 1952, one month after his letter to Shivers. These workers fulfilled their contract and returned to Mexico with no complaints from Parliman. In June of that same year he contracted eight more. After less than a month Parliman complained to the local office of the U.S. Employment Service (USES) that these braceros had drunkenly damaged irrigation pipes and other items on his property. He demanded that the federal agency cancel his contracts immediately, releasing him from the need to pay off the remainder of the money he owed the workers. The local field representative of the USES found no corroborating evidence of any destruction caused by the braceros and refused to release Parliman from his contractual obligations. Instead, it became clear that Parliman had contracted too many workers and did not want to pay for the minimum number of hours stipulated in the contracts. Desperate, Parliman took the issue to the local court system. After two weeks in prison waiting for their trial, each of the braceros was found not guilty for lack of evidence by South Texas jurors. A friend and associate of Parliman complained that this episode proved that "unless these contracts in respect to the farmer and worker are changed, and changed immediately, then they perpetrate a tremendous injustice against the farmer, give the whip hand to the common uneducated farmhand and deny the farmer any right of control, similar to the Russian system behind the Iron Curtain and they definitely demand severe penalties be paid by the farmer if he attempts to exert control of his men and discharge the unruly ones."[2]

In many ways the complaints raised by Clifford Parliman against the Bracero Program at the same time he utilized it as a supply of cheap foreign labor perfectly illustrate the contentious relationship between South Texas agricultural interests and the Bracero Program. For more than two decades, growers in the Lower Rio Grande Valley and other areas of South Texas never stopped complaining about what they deemed the unfair restrictions of the program. While these complaints did not tend to go quite as far as Parliman's demand for immediate secession, they all evinced a palpable anger over government regulation of Mexican labor migration, none of which stopped the farmers from annually hiring thousands of braceros through the binational contract labor scheme.

Hidden by this gnashing of teeth and public displays of righteous indignation was the Bracero Program's Lone Star heritage. The gradual dissipation of the Great Depression and the specter of war in Europe and the Pacific led the growers of South Texas, along with their compatriots in California and Arizona, to demand that the federal government allow them to contract seasonal labor from Mexico. These cries in 1940 and 1941 differed little from their requests in 1936 (see chapter 5), but the entry of the United States into World War II at the end of 1941 provided the excuse for putting their prewar demands into effect. The program that emerged in 1942 from the negotiations between the governments of the United States and Mexico was much different from the wholly unregulated recruitment scheme desired by the growers of South Texas, not least because Mexico refused to place its citizens in Texas until the chronic discrimination suffered by Mexicans and Mexican Americans in that state had been substantially reduced.

Despite the efforts of the Mexican government to protect its citizens during the Bracero Program, however, over the course of more than two decades the contract labor scheme evolved beyond its control. As the U.S. government wrested control from the Mexican government and southwestern agricultural interests got their hands on the Bracero Program, the South Texas model of labor relations gradually spread to the rest of the nation. Despite the restrictions written into the initial agreement, by the 1950s it had developed into a source for foreign, surplus labor that lacked the basic free labor rights of mobility and negotiation. Further, at almost every step of the evolution of the Bracero Program from 1942 to 1964, Texas remained central: as an obstacle to binational agreements, as a voracious exploiter of contract labor after the blacklist expired, and, when Texas growers turned to mechanization rather than pay the minimum bracero wage, as the primary cause of the program's death.[3]

IN 1940 SECRETARY of Agriculture Henry Wallace testified before a Senate committee that there was a glut of agricultural labor on the nation's farms as a result of mechanization and technological advancement. He claimed that the agricultural economy required 1.6 million fewer workers than it had a decade earlier.[4] One year later, in 1941, the Bureau of Agricultural Economics published a report claiming that 1.5 million workers could leave agriculture without threatening the nation's agricultural output.[5] Despite these assertions that the end of the Great Depression and the recovery of the nation's industrial economy did not threaten the existence of an agricultural labor force, growers throughout the nation complained that they found themselves in a dire situation that could only be solved by the importation of workers from Mexico.

Throughout 1940 and 1941 the growers of South Texas fretted that Mexican American workers had abandoned their fields permanently for the lure of higher wages further north. Some sought to deal with this problem with more stringent enforcement of the Emigrant Labor Agency Law of 1929.[6] Most demanded, as they had in 1936, that the federal government eliminate the immigration regulations that excluded the entry of illiterates and contract laborers. In effect, they demanded an open border and the right to take as many workers as they pleased out of Mexico. Agribusiness interests and their adjuncts in the state government pleaded for the Texas delegation in the U.S. House and Senate to introduce legislation creating a contracting system similar to the one established during World War I.[7] Growers from California and Arizona soon joined in these demands for an open border for labor.[8]

Complaints about labor shortages in 1940 and 1941 hid a much different reality. Growers were correct in asserting that their bottomless surplus labor pool of the Great Depression years had disappeared, but agricultural workers had not vanished. Instead, farmworkers had options in the growing economy of the early 1940s, even before the United States entered World War II, that they had not enjoyed in the 1930s. Those options gave them leverage to negotiate for higher wages and better treatment. Growers had no intention of granting these demands, however. In South Texas, this could be seen most clearly in the 1941 cotton harvests. An official with the Texas Farm Placement Service noted, "The conflict between farmer and worker concepts of wages in South Texas has been a major factor in the farm labor controversies of the 1941 season. To start with, the farmers of the Lower Rio Grande Valley, when the cotton season started out to be late, rather than holding the milling workers throughout the region with promise of increased and prevailing wages obtaining elsewhere, clung to the 75 cent scale and made no effort to keep them for the Valley cotton harvest." As a result, "the Mexicans scattered out all over the State and into Mississippi and Arkansas, where wages were better. The South Texas farmers would have had ample supply of labor to harvest their cotton and other crops had they handled the situation and the workers sensibly and practically."[9]

Rather than debate whether they should pay competitive wages, however, South Texas farmers looked again to limit worker mobility as a way to deal with the changing economy. An editorial in the *Corpus Christi Caller-Times* suggested that farmers "hold the labor that they already have on the farm. With government help a condition close to conscripting available labor can be worked out to prevent the lost-motion migration which threw the South Texas cotton harvest out of gear" in 1941. This author did, however, provide another option: "The second choice (and with conditions being what they are, it seems a poor second choice) is for organized farmers to go ahead with their efforts to import workers from Mexico."[10] Competitive wages, even compared to notoriously low-wage states like Arkansas and Mississippi, never entered the equation. Instead, the choice came down to forced immobility or the introduction of surplus workers to artificially replicate the labor conditions of the previous decade.

Initially the Department of Agriculture denied that a shortage of farm labor existed, while President Roosevelt reminded the congressmen from Texas that the Texas Farm Placement Service had been established a decade earlier to assist in alleviating labor shortages.[11] But any argument over whether there was or was not a shortage of labor in 1940–41 is irrelevant. The salient point is that growers had relied on an overflowing labor pool for so long that they saw any decrease in the supply of available workers as a catastrophic shortage. For the growers of South Texas these beliefs went back to the very beginning of large-scale agricultural growth around the turn of the century, when farmers had declared an inalienable right to Mexican immigrant labor that coincided quite conveniently with their equally fervent desire to continually slash wages. In the end, this desire to maintain a surplus labor pool as a protection against higher labor costs motivated calls for the lifting of immigration restrictions from Mexico. Notions of labor shortage were entirely impressionistic, mouthed piously by farming interests transfixed by rising market prices and federal agricultural subsidies that seemed certain with the expansion of war in Europe.[12] Pearl Harbor and the U.S. entry into the war only added to the formidable artillery at the command of lobbyists and politicians seeking to grant farm interests their desired foreign labor supply. Early in 1942 the U.S. government moved forcefully to appease growers' desires for Mexican labor.[13]

Meanwhile, Mexico continued to suffer under the weight of economic crisis and instability. Industrial and agricultural output grew substantially in the early 1940s, and the massive land reform undertaken during the presidency of Lázaro Cárdenas temporarily blunted the agrarian radicalism that had plagued rural areas since the revolutionary era, but the capital-intensive nature of economic growth in each sector only exacerbated the class stratification of the rural majority. Mexican agricultural output grew at an annual rate of 6.3 percent from 1940 to 1960, one of the highest rates in the world, but the benefits of this growth did not trickle down.[14] Instead, in the words of scholar Roger Bartra, the "development of Mexican agriculture since the Cardenista years of agrarian reform has been characterized by the rise of a powerful sector of capitalist farmers situated in the middle of a sea of semi-proletarianized and pauperized peasants and of landless day laborers."[15] Small farmers found themselves unable to compete with the irrigated agribusiness enterprises growing around them. Many saw migration and wage labor as the only means of subsistence.

The vast majority of these migrants looked not to the United States but to the growing urban areas of Mexico, especially Mexico City.[16] For a substantial minority of migrants, however, the burgeoning wartime economy north of the Rio Grande created a powerful justification for international migration. Thus, as Harry Cross and James Sandos argued, altering Eyler Simpson's classic formulation of agrarian reform, "Migration, not the ejido, proved to be Mexico's 'way out' of its development crisis of the mid-twentieth century."[17] As with previous eras, it is impossible to state with any certainty the number of people who crossed the U.S.-Mexico border from 1940 to 1941, but large numbers resumed the northward migrations that had all but stopped during the depths of the Great Depression. This resumption of emigration to the United States forced the Mexican government to face the same problem it had in the decades before the Great Depression. How could policymakers turn this out-migration to the advantage of the Mexican state and nation without entirely discarding the artifice of protective, if defensive, nationalism?

Shortly after the official entry of the United States into World War II in December 1941 the two nations began negotiations for the construction of a binational contract labor program. The growers who demanded access to Mexican workers had no intention of letting either government dictate the terms by which this access was granted, but the unilateral contracting of labor from south of the border that had been acceptable during World War I was not diplomatically possible in the context of World War II and the Good Neighbor Policy.[18] For its part, the Mexican government remained wary of allowing its citizens to work in the United States, remembering the humanitarian crises created when

Mexicans found themselves stranded and destitute in the United States during the 1920s and 1930s. Before the official negotiations began, for instance, the Mexican consul at Eagle Pass, Francisco Polin Tapia, expressed a common belief among officials in Mexico that there would be no guest worker program: "We know that this is only an attempt to hold down wages on the Mexican agricultural workers who live in the United States; and I feel sure that before my government agrees to any movement of agricultural workers to the United States, the restrictions placed on the movement including transportation, wage contracts, and cash bond to insure the safe return of workers to Mexico, and the carrying out of all terms of the contract will make the terms prohibitive to the people who are trying to hold down wages." He then added, "We have recently spent several million dollars returning 25,000 workers to farms in Mexico, and we shall not soon forget this experience."[19]

Mexican policymakers worried that an increased migration of Mexicans to the United States would only multiply the instances of discrimination and violence against ethnic Mexicans throughout the United States, but especially in Texas. Despite these misgivings about authorizing the transport of Mexican workers to the United States, the Mexican government ultimately acquiesced because it had little choice. The potential financial and social benefits of the guest worker program overrode the fears of its negative consequences.[20] The Mexican secretary of foreign relations put a more patriotic spin on it: "The immigration of braceros can be considered as one of the ways in which Mexico aided the effort of the Allied Nations for total victory, despite negative effects on production in Mexico, by helping sustain levels of production in the United States as necessary in the war."[21]

The result was the Emergency Farm Labor Supply Program, originally meant as a temporary mechanism for solving the supposed agricultural labor shortage in the United States. The agreement drawn up between the two governments allowed for contracting of agricultural laborers in Mexico by the U.S. government, which then subcontracted to U.S. farming interests. The agreement came with a few important restrictions that the Mexican government hoped would guarantee fair wages and treatment for its citizens abroad. First, the agreement stated that Mexican workers could not be used to displace native workers. Second, braceros were guaranteed the prevailing wage in the area for which they were contracted, with a thirty-cent minimum wage, as well as suitable housing and food.[22] Third, any signs of discrimination by employers would result in cancellation of their contracts. Chronic discrimination in any town or region would lead to unilateral blacklisting by the Mexican government. As a result of this provision, officials in Mexico City refused to allow braceros into the state of Texas throughout the wartime program. Finally, any grower who employed undocumented Mexican workers would not be allowed to contract braceros. In theory, these regulations should have protected against any adverse effect caused by the introduction of large numbers of guest workers into the agricultural labor pool. In practice, however, the Bracero Program realized Consul Polin Tapia's fears. As Cindy Hahamovitch has argued, "All those protections failed because they weren't meant to succeed."[23]

DESPITE THE BLACKLISTING of Texas, wartime conditions in the state were important for the operations of the Bracero Program. Widespread discrimination, pervasive and unapologetic employment of undocumented Mexican laborers by the region's growers, and the state government's efforts to have Texas removed from Mexico's bracero blacklist all had a profound effect on the workings of the international labor agreement during the war. The ways these different strands of social and labor relations came together in South Texas in these years not only dictated how the original wartime program operated but also proved pivotal in the program's evolution in the postwar years.

The most obvious and visible aspect of wartime conditions in Texas, at least from the point of view of Mexico, was the continued segregation of and discrimination against Mexicans and Mexican Americans. While these conditions had a long and well-documented history before the outbreak of World War II, added scrutiny from Mexico, the U.S. government, and an energized Mexican American civil rights movement helped turn these instances of discrimination into episodes of national and international importance. The constant empty recitations by politicians and community leaders in Texas of the ideals of the Good Neighbor Policy only made these shortcomings more glaring.

At its most brutal, this racial system still held the potential for violence, even if Texas witnessed no single episode like the 1942 Zoot Suit Riots in Los Angeles.[24] Mexican consular officials in Texas published a seemingly never-ending series of updates on discriminatory actions throughout the state to justify their nation's refusal to send braceros to Texas, including acts of violence against Mexicans moving to Anglo neighborhoods, school segregation, police misconduct against

Mexicans and Mexican Americans, and dozens of other instances of racial discrimination. The most shocking actions detailed in these reports include the machine-gunning of a Mexican family by the sheriff of Bee County and the fire-bombing by Anglos of a house in the Mayfield Park section of San Antonio recently purchased by a Mexican American family.[25]

Less dangerous, though no less galling for the Mexican government and the ethnic Mexican populations in South Texas, was the continuation of segregation in education and public accommodations. Longtime civil rights activist Alonso Perales testified before Congress that he had a list of 150 towns and cities in Texas "where there exist from 1 to 10 public places of business and amusement, where Mexicans are denied service, or entrance," leading him to declare that the "discriminatory situation in Texas is truly a disgrace to our Nation."[26] The state of Texas made token efforts to deal with these issues but rarely moved beyond expressions of feigned horror at press conferences.[27]

Journalist Hart Stilwell noted in 1946 that "if an Anglo-American has served one day in the penitentiary [in Texas] for the killing of a Latin-American during [the previous twenty-five years], I have not heard of it." Further, he asserted, "It may be accepted as an established fact in Texas that an Anglo-American can kill a Latin-American with impunity. The day has passed when the Anglo-American received a bounty for such an act, and the day has passed, in most of Texas, when the killing of Latin-Americans was considered a sport."[28] Needless to say, Mexicans and Mexican Americans failed to view this as substantial progress.

The state of Texas finally reacted to these protests against chronic discrimination in 1943, but not because of any pangs of conscience. Instead, the state was under pressure to break Mexico's blacklist, both to erase the embarrassment of being singled out by Mexico as the most discriminatory state and to allow the state's large growers to avail themselves of bracero labor.[29] Mexico's reasons for targeting Texas were even clearer: Texas had the largest Mexican-origin population in the United States, a greater dependence on ethnic Mexican laborers than any other state, and the worst history of chronic anti-Mexican racism. No other place in the United States carried as much political and symbolic importance for Mexico in the effort to exert influence over the binational agreement.[30]

The first attempt by the government of the state of Texas to convince Mexico to reconsider its position was the passage of the "Caucasian

Race Resolution" by the state legislature, which banned discrimination against "Caucasians" (which legally included Mexicans and Mexican Americans) in public accommodations. As historian George Green noted, this resolution implied "that it was all right with the state if discrimination against black Texans continued unabated."[31] This nonbinding proclamation did not change the minds of officials in Mexico, who saw how empty these affirmations were.

Governor Coke Stevenson next wrote to the Mexican secretary of foreign relations, Ezequiel Padilla, that "it has recently come to my attention that the Mexican Government has contemplated that in view of discrimination which may exist against Mexicans resident in this State, Mexican laborers who are being sent elsewhere in the United States under existing agreements between the Mexican and United States Governments will not be sent to Texas." While he mentioned efforts to legislate an end to discrimination, Stevenson made his intentions clear in informing Padilla that the cotton-growing areas around Corpus Christi expected a large harvest in 1943 and therefore required Mexican labor. He concluded by assuring Padilla, "I desire further to assure Your Excellency that the people of this State will wait with the highest interest the decision of the Mexican Government which I hope will permit Mexican workers to come to Texas in order to work on our farms, where they are so desperately needed." Padilla responded a few days later, writing that he appreciated the governor's efforts, but that only when chronic discrimination was eliminated would Mexico consider lifting the blacklist.[32]

When the Caucasian Race Resolution and a vaguely apologetic letter did not cause Mexico to budge, the state government formed the Good Neighbor Commission.[33] The executive secretary, Pauline Kibbe, wrote to other members of the commission a year after its founding and made clear that the commission's primary job was to convince Mexico to allow braceros into the state: "As you know, the occurrence which actually brought on the creation of the Good Neighbor Commission was the refusal of the Mexican Government, in the spring of 1943, to allow emergency agricultural labor to come into Texas to assist in harvesting the crop because of the 'conditions' which existed here. When the Commission was set up, we agreed that our first responsibility was to ascertain exactly what those 'conditions' were and then formulate some program of action to permanently clear up the situation, not only with regard to farm laborers, but as concerned all Latin Americans in Texas."[34]

The commission's efforts to discover these "conditions" led them to the following realizations several years later that nicely capture the nature of its activities: "The Second World War brought another wave of immigrants to Texas to work on farms, ranches, and in industry. Those brought in legally were augmented by waves of 'wet-backs' and *for the first time*, state-wide physical evidence of discrimination appeared in public places—restaurants, schools, hotels, movie houses and rental properties—and this brought about a wave of incidents, particularly from Mexicans of improved economic circumstances and from soldiers."[35] While the author of this report seemed to have forgotten that there was no legal contracting of workers in Texas from Mexico during World War II (though it is unclear if he referred to braceros or legal immigrants), he also made the argument that wartime immigration *created* discrimination against Mexicans and Mexican Americans. This type of superficial investigation into issues of discrimination led scholar George I. Sánchez to complain that the commission was nothing more than a "glorified tourist agency" meant to paper over incidents so that Mexico would eliminate the bracero blacklist.[36] It also confirms historian Emilio Zamora's comment that the state of Texas was only "interested in conceding the necessary measure of good neighborliness to lift the ban."[37] Discrimination was only a problem once it entered the glare of public attention.

Two episodes in particular illustrate the way the commission operated. The most notorious instance of discrimination in which the commission found itself embroiled was the Felix Longoria affair. Longoria was a Mexican American from Three Rivers, south of San Antonio, who entered the military in 1944 and shipped out to the Pacific.[38] He died in action, but his body did not return to Three Rivers until January 1949. When his widow and family tried to arrange for a wake at the only funeral home in Three Rivers, they were told by the owner that he did not provide such services for Mexicans because the town's "whites wouldn't like it."[39]

Word of this denial quickly reached Dr. Hector Garcia, a military veteran and founder of the American G.I. Forum, in nearby Corpus Christi. Several months earlier Garcia and his group had undertaken a study of conditions in South Texas labor camps and segregated schools. The reports of their findings revealed shocking conditions, but these revelations received little attention from the press or politicians.[40] With the Longoria affair, however, Garcia found an issue that finally gained traction in his effort to push for Mexican American civil rights. Racist treatment of a dead serviceman roused greater anger, apparently, than that same treatment inflicted every day on migrant farmworkers and schoolchildren. The local, state, national, and international press began to take notice when Garcia demanded that the funeral home allow Longoria's wake, but the episode received even more notoriety when recently elected Senator Lyndon Johnson publicly objected to the treatment of Longoria and his family, eventually receiving permission from President Harry S. Truman to have Longoria's body interred at Arlington National Cemetery.

Beyond the obvious civil rights implications of this case, it complicated the ongoing negotiations to extend the bracero program between the United States and Mexico. As a concrete example of anti-Mexican discrimination in Texas, it gave more ammunition to those in Mexico who sought to maintain the blacklist against bracero contracting to Texas. The Good Neighbor Commission took this threat to Texas's standing in relation to the bracero program as its point of departure. An official memorandum from the commission after Johnson's intervention stated that Garcia "was right to insist on the availability of the funeral home chapel for services for Felix Longoria. However, he could have adjusted the case without publicity; for instance, by appealing to the Good Neighbor Commission." The memorandum then continued, "National news is, in the 20th Century, international news. United States prestige and good will were damaged abroad by the ever-ready anti-United States press agents. Specifically, diplomatic conversations with Mexico on the subject of a labor contract were stopped." Turning to the Anglos of Three Rivers, the commission stated that the latter "did not recognize the serious international dangers of their customs of discrimination against Mexicans."[41] In other words, the Good Neighbor Commission remained unconcerned with discrimination as such. Only when its impact moved beyond the local level and into the realm of international politics did it confront the situation.[42]

The second episode, while far less important than the Longoria affair, provided a glimpse of the commission's everyday affairs and concerns. Neville Penrose, who was appointed chairman of the commission by archconservative governor Allan Shivers, wrote to another member of the commission in August 1952, after Mexico had lifted the blacklist against braceros in Texas, with a new idea he called the "Bracero Sample Project." He wrote, "I am sending you a bundle of Mexico City newspapers. I wish you would pore over them and get the names of some nationally advertised products in this country, also being marketed down there. Something like Life Buoy Soap, and Phillips Milk of Magnesia. Write to some of these organizations and see what we can do about collecting a little kit to hand these braceros as they go back to Mexico. I do not think it should be very large or expensive. If it is just 25 cents or 50 cents worth of merchandise it will serve our purpose and I think it would be very good advertising for the donors and a perfect place for the letter we contemplate." He then continued, "I am completely sold on the idea that we must do something with a quarter of a million potential salesmen. They come up here, they stay for a while and go back to Mexico. We must—we positively must—do everything we can to send these laborers back singing our praises. I can think of nothing more important for the Good Neighbor Commission than this project."[43] While the project never actually occurred, it provides a stunning example of how the commissions' members viewed their responsibilities. They sought not to protect Mexicans and Mexican Americans in Texas but rather to muffle news of discriminatory acts and help the state's economic elites secure cheap labor and new customers.

The Good Neighbor Commission lasted until the 1980s, but never as anything more than an underfunded public relations body. As the assistant director of the commission wrote to a local group in Eagle Pass, its primary job was to "look into matters of reported discrimination against Latin Americans and to smooth them over on the local level to the satisfaction of all, thus avoiding widespread and unfavorable publicity for your city."[44] In the end, however, the Good Neighbor Commission served its purpose, as the Mexican government finally allowed the contracting of braceros for employment in Texas.

WHILE THE GROWERS of Texas griped about not having the option of legally contracting workers from Mexico during the war, the Bracero Program was operating in the rest of the nation. Through a complex arrangement of overlapping jurisdictions among the Department of Agriculture, the Department of State, the U.S. Employment Service, and the Immigration and Naturalization Service, the wartime program operated as an executive branch effort with very little oversight from the legislature. Congress's belated approval came with the passage of Public Law 45 on April 29, 1943, which accepted the basic parameters of the international agreement.[45] These basic standards continued until 1947, when the wartime program came to an end, two years after the war itself.[46]

During the program's first year, 1942, only 4,203 braceros came to the United States. The number of braceros increased sharply after 1942, however, with more than 200,000 coming from 1942 to 1947: 53,098 in 1943, 62,170 in 1944, 49,494 in 1945, 32,043 in 1946, and 19,632 in 1947.[47] More important than the total numbers, however, is where these workers were sent. The Pacific Northwest and California received the vast majority of braceros during the war (63 percent for California, 15 percent for the Northwest), though a total of twenty-four states received workers from Mexico.[48] As the President's Commission on Migratory Labor noted in its 1951 examination of the Bracero Program, "The areas served by the war emergency program were high-wage States which had been gaining population by in-migration during the preceding decade."[49] As a result, farm interests used the foreign contract laborers to stall the upward trend in wages caused by the increase in employment opportunities in war production in many of these states. Growers in Texas noticed this, fueling their efforts to break the blacklist.

These shrinking wage levels did not go far enough for agribusiness interests, however. Edward O'Neal of the American Farm Bureau Federation made a series of complaints before a Senate subcommittee in 1943 that growers continued to repeat throughout the life of the Bracero Program. He argued that the unregulated employment of workers from Mexico, both under the semiorganized World War I program and the hiring of undocumented workers along the border, "worked just fine until the Administration got to fooling with it." He rejected the need for or the utility of the standards set by the Mexican government for minimum wages and living and working conditions of contracted workers, instead declaring that, "in former years all you had to do was go to Mexico and look at the men who came in and worked under the old conditions. . . . they got Mexicans in large numbers to come over and do this work."[50]

In fact, many growers continued to employ unauthorized Mexicans in large numbers. Most prominent were the Texas growers left outside of the agreement, who simply shrugged off the official rebuke of the Mexican government and went back to employing unauthorized foreign workers in larger numbers than ever as wartime demands sent crop prices back up to levels not seen since the end of World War I. Even though the agreement with Mexico ostensibly bound the United

States to keep undocumented immigrants from crossing north of the border, the Border Patrol and the INS took a hands-off approach with regards to the labor needs of border area growers, especially in South Texas. As historian Otey Scruggs argued, "Since Texans were unable to acquire braceros, the American government was more easily persuaded to acquiesce in their use of wetbacks."[51] Similarly, the assistant commissioner of immigration, W. F. Kelly, later wrote, "At times, due to manpower shortages and critical need for agricultural production brought on by the war, the Service officers were instructed to defer the apprehension of Mexicans employed on Texas farms where to remove them would likely result in loss of the crops. . . . This situation resulted first in an increased illegal migration and second in [encouraging] Texas farmers, particularly in the border areas, to rely more and more on 'wetback' labor for producing their crops."[52]

Texas growers did not worry about the blacklist creating labor shortages because Mexican farmworkers continued to come on their own. Farmers knew that the seemingly endless supply of workers crossing the border from Mexico guaranteed a steady oversupply of potential field workers. Concerns over the continuation of the Bracero Program and the Mexican blacklist had little effect on the day-to-day operations of South Texas growers. Still, farmers viewed any restriction on their available labor supply as problematic. Objectively, they did not need braceros to supplement an already overflowing labor pool of mobile farmworkers, but they did not view it that way. The blacklist was, to them, an outrageous limitation on their ability to recruit workers. As World War II receded further into the past, however, the nature and terms of the program continued to change, and Texas became more central to these alterations in the international agreement.

THE BRACERO PROGRAM definitively shed its origins as an emergency measure in the years from 1947 to 1951 and became a semipermanent feature of U.S.-Mexican relations and the agricultural economy. These years also witnessed a slow evolution of the program as each nation tried to gain an upper hand in the administration of the increasingly contentious agreement. Growers in the United States sought to mold the accords to their needs. Mexico sought to gain leverage over negotiations during this brief interregnum but found its efforts frustrated time and again by the increasingly aggressive, unilateral actions of the U.S. government and U.S. growers. As a result, by 1951 the United States and its growers had gained an upper hand in their dealings with the Mexican government and had begun to shed the earlier protections against wage deflation, job displacement, and the hiring of illegal labor that served as cornerstones of the original wartime agreement.

The general terms of the wartime program remained until 1949.[53] On the ground, however, the basic nature of the Bracero Program changed drastically from 1947 to 1949. The most important of these changes was the institution of a process known officially as "drying out the wetbacks," which converted illegal immigrants into legal braceros. One of the primary reasons that the Mexican government had agreed to the wartime program in the first place had been the hope that it would drastically reduce, if not eliminate, the flow of unauthorized migrants leaving for the United States without any legal protections. The lack of stringent border controls and the blacklist on Texas growers combined to do the opposite. The flow of undocumented immigrants into the United States dramatically increased. As a result the Mexican government proposed a new system by which these unauthorized entrants could be incorporated into the bracero system so that they would not fall outside of the protections written into the bracero contracts. The U.S. government and growers agreed to "drying out" as a simple way to legitimize the continued use of whichever laborers they pleased.[54]

The two nations signed new agreements in 1947 that authorized the process of "drying out."[55] While many growers in Texas remained skeptical of the Bracero Program, fearing that it represented a dangerous precedent for government regulation of agricultural labor, they still took advantage of the new agreement to enter the Bracero Program on their terms. Through this innovation, farm interests found that the Mexican government and the Bracero Program as a whole had come to them, allowing growers to simply legalize the workers they would have employed anyway. In theory, "drying out" should also have forced Texas growers to live up to the minimum wage and adverse-effect standards established in the original agreement, but lack of enforcement allowed these growers to maintain the same employment practices they had followed during the blacklist period. According to two scholars examining the situation in South Texas during these years, "It is a matter of common knowledge in the Valley that many of the growers who used contract workers at the same time used wetbacks yet we were not able to trace a single case where a contract has been broken in the Valley for this reason."[56] They further observed, "No official word is given that the farmers are to be left alone, but the Inspectors soon learn that they are apt to be called before some kind of investigating board if they are too zealous in doing their jobs. . . . One Inspector, for example, stated that he never picks up a wetback engaged in irrigating. . . . One of the older Inspectors has a policy of not picking up anyone who is working or who is carrying any agricultural implement that would indicate that he had been working."[57]

As a result, the INS legalized 55,000 unauthorized workers in Texas alone during 1947. By comparison, the other bracero states imported or reauthorized only 31,331 braceros during that same year. Thus, while the blacklist remained in effect for Texas, the shift had already begun by which the state became the primary user of legal Mexican labor. As historian Arthur Corwin argued, "By that date Mexico plainly had lost control of the migratory labor program, and many a Texas employer was grinning with satisfaction."[58] The same trend continued during the next two years. From 1947 to 1949 only 74,600 Mexicans came under contract from Mexico compared to 142,200 workers legalized within the United States through "drying out."[59] Thus, by virtue of the process of legalization of unauthorized workers alone, Mexico had lost much of its leverage in dictating (or even negotiating) the terms of the Bracero Program.

The "drying out" process also led directly to the first diplomatic showdown between the two nations over the future of the program. Throughout 1948 more and more prospective braceros crowded into border towns in hopes of working in the United States—either as regularly contracted braceros or as unauthorized entrants who gained legitimacy through the alchemy of "drying out."[60] This crush of aspiring guest workers strained the capacity of already overcrowded border towns like Ciudad Juárez. In an effort to alleviate the crowding in Ciudad Juárez the Mexican government authorized the recruitment of 2,000 braceros on October 1, 1948. The Mexican government had resisted border recruitment for years for fear that it would increase undocumented migration among those who did not receive bracero contracts, but by 1948 officials felt that they had no other option.[61]

Cotton growers in the El Paso region announced to Mexican officials that the prevailing wage for cotton picking was $2.50 per hundredweight. Mexican officials rejected this rate as a transparent effort to slash wages, instead insisting on $3.00 per hundredweight for all braceros. INS officials in El Paso, angry over what they deemed "an outright breach of the labor agreement," decided to open up the border (and a much larger breach in the agreement) to all willing Mexican farm-workers, bypassing the formal structures and protections of the inter-national accord.[62] INS officials passed word to workers massed on the Mexican side that work was available at $2.50. From October 16 to 18, approximately 6,000 flowed across the border at El Paso, were herded together by the Border Patrol, arrested for illegal entry, sent to tempo-rary enclosures, and then paroled to cotton growers.[63] Grover Wilmoth, the district director of the INS at El Paso, justified the opening of the border by arguing that "they need the work, our farmers need them and the crops were going to waste."[64] Robert Goodwin, director of the U.S. Employment Service, testified that Wilmoth created the "El Paso incident" (as it came to be known) "on the allegation that the present treaty is not working in that we are not getting needed farm labor from Mexico."[65] The Department of Labor added its two cents on the matter when Don Larin, head of the Farm Placement Service, declared, "Mex-ico agreed to send braceros who would receive the prevailing wages. But Mexican officials came up with a demand that the laborers receive $3.00 a hundred pounds for the first cotton picking. These Mexican officials were pointing a pistol at the American farmers' head."[66] While this bureaucratic wrangling took place, the 6,000 workers brought across the border unilaterally went to work and, according to Ernesto Galarza, glutted the local labor market, reducing cotton-picking wages to $1.50 per hundredweight.[67] Once again, the growers received exactly what they wanted.

The Mexican government reacted to this breach of the agreement by immediately canceling the bracero accord, though the flow of workers continued for several months through a unilateral program operated by the INS and the Department of Labor, the agencies responsible for the El Paso incident. For its part, the U.S. government informed Mexico that any new agreement must not include unilateral blacklist-ing, clearly meant to lift the continuing ban on contracting to Texas. For months the two countries tried to gain leverage over the other in crafting a new agreement, which finally took shape in 1949, eight months after the previous accord had been voided.[68]

With the El Paso incident as an object lesson of what a unilateral program might look like if Mexico did not accede to the demands of growers and the U.S. government, the 1949 agreement eliminated uni-lateral blacklisting, in essence ending the exclusion of Texas from the program, while also extending the "drying out" process.[69] Mexico continued to hold out against growers' demands that they place contracting centers along the border, but that effort too collapsed in August 1950 when Mexico quietly agreed to allow contracting from the border towns. As a result, the traffic through interior contracting centers decreased drastically and a larger flow of prospective braceros moved toward the U.S.-Mexico border, producing a larger number of potential undocumented immigrants and crushing the Mexican government's hopes to eliminate (or at least slow down) the flow of unauthorized migrants north of the border.

Despite the end of the bracero blacklist, however, scholars Lyle Saunders and Olen Leonard argued at the time that the 1949 agreement "had little effect on the [Rio Grande] Valley." South Texas growers only reluctantly contracted braceros. Employers gave two primary reasons for this hesitancy: they abhorred the inclusion of a minimum wage in the agreement, which rose to forty cents per hour in the new contract, and they disliked the requirement that employers pay transportation costs to and from Mexico.[70] Farm owners had never paid transportation costs for undocumented workers or "dried out" braceros, so they saw no reason to do any different for contract labor. As a result, Valley growers requested few braceros from contracting centers in Mexico. Lower Rio Grande Valley farm associations requested only 1,500 workers from the U.S. Employment Service in 1950. They remained interested only in legalizing their unauthorized workers already in the fields. Even after a sizeable deportation campaign in 1950 in the Lower Valley, the growers showed little interest in curbing their employment of unauthorized labor.[71] Instead they claimed that the Border Patrol was a "Gestapo outfit" that was "siding with Mexico."[72] As with the Bracero Program, Texas growers whined incessantly about the activities of the Border Patrol even as they used them to their benefit.

The postwar Bracero Program nonetheless continued to evolve toward the wishes of growers and away from the desires of the Mexican government. These changes resulted in a drastic shift in the geographic dispersal of braceros in the United States. As the President's Commission reported, change proceeded at an astonishing rate:

California which in 1945 received 63 percent of the Mexican
workers had only 8 percent in 1949. The States of the Northwest,
which with California, had 78 percent of the Mexican program in

1945, had no Mexican workers in 1949. Texas, which had no legally contracted Mexicans in wartime, had 46 percent of all Mexican nationals under contract in 1949. New Mexico and Arkansas, which had none of the Mexican workers in wartime, had 17 and 16 percent, respectively, in 1949. Together, Texas, New Mexico, and Arkansas had 79 percent of the 1949 Mexican labor program.[73]

These same trends continued in 1950, as only 19,813 new braceros came through contracting centers, while 96,239 became braceros through "drying out," primarily in South Texas.[74] As a result, Texas growers, who were denied braceros during the war, dominated the Bracero Program for much of the rest of its existence. They may have complained that it was a flawed system that gave Mexico too much influence, but they also began to understand that it could guarantee the surplus labor that allowed them to maintain, or even lower, wage rates. Adverse-effect clauses in the agreements came to be seen as little more than rhetorical decoration without any capacity for enforcement, vestigial artifacts of a past multilateralism.

By 1950, however, problems within the Bracero Program had become more glaring. Conflicting complaints from the Mexican government, Mexican American civil rights groups, the INS, and growers over the program's workings became public and forced the White House to respond. As Cindy Hahamovitch has argued, "The Depression was over, the war had ended, the economy was booming, and, in the richest country in the world, farmworkers got poorer."[75] The Bracero Program was a major factor in creating and sustaining this situation. As a result, Harry Truman signed an executive order that created the President's Commission on Migratory Labor in order to study conditions of agricultural labor and the ways the Bracero Program, and foreign labor in general, affected the agricultural labor market and labor relations.[76]

Commissioners traveled around the country investigating these conditions in 1950 and published their findings in 1951. The report began by examining growers' claims that they required foreign labor to combat rising prices and increased international competition. "Normally, if there were a labor shortage, wages would rise," the report stated. "Since on the contrary they have declined, it seems reasonable to infer that the supply of illegal alien labor, plus the contract labor the Government admitted or imported, has helped to depress farm wages relative to factory wages."[77] The commission argued that the process of "drying out" assured a continued flow of unauthorized immigrants.[78] Not surprisingly, the commission pointed to the growers of South Texas as the worst threats to the proper functioning of the program. It rejected the constantly repeated assertion that domestic labor would not do field work, instead arguing that the employment of undocumented workers had reduced the wage level below the subsistence level of U.S. residents.[79] The commission's recommendations were clear: "Foreign labor importation and contracting [should] be under the terms of intergovernmental agreements which should clearly state the conditions and standards of employment under which the foreign workers are to be employed. These should be substantially the same for all countries. No employer, employer's representative or association of employers, or labor contractor should be permitted to contract directly with foreign workers for employment in the United States."[80] Clearly, the authors of this report hoped that its conclusions would be applied in the 1951 renewal of the bracero agreement. Instead, a much different agreement emerged that continued the trends of the previous few years and resulted in an almost complete rejection of the commission's recommendations.

WHEN U.S. AND Mexican officials negotiated a renewal of the Bracero Program and Congress considered a new bill that would set the parameters of government regulation of guest workers in mid-1951, they faced a complex set of choices and options. A cacophony of opposed interests and proposals inundated negotiators and policymakers. Mexican officials demanded that the United States pass a law that made the federal government the guarantor of the contracts, rather than the employers, as it had been during the Second World War. They hoped that this shift would compel U.S. officials to enforce bracero regulations. At the same time, Texas State Federation of Labor official Andy McClellan reported that "we're pouring the messages and wires into Mexico City asking all of the big labor leaders to try to stop the signing of the new bracero accord. . . . In the meantime, however, the Valley farmers are threatening rebellion if nothing is done to get labor for the cotton picking. They have behaved like a bunch of spoiled kids since this deal started, and their 'squawking' is turning a lot of good people against them."[81] Not to be outdone, growers' interests inundated officials in Washington with demands that the Bracero Program be extended and deregulated. The President's Commission report served as a possible guide to how the

Bracero Program might be improved. Congress reacted to these disparate demands by largely ignoring them and passing a bill that made few concrete changes in the guest worker program.

That bill, known as Public Law 78, disregarded the recommendations laid out by the commission, instead providing only a cosmetic stabilization of the program that did nothing to solve issues of adverse effect. It reiterated the restrictions placed on the wartime program—contracting required the certification of nonavailability of domestic labor, braceros could create no adverse effect to domestic labor, and employers had to make reasonable efforts to attract domestic workers—but did little to improve the mechanisms for ensuring that employers lived up to these restrictions.[82] Instead, the law permanently erased the decades-old tradition of prohibiting foreign contract labor from entering the United States, while providing no methods for determining labor shortages or prevailing wages. PL 78 thus maintained and expanded the Bracero Program, with all of its problems left to continue for the life of the agreement. This new law also added an air of permanence and stability to what had a few years earlier been nothing more than a temporary emergency program.[83] According to Ernesto Galarza, who vehemently opposed the Bracero Program, "Ten years of employer experimentation with braceros concluded with Public Law 78. . . . In a sense, these were years of trial and error as growers made one delightful discovery after another. Like the sprinkling systems of mechanized irrigation, braceros could be turned on and off."[84]

This institutionalization of the Bracero Program also coincided with the Mexican government's continuing loss of leverage in shaping its future. While PL 78 made the U.S. government the ultimate guarantor of contracts, officials, prodded by growers' demands for cheaper and more plentiful labor, continually worked to erode the Mexican government's control over the agreement. Mexican officials tried to reverse this long-term trend in late 1953 when the two nations entered into negotiations for an extension of the agreement. They sought slight alterations in the program like a higher minimum wage, the end of border recruitment, and a larger role for the Mexican government in determining prevailing wages and labor shortages. By January 1954, however, these negotiations had fallen apart as U.S. negotiators refused to accede to any Mexican demands. On January 16, U.S. border officials ended this standoff by rolling the clock back to 1948. They announced that braceros could be unilaterally contracted at the border until a new bilateral agreement was worked out. For the next few weeks, U.S. officials stood at the border and called out the number of workers needed that day, creating near-riots as thousands crowded at entry points for the chance at legal employment north of the border.[85] The effects of this open-border incident were profound—it proved definitively that the United States possessed a trump card in negotiations with Mexico. As long as thousands of Mexicans crowded along the border for the chance to become braceros, the United States and its growers could control the program regardless of the desires of the Mexican government. By again violating the international agreement, the United States gained complete control over its future operation. This incident was an "irrefutable demonstration of Yankee imperialism," according to Mexican scholar José Lázaro Salinas.[86]

The border incident was just the first move made by the U.S. government in 1954 to consolidate control over the functioning of the Bracero Program. With the Mexican government removed as an obstacle to unilateral operation of the guest worker scheme, U.S. policymakers looked to eliminate the continued use of undocumented workers in the Southwest, especially in Texas, and consolidate federal control over foreign labor. Growers continued to argue, as they had for decades, that they had an inherent right to Mexican labor, regardless of international accords or immigration law. They thus viewed the Bracero Program as a violation of their rights, even as they availed themselves of contract laborers. As one South Texas landowner explained, "I could go across the border and within a radius of 50 miles hire 12 to 15 good, experienced cowhands. That's the way we used to do it, we knew these people and they knew us. . . . As it is under the program, we have to take whatever Mexican nationals they give us, and hope they can do the job."[87] Another grower, looking back on these years, wrote that "the Valley cotton farmer became completely dependent upon the wetbacks to harvest his cotton. This seemed to be satisfactory to everyone concerned. . . . A few farmers considered themselves to be farsighted and purchased some of the newfangled cotton picking machines. Their investment was so high that they were reluctant to admit they had bought white elephants and held out until they could find suckers to sell the machines to."[88] As long as the option of hiring unauthorized entrants from Mexico remained, mechanization and braceros remained secondary for the growers of South Texas, who decried any efforts to curtail their well-worn practices as illegal and communist-inspired.[89]

In spite of Texas growers' constant complaints, the lack of Border Patrol activity in South Texas remained a poorly guarded secret in the early 1950s. Rumors circulated, for instance, that the head of the patrol ordered his officers to stay away from the South Texas farm of Governor Allan Shivers, a well-known and unapologetic employer of undocumented Mexican labor.[90] This sort of arrangement had a long history in the region, but the growers' interests became much more aggressive in the 1950s in trying to rein in any trouble that the INS might cause if it began enforcing the law. The simplest method for accomplishing this feat came through Congress. By cutting appropriations for the Border Patrol, legislators hoped to limit its activities. As scholar and activist Ernesto Galarza wrote, "It never appeared to be the intention of Congress to finance the Service adequately so that the gateway to illegal labor could be firmly closed. . . . With the purse half shut the gate could remain half open."[91] Border Patrol chief Willard Kelly responded to the loss of an appropriation in 1952 by declaring that the Border Patrol would have to abandon the Lower Rio Grande Valley altogether and pull patrols back to a "line 10 miles to the north of Kingsville, Falfurrias, and Hebbronville."[92] The Mexican government filed a complaint with the Department of State immediately after learning of this decision, angry that it would make enforcement of the Bracero Program even more difficult.[93] The withdrawal of the Border Patrol from the Lower Valley did not happen, however, as countervailing pressures soon came to bear on the situation.

The response came from the INS in 1954 with Operation Wetback, a massive public relations campaign that masqueraded as a military operation. The newly appointed head of the INS, General Joseph Swing, launched the operation in the summer of 1954 as a campaign to deport massive numbers of undocumented Mexicans throughout the Southwest. While Swing depicted this effort as a break from the INS's recent past, Operation Wetback was little more than a slight increase in manpower, a liberal usage of overtime, and a massive public relations blitz meant to convince the public that the INS and the Border Patrol were gaining control of the border.[94] With the support of President Eisenhower and Attorney General Herbert Brownell, the operation began in California in early June, rounding up and repatriating thousands as officers moved north from the Imperial Valley. Before the operation began Swing assured employers that they could legally contract braceros through the INS, but he warned them that he intended to rid the

Southwest of all illegal entrants: "I am quite emphatic about this because I know I am going to run into some opposition in southern Texas."[95]

Word of the operations in California spread rapidly to Texas, as was Swing's goal, leading tens of thousands of Mexicans to return to Mexico ahead of the deportation force.[96] South Texas growers, however, either ignored the warnings that Operation Wetback would eventually come to Texas, or simply believed that the INS would not dare take their workers away.[97] The INS district director in San Antonio reported that the Valley Farm Bureau "intend[s] to destroy our effort at enforcement of the law here in the Valley."[98] Some growers, like Governor Shivers, did take the INS seriously and began removing their undocumented workers by the end of June.[99] But most had done nothing by the time the Mobile Task Force arrived in South Texas in early July to begin the operation. Starting on July 3 the task force set up roadblocks and patrolled rail traffic, arresting any illegal entrants attempting to travel north ahead of the deportation sweeps. These efforts led to the apprehension of approximately 800 migrants before the full operation began. The full sweeps began on July 15. By the end of the month more than 40,000 had been captured in South Texas.[100]

The opposition that Swing had anticipated from the growers of South Texas was not long in coming. Growers and their allies not only claimed again that the federal government was trampling their rights, but some viewed the operation as a far more insidious undertaking. A writer for the *San Benito News* surmised that the "CIO may be getting lists of union membership prospects from the bracero centers. If the Border Patrolmen were racing through cotton fields with pistol in one hand and union membership application in the other, the union bosses in Washington might be content."[101] The editor of the *Weslaco News* went even further a few weeks after the operation began, writing, "After watching the tactics of Uncle Sam's invading force of crack tan-shirts for 14 days, it becomes our opinion that the whole situation amounts to about the same thing as undeclared martial law."[102] For some reason, an editorial in the *Valley Monitor* (McAllen) referred to the architects and supporters of the deportation drive as "longhairs."[103] One grower, who described Operation Wetback as an "old-fashioned West Texas rabbit drive," wrote, "It is amazing that the [Task Force] did not meet resistance, even armed resistance, for in four short days the way of life for more than a million people was drastically and irrevocably changed."[104]

Braceros being sprayed with DDT upon entering the United States at Hidalgo, Texas, processing center. (Photograph by Leonard Nadel, 1956. Leonard Nadel Bracero Photographs, Archives Center, National Museum of American History, Smithsonian Institution.)

By the time the campaign came to an end in September more than 100,000 Mexicans had been deported from South Texas, and an unknown number had left for Mexico just ahead of the task forces.[105] As General Swing had intended when he launched the operation, the removal of unauthorized workers forced South Texas growers to accept the need to recruit braceros. Between July 1 and July 15 the threat of Operation Wetback led Valley growers to send requests for 30,000 braceros to the Hidalgo reception center, with more than 15,000 Mexicans contracted by the middle of the month. The previous year, by contrast, only 700 had been contracted in the first two weeks of July.[106] The increased use of braceros in the nation as a whole, and South Texas in particular, was the primary result of Operation Wetback. When the Bracero Program reached its peak of contracted workers in 1956, Texas received 43 percent of the total of 445,197, almost twice as much as second-place California.[107]

Rather than seeking to keep these farmers from hiring foreign workers, Operation Wetback shifted the source of those foreign workers. Swing and the INS sought to consolidate the Bracero Program by making it the only game in town. As such, the deportation campaign complemented the border incident in January of the same year—the first subjugated Mexican desires to U.S. labor supply needs, while the second disciplined growers who sought to avoid federal regulation of their workforce. No steps were taken to improve methods for determining adverse effect, labor shortages, or prevailing wages. Instead, the INS focused solely on the issue of managed supply and ignored entirely the festering problems of treatment and need. More than ever before, the federal government assumed the narrow role of labor contractor, maintaining within the executive branch a monopoly on the recruitment of foreign labor. "The most skeptical of farm employers could see that the private black market was no longer vital, now that a public one could be created at will," according to Ernesto Galarza. "The Wetback obbligato thus ended on a harmonious chord. In the difficult transition from clandestine to legal labor which it had marked, the essential controls over the labor pool had not been jarred and the principles of employer determination of wages had not been undermined."[108]

In the end, the events of 1954 were not terribly important in a law enforcement sense. A brief spike in apprehensions enabled General Swing to declare, incorrectly, that he had erased the issue of undocumented workers in the Southwest.[109] The importance of these events instead lay in the ability of federal authorities to produce the credible fiction of a controlled border. In Operation Wetback and the expansion of the Bracero Program, authorities found a way to quiet the fears of nativists and employers (who were by far the loudest lobbying groups on these issues) by fabricating the image of both enforcement and managed temporary migration. These notions of control and strict management were illusory, of course, but they served a very specific political purpose. As Galarza noted, agricultural employers found that this new image of control had very little negative effect on their ability to dictate terms to their workers.[110]

Not surprisingly, while this system hummed along for the remainder of the 1950s, Texas was the primary recipient of braceros. The slight change in the source of their labor did little to change growers' general employment practices and wage rates, however. According to Andrew McClellan, a Texas State Federation of Labor official well versed in the Valley labor situation, a number of bracero users ignored the fifty-cent minimum bracero wage and substituted a standardized wage of thirty cents an hour (which dropped even lower in some areas). Employers simply forced workers to sign falsified payroll documents.[111] In April 1955 the Mexican consul at McAllen stated in an interview that 40 percent of the bracero users in his consular district, which covered much of the Lower Rio Grande Valley, violated the minimum wage. A few months later he claimed that the percentage was even higher.[112] As a result, the Rio Grande Valley had the highest bracero desertion rate in the nation, at 20–35 percent in the mid-1950s.[113] For its part, the federal government did little to solve the problem, sometimes issuing warnings but rarely punishing minimum wage violators.[114]

By the early 1960s, however, the trajectory of the Bracero Program changed. What had seemed a permanent part of the U.S. agricultural economy in the late 1950s suddenly ran up against pressure from two sides: demands for the end of the program from Mexican Americans and organized labor, and increased use of mechanization in the cotton fields of Texas that made braceros superfluous. While the AFL-CIO and Mexican American groups like the G.I. Forum and LULAC had long criticized the Bracero Program, growers in South Texas and elsewhere also slowly turned against it as bracero minimum wages increased and agricultural technology improved. Both forces came together at the beginning of the decade to bring the international agreement to an anticlimactic end when Congress failed to renew it in 1964.

Texas growers proved as important to the disappearance of the program as they were to its beginning and its enormous growth during the 1950s. The majority of braceros in Texas worked in the cotton fields, and when cotton growers turned against the program they eliminated their state as the primary bracero recipient almost overnight. In 1961 Texas received 40 percent (approximately 116,000) of all braceros, while California received 34 percent (approximately 100,000). A year later, after Congress passed a seventy-cent minimum wage for the program, Texas received only 15 percent (29,000) of the braceros while California received 60 percent (116,000).[115] Total numbers decreased even further in 1963, when Texas growers contracted only 17,700 braceros for 20 percent of the national total, barely more than Florida and Michigan and only a third of California's total.[116] In 1964, the final year of the Bracero Program, braceros made up a negligible force in the Texas cotton fields. In their stead came the much-delayed mechanization of Texas cotton.[117] The Good Neighbor Commission reported in 1967 that "Texas cotton farmers, anticipating the day when Braceros would no longer be available as shock troops in the fields, started converting to machine harvesting several years ago. Thus the gradual annual reduction in the number of Braceros allowed to enter, and the final termination of Public Law 78, found Texas growers relatively well prepared to carry on without them."[118]

The growers themselves, who had pleaded so fervently for these braceros just a few years earlier, expressed little nostalgia at the end of the program. Newspapers throughout Texas echoed these sentiments. The *Dallas Times Herald* editorialized that "Texas' farm labor will not be much affected by the end of the bracero farm program, farmers have predicted, because the federal 70-cent hourly wage minimum for braceros had already priced them out."[119] Likewise, a writer for the *Corpus Christi Caller* argued, "The U.S. Congress may think it killed the Mexican contract worker program last week. All it actually did was write the obituary."[120]

Growers had not killed the Bracero Program alone, however. Organized labor and Mexican American civil rights groups had been arguing against it for years before politicians finally seemed to pay attention in the early 1960s once Texas agricultural lobbyists silenced themselves. Henry Muñoz, the director of the Department of Equal Opportunity for the Texas AFL-CIO, succinctly summarized Mexican American and labor opposition to the foreign labor program when he argued, "We imported 195,000 Mexican workers [in 1963] at a time when our total rate of unemployment is almost 5 million—4,846,000. I doubt if history offers any other example of any nation suffering from massive unemployment recruiting hundreds of thousands of foreign workers of an unskilled character, to do unskilled work in the nation of recruitment."[121]

The fight against the Bracero Program also entered into the larger movement for civil rights. In one of the stranger debates in the waning days of the agreement, Congressman Henry B. Gonzalez tried to browbeat southern conservatives into voting against renewal of the Bracero Program by arguing that it was not consistent with their opposition to federal civil rights legislation. Public Law 78 gave the federal government authority to investigate instances of racial discrimination against Mexican workers, so Gonzalez demanded that prosegregation legislators show some consistency. They could not, he argued, vote for an extension of PL 78 and against the Civil Rights Act.[122] This line of argument ultimately had no effect on the longevity of the guest worker program, but it does point to how the waning of the Bracero Program became tied into the Kennedy and Johnson administrations' focus on civil rights. As Secretary of Labor Willard Wirtz argued, "It is much more than a coincidence that Congress terminated Public Law 78 . . . just at the time when the Nation was writing the dictates of decency into the Civil Rights Act and declaring war on poverty and ignorance in this country."[123] As the Bracero Program's effects became clearer and its defenders seemed to fade away, its future vanished. Though organized labor, civil rights advocates, and agribusiness interests seldom made comfortable bedfellows, they combined quite effectively to end the Bracero Program.[124]

WITH THE BENEFIT of hindsight, a few facts about the effects of the Bracero Program stand out. While Mexican braceros poured into South Texas during the peak years of the international agreement, Mexican Americans poured out. The proper functioning of the international agreement should have made this impossible, or at least less likely, since braceros were not supposed to replace domestic workers, but the failure of enforcement mechanisms and the lack of concern for domestic labor that animated the primary supporters of the Bracero Program meant that these two massive population shifts occurred simultaneously, each reinforcing the other.

Looking back over the entirety of the program, some patterns become clear. An increase in out-of-state migration occurred during World War II as many Mexican Americans left Texas for employment in the booming war industries and the fields of the Midwest and West. Rather than decrease after the war, however, the number of out-of-state migrants who registered with the state jumped from 22,460 in 1945 to 39,801 in 1947 and 71,353 in 1949, not to mention the unknown number who left without registering. While this outward flow grew, undocumented workers made up a substantial portion (if not a majority) of the South Texas agricultural workforce, as tens of thousands of these unauthorized foreign workers became braceros through the "drying out" process.[125] As civil rights lawyer and activist Gus Garcia wrote in an unpublished letter to the editor of the *Corpus Christi Caller*, "So long as stalwart champions of the people—like your idolized Mr. Allan Shivers [governor of Texas]—continue to hire wetback labor and to harass the Immigration Officials in their attempts to enforce the law, thousands upon thousands of South Texas families will continue to be uprooted year after year from their homes and forced to wander about the country, seeking a living, or at least a subsistence wage."[126]

When Texas growers first gained access to workers legally contracted from Mexico in the early 1950s, the migrant stream out of Texas only grew. Underlying this amplification of previous migration patterns was an unchanging assertion by the political and economic elites of South Texas that Mexican Americans refused to do field work, necessitating their reliance on foreign labor, whether legal or illegal. Even while Tejanos worked in fields throughout the nation, farmers in South Texas claimed that they refused to do agricultural work. As the President's Commission on Migratory Labor reported, "Texas farm employers told us that Texas-Mexicans were 'no good,' but farm employers in Arizona, Colorado, and other States told us with equal emphasis that the Texas-Mexicans are good and reliable workers."[127] During the early 1950s, before the crackdown of Operation Wetback, a state representative from the Lower Valley echoed this feeling in justifying the employment of undocumented workers: "The farmers need labor; the wetbacks need work; and the local Spanish-speaking people have a gypsy spirit which makes them want to travel. They just can't resist going north each year, and it is fortunate that there are wetbacks around to take their place. Then, too, the local Spanish-speaking people are tending to leave agriculture. They don't like the hard work."[128] An employee of the Texas Employment Commission likewise reported that local Mexican Americans were "extremely lazy and won't work, even for 50 or 60 cents an hour."[129] Whether these opinions came from willful ignorance or not, Secretary of Labor Willard Wirtz came closer to the truth when he wrote, "The false notion that 'Americans won't do stoop labor' was carefully nurtured from the truer fact that they won't work for stoop wages."[130]

In 1955, the first full season after Operation Wetback, Texas growers imported just over 150,000 braceros. Of these, 75,000 went to the four counties of the Lower Rio Grande Valley and another 19,000 went to the seven-county area stretching from Laredo north through the Winter Garden. These same counties sent almost 70,000 Mexican Americans into the interstate migrant stream. In such a situation, growers could complain that they suffered from a labor shortage, but only because their reliance on foreign labor had long since pushed local Mexican Americans out of the local employment market. Thus, the bracero minimum became the prevailing wage, as there was no local workforce against which adverse effect could be measured. As a result, with the rapid buildup of a bracero workforce, by the late 1950s agricultural wages in South Texas dropped below the rates of the late 1940s (the peak years of undocumented workers).[131] Mechanization remained negligible during the 1950s, however, as farmers still found little economic utility in the purchase and maintenance of expensive harvesting machinery.[132] In other words, the Bracero Program clearly maintained an artificially low wage rate in South Texas, pushing local workers into the migrant stream. Growers' preference for foreign labor and desire to slash wages, not a "gypsy spirit" or refusal to do farmwork, made these entries into the migrant stream almost inevitable.

The decrease in bracero recruitment by South Texas growers in the early 1960s did not reverse this trend, however. The 1961 migration included an estimated 127,000 from South Texas, up from approximately 105,000 each of the previous two years.[133] The next two years witnessed similar numbers of migrants—127,800 in 1962 and 128,000 in 1963. Importantly, however, the nature of these migrations had changed, as the number of interstate migrants increased from 91,000 in 1962 to 95,000 in 1963, while intrastate migrants decreased from 36,800 in 1962 to 33,000 in 1963.[134] The combined effects of widespread mechanization and the return of South Texas farmers to undocumented workers blunted any improvement for domestic farm labor that could have come with the end of the Bracero Program.

The upward trends in interstate migration continued after the end of the Bracero Program. The number of registered migrants grew to 167,000 in 1965, 38,000 more than the previous year. Interstate migration grew to 128,500, 24 percent more than the previous year, but the intrastate stream grew from 25,000 in 1964 to 38,600 in 1965, an increase of 54 percent, as jobs previously closed to domestic workers opened with the end of the Bracero Program.[135] The migrant stream shrank slightly in 1966, down to 162,000. Interstate migration remained roughly the same, but intrastate migration reversed the trend of the previous year and declined drastically (16%) as fewer South Texas migrants accepted employment from Texas growers.[136] These trends continued for the rest of the decade, so that by 1972 only 30,000 registered as migrants, and almost all of these traveled out of state.[137] In a sort of reflex response, echoing their predecessors' claims during the 1920s, some growers claimed that labor contractors threatened their livelihood by sending Mexican Americans elsewhere for employment, but most simply returned to their time-honored practice of hiring undocumented workers with little concern for the Mexican Americans in their midst. When the Good Neighbor Commission predicted in

1966 that "other states will intensify and perfect still more their methods of recruiting in Texas, since Texas has far more surplus farm labor than any other state," most growers ignored it.[138]

WHEN THE BRACERO Program came to a halt after two decades in 1964, all of the justifications that politicians and growers had repeated since the beginning of World War II for their continued use of foreign contract labor disappeared, replaced by quiet resignation and shrugged shoulders.[139] Despite its hushed ending, however, the Bracero Program had been essential to the development of the postwar economic order in the United States. While it only provided labor for agriculture after World War II, never again moving into the realm of industrial employment, it served as the nexus of two economic forces with enormous consequences for the future. The Bracero Program both (1) implemented a regional variant of a global trend toward reliance on guest workers and (2) facilitated the widespread adoption of a local variant of labor relations, applying conditions eerily reminiscent of agricultural labor in South Texas to the rest of the nation. As such, the Bracero Program's importance extends beyond the fields of the Southwest, instead impacting directly on the development of modern labor relations.

In the aftermath of World War II, several European nations and South Africa (a longtime employer of guest workers) joined the United States as habitual users of temporary foreign labor, with systems in each nation operating as "variations on a theme: each program stabilized (or depressed) wages by enlarging the workforce available to certain target industries."[140] Supporters in all of these nations rationalized the programs as the sole source of labor for jobs that native workers would not perform.[141] The comparison made by the Agricultural Workers Organizing Committee of the AFL-CIO is remarkable as one of the few voices of dissent during the life of the Bracero Program that considered the global nature of the guest worker phenomenon: "We believe that America deserves a more honorable place in the world community than the Union of South Africa, but at the present time we and South Africa are the only countries on earth which tolerate large-scale alien contract labor programs." The author extended the analogy: "South African mine owners import Negroes from segregated kraals, under contract, and return them home to their kraals when their labor is no longer needed. Southwest farm owners import Mexicans, under contract, and return them to Mexico when their labor is no longer needed."[142]

All guest worker programs are not the same, of course, but they have had a number of similarities wherever and whenever they have operated.[143] They have existed at the intersection of several competing interests and have been justified for many different reasons. First and foremost, they provide employers with an artificially enlarged labor supply in low-wage sectors. This aspect of these programs is both the most obvious and the one most fervently hidden under contractual protections and the rhetoric of diplomatic multilateralism. Second, they provide the image of control, depicting guest workers as an ordered, temporary migration that erases the messiness of most population movements. This notion of control is largely fraudulent, but it has been a key rhetorical weapon for those who employ guest workers. Managed migration is also supposed to cut down on undocumented entry by providing a legal alternative. This point is even more clearly wrong, but it has remained a key selling point for guest worker programs. Finally, foreign contract labor provides a source of capital for sending nations. Sending and receiving countries often join hands to repeat this mantra which, like the other rationales, holds a kernel of truth that obscures the much larger problems inherent in such a system.[144]

All of these rationales miss the most important aspect of guest worker programs, however. By the very nature of such a system, guest workers enjoy no inherent rights of free labor. They cannot quit, they cannot negotiate, and they cannot change employers. Guest workers can run away, and many do, but that immediately transforms them into undocumented migrants without even the thin legal protection afforded to guest workers. If they complain or try to bargain, they can simply be deported, ridding the employer of the immediate problem. This creates, in the words of Cindy Hahamovitch, "the perfect immigrant," stripped of all rights but blessed with the imprimatur of a legal temporary migration scheme.[145] The supporters of guest worker programs, it seems, are more than happy to ignore the implications of creating a managed workforce that lacks the basic rights of free labor.[146]

This international backdrop provides only part of the explanation for the existence and longevity of the Bracero Program, however. The global context existed in tandem with a more localized heritage that applied the labor practices developed in South Texas during the 1910s and 1920s to the rest of the nation. While agricultural and industrial interests in the Midwest and West had contracted thousands of workers from South Texas during the 1920s, creating a small and unregulated version of an international labor system, World War II provided the opportunity to stabilize and nationalize this method of artificially creating a surplus labor pool through international migration. And in the best tradition of Lone Star democracy, political elites helped assure the availability of this excess labor pool at every step, nationalizing the spirit of the Emigrant Labor Agency Law.

Despite growers' constant complaints against it, the Bracero Program witnessed "the most complete coincidence between government intervention and the interests of agribusiness to date."[147] In the words of Mae Ngai, the essential political aspects of the Bracero Program "signaled consolidation of industrial farm production as a low-wage enterprise beyond the reach of federal labor standards and workers' rights. In 1955 farm wages in the United States were 36.1 percent of manufacturing wages, a decline from 47.9 percent in 1946. That downward trend in large part resulted from the semicolonial use of foreign contract and undocumented laborers—workers who had no legal standing in the society in which they worked."[148]

With agricultural interests able to dictate how their labor needs were filled, especially during the peak years of the Bracero Program in the late 1950s, when the United States had wrested any leverage out of the hands of the Mexican government, they simply recreated the practices of South Texas growers they had long envied and sought to emulate. At the most basic level, South Texas labor relations had long denied workers' basic rights. By emulating this model, the Bracero Program and other guest worker schemes inevitably stripped individuals of the rights of movement and choice in the name of cheap labor for the employing country and supplemental income for the sending country.

ERNESTO GALARZA CONCLUDED his analysis of the Bracero Program by arguing that "the ideal worker" for bracero users and their supporters was "the man of the barracks, the man in a camp who spent all his time under supervision if not under surveillance. . . . Outside the barracks the limits of freedom were prescribed, and they were also the limits of the job. Liberty had found its economic determinant."[149] Likewise, the Agricultural Workers Organizing Committee declared, "We are convinced that foreign contract labor programs, whatever their announced purpose, by their very nature wreck vast harm upon the general farm labor market. These programs contain inescapable contradictions between purported purpose and practical effect—contradictions which cannot be removed legislatively or administratively."[150]

In the decades since these observations the Bracero Program has disappeared from the public consciousness, only to appear again in recent years as a nostrum to solve the "immigration crisis." "In an era in which governments seem to be racing each other to throw up obstacles to free movement across borders," Hahamovitch has explained, "guest-worker programs have been promoted as an alternative to illegal immigration."[151] Guest worker programs have never entirely disappeared (a variety of H-1 and H-2 programs still bring foreign workers into the United States), but calls for enlarged and less regulated methods for procuring foreign labor always seem to reappear at the same time that politicians declare a need to deal with "illegal immigrants." Unfortunately, the proponents of such a system seem never to have examined the history of the Bracero Program. They not only ignore the rampant violations of the spirit and letter of the law that were endemic to the Mexican labor agreement, but they also fail to realize that the Bracero Program *created* undocumented migration by intensifying the pressure to emigrate, "institutionalizing migration to the United States as an accepted and expected life experience," according to Harry Cross and James Sandos.[152] In the place of research and reasoned evaluation of guest worker programs, intellectual sophistry and disingenuous demagoguery have dominated these debates over the current immigration situation. A new bracero program has thus improbably emerged decades after the original was killed off as a deus ex machina for complicated issues of labor relations and international migration. As has been the case since at least the early twentieth century, the search for exploitable labor has been allowed to masquerade as an immigration policy while notions of citizenship or human rights have continued to recede into the background.[153] Gone are both the crude racism and the references to "the hewers of wood and the carriers of water" that littered discussions of who should be allowed entry into the United States in the twentieth century. But the same spirit of exclusion has survived with modernized forms of control and a new vocabulary. The difference is that the excluded worker has now become the employers' ideal. For agricultural workers (and increasingly for nonagricultural workers), the entire nation looks more and more like Texas.

Epilogue

In February 1991 twenty-two men met at a home in Edinburg, Texas. They had been lured there by a radio advertisement on a Spanish-language radio station in McAllen that promised employment opportunities for experienced field workers interested in working in the pineapple fields of Maui. At this informal meeting, labor contractor Cristobal Gómez showed the gathered men a videotape supplied by the Wailuku Agribusiness Corporation that depicted an idyllic tropical work environment. Gómez also promised the potential pineapple workers free housing, affordable food, $5.00 an hour as a base salary, and ample opportunity to earn time-and-a-half for working more than forty-eight hours per week. Finally, he promised that they would each return to Texas after four months with at least $4,000 in net earnings, far more than they could hope to earn at home. These twenty-two workers all signed up with Gómez and arrived in Maui in March.[1]

On arriving in Hawaii, however, the workers found that they had been lured across the Pacific with exaggerated claims of work hours and conditions. None of them ever worked enough to earn overtime, they were continually forced to speed up their pace through the fields, and there were no toilet facilities in the fields. Even more galling, however, was the fact that the workers from South Texas toiled in the fields next to local unionized labor working for almost twice as much per hour at half the pace. On some occasions, the workers from South Texas did not enter the fields at all (and therefore did not earn any wages) because all necessary labor was provided by local employees. Wailuku clearly viewed them as a flexible surplus labor force that could be used when required and ignored when necessary.

Even worse, the recruited workers were locked within a razor-wire-surrounded compound each night at 11:00 P.M. When they complained about these working and living conditions, Gómez informed the workers that they could be expelled from the dormitory with no means to fly back to the mainland (Gómez held on to their return tickets) if they continued to complain. After more than a month of this treatment, the South Texans simply refused to continue working and

223

contacted Texas Rural Legal Aid to help get them back to the mainland. After their strike had attracted the attention of Hawaiian news agencies, Wailuku and Gómez decided to give the workers their return tickets back to Texas. Once there, Texas Rural Legal Aid filed suit against both Wailuku and Gómez, claiming numerous violations of labor and civil rights law. Days before a jury trial was set to begin in McAllen, Wailuku and Gómez agreed to a settlement of $175,000 for violations of the Agricultural Workers Protection Act, the Fair Labor Standards Act, and Title VII of the Civil Rights Act, as well as breach of contract, fraud, and "intentional infliction of emotional distress," after the judge warned them that a South Texas jury was not likely to look kindly on an agribusiness corporation that abused and lied to local farmworkers.[2]

The federal judge's warning to the plaintiffs provides one point of entry into the larger importance of this case, which is at once both exotic and mundane. In one sense, Hawaiian employers reaching all the way to South Texas to fill their labor needs seems bizarre given the enormous distances involved. In fact, however, Hawaiian growers had been seeking nonlocal labor for several years when they took up Cristobal Gómez's offer to bring workers from the Lower Rio Grande Valley.[3] Pineapple harvesting was a simple process that took a few minutes to learn, but it was labor intensive. In Maui's rapidly expanding tourist economy, many locals sought to avoid agricultural work even though most field workers in Hawaii were protected by union membership.[4] In addition, Wailuku had only been growing pineapples for a few years after the collapse of the Hawaiian sugar industry. In 1987 it converted 2,500 acres of sugar fields to pineapples.[5] Wailuku looked to nonlocal workers, the cheaper the better, to fill what it feared was an impending lack of surplus labor for its relatively new undertaking. In drawing workers out of South Texas, Wailuku joined a decades-long tradition of distant employers who sought to take advantage of the low wage standards of the migrant labor pool that moved to and from the Lower Rio Grande Valley annually. So in another sense, the Wailuku case looks exactly like thousands of other cases of inflated claims, unfulfilled promises, and intentional mistreatment that plagued workers caught in the migrant stream, a fact that the judge in this case rightly warned would color the jury's decision.[6]

The way Wailuku tried to defend itself in this case provides another point of entry. Wailuku officials and lawyers claimed that the labor contractor, Cristobal Gómez, was the sole employer and was responsible for all of the violations. He had contacted the workers in Texas, he had arranged for their transportation, and therefore he maintained all liability and blame for their treatment in Hawaii. Wailuku officials wanted the case dismissed even though the company purchased the airline tickets to and from South Texas, provided all of the money for payroll, kept all of the records, owned all of the equipment and facilities used by the recruited workers, and was Gómez's only client.[7] Wailuku was not breaking new ground with its defense, which low-wage employers had been using for years. The Southern Pecan Shelling Corporation had done exactly the same thing sixty years earlier in the dispersed shelling sheds on the West Side of San Antonio. Wailuku officials were simply trying to insulate themselves from their own questionable recruiting and employment practices by introducing a contractor who could serve as their front man if anything went wrong. More important, they sought to use field workers from South Texas as, in essence, internal guest workers who could undercut and eventually replace local unionized workers, but without any messy liability should their plan fail. As an ethnically distinct workforce with no right to find a new employer or even to leave their compound after dark, these workers found themselves cast unwittingly in the role of late-twentieth-century domestic braceros, while Cristobal Gómez was little more than a poorly paid employee made to look like an employer.

This case, then, reveals two related but distinct issues in contemporary labor relations. First, it points out the continuity of agricultural labor practices since the early twentieth century. Left outside of normal labor rights protections, farmworkers continue to be poorly paid, abused, lied to, and exploited in every way imaginable. The conditions of employment at Wailuku would have confounded the workers who built the agricultural economy of South Texas in the early twentieth century, but the treatment they received would have looked quite familiar. Second, as we will see, this case opens a window onto the increasing use of the labor relations of agriculture by employers in the service and industrial sectors. The migrant farmworker, highly exploitable and rootless as far as employers are concerned, has become the ideal.[8]

This increased "farmworkerization" can be seen in a few important ways.[9] The first, given Wailuku's failed but common strategy, is the continued effort by employers to claim that they are not really employers. This contractor ruse, pioneered out of necessity by early capital-intensive industries like canal and railroad corporations, then adapted by agribusiness operators in the twentieth century, operates within a pernicious, but increasingly important, blind spot in U.S. labor laws that allows the exploitative labor practices of agriculture to spread into nonagricultural labor.[10]

An essential case bearing on this corner of employment law originated in South Texas in the 1970s. One of the largest onion producers in the world, Griffin and Brand of McAllen Inc., secured all of its field labor for onion clipping through "crew leaders." These contractors recruited all of the field laborers at nearby border crossings, drove them to the fields, and had them clip onions according to directives from the company. The company then paid a lump sum to the crew leader according to piece rates, which was distributed to the individual workers. Griffin and Brand employed field supervisors, but it communicated only with the crew leaders and not with the individual workers. As a result, when this arrangement led to multiple violations of child labor, minimum wage, and record-keeping provisions of the Fair Labor Standards Act, Griffin and Brand officials simply argued that they were not the employers and that all of the resultant violations were the fault of the crew leaders' negligence. In *Hodgson v. Griffin and Brand*, the Fifth Circuit Court of Appeals rejected this argument, ruling that Griffin and Brand wielded almost complete control over the crew leaders and therefore was a negligent employer.[11]

Although this decision, which predates the Wailuku case by two decades, would seem to have settled the matter, things have not worked out that way. Instead, employers throughout the nation have continued to hide their own clear violations of labor law under a veneer of innocence provided by straw contractors on whom they can dump all liability. Even Griffin and Brand continued to indulge in this useful fiction for decades after the 1973 decision.[12] When employers are willing to use straw contractors in this race to the bottom, successful prosecutions are exceedingly difficult. Employers know that few migrant agricultural workers or poor service sector employees can afford to hire a lawyer to argue their case, especially noncitizen workers. In each and every situation, the burden of proof lay with the workers to establish a direct employment relationship with the company, and then to provide proof of overdue wages, negligent treatment, or any other claim they might make against employers. Since these cases take years to crawl through the court system, employers realize that continued violations of the law will save them more money than prosecution of these violations will ever cost them.[13]

Workers far removed from the farms have had to confront this issue with more frequency in recent years. Retailers provide the most obvious examples.[14] For instance, janitorial services for corporations like Walmart, Target, and Outback Steakhouse have frequently been farmed out to contractors, many of whom have violated all manner of labor laws in fulfilling their contracts.[15] The corporations just point their fingers at the contractor as the true employer who is responsible for abuses such as child labor, unpaid wages, unsafe conditions, and on and on. Even more insidious have been the many other ways that Walmart has used variants of the contractor ruse to avoid liability for its business and employment practices. Most of these excuses have to do with the size of Walmart, which argues that its operations are so massive and complex that contractors are as necessary as their mistakes are inevitable. Those mistakes, however, cannot be blamed on Walmart in any legally binding way because of the convenient legal fiction of the contractor. Similarly, Walmart has claimed that it cannot be blamed for violations like the hiring of large numbers of undocumented workers or widespread discrimination in wages and hiring because its size makes centralized decisions impossible. Such problems arise from the mistakes or negligence of local employees.[16] Walmart fell back on these excuses in late 2012, when hundreds of workers died in a factory fire in Bangladesh while producing clothes for sale in U.S. Walmarts. The corporation denied any responsibility by pointing to the many contractors, subcontractors, and subsubcontractors who stood between Arkansas and Bangladesh.[17] These conditions, and the legal arguments that allow them to persist, owe much to conditions in the fields.

Closely related to the proliferation of straw contractors has been the effort to use agricultural recruitment methods. No industries have gone further down this path than chicken and beef processors. For decades, the meatpacking and processing industries had some of the highest wages and unionization rates in the nation.[18] Since the 1980s, however, corporations like Nebraska Beef and Tyson Foods have sought to slash wages and gut unions by attracting workers in much the same way as early twentieth-century farmers in South Texas or sugar beet corporations in the 1920s. Tyson provided the most brazen example throughout the 1990s when its managers conspired to smuggle large numbers of unauthorized immigrants from Mexico to more than a dozen different plants, where they were provided with fraudulent documentation. An operation of that scale did not go unnoticed, and the Immigration and Naturalization Service launched an undercover investigation into Tyson's illegal hiring practices.[19] Undercover INS agents posing as smugglers received official Tyson checks for bringing in undocumented workers. This investigation, the first time that the INS and Justice Department had gone after corporate violators rather than undocumented workers, led to dozens of indictments against the corporation for a host of illegal activities in late 2001.[20] Nebraska Beef operated a remarkably similar system, paying smugglers to bring workers from Mexico and provide them with fraudulent papers. An INS raid on a Nebraska Beef factory in December 2000 led to a number of indictments and hundreds of deportations. In both cases, however, the corporations escaped with minimal punishment because most of the witnesses had been deported.[21] Blatant and numerous violations of the law, in other words, paid off for both companies.[22]

This workforce allowed chicken and beef processors to speed up processing lines, slash wages, reduce bathroom breaks, eliminate mandated safety precautions, and numerous other cost-cutting measures. These changes inevitability led to higher rates of injury and employee turnover, but those problems did not hurt the bottom line. Conditions have been so deplorable that Human Rights Watch, an organization that typically focuses on the most unsavory and totalitarian nations on the planet, published a report on the conditions endemic to the U.S. meatpacking industry.[23] The report found that conditions in these plants worsened in direct relation to the hiring of undocumented labor, while also adding that meatpacking corporations had eliminated the need to move production facilities overseas by "reproducing developing country employment conditions here."[24] Agribusiness interests had made precisely the same cynical calculation decades earlier. Workers who lacked citizenship rights were less likely to complain about dangerous conditions, blatant discrimination in job placement, or unpaid wages. They would either endure these circumstances or they would leave, opening up a job for some other faceless worker. Fear would help keep costs down—fear of deportation, fear of losing one's job, fear of the unknown. As Mike Davis has argued, "a cheap labor flux without the necessary quotient of fear and uncertainty imposed by illegality might cease to be cheap labor."[25]

Fear and uncertainty have been handed down as the primary legacy of the South Texas farm boom, the ever-lingering shadow of the revolution in Texas. The Tyson executives seeking to cut costs and bump up their own paychecks probably know nothing about the labor relations of early twentieth-century Texas agriculture. They may not even consciously see their policies as imitating agricultural practices. So thoroughly have these practices been ingrained that they are simply accepted as unsavory but constant, a messy but unavoidable aspect of low-wage industries. Whether they realize it or not, these employers are walking down the same path of exploitation as many who came before them: early twentieth-century Texas cotton growers, midwestern sugar beet corporations, pecan company executives, and bracero users, among many others. The preference for workers unable to exercise the basic rights of citizenship—choice of employer, mobility, ability to confront employers for violations of labor law—has been the constant. Texas growers were not the first to realize the exploitability of noncitizen workers, but they were the most enthusiastic users of such labor. Tyson and Walmart will not be the last to make this same realization, but they are the most obvious inheritors of this tradition.

There are many reasons for this continuity. The most obvious cause has been agricultural workers' continued lack of legal status. With few exceptions, farm laborers have enjoyed none of the basic labor protections that most other workers enjoy. When farmworker issues have come to the attention of the general public, such as during the Great Depression and the years of United Farm Workers activities in California, they have been treated as issues of poverty. The New Deal and Great Society dealt with them through temporary relief programs but did nothing to attack the roots of the problem. They dispensed some money, spoke solemnly about rural poverty, but then forgot about the farmworkers who continued to travel along the migrant circuit year after year. This shameful bait-and-switch, with the rightful protections of labor rights and civil rights replaced by the bland rhetoric of alleviating rural poverty, has continued to the present day. Even when the public has paid attention to the plight of farmworkers, issues of labor supply have always taken precedence as politicians bend over backward to appease agribusiness interests.[26] Agricultural workers have, therefore, remained as an ever-present example for employers in other industries. Until that example no longer exists, there is no reason to think that copycat tactics will not continue.

Just as important as the continuation of the exploitative nature of agricultural labor has been the way immigration policies have consistently been used as labor market tools. Hidden under the numerous declarations of "immigration crises" since the early twentieth century has been the clear hand of employers seeking to thwart aspects of immigration control that would hurt their businesses. The fight between restrictionists and antirestrictionists in the 1920s over whether Mexico should be included under immigration quotas has continued, stripped only of its eugenic vocabulary, into the twenty-first century.[27] At their core these debates still boil down to simplistic notions of border control versus border anarchy that completely misunderstand the reality of immigration. Within this discursive reality, Latinos have remained the quintessential objects of surveillance and control.[28]

While these recurrent waves of nativist mania would seem to hurt employers, the result has typically been the opposite. They have been able to redirect antiforeign sentiment into a powerful method of control by simply ignoring it. Workers are the ones who face the immediate consequences of nativism, not employers. Nativist efforts to strip undocumented workers of government services or the right to rent housing have only strengthened the hand of those who seek to employ foreign labor. Texas growers realized this in the 1920s and 1930s, and the rest of the nation has figured it out in the intervening years.

The solutions that have been presented for these issues have, more often than not, just been variations on old schemes that did not work. Calls for beefing up the Border Patrol and closing the border to illegal entry are little more than calls for a new Operation Wetback, which solved nothing other than a short-term public relations problem for the INS. Those demands for a closed border are typically made in tandem with calls for a new guest worker program to deal with any future labor shortages, especially but not exclusively in low-wage industries like agriculture and food processing. Time and time again, the mechanisms that stripped workers of the ability to claim basic rights in the past are recycled as the only rational response to an immigration system that has veered out of control. Lost in these discussions is any notion of what "border control" actually entails and the very serious price born by workers whose rights are trampled beneath these empty notions. All these incessant, empty debates accomplish is tying the taint of illegality more tightly to the most poorly paid workers.

The condition of Mexican and Mexican American farmworkers in South Texas changed little from the beginning of the farm boom in the 1910s until the post-Bracero era. From the beginning of large-scale migration from Mexico during the Revolution, Mexicans and Mexican

Americans were viewed by potential employers as a never-ending supply of labor power, more beasts of burden than citizens. This system was merely amplified over the next several decades, even as massive economic and political changes occurred in both nations. Temporary shifts in migration flows, immigration legislation, and demographic changes may have altered some of the specifics of these trends, but they have not changed their broad outlines. Migrants have continued to flow from northern Mexico to South Texas and the rest of the United States, while employers have continued to formulate countless methods to put these migrants to work. Migration flows, in fact, have only increased in the years since the end of the Bracero Program, with little thought or energy given to improving the treatment meted out to those who migrate.

Only rigid enforcement of civil rights and labor laws can improve this situation. Hopefully, the latest wave of nativism, with its red-faced calls for border walls and massive deportations, will recede as all others have, but the disappearance of overt racism is just a beginning. Only when the civil rights of all workers, regardless of citizenship or country of origin, are honored can South Texas, the U.S.-Mexico border region, and the United States as a whole avoid repeating the history of labor repression and racial segregation in South Texas.

Notes

ABBREVIATIONS

ITC   Institute of Texas Cultures Library, San Antonio

PST   Paul S. Taylor Collection, Bancroft Library, University of
                        California at Berkeley

Ranger Investigation   "Proceedings of the Joint Committee of the Senate and
                        the House in the Investigation of the Texas State Ranger
                        Force," 36th Legislature, Regular Session (January 14–
                        March 19, 1919), Harbert Davenport Papers, Texas State
                        Archives, Austin

STA-TAMUK   South Texas Archives, Texas A&M University–Kingsville

TAMU-CC   Texas A&M University–Corpus Christi

TLA   Texas Labor Archives, University of Texas at Arlington

TSA   Texas State Archives, Austin

USNA-CP   U.S. National Archives—College Park, Maryland

USNA-DC   U.S. National Archives—Washington, D.C.

UT-Benson   Benson Latin American Collection, University of Texas
                        at Austin

UT-CAH   Dolph Briscoe Center for American History, University
                        of Texas at Austin

UTPA   University of Texas–Pan American Library Special
                        Collections, Edinburg

INTRODUCTION

1. *HemisFair 1968 Official Souvenir Guidebook*, 21.
2. Ibid.
3. "Big Daddy of All Fiestas Is a Gusher," *San Antonio Express-News*, April 7, 1968.
4. *HemisFair 1968 Official Souvenir Guidebook*, 24.
5. "Spain Returns to Texas," *San Antonio Express-News*, April 7, 1968.
6. "Mariachi Music Will Lure You to Mexican Pavilion," *San Antonio Express-News*, April 7, 1968.

7. The ultimate example of this older historiography is Webb, *Texas Rangers*. Webb famously wrote, "Without disparagement it may be said that there is a cruel streak in the Mexican nature, or so the history of Texas would lead one to believe. This cruelty may be a heritage from the Spanish of the Inquisition; it may, and doubtless should, be attributed partly to the Indian blood. Among the common class, ignorance and superstition prevail, making the rabble susceptible to the evil influence of designing leaders. Whatever the reasons, the government of Mexico has ever been unstable, frequently overturned by civil war, and changed but seldom improved by revolution. . . . [The Mexican] won more victories over the Texans by parley than by force of arms. For making promises—and for breaking them—he had no peer" (14). Slightly more updated, though no less reliant on mythology, is Fehrenbach, *Lone Star*. Walk into any chain bookstore and you are more likely to find these two books than any of the more recent or insightful books on Texas history in the footnotes of this study.

8. "West San Antonians Divided on Fair," *San Antonio Express-News*, July 14, 1968.

9. Montejano, *Anglos and Mexicans in the Making of Texas*; Foley, *White Scourge*; and Zamora, *World of the Mexican Worker in Texas*.

10. Johnson, *Revolution in Texas*; Tijerina, *Tejano Empire*; and Young, *Catarino Garza's Revolution on the Texas-Mexico Border*.

11. Gutiérrez, *Walls and Mirrors*; Hernández, *Migra!*; Vargas, *Labor Rights Are Civil Rights*; Zamora, *Claiming Rights and Righting Wrongs in Texas*. See also Pastrano, "Industrial Agriculture in the Peripheral South"; and Garcia, *Rise of the Mexican American Middle Class*.

12. Hahamovitch, *No Man's Land*; Hahamovitch, *Fruits of Their Labor*; Ngai, *Impossible Subjects*; and Peck, *Reinventing Free Labor*. See also Higbie, *Indispensable Outcasts*.

13. This definition is based on my understanding of the region as a native of San Antonio as well as on the work of cultural geographer Daniel Arreola. See Arreola, *Tejano South Texas*.

14. For a much fuller explanation of the cultural geography of South Texas, see Arreola, *Tejano South Texas*.

15. See Weber, *Myth and the History of the Hispanic Southwest*.

16. There was also an East Coast agricultural migrant stream, though the historiography of migrant labor still seems curiously fixated on California. See Hahamovitch, *Fruits of Their Labor*. These migrants along the Atlantic Coast were most famously depicted in the 1960 CBS News documentary *Harvest of Shame*.

17. See Daniel, *Bitter Harvest*; and Mitchell, *Lie of the Land*.

18. See Andradet, "Biting the Hand That Feeds You"; Linder, *Migrant Workers and Minimum Wages*; Ruckelshaus, "Labor's Wage War"; Brunn, *Wal-Mart World*; Compa, *Blood, Sweat, and Fear*; Striffler, *Chicken*; and Tanger, "Enforcing Corporate Responsibility for Violations of Workplace Immigration Laws." There is also a massive body of recent case law that deals with these issues of labor relations and efforts to strip workers of rights and ability to negotiate. See, for instance, *Vizcaino, et al., v. Microsoft Corporation*, 97 F.3d 1187 (9th Cir. 1995) and 120 F.3d 1006 (9th

Cir. 1997); and *Daniel Reyes, et al., v. Remington Hybrid Seed Company, Inc., et al.*, 495 F. 3d 403 (7th Cir. 2007).

PART I

1. Barton, "Borderland Discontents," 160; Katz, *Secret War in Mexico*, 31; Katz, "Liberal Republic and the Porfiriato," 110; Meyers, *Forge of Progress, Crucible of Revolt*, 179–86; Zamora, *World of the Mexican Worker in Texas*, 65.

2. The Laguna was therefore very much like the Lower Rio Grande Valley and the Winter Garden in Texas, and the Imperial Valley in California. All were too dry for large-scale, profitable cultivation without irrigation. Importantly, however, none of these regions in the United States had large-scale irrigation until after the turn of the century, at least twenty years after the Laguna. On irrigation in the Lower Rio Grande Valley, see Sandos, *Rebellion in the Borderlands*, 66–72; and Sandos, "Mexican Revolution and the United States," 95–136. On irrigation in the Winter Garden, see Taylor, "Mexican Labor in the United States: Dimmit County, Winter Garden District, South Texas," 293–464. On irrigation in the Imperial Valley, see Taylor, "Mexican Labor in the United States: Imperial Valley," 1–94; and Starr, *Material Dreams*, 18–43.

3. Meyers, *Forge of Progress, Crucible of Revolt*, 33.

4. Ibid., 34.

5. Ibid., 7.

6. For broader studies of Liberal and Porfirian development, see Hart, *Revolutionary Mexico*, 1–240; Hart, *Empire and Revolution*, 1–270; Katz, *Secret War in Mexico*; Katz, "Liberal Republic and the Porfiriato," 49–124; Knight, *Mexican Revolution*, 1:1–71; Mora-Torres, *Making of the Mexican Border*; Tutino, *From Insurrection to Revolution in Mexico*, 268–336; and Vanderwood, *Disorder and Progress*.

7. Meyers, *Forge of Progress, Crucible of Revolt*, 117.

8. At the same time, these employers complained that laborers had become increasingly combative, especially those who had traveled to work in the United States. One hacienda administrator complained in 1905, "In the last five years everything has changed with respect to workers in the Laguna; before the peon was content with simply a reed hut and 32 centavos a day. Now he demands an adobe house and a salary two or three times larger. All the haciendas in the Laguna are constructing hundreds of fincas for their workers and you can understand that if we don't do the same we will not be able to attract workers." Quoted in Meyers, *Forge of Progress, Crucible of Revolt*, 131–32; and Zamora, *World of the Mexican Worker in Texas*, 65.

9. Meyers, *Forge of Progress, Crucible of Revolt*, 178.

10. Ibid., 126–38.

11. For an interesting discussion of the importance of these droughts, see Davis, *Late Victorian Holocausts*, 261.

12. Cahill, "U.S. Bank Panic of 1907 and the Mexican Depression of 1908–1909," 795–811.

13. See Tutino, *From Insurrection to Revolution in Mexico*, 304.

14. While many of these departures were voluntary, many were not. Many railroad companies simply sent their former employees south to the border and left them, while mining companies removed them from company housing and threatened them with vagrancy arrests if they did not leave on their own. See Barton, "Borderland Discontents," 160; Hart, *Revolutionary Mexico*, 143; Katz, *Secret War in Mexico*, 31; Katz, "Liberal Republic and Porfiriato," 110; and Zamora, *World of the Mexican Worker in Texas*, 65.

15. Meyers, *Forge of Progress, Crucible of Revolt*, 186.

16. Ibid., 188; Zamora, *World of the Mexican Worker in Texas*, 65. No evidence has been produced that the "Mexican Cotton Pickers" were anything but the creation of overactive imaginations in an increasingly tense environment. Still, members of the armed band that attacked Viesca most likely purchased their arms north of the Rio Grande in Del Rio and Eagle Pass, so there could have been some validity to the Mexican Cotton Picker scare. See "Attacking Mexican Towns," *New York Times*, June 29, 1908.

17. For more on the Viesca attack, see Albro, *Always a Rebel*, 105; Albro, *To Die on Your Feet*, 40–42; Meyers, *Forge of Progress, Crucible of Revolt*, 188–92; and Zamora, *World of the Mexican Worker in Texas*, 65.

18. The Mexican government claimed that this attack was prompted by Ricardo Flores Magón and the exiled leaders of the anarchist Mexican Liberal Party (Partido Liberal Mexicano, or PLM). While attacks a few days later near the border were instigated by the PLM, direct ties with the Viesca raid are lacking. This does not mean that PLM agitation in the region had no effect, only that there is no evidence that these events were orchestrated by Flores Magón. See "Mexican Raiders Trapped," *New York Times*, June 28, 1908.

19. Katz, *Secret War in Mexico*, 7.

CHAPTER 1

1. See Utley, *Lone Star Justice*, 160; de León, *They Called Them Greasers*, 59–60; Tijerina, *Tejano Empire*, 125–26; and Montejano, *Anglos and Mexicans in the Making of Texas*, 53.

2. The main exception to this statement was the Garza Rebellion in the early 1890s. Led by Catarino Garza, a crusading journalist from the Texas-Mexico border region, this rebellion sought to overthrow the Díaz regime but soon became a running battle with state and federal forces north of border. See Young, *Catarino Garza's Revolution on the Texas-Mexico Border*.

3. De León and Stewart, *Not Room Enough*, 25. *Carreteros* were cart-drivers who dominated the trade network of South Texas, providing the only reliable mode of transporting supplies throughout the region. These Mexican and Mexican American *carreteros* dominated the commercial trade in South Texas and white teamsters were never able to compete with them. This one-sided rivalry led to the outbreak of the "Cart War" in 1857, when white terrorists attacked and killed a number of *carreteros* in the counties south of San Antonio. *Arrieros* carried smaller loads across the region, using mules rather than the enormous wooden wagons used by

the *carreteros*. For an examination of the *carreteros* and *arrieros* and their importance in South Texas, see Tijerina, *Tejano Empire*, 67–71.

4. See Alonzo, *Tejano Legacy*.

5. Montejano wrote this about the sheriff's sales: "One legal method characterized by considerable ambiguity, for example, was the so-called sheriff's sale ordered by county courts to settle tax arrears and outstanding private debts. These sales were formally auctions where the land was sold to the highest bidder, but the bids obtained were often so low that the entire court-ordered proceedings were suspect. Examples of this practice are plentiful. In June 1877, for instance, the Hidalgo County sheriff sold 3,000 acres of the Hinajosa grant for a total cash price of $15 in order to cover tax arrears, and the following year an additional 4,000 acres from the grant were auctioned for $17.15. The question about legality, thus, was often an ambiguous and pointless matter." Montejano, *Anglos and Mexicans in the Making of Texas*, 52.

6. Ibid., 44.

7. Evan Anders, quoted in ibid., 44.

8. Ibid., 98.

9. See Falcón, "Force and the Search for Consent."

10. Montejano, *Anglos and Mexicans in the Making of Texas*, 94–95.

11. Anders, *Boss Rule in South Texas*, 89.

12. Ibid., 14.

13. Bailey, *Viva Cristo Rey*; Meyer, *Cristero Rebellion*.

14. See Voss, "Nationalizing the Revolution"; Salamini, "Tamaulipas"; and Ankerson, "Saturnino Cedillo."

15. Wasserman, "Chihuahua: Politics in an Era of Transition," 221.

16. Ibid., 229.

17. Pablo Mares, in Gamio, *Life Story of the Mexican Immigrant*, 2.

18. Knight, *Mexican Revolution*, 2:406–7.

19. Official correspondence of May 26, 1919, Box 1, Record Group 76, Entry 154, *United States and Mexican Claims Commission—Reports on Conditions along the Mexican Border, 1911–1919*, USNA-CP.

20. Knight, *Mexican Revolution*, 2:409.

21. Weekly Border Condition Report, Brownsville, Texas, September 2, 1916, Box 1, Memorandum 7. Entry 825—Records of United States Commissioners of American and Mexican Joint Commission—Memorandums Furnished by the Department of State, 1916 (hereafter, Gray-Lane Files), Department of State, Record Group 43, USNA-CP.

22. Knight, *Mexican Revolution*, 2:415. See also Dudley Dwyre (U.S. consul in Guadalajara), American Foreign Service Report, March 7, 1925, File 52903/66, Box 894, Record Group 85, USNA-DC.

23. See Gonzalez and Fernandez, *Century of Chicano History*. Gonzalez and Fernandez argue that the Mexican Revolution had very little effect on migration to the United States. Instead, they point to the Porfirian era and the growth of U.S. economic interests in Mexico as the essential cause of large-scale emigration. The primary problem with this analysis is that it overstates the importance of

U.S. corporations and financiers and casts the Porfirian regime as little more than a helpless adjunct of foreign capital. In their telling, international boundaries and the structures of state control essentially disappear or are subsumed beneath the power of capital.

24. The INS archives are filled with evidence of this displacement into the United States, primarily Texas. See esp. Files 53108/71–71P, Boxes 1110–112, Record Group 85, USNA-DC.

25. Galarza, *Barrio Boy*, 1.

26. "Report of Conditions Existing in Europe and Mexico Affecting Emigration and Immigration," n.d., File 51411/1, Box 23, Record Group 85, USNA-DC.

27. Ibid.

28. According to Anna Pegler-Gordon, immigration officials also feared that Asian immigrants might successfully pass themselves off as Mexicans at the border and overcome Asian exclusion through the "manipulation of racial identities." Pegler-Gordon, *In Sight of America*, 178.

29. Secretary of Labor and Commerce Oscar Strauss to Secretary of State Elihu Root, February 12, 1908, File 41463/B, Box 53, Record Group 85, USNA-DC.

30. See Peck, *Reinventing Free Labor*, 103–14.

31. Commissioner-General of Immigration to Secretary of Labor, March 12, 1913, File 52546/31G, Box 671, Record Group 85, USNA-DC.

32. Quoted in Sandos, *Rebellion in the Borderlands*, 85.

33. J. W. Berkshire to Commissioner-General of Immigration, October 21, 1913, File 53108/71G, Box 1111, RG 85, USNA-DC.

34. Ibid.

35. Ibid.

36. Ibid. Women were especially targeted for exclusion. Officials often claimed that poor Mexican women tended to become prostitutes once they entered the United States. See J. W. Berkshire to Commissioner-General of Immigration, May 18, 1911, 53108/71A, Box 1110, RG 85, USNA-DC.

37. Two recent books provide more in-depth studies of public health concerns and quarantines on the U.S.-Mexico border during this same era. See McKiernan-González, *Fevered Measures*; and Molina, *Fit to Be Citizens?*

38. See Sandos, *Rebellion in the Borderlands*, 66–72; and Sandos, "Mexican Revolution and the United States," 95–136.

39. Sandos, "Mexican Revolution and the United States," 135–36.

40. Sandos, *Rebellion in the Borderlands*, 71.

41. Sandos, "Mexican Revolution and the United States," 4. See also Walsh, *Building the Borderlands*, 72.

42. Johnson, *Revolution in Texas*, 31–32; Zamora, *World of the Mexican Worker in Texas*, 33; Anders, *Boss Rule in South Texas*, 139–40.

43. Knight, *Mexican Revolution*, 2:376.

44. Francisco Chapa was particularly open in his efforts to help Reyes, shortly after he had been instrumental in mobilizing anti-Prohibition voters to support Oscar Colquitt's successful gubernatorial campaign. Chapa's business partners in San Antonio also aided the Reyes movement, though they could do nothing to keep

the federal government from hounding Reyes for his blatant violations of neutrality laws. See Raat, *Revoltosos*, 244–45; and Coerver and Hall, *Texas and the Mexican Revolution*, 17–29. Equally important was Amador Sanchez, sheriff of Webb County (Laredo), who stored arms for a planned invasion and acted as a go-between for Reyista agents in Mexico and Chapa in San Antonio. See Harris and Sadler, *Texas Rangers and the Mexican Revolution*, 79.

45. Henry Hutchings to Oscar Colquitt, December 1, 1911, File 301-252-6, Oscar B. Colquitt Gubernatorial Papers, TSA.

46. On the activities of the Mexican Liberal Party and other radical groups in Texas during the Revolution, see Emma Tenayuca, interviewed by Gerry Poyo, February 21, 1987, Oral History Collection, ITC; Raat, *Revoltosos*; Albro, *Always a Rebel*; Cockcroft, *Intellectual Precursors of the Mexican Revolution*; Langham, *Border Trials*; and MacLachlan, *Anarchism and the Mexican Revolution*.

47. Katherine Benton-Cohen describes similar fears of revolutionary violence and ideology spreading over the border in Arizona during the Bisbee Deportation episode. Benton-Cohen, *Borderline Americans*, 223–25.

48. Coerver and Hall, *Texas and the Mexican Revolution*, 23.

49. Ibid., 123.

50. Years later, former Texas Ranger William Warren Sterling declared that the federal government's "vacillating policy" led almost inevitably to violence. "Nowhere in their history have people of Spanish extraction had any respect for weaklings," he declared. "This trait in their character and the value of the iron hand was demonstrated during the long regime of Don Porfirio Diaz. Each new gesture of appeasement merely added to the audacity of potential bandits." Sterling, *Trails and Trials of a Texas Ranger*, 24–28.

51. Colquitt quoted in untitled, *Denver Weekly*, December 6, 1913, May–December 1913 Clippings File, Box 2E205, Oscar Colquitt Papers, UT-CAH.

52. "Gas-Bag Patriotism," *Chicago Record-Herald*, September 3, 1913, May–December 1913 Clippings File, Box 2E205, Colquitt Papers, UT-CAH; "The President's Wise Policy toward Mexico," *Dallas News*, March 17, 1914, May–December 1913 Clippings File, Box 2E205, Colquitt Papers, UT-CAH.

53. "Texas and Mexico," *New Orleans Times-Democrat*, November 20, 1913, May–December 1913 Clippings File, Box 2E205, Colquitt Papers, UT-CAH.

54. "Foolish Criticism of Colquitt," *Houston Post*, March 11, 1914, May–December 1913 Clippings File, Box 2E205, Colquitt Papers, UT-CAH.

55. John R. Hughes to Henry Hutchings, June 1911, File 301-252-2, Colquitt Papers, TSA.

56. The Texas Rangers, like the Alamo, are so enveloped in mythology that it is often difficult to disentangle their history from the folklore that grew up around them. In addition, the Rangers meant very different things to Anglos and Mexicans. On one extreme, state Representative W. W. Stewart declared in 1919 that the Rangers were, along with the Alamo and San Jacinto, the "three great monuments to Texas liberty." Ribb, "José Tomás Canales and the Texas Rangers," 198. See also Webb, *Texas Rangers*, 3–15. Mexicans and Mexican Americans, however, often viewed the Rangers as a bloodthirsty yet cowardly military force of occupation, who

would not hesitate to kill Mexicans, whether innocent or not. The term "rinche," a local corruption of the word "Ranger," was a common and important part of the border vocabulary, meant as an epithet that was applied to all armed Anglos who attacked Mexicans. A number of works have dealt with these nonmythic depictions of the Rangers, but the most important is Paredes, *"With His Pistol in His Hand."* See also Samora, Bernal, and Peña, *Gunpowder Justice.*

57. All Rangers served at the sufferance of the governor, which made the force a source of political patronage. When James Ferguson became governor in January 1915, replacing Oscar Colquitt, he immediately moved to put his own men into the Ranger force. While the force had diminished since the late nineteenth century, and had in fact almost disappeared in the first fifteen years of the twentieth century, Ferguson halted this trend and installed loyal subordinates as Ranger captains. His predecessor had only hesitantly funded the Rangers, but Ferguson saw the possibility of political gifts and patronage opportunities in the legendary force. Still, despite the increased demands for Ranger protection during the early years of the Revolution, Ferguson did little to increase the size of the force. The events of 1915 would compel him to increase the size and funding of the Rangers, but most important Ferguson instilled in them an indisputable partisanship. While this had been the case to some degree for the life of the Rangers, the 1910s would see the force become fully politicized as a sort of paramilitary arm of the Governor's House. How the Rangers reacted to groups in South Texas, and especially the Valley, depended on who was in the governor's mansion. During the Ferguson administration, which ended with his impeachment in September 1917, the Rangers continued their long history of aiding the ranching elites of South Texas. But Ferguson's replacement, William Hobby, would again purge the force and fill the captaincies with his own men. During the Hobby administration, the Rangers became even more overtly political, acting as a blunt instrument wielded by the new farming elites against the remnants of the once dominant political machines and their Mexican American supporters.

58. T. W. Dee to J. M. Fox, December 9, 1913, File 301-253-7, Colquitt Papers, TSA.

59. O. H. Grigg to J. M. Woods, November 25, 1913, File 301-253-7, Colquitt Papers, TSA.

60. W. C. Linden to Oscar Colquitt, December 3, 1913, File 301-253-6, Colquitt Papers, TSA.

61. Dudley K. Lansing to Henry Hutchings, November 17, 1913, 301-253-5, Colquitt Papers, TSA.

62. W. T. Gardner to Oscar Colquitt, November 20, 1913, 301-253-5, Colquitt Papers, TSA. William H. Davis to Oscar Colquitt, 301-253-5, Colquitt Papers, TSA.

63. A full account of the violence that surrounded the Plan de San Diego is beyond the scope of this study. There are a few excellent studies of the plan, its roots, and its effects. Sandos, *Rebellion in the Borderlands*, and Sandos, "Mexican Revolution and the United States," both provide an in-depth analysis of the roots of the plan and the violence that occurred in 1915 and 1916. Johnson, *Revolution in Texas*, gives a detailed summary of the violence in South Texas but also looks at the effects of the Border War, arguing that it caused Tejanos to articulate their American citizenship more clearly as a defense against future racially motivated violence.

Richard Ribb also deals with the plan in "José Tomás Canales and the Texas Rangers." Finally, Harris and Sadler, *Texas Rangers and the Mexican Revolution*, gives an encyclopedic summary of every gunfight during the Border War, but as with all aspects of their book, the authors maintain an unfortunate unwillingness to jettison the mythology that envelops the Rangers and all of Texas history.

64. Johnson, *Revolution in Texas*, 72–73.

65. Plan de San Diego, Box 1, Memorandum 11, Gray-Lane Files, USNA-CP. Also reprinted in Joseph and Henderson, *Mexico Reader*, 689–91.

66. Nafarrate has long served as the link some historians have attempted to draw between the Plan de San Diego and Venustiano Carranza. According to this version of the story, Carranza used the border raids of the plan as a way to force the Wilson administration to recognize his government. In other words, Carranza orchestrated the astounding violence that engulfed South Texas in 1915 and 1916 for his own political gain, using Nafarrate as his local organizer to ensure that the scheme came off as planned. For the earliest account of this theory, see William M. Hanson to Francis J. Kearful, November 7, 1919, Box 15, Folder 4, Subject #225.34, William J. Buckley Sr. Papers, UT-Benson. The foremost (and really the only) historians advocating this position have stated their argument as follows: "Why would Carranza sponsor raids into Texas? Because he desperately needed United States diplomatic recognition. At first glance this seems a counterproductive policy, but in reality it was brilliant. . . . He could, and did, argue that Mexican exiles and other malefactors were causing all the trouble and suggest strongly that were he recognized as president he would quickly put a stop to these incursions." Harris and Sadler, *Texas Rangers and the Mexican Revolution*, 252–53.

67. Sandos, "Mexican Revolution and the United States," 213–14.

68. The Zimmerman Telegram, which made a proposal to Carranza similar to the Plan de San Diego, was used as proof of German-Mexican connivance when it was discovered in 1917. In his study of German-Mexican relations during the Revolution, Friedrich Katz noted that the plan "certainly is the type of plot the Germans would have liked to be involved in," but he found no evidence of any connection. Katz, *Secret War in Mexico*, 341. Anglos also saw signs of pro-German sentiment among Mexicans and Mexican Americans when large numbers of Valley residents fled to Mexico in 1917. While this exodus was caused by a combination of Ranger-led violence and unwillingness to be drafted into the U.S. military, many saw it as prima facie evidence that Mexicans were not reliable American citizens. The investigation into the activities of the Texas Rangers led by José Tomás Canales in 1919 featured almost constant assertions by Ranger supporters that Mexicans brought much of the violence on themselves by not living up to the standards of American citizenship. See "Proceedings of the Joint Committee of the Senate and the House in the Investigation of the Texas State Ranger Force," 36th Legislature, Regular Session (January 14–March 19, 1919), Harbert Davenport Papers, TSA, 345–47, 467–69, 481–510 (hereafter, "Ranger Investigation").

69. A revised version of the plan appeared on February 20, which clarified many of the generalities of the first document. It called for the war to begin in Texas and move on from there. It also put the fight in class-based terms, using the term

"proletarian" to describe the plan's allies. Additionally, issues of land and labor became more central to the document, joining the original's obvious basis in racial solidarity. The ends of the plan remained the same.

70. Quoted in Johnson, *Revolution in Texas*, 74.

71. I will refer to the violence of 1915 and 1916 as the Border War for a few reasons. First, the alternatives are problematic. Referring to the entire episode as the Plan de San Diego can distort the importance of that conspiracy for the violence that ensued. While the plan was clearly an important impetus for the race war that ensued, using its name to denote these struggles could be seen as ignoring the reactionary violence launched by Anglo vigilantes and law enforcement officials. The problems with "the Bandit War," preferred by Harris and Sadler, should be clear. Second, the term "Border War" identifies the importance of the border and the borderlands in the uprising and subsequent suppression. Third, it correctly identifies the violence as a legitimate "war," in which thousands were killed in a matter of months and an even greater number abandoned large swaths of the Lower Rio Grande Valley to avoid the wanton bloodshed. Richard Ribb has likewise referred to this period as the Border War in his study of J. T. Canales. Ribb, "José Tomás Canales and the Texas Rangers."

72. "Chronological List of Raids and Outrages between July 6th and October 29th, 1915 in the Lower Rio Grande Valley Section of Texas," Box 1, Memorandum 11, Gray-Lane Files, USNA-CP.

73. Ibid.

74. See Adjutant General Department, General Correspondence, Files 401-550-11 to 401-550-22 and 401-551-3 to 401-551-21, TSA.

75. Harris and Sadler, *Texas Rangers and the Mexican Revolution*, 555.

76. Ribb, "José Tomás Canales and the Texas Rangers," 92. See also Sterling, *Trails and Trials of a Texas Ranger*, 47–48.

77. Quoted in Ribb, "José Tomás Canales and the Texas Rangers," 92.

78. Joseph Nichols to Henry Hutchings, May 13, 1916, File 401-554-18, TSA.

79. Johnson, *Revolution in Texas*, 86. The State Department records and Johnson refer to Adolfo Muñoz, but Ribb refers to him as Rodolfo Muñiz. For sake of clarity, I will use Adolfo Muñoz, though it would certainly not be outside of the realm of possibility that federal authorities misspelled his name.

80. J. T. Canales also pointed out that Muñoz had been arrested earlier in the day, but kept in San Benito until nightfall. Thus, he claimed that Carr and Hinojosa had killed Muñoz and fabricated their story about masked vigilantes. "Ranger Investigation," 27–28.

81. Ibid., 859.

82. Ibid., 28.

83. "Chronological List of Raids and Outrages between July 6th and October 29th, 1915 in the Lower Rio Grande Valley Section of Texas," Box 1, Memorandum 11, Gray-Lane Files, USNA-CP.

84. Brownsville attorney Harbert Davenport asserted that the conflict between Pizaña and Scrivener could have resulted from competing cattle rustling operations, though I know of no other evidence to support this claim. Ribb, "José Tomás Canales

and the Texas Rangers," 98. Later, police found the corpses of twenty Mexicans buried on Scrivener's property. It is not clear whether Scrivener or the Rangers were responsible for these killings. H. J. Kirk, in "Ranger Investigation," 599–604.

85. William Hanson, in his capacity as an investigator looking into the violence surrounding the Plan de San Diego for Senator Albert Bacon Fall, incorrectly testified that the Los Tulitos fight was a "battle with invaders." See Sworn Statement of William M. Hanson, November 24, 1919, Box 18, Folder 10, Subject #235, Buckley Papers, UT-Benson. Aniceto's brother, Ramón, went on trial for murder but was acquitted on grounds of self-defense. Canales served as his defense attorney.

86. Ribb, "José Tomás Canales and the Texas Rangers," 97, 101.

87. Américo Paredes referred to the Border War as the Pizaña Uprising, showing the prominence of Pizaña in the later stages of the violence. Likewise, federal investigators viewed Pizaña and de la Rosa as the primary masterminds of the uprising, despite their lack of involvement in the initial stages. Paredes, *"With His Gun in His Hand,"* 26.

88. "Chronological List of Raids and Outrages between July 6th and October 29th, 1915 in the Lower Rio Grande Valley Section of Texas," Box 1, Memorandum 11, Gray-Lane Files, USNA-CP.

89. Ibid.

90. Ibid.

91. J. W. Berkshire to Commissioner-General of Immigration, October 4, 1915, File 532108/71O, Box 1112, RG 85, USNA-DC.

92. Ribb, "José Tomás Canales and the Texas Rangers," 328–30.

93. "Chronological List of Raids and Outrages between July 6th and October 29th, 1915 in the Lower Rio Grande Valley Section of Texas," Box 1, Memorandum 11, Gray-Lane Files, USNA-CP.

94. W. T. Vann, in "Ranger Investigation," 574–75.

95. R. B. Creager, in "Ranger Investigation," 355.

96. Claude Adams to Henry Hutchings, September 6, 1915, File 401-551-11, TSA.

97. E. P. Reynolds to Supervising Inspector, December 2, 1915, File 53108/71P, Box 1112, RG 85, USNA-DC; James E. Trout (Laredo Inspector in Charge) to Supervising Inspector, June 13, 1916, File 541252/79A, Box 64, RG 85, USNA-DC. The State Department continued to trace the activities of Pizaña and de la Rosa. "Activities of Luis de la Rosa," n.d., Box 7, Memorandum 69, Gray-Lane Files, USNA-CP.

98. "Mexicans Flee from Border to Mexico Side," *San Antonio Light*, September 11, 1915.

99. Ibid.

100. "Believed 158 Mexicans Shot along Border," *San Antonio Light*, September 21, 1915.

101. "All Is Quiet on Mexican Border," *San Antonio Light*, September 22, 1915.

102. Harbert Davenport, as quoted in Johnson, *Revolution in Texas*, 124.

103. Johnson, *Revolution in Texas*, 144. It is worth noting that, in addition to the regular Rangers, a group known as the Special Rangers also formed during these years. They served without pay but were deputized as Rangers and therefore could act with impunity during the Border War. A number of these Special Rangers gained

handsomely from the Border War, taking advantage of the violence to seize the land of dead and departing Mexicans and Tejanos. Lon Hill, in "Ranger Investigation," 1145–61.

104. Harris and Sadler, *Texas Rangers and the Mexican Revolution*, 210.

CHAPTER 2

1. *Missionite*, Mission, Texas, vol. 1, no. 10, December 3, 1909, Box 2, Folder 17, Publications Subcollection, John H. Shary Collection, UTPA. John Shary owned the Southwestern Land Company and his massive collection provides an invaluable view of the operations of these land companies. Thanks to Tim Bowman for sharing information with me on the Shary Collection.

2. Southwestern Land Company, "Sharyland Song Book," n.d., Box 2, Folder 38, Publications Subcollection, Shary Collection, UTPA.

3. Maril, *Poorest of Americans*, 36.

4. Max Dreyer, interviewed by Joan Ballard and Sid Ballard, December 1987, Oral History Collection, ITC.

5. Commissioner-General of Immigration to Secretary of Labor, March 12, 1913, File 52546/31G, Box 671, Record Group 85, USNA-DC. See also Corwin, "Early Mexican Labor Migration," 29–30.

6. Customs Inspector George Head to Commissioner-General of Immigration, October 28, 1913, File 53108/71H, Box 1111, Record Group 85, USNA-DC.

7. Similar concerns cropped up annually in reports of the supervising inspector at El Paso (whose district covered the entire U.S.-Mexico border) during the Mexican Revolution. In 1915 he complained that the number who entered the United States from Mexico "during the past year has been far in excess of the opportunities afforded for lucrative employment. The dearth of employment, caused by inactivity in railroad construction work in this section of the country, has been particularly unfortunate in its bearing upon the growing distress in Mexico." U.S. Department of Labor, *Annual Report of the Commissioner General of Immigration to the Secretary of Labor: Fiscal Year Ended June 30, 1915*, 265.

8. *Carrizo Springs Javelin*, April 27, 1912, Series 3, Carton 12, Folder 27, PST.

9. Arreola, *Tejano South Texas*, 45; U.S. Bureau of the Census, *Thirteenth Census of the United States: 1910*.

10. Quoted in Taylor, "Mexican Labor in the United States: Migration Statistics, IV," 26, footnote 4.

11. Arreola, *Tejano South Texas*, 45; U.S. Bureau of the Census, *Thirteenth Census of the United States: 1910*.

12. U.S. Bureau of the Census, *Fifteenth Census of the United States: 1930*.

13. Arreola, *Tejano South Texas*, 45–55.

14. Ibid., 44.

15. California also had a more self-contained migrant population that cycled from harvest to harvest within California, unlike Texas workers, who had to move well beyond the state to maintain even the barest subsistence. On these changes in California, see Mitchell, *Lie of the Land*. For a narrative history of the evolution of California agriculture, see Starr, *Inventing the Dream*; and Starr, *Material Dreams*.

16. See Handlin, *Uprooted*.

17. See Willard, *Status of Farming in the Lower Rio Grande Irrigated District of Texas*, 22–23.

18. Weber, *Dark Sweat, White Gold*, 49.

19. Foley et al., *From Peones to Politicos*, 12.

20. Willard, *Status of Farming in the Lower Rio Grande Irrigated District of Texas*, 1–2.

21. Ibid., 4.

22. Walsh, *Building the Borderlands*, 71–72. Foley et al., *From Peones to Politicos*, 13; McWilliams, *North from Mexico*, 163; Taylor, "Mexican Labor in the United States: Dimmit County, Winter Garden District, South Texas," 295.

23. Sam Robertson, quoted in "Exodus across Border Will Create Acute Labor Shortage for Planters—Mexico Liable to Retaliate with Boycott," *San Antonio Express*, October 20, 1929.

24. Zamora, *World of the Mexican Worker in Texas*, 33.

25. The Rio Grande remained the main source of water for the border counties, but secondary rivers and subterranean limestone reservoirs that lie beneath the region were important for farms further removed from the border. "Survey of the Underground Waters of Texas," February 16, 1931, Series 3, Carton 12, Folder 35, PST; Willard, *Status of Farming in the Lower Rio Grande Irrigated District of Texas*, 20–21. It is also worth noting that irrigation in South Texas was accomplished primarily through private investors, unlike in California and the West, where the federal government paid for much of development of irrigation works. This also meant, however, that there was no centralized control over the dozens of private irrigation companies that quickly emerged in South Texas. See Walsh, *Building the Borderlands*, 72. For a full survey and analysis of water and irrigation in the development of the U.S. West, see Worster, *Rivers of Empire*.

26. Sandos, "Mexican Revolution and the United States," 135.

27. Many South Texas growers, however, continued to use immigrant workers well past the 1920s, since they feared damaging their machinery and hand labor remained cheaper than machines. Foley, "Mexicans, Mechanization, and the Growth of Corporate Cotton Culture in South Texas," 281–82, 292–93.

28. Nick Doffing Company Inc., "Golden Groves: Lower Rio Grande Valley," n.d., Box 1, Folder 63, Publications Subcollection, Shary Collection, UTPA.

29. O. H. Stugard and Sons, Alamo, TX, "The Land of Continuous Crops: The Lower Rio Grande Valley," n.d., Box 1, Folder 23, Publications Subcollection, Shary Collection, UTPA.

30. John H. Shary, "The Treasure Land of the Lower Rio Grande Valley: Where Nature's Smiles Are Brightest," n.d., Box 2, Folder 36, Publications Subcollection, Shary Collection, UTPA.

31. John H. Shary, "Resources and Development of the Lower Rio Grande Valley," November 1927, Box 1, Folder 13, Publications Subcollection, Shary Collection, UTPA.

32. Quoted in Taylor, *American-Mexican Frontier*, 105–6.

33. George Weymouth in Missouri Pacific Lines, "What Editors of Some of the Country's Leading Farm Journals Saw on a Tour of the Lower Rio Grande Valley," n.d., Box 1, Folder 16, Publications Subcollection, Shary Collection, UTPA.

34. Quoted in Taylor, "Mexican Labor in the United States: Dimmit County, Winter Garden District, South Texas," 240.

35. While Donald Worster focused primarily on the Far West and only dealt with Texas sparingly, much of his argument about the central place of irrigation in the history of the West also holds for Texas. Worster, *Rivers of Empire*.

36. The Shary Collection at the University of Texas–Pan American Special Collections provides a surprisingly complete picture of the way this system emerged.

37. Drafts of Southwestern Land Company promotional literature, n.d., Box 2, Folder 13, Publications Subcollection, Shary Collection, UTPA.

38. Ibid.

39. McWilliams, *Factories in the Field*, 168–69.

40. Texas Agricultural Experiment Station, "Bermuda Onion Culture in Texas," November 1932, Quarters Project Collection, STA-TAMUK.

41. Tiller, *Texas Winter Garden*, 31, 54, 113–14.

42. Texas Agricultural Experiment Station, "Spinach under Irrigation in Texas," November 1932, Quarters Project Collection, STA-TAMUK.

43. McWilliams, *Ill Fares the Land*, 241–42.

44. U.S. Bureau of the Census, *United States Census of Agriculture: 1925*, Summary Statistics, by States, Final Figures, 25, 27.

45. Ibid., 46–47.

46. U.S. Bureau of the Census, *United States Census of Agriculture: 1925*, 1144, 1154.

47. Ibid., 1210, 1220, 1229, 1239.

48. Coalson, *Development of the Migratory Farm Labor System in Texas*, 7–8; Johnson, *Revolution in Texas*, 176–77.

49. McWilliams, *Factories in the Field*.

50. Roediger, *Wages of Whiteness*.

51. Foley, "Mexicans, Mechanization, and the Growth of Corporate Cotton Culture in South Texas," 292; Foley, *White Scourge*, 6–7, 35–41, 70; Taylor, *American-Mexican Frontier*, 131; Taylor, "Mexican Labor in the United States: Dimmit County, Winter Garden District, South Texas," 340.

52. Many farmers maintained an important, if ever-shrinking, number of share-croppers who remained throughout the year. "The primary purpose of maintaining Mexican sharecroppers on halves is to immobilize them so that ample labor will be on hand through the year and a large nucleus to start the picking season," wrote Paul Taylor. "Thus farmers, in the manner of many industrial employers, maintain individual labor reserves." Taylor, *American-Mexican Frontier*, 121. Often kept in place by debt peonage, these sharecroppers served as an unpaid labor force throughout the year. By the onset of the Great Depression, however, the number of sharecroppers and tenants dwindled to the point of irrelevance as the migrant work force grew throughout the South Texas agricultural regions. See Montejano, *Race, Labor Repression, and Capitalist Agriculture*, 8. The persistence of sharecropping

also depended on the region and crop. The cotton belt around Corpus Christi had the highest rate of tenancy, the Winter Garden with its vegetable farms had the lowest rate, while the Lower Rio Grande Valley fell in between these two extremes. See Montejano, *Anglos and Mexicans in the Making of Texas*, 172–73.

53. Testimony of Emilio Flores, in U.S. Commission on Industrial Relations, *Final Report and Testimony Submitted to Congress by the Commission on Industrial Relations*, 9201–202.

54. Taylor, "Mexican Labor in the United States: Dimmit County, Winter Garden District, South Texas," 325.

55. Ibid., 304.

56. Taylor, *American-Mexican Frontier*, 101.

57. Quoted in Foley, *White Scourge*, 47–50.

58. Labor Commissioner E. J. Crocker to Governor Miriam Amanda Ferguson, December 5, 1925, File 301-426-25, Miriam Amanda Ferguson Gubernatorial Papers, TSA.

59. Foley, "Mexicans, Mechanization, and the Growth of Corporate Cotton Culture in South Texas," 279.

60. Ibid., 278–79; McWilliams, *North from Mexico*, 158–60; Taylor, *American-Mexican Frontier*, xi; Taylor, "Mexicans North of the Rio Grande," in Taylor, *On the Ground in the Thirties*, 5.

61. Mr. Baylor, interviewed by Paul Taylor, November 30, 1928, Series 3, Carton 12, Folder 13, PST.

62. Louis Bailey, interviewed by Paul Taylor, August 1929, Series 3, Carton 12, Folder 23, PST.

63. Taylor, *American-Mexican Frontier*, 113.

64. Ibid., 110.

65. Foley, "Mexicans, Mechanization, and the Growth of Corporate Cotton Culture in South Texas," 289.

66. Ibid., 290.

67. Ibid., 287; Fitzgerald, *Every Farm a Factory*, 116.

68. Fitzgerald, *Every Farm a Factory*, 107.

69. Coalson, *Development of the Migratory Farm Labor System in Texas*, 34.

70. See Corwin, "Early Mexican Labor Migration," 29–30.

71. Vargas, *Proletarians of the North*, 18.

72. McWilliams, *Ill Fares the Land*, 259–60.

73. Ibid., 260–62.

74. Ibid., 267.

75. Ibid.

76. Ibid., 267–68.

77. Ibid., 271.

78. Coalson, *Development of the Migratory Farm Labor System in Texas*, 34; Reisler, *By the Sweat of Their Brow*, 78.

79. There are two recent studies of the sugar beet industry: Mapes, *Sweet Tyranny*; and Norris, *North for the Harvest*.

80. McWilliams, *Ill Fares the Land*, 109.

81. Taylor, "Mexican Labor in the United States: Valley of the South Platte, Colorado," 115; Valdés, *Al Norte*, 4.

82. Mapes, "Special Class of Labor," 78. See also Vargas, *Proletarians of the North*, 13–14.

83. Mapes, *Sweet Tyranny*, 122.

84. Quoted in ibid., 122.

85. Mapes, "Special Class of Labor," 71. In 1922, more than 30 percent of all sugar beet field workers in the Midwest had been recruited in Texas. Norris, *North for the Harvest*.

86. Mapes, *Sweet Tyranny*, 123.

87. Menefee, *Mexican Migratory Workers of South Texas*, xiii–xiv.

88. Quoted in Taylor, "Mexican Labor in the United States: Valley of the South Platte, Colorado," 140–41; emphasis added.

89. Mapes, "Special Class of Labor," 79.

90. Valdés, *Al Norte*, 13.

91. Mapes, "Special Class of Labor," 80.

92. Ibid.

93. Valdés, *Al Norte*, 13.

94. Ibid., 15–16.

95. Ibid., 16.

96. Ibid., 17.

97. McWilliams, *Ill Fares the Land*, 280.

98. Mapes, "Special Class of Labor," 84.

99. Vargas, *Proletarians of the North*, 33.

100. Ibid., 19, 103.

101. Taylor, "Mexican Labor in the United States: Bethlehem, Pennsylvania," 1–24.

102. See Vargas, *Proletarians of the North*.

103. Quoted in Taylor, "Mexican Labor in the United States: Chicago and the Calumet Region," 73.

104. Ibid., 25.

105. Vargas, *Proletarians of the North*, 86.

106. Ibid., 61–62, 117.

107. Mapes, "Special Class of Labor," 86.

108. Mexicans engaged in urban labor also had to deal with the deportation drive of 1921, which especially targeted Chicago, sending many who lacked proof of permanent residence back to Mexico. While this deportation campaign paled in comparison to what would come in the late 1920s and 1930s, Vargas is correct in arguing that the 1921 deportations foreshadowed things to come for the Mexican communities of the urban Upper Midwest. Vargas, *Proletarians of the North*, 83–86.

109. Ibid., 98–99; Mapes, "Special Class of Labor," 87.

110. Taylor, "Mexican Labor in the United States: Chicago and the Calumet Region," 74–75.

111. Ibid., 75–76.

112. Taylor, "Mexicans North of the Rio Grande," in Taylor, *On the Ground in the Thirties*, 2.

113. Gamio, *Mexican Immigration to the United States*, 27.

114. Sánchez, *Becoming Mexican American*, 66.

115. Rouse, "Mexican Migration and the Social Space of Postmodernism," 251.

116. Ibid., 247–63. See also Rodriguez, *Tejano Diaspora*. Another study that examines the complex and often circular paths taken by Mexican and Mexican American communities within the United States is Deutsch, *No Separate Refuge*. Deutsch argued that "a group with as large a migratory element as Chicanos calls out for a study that will go beyond the bounds of a single geographically defined community, a study that will link, as the migrants themselves did, the disparate sites of Chicano experience: the home village, the city, the fields, and the mining camps" (9).

117. McWilliams, *Ill Fares the Land*, 208.

PART II

1. John Willson to John Nance Garner, May 10, 1930, File 55409/22A, Box 6068, Record Group 85, USNA-DC.

2. John Willson to John Nance Garner, May 10, 1930, File 55409/22A, Box 6068, RG 85, USNA-DC. It is not clear if Garner responded. Unfortunately, he destroyed almost all of his personal papers after leaving the vice presidency in 1940.

3. See Hernández, *Migra!*, 17–60.

4. The foundational recent texts on the politics of mobility are Ngai, *Impossible Subjects*; Peck, *Reinventing Free Labor*; Hahamovitch, *No Man's Land*; and Hahamovitch, *Fruits of Their Labor*.

CHAPTER 3

1. Elias Garza, as quoted in Gamio, *Life Story of the Mexican Immigrant*, 150.

2. Elias Garza, as quoted in ibid., 151.

3. The best studies of these political changes are Anders, *Boss Rule in South Texas*; and Montejano, *Anglos and Mexicans in the Making of Texas*, 129–52.

4. Alba Heywood, "Ranger Investigation," TSA, 66.

5. *Carrizo Springs Javelin*, October 4, 1913, Series 3, Carton 12, Folder 27, PST.

6. *Carrizo Springs Javelin*, May 8, 1914, Series 3, Carton 12, Folder 27, PST.

7. Montejano, *Anglos and Mexicans in the Making of Texas*, 139–40.

8. Ibid., 140.

9. Hanson, the captain of this newly created force, had spent the last several years of the Porfirian era in Mexico engaging in farming and oil investments. When the Revolution began, Hanson entered into the pay of the faltering Díaz regime, organizing a spy ring in northern Mexico in 1911. After the fall of Díaz, Hanson remained in Mexico, trying to salvage what was left of his farming and oil interests. Carranza's forces arrested Hanson in 1914 and, after a court-martial, sentenced him to death. Pressure from the U.S. consul saved him from execution, but he was forced

to leave Mexico. Hanson continued to press for repayment of his losses for the next several years, but to no avail. Hanson's anger at Mexico and Mexicans because of these events was so intense that one Ranger, later appointed adjutant general, hypothesized that Hanson had written the Plan de San Diego as a pretext for a race war. See Sterling, *Trails and Trials of a Texas Ranger*, 28; and Ribb, "José Tomás Canales and the Texas Rangers," 139–47.

10. James A. Harley, *Adjutant General Annual Report for 1918*, 7, TSA.

11. Not all political bosses received the same treatment from Hobby. Jim Wells and some of his associates supported Hobby in the primary against Ferguson, shielding themselves for the time being from the Progressive onslaught.

12. Ribb, "José Tomás Canales and the Texas Rangers," 156.

13. Johnson, *Revolution in Texas*, 166–67.

14. Clark, *Fall of the Duke of Duval*, 34–37; Ribb, "José Tomás Canales and the Texas Rangers," 156–72.

15. Anders, *Boss Rule in South Texas*, 9–10.

16. The last gasp of the old machines in the farming counties came in 1928 with the "Hidalgo County Rebellion." Hidalgo County sheriff and former Texas Ranger A. Y. Baker maintained tenuous control of the county into the late 1920s. Newcomer farmers created a rival faction called the Good Government League to oust Baker's allies in the 1928 elections. They especially coveted the position of county judge, the most powerful position in local South Texas government during these years. The machine counted the votes, however, and when the final tally went in favor of the GGL candidate, Baker threw out the ballot box from Weslaco, a town firmly in the control of newcomers since its founding in 1921. After complaints about these irregularities, the U.S. Congress investigated the episode and found evidence of illegal activities. When the case went to trial, Baker was found guilty of falsifying election results, but before sentencing he disappeared, never to be seen again. It is still not known what happened to Baker, but his disappearance signaled the definitive end of the machine era. Montejano, *Anglos and Mexicans in the Making of Texas*, 147–48.

17. Littleton Richardson, interviewed by Paul Taylor, April 16, 1929, Series 3, Carton 12, Folder 14, PST.

18. Foley, "Mexicans, Mechanization, and the Growth of Corporate Cotton Culture in South Texas," 291.

19. Quoted in Taylor, "Mexican Labor in the United States: Dimmit County, Winter Garden District, South Texas," 438.

20. The ethnic Mexican majority did not simply accept these new elites and their consolidation of power. A number of historians have examined the efforts of mutual aid societies and ethnic Mexican political organizing that challenged Anglo dominance. The best example of this scholarship is Zamora, *World of the Mexican Worker in Texas*.

21. Montejano, *Anglos and Mexicans in the Making of Texas*, 162.

22. Ibid., 195–96.

23. G. A. Tallmadge, interviewed by Paul Taylor, September 1929, Series 3, Carton 12, Folder 27, PST.

24. John Stone, interviewed by Paul Taylor, April 8, 1929, Series 3, Carton 12, Folder 14, PST.

25. Ibid.

26. Louis Bailey, interviewed by Paul Taylor, August 1929, Series 3, Carton 12, Folder 23, PST.

27. Quoted in Taylor, "Dimmit County," 422.

28. Montejano, *Anglos and Mexicans in the Making of Texas*, 168. The best survey of school segregation in South Texas and the efforts to overturn it remains San Miguel, *"Let All of Them Take Heed,"* 1–63.

29. African Americans, however, were always segregated in separate schools, despite the fact that their numbers were low in South Texas.

30. John Stone, interviewed by Paul Taylor, April 8, 1929, Series 3, Carton 12, Folder 14, PST.

31. Taylor, "Mexican Labor in the United States: Dimmit County, Winter Garden District, South Texas," 389.

32. Taylor, *American-Mexican Frontier*, 200.

33. Littleton Richardson, interviewed by Paul Taylor, April 16, 1929, Series 3, Carton 12, Folder 14, PST.

34. Taylor, "Mexican Labor in the United States: Dimmit County, Winter Garden District, South Texas," 372.

35. Ibid.

36. Taylor, *American-Mexican Frontier*, 201.

37. John Stone, interviewed by Paul Taylor, April 8, 1929, Series 3, Carton 12, Folder 14, Paul S. Taylor Collection, Bancroft Library, University of California–Berkeley.

38. Mr. Baylor, interviewed by Paul Taylor, November 30, 1928, Series 3, Carton 12, Folder 13, Paul S. Taylor Collection, Bancroft Library, University of California–Berkeley.

39. Quoted in Taylor, "Mexican Labor in the United States: Dimmit County, Winter Garden District, South Texas," 390.

40. See Johnson, Booth, and Harris, *Politics of San Antonio*, vii–xi, 3–71; and Rosales, *Illusion of Inclusion*, 1–33.

41. "How the Mexican Lives," *Texas Argus* (San Antonio), January 1928, Box 2, Folder 11, Oliver Douglas Weeks Papers, League of United Latin American Citizens Collection, UT-Benson.

42. On the environmental history of San Antonio, see Miller, *On the Border*; and Miller, *Deep in the Heart of San Antonio*.

43. "Flood Wave on a Texas River—San Antonio in Ruins," *London Times*, September 12, 1921.

44. For two fairly useful oral histories that touch on the San Antonio flood, see Vicente Flores, interviewed by Diana Garza, May 5, 1977, Oral History Collection, ITC; and James Maverick, interviewed by Clyde Ellis, July 8, 1977, Oral History Collection, ITC.

45. "40 Known Dead, Fear 250 Perished, in Flood That Sweeps San Antonio; Property Loss Is Put at $3,000,000," *New York Times*, September 11, 1921.

46. The mayor of San Antonio sent a telegram to the *New York Times* stating, "Condition in San Antonio is exaggerated. The loss of life is less than fifty. . . . The city is able to care for itself and does not need outside help." "Outside Aid Not Needed, San Antonio Mayor Wires," *New York Times*, September 12, 1921. The city government had also installed wooden blocks coated in asphalt on many of the busiest streets downtown shortly before the 1921 flood. The streets of Philadelphia used the same materials, but in a city as flood-prone as San Antonio it was just a matter of time before the blocks, much lighter than normal paving stones, floated away to serve as projectiles to batter people and buildings caught in the flood waters.

47. For a recent study of the expanding importance and precarious existence of slums on a global scale, see Davis, *Planet of Slums*, esp. "Slum Ecology," 121–50.

48. A political machine very much in the tradition of Tammany Hall maintained control of San Antonio throughout these years. Progressive attempts to topple the machine, which had run the city since the late nineteenth century, did little more than force it to slightly alter its methods of operation. It remained in charge until the 1950s (the Maury Maverick government from 1939 to 1941 being the only exception), when a group called the Good Government League seized control of the city and operated it in the Progressive machine manner.

49. "Find 109 More Dead in Texas Lowlands," *New York Times*, September 13, 1921; "Find More Flood Victims," *New York Times*, September 14, 1921.

50. Davis, *Planet of Slums*, 122.

51. Miller, *Deep in the Heart of San Antonio*, 65.

52. Mitchell, *Lie of the Land*, 195.

53. A number of scholars have examined these issues in the context of California agriculture. See, for example, Daniel, *Bitter Harvest*; and Mitchell, *Lie of the Land*. While migrant labor was certainly important for the growth of California agriculture, the almost complete domination of California in this historiography is puzzling. Texas was every bit as dependent on migrant labor but consistently went further in its efforts to immobilize that labor. Likewise, the sheer scale of the migrant stream that went through and out of Texas dwarfed the much smaller, more self-contained migrant stream in California agriculture.

54. Montejano, *Race, Labor Repression, and Capitalist Agriculture*, 31. See also Zamora, *World of the Mexican Worker in Texas*, 30.

55. Taylor, *Spanish-Mexican Peasant Community*, 49–50. While this man eventually left the Nueces County farm, he later took a job as a sharecropper on halves at another cotton farm in the same county but was driven from his tract before picking, without pay, after a disagreement with the owner's wife. Rather than fall victim to these practices again, he returned to Mexico.

56. Quoted in Taylor, "Mexican Labor in the United States: Chicago and the Calumet Region," 34–35.

57. Casefile 50-394 (163721), frames 500–519, Reel 18, *Department of Justice Peonage Files, 1901-1945* (microfilm).

58. Commissioner-General of Immigration to Samuel Gompers, January 16, 1912, File 52546/31D, Box 671, Record Group 85, Immigration and Naturalization Service, USNA-DC.

59. The *Carrizo Springs Javelin* registered its typical acerbic denunciation of any attempt to protect Mexicans: "The Mexican consul at San Antonio is registering a large kick on the treatment he alleges his unfortunate countrymen receive from the large contractors of labor, and we understand that he has appealed to the state department for redress. He states that the Mexicans are held in a state of peonage, and are maltreated in other ways. The Medina dam contractors are among the people complained of. In this immediate section it is a hard job to get the hombres to do the work they are paid for, much less get them to do work they are not paid for. We might file a complaint with the consul to see if that situation might not be relieved also." *Carrizo Springs Javelin*, September 7, 1912, Series 3, Carton 12, Folder 23, PST.

60. A. Bruce Bielaski to Attorney General, November 20, 1912, Casefile 50-394 (163721), frames 496–99, Reel 18, *DOJ Peonage Files*.

61. Bielaski to Attorney General, November 20, 1912, *DOJ Peonage Files*.

62. Obviously, these methods were not unique to South Texas. Carey McWilliams pointed out similar systems in California, including a statement from the State Council of Defense in 1918 that "urged the passage of a more drastic law against vagrants as a means to compel men who are offered employment in orchards and farms to accept such work under penalty of prosecution." McWilliams, *Factories in the Field*, 180–81.

63. Montejano, *Anglos and Mexicans in the Making of Texas*, 205; Taylor, *American-Mexican Frontier*, 149.

64. Taylor, *American-Mexican Frontier*, 149. See also Mr. Miller, interviewed by Paul Taylor, September 1929, Series 3, Carton 12, Folder 23, PST.

65. Quoted in Taylor, *American-Mexican Frontier*, 149.

66. Quoted in ibid., 150.

67. Ibid.

68. McWilliams, *Ill Fares the Land*, 253; McWilliams, *North from Mexico*, 167–68.

69. Taylor, "Mexican Labor in the United States: Dimmit County, Winter Garden District, South Texas," 451.

70. Ibid., 330.

71. Morris Dupree, interviewed by Paul Taylor, April 10, 1929, Series 3, Carton 12, Folder 14, PST.

72. Taylor, "Mexican Labor in the United States: Dimmit County, Winter Garden District, South Texas," 331. See also McWilliams, *Ill Fares the Land*, 253.

73. Texas growers had long fought to keep their workers from drifting away to do railroad work, but the low wages available as a track worker always made this little more than a slight irritant compared to the competition from the sugar beet growers and other far-away opportunities in the 1920s.

74. "Origins and Problems, Texas Migratory Farm Labor," September 1940, 23, Farm Placement Service, TSA.

75. Testimony of S. Maston Nixon, in U.S. Congress, House Committee on Immigration and Naturalization, *Seasonal Agricultural Laborers from Mexico*, 42.

76. E. J. Crocker, "Internal History of the Labor Commission," March 1925, File 301-416-25, Miriam Amanda Ferguson Gubernatorial Papers, TSA.

77. Slightly more charitable was a man named "Stubbs" interviewed by Paul Taylor at the Chamber of Commerce in Robstown, near Corpus Christi, who stated, "They should let the four border states have the Mexicans, and not let them go north." Series 3, Carton 12, Folder 27, PST.

78. Similar bills passed in 1923 and 1925 had done little to slow the flow of workers heading north, as their wording dealt more with charges of exploitation by labor agencies than with explicitly attempting to outlaw emigration to the North, as did the 1929 law.

79. Montejano, *Race, Labor Repression, and Capitalist Agriculture*, 33–34; Taylor, "Mexican Labor in the United States: Dimmit County, Winter Garden District, South Texas," 331.

80. See Texas Bureau of Labor Statistics, *Eleventh Biennial Report of Texas Bureau of Labor Statistics, 1929–1930*, TSA.

81. Montejano, *Anglos and Mexicans in the Making of Texas*, 210–13.

82. A. P. Johnson, quoted in Montejano, *Race, Labor Repression, and Capitalist Agriculture*, 34.

83. Ibid., 35.

84. J. R. Steelman to Frances Perkins, March 24, 1938, Record Group 174, General Records of the Department of Labor, Office of the Secretary, Secretary Frances Perkins, General Subject File, 1933–1941, USNA-CP; emphasis in original.

85. McWilliams, *Ill Fares the Land*, 259–67.

86. McWilliams, *North from Mexico*, 167–68.

87. Taylor, "Mexican Labor in the United States: Dimmit County, Winter Garden District, South Texas," 332.

88. Valdés, *Al Norte*, 54.

89. Norris, *North for the Harvest*, 63.

90. "Valley Farm Labor Migration to Mid-West May Be Stopped," *Corpus Christi Caller-Times*, April 7, 1942.

91. For a far more thorough discussion of this "freezing" policy, see Zamora, *Claiming Rights and Righting Wrongs*, 24–61.

92. Montejano, *Race, Labor Repression, and Capitalist Agriculture*, 34–35.

CHAPTER 4

1. John Wilde to Governor Miriam Ferguson, n.d., File 301-495-23, Miriam Amanda Ferguson Gubernatorial Papers, TSA; Court document notarized by S. C. Bates, August 26, 1929, File 301-495-23, Ferguson Gubernatorial Papers, TSA; Espiridión de León to Miriam Ferguson, March 2, 1933, File 301-495-23, Ferguson Gubernatorial Papers, TSA. I have not been able to determine what happened to de León or his family after the deportation.

2. The classic study of Mexican repatriation and deportation during the Great Depression remains Hoffman, *Unwanted Mexican Americans in the Great Depression*, though it deals almost entirely with Los Angeles. See also Balderrama and Rodriguez, *Decade of Betrayal*; González Navarro, *Los extranjeros en México y los mexicanos en el extranjero, 1821–1970*, vol. 3, 294–302; and Guerin-Gonzales,

Mexican Workers and American Dreams. These studies, however, ignore Texas and fail to connect the deportations with the nativist agitation of the 1920s. The only full-length study of repatriation from Texas, which has never been published, is McKay, "Texas Mexican Repatriation during the Great Depression." Too many other studies to list have accepted the traditional narrative of deportations following the economic collapse, including two recent books that deal specifically with the history of U.S. deportation policy: Kanstroom, *Deportation Nation*; and Moloney, *National Insecurities.*

3. Nativist forces sought a literacy test for decades, but failed to secure its passage since first attempting such a bill in 1897. See Higham, *Strangers in the Land,* 162.

4. Reisler, *By the Sweat of Their Brow,* 24.

5. E. S. Orgain to Charles Culberson, n.d., File 54261/202, Box 271, Record Group 85, USNA-DC.

6. See File 54261/202, Box 271, RG 85, USNA-DC. It is worth noting that the vast majority of these entreaties to the federal government came from Texas. Complaints came from other states as well, but not on the same scale.

7. Departmental Order, Secretary of Labor, June 12, 1918, File 52461/202, Box 271, RG 85, USNA-DC; Reisler, *By the Sweat of Their Brow,* 25–33; "Contract Labor Admitted for Farmers," *Survey,* June 30, 1917, 295–96.

8. Commissioner-General of Immigration Service to Secretary of Labor, June 11, 1918, File 54261/202, Box 271, RG 85, USNA-DC; Departmental Order, Secretary of Labor, July 10, 1918, File 52461/202, Box 271, RG 85, USNA-DC. Smaller numbers of workers also came in from the Bahamas and Jamaica under these same exemptions.

9. Secretary of Labor to Samuel Gompers, December 20, 1918, File 54261/202E, Box 273, RG 85, USNA-DC.

10. Departmental Order, Secretary of Labor, June 12, 1918, File 52461/202, Box 271, RG 85, USNA-DC; Commissioner-General of Immigration Service to Secretary of Labor, June 11, 1918, File 54261/202, Box 271, RG 85, USNA-DC.

11. Herbert Hoover to Felix Frankfurter, June 4, 1918, File 54261/202, Box 271, RG 85, USNA-DC; "Mexican Laborers Admitted under Order of Secretary of Labor, June 1, 1917 to March 1, 1918," n.d., File 54261/202A, Box 273, RG 85, USNA-DC; E. P. Reynolds to Supervising Inspector, February 26, 1918, File 54261/202A, Box 273, RG 85, USNA-DC; Inspector in Charge at Hidalgo, Texas, to Supervising Inspector, n.d., File 54261/202A, Box 273, RG 85, USNA-DC; Reisler, *By the Sweat of Their Brow,* 30.

12. Secretary of Labor to Herbert Hoover, June 11, 1918, File 54261/202, Box 271, RG 85, USNA-DC.

13. L. B. Leighton to William Hollis, July 10, 1918, File 54261/202, Box 271, RG 85, USNA-DC.

14. The Chambers of Commerce across the state clearly had a form telegram they each sent in with a few variations according to the interests of the locality. Corsicana Chamber of Commerce to Commissioner-General of Immigration, July 25, 1918, File 54261/202, Box 271, RG 85, USNA-DC.

15. For final statistical breakdowns of workers imported through two ports of entry in Texas, see "Mexican Laborers Imported Departmental Exceptions

through the Port of Del Rio," January 13, 1919, File 54261/202, Box 272, RG 85, USNA-DC; "Mexican Laborers Imported Departmental Exceptions through the Port of Hidalgo," January 13, 1919, File 54261/202, Box 272, RG 85, USNA-DC; Reisler, *By the Sweat of Their Brow*, 33; Commissioner-General of Immigration to all Commissioners and Inspectors of Bureau of Immigration, December 17, 1918, File 54261/202, Box 272, RG 85, USNA-DC; Departmental Memo, Information and Education Service of the Department of Labor, December 26, 1918, File 54261/202E, Box 273, RG 85, USNA-DC.

16. Quoted in Reisler, *By the Sweat of Their Brow*, 33.

17. Statement of Fred Roberts, in U.S. Congress, Senate Committee on Immigration, *Admission of Mexican Agricultural Laborers*, 3, 4, 11.

18. Statement of Roy Miller, in ibid., 16.

19. Ngai, *Impossible Subjects*, 10.

20. Ibid., 19.

21. Deutsch, *No Separate Refuge*, 124; Ngai, *Impossible Subjects*, 72; Vargas, *Proletarians of the North*, 83.

22. Gutiérrez, *Walls and Mirrors*, 49. See also Guerin-Gonzales, *Mexicans Workers and American Dreams*, 45; Deutsch, *No Separate Refuge*, 126; Mapes, "Special Class of Labor," 67–77; McWilliams, *Factories in the Field*, 126; Sánchez, *Becoming Mexican American*, 83; and Corwin, "Story of Ad Hoc Exemptions," 143.

23. Statement of John Garner, in U.S. Congress, House Committee on Immigration and Naturalization, *Seasonal Agricultural Laborers from Mexico*, 189.

24. George Clements, quoted in Gutiérrez, *Walls and Mirrors*, 48–49.

25. Deutsch, *No Separate Refuge*, 126. See also Aguila, "Mexican/U.S. Immigration Policy prior to the Great Depression," 207–12; and Mapes, *Sweet Tyranny*, 146.

26. Ngai, *Impossible Subjects*, 7, 71.

27. Hernández, *Migra!*

28. Ngai, *Impossible Subjects*, 89.

29. Higham, *Strangers in the Land*, 325.

30. A writer for the *El Paso Evening Post* described Box's efforts to include Mexico under the quotas as driven by "the blind enthusiasm of a fanatic." "Let's Not Blindly Cut Immigration," *El Paso Evening Post*, January 15, 1930.

31. Timothy Turner, quoted in Sánchez, *Becoming Mexican American*, 83.

32. Statement of Congressman Edward Taylor, in U.S. Congress, House Committee on Immigration and Naturalization, *Seasonal Agricultural Laborers from Mexico*, 260. See also Mapes, *Sweet Tyranny*, 145.

33. Statement of Congressman Carl Hayden, in U.S. Congress, Committee on Immigration and Naturalization, *Seasonal Agricultural Laborers from Mexico*, 191. See also Reisler, *By the Sweat of Their Brow*, 200–203; and Mapes, "Special Class of Labor," 74–75.

34. Reisler, *By the Sweat of Their Brow*, 204.

35. Foerster, *The Racial Problems Involved in Immigration from Latin America and the West Indies to the United States*, 14.

36. Ibid., 57.

37. Ibid., 60.

38. Ibid., 60.

39. Ibid., 59.

40. John Box, in U.S. Congress, House Committee on Immigration and Naturalization, *Seasonal Agricultural Laborers from Mexico*, 46.

41. S. Maston Nixon, in ibid., 46.

42. Reisler, *By the Sweat of Their Brow*, 204.

43. Oliver Douglas Weeks, a professor at the University of Texas, transcribed all of these letters. See Oliver Douglas Weeks Papers, League of United Latin American Citizens Collection, UT-Benson.

44. J. H. Powell to John Box, January 29, 1926, Box 2, Folder 3, Weeks Papers, UT-Benson.

45. W. F. Cottingham to John Box, February 4, 1928, Box 2, Folder 9, Weeks Papers, UT-Benson.

46. Morrison Swift, "Strengthen the Immigration Law and Improve the American Race," March 1926, Box 2, Folder 3, Weeks Papers, UT-Benson.

47. C. M. Goethe to John Box, February 4, 1928, Box 2, Folder 11, Weeks Papers, UT-Benson.

48. Reisler, *By the Sweat of Their Brow*, 207.

49. Statement of C. B. Moore, in U.S. Congress, Senate Committee on Immigration, *Restriction of Western Hemisphere Immigration*, 60. In the same hearings, see also statements of Senator John Kendrick (69–72), Alfred Thom (87–99), and E. E. McInnis (99–109).

50. Quoted in Reisler, *By the Sweat of Their Brow*, 206.

51. Statement of George Kreutzer, in U.S. Congress, Senate Committee on Immigration, *Restriction of Western Hemisphere Immigration*, 184.

52. Quoted in Reisler, *By the Sweat of Their Brow*, 211.

53. For his part, Mexican president Alvaro Obregón announced that his government would drastically reduce legal entries from the United States in retaliation if Mexico was placed under a quota. See Martinez, *Mexican Emigration to the United States*, 76; and Corwin, "Mexican Policy and Ambivalence toward Labor Emigration to the United States," 183.

54. Statement of Secretary of State Frank Kellogg, in U.S. Congress, Senate Committee on Immigration, *Restriction of Western Hemisphere Immigration*, 155–72. See Zolberg, *Nation by Design*, 257–68.

55. Quoted in Reisler, *By the Sweat of Their Brow*, 213–14; Corwin, "Story of Ad Hoc Exemptions," 146.

56. Hodgdon, "Extension of Administrative Authority in Immigration Regulation," 48.

57. A writer for the *El Paso Evening Post* even argued, "Rep. Box has done a good job of restricting our oversupply of peon labor. For it has been his agitation, largely, which has forced the greater limitation now in effect." "Let's Not Blindly Cut Immigration," *El Paso Evening Post*, January 15, 1930.

58. Council on Foreign Relations, *Survey of American Foreign Relations*, 4:221–22.

59. See also ibid., 209–28.

60. U.S. Department of Labor, *Annual Report of the Commissioner General of Immigration to the Secretary of Labor: Fiscal Year Ended June 30, 1927*, 22.

61. U.S. Department of Labor, *Annual Report of the Commissioner General of Immigration to the Secretary of Labor: Fiscal Year Ended June 30, 1929*, 21.

62. Statements of William Whalen and T. W. Hooks, May 26, 1928, File 55609/358, Box 438, RG 85, USNA-DC.

63. Statement of Mrs. M. M. Huffer, May 26, 1928, File 55609/358, Box 438, RG 85, USNA-DC.

64. Acting Commissioner-General George Harris to John Garner, June 12, 1928, File 55609/358, Box 438, RG 85, USNA-DC.

65. McKay, "Texas Mexican Repatriation during the Great Depression," 109; Balderrama and Rodriguez, *Decade of Betrayal*, 49.

66. "Exodus across Border Will Create Acute Labor Shortage for Planters—Mexico Liable to Retaliate with Boycott," *San Antonio Express*, October 20, 1929.

67. This same line of argument would reappear in the 1950s when the next major deportation drives occurred. See Hernández, *Migra!*, 151–95.

68. Walsh, *Building the Borderlands*, 99. Walsh makes clear that Mexican authorities were well aware that large-scale deportations and the harassment of Mexican workers began in South Texas in 1928.

69. This procedure did not change until 1934, when immigration officials changed the regulations to require a warrant before raids and arrests. McKay, "Texas Mexican Repatriation during the Great Depression," 111–12, 130, 133, 146.

70. Deportation campaigns began in California in the summer of 1930, but the most famous raid did not occur until February 1931 at La Placita in one of the largest Los Angeles barrios. See Balderrama and Rodriguez, *Decade of Betrayal*, 57–58; and Hoffman, *Unwanted Mexican Americans in the Great Depression*, 71–83.

71. In 1929 Ernesto Galarza made exactly this argument regarding the quota debates: "The restrictionists have mustered the familiar artillery of racial dilution and the color flood, while those who seek to keep the gates open, as they have been for the last eighteen years, are once more pressing the equally old argument that the very economic structure of the United States rests on the brawn and sweat of the immigrant. . . . For the moment let it be accepted as true that everyone has presented his side of the case except the Mexican worker himself." Galarza, "Life in the United States for Mexican People: Out of the Experience of a Mexican," in Galarza, *Man of Fire*, 27, 28.

72. See Gutiérrez, *Walls and Mirrors*.

73. Ngai, *Impossible Subjects*, 8.

PART III

1. For newspaper coverage of the riot and its aftermath, see Don Politico, "Personality of the Week," *San Antonio Light*, August 25, 1939; "Violence at Red Rally Feared by S.A. Police," *San Antonio Light*, August 25, 1939; "Mob Storms Red Rally in S.A.," *San Antonio Light*, August 26, 1939; "Riots, Prayers Alternate in Parade to Alamo," *San Antonio Light*, August 26, 1939; "Anti-Red Crowd Takes

It, Dishes It Out," *San Antonio Light*, August 26, 1939; "Communists Flee from 5,000 Texans," *New York Times*, August 26, 1939; "Recall of Maverick Is Sought," *San Antonio Light*, August 27, 1939; "Ouster of Maverick as Mayor Is Sought," *New York Times*, August 27, 1939; "Urges Maverick Recall," *New York Times*, September 1, 1939; Alex N. Murphree, "Maverick Encounters Free-Speech Troubles," *New York Times*, September 3, 1939; "Five Marx Brothers" (editorial), *Washington Post*, August 27, 1939; and Don Politico, "Big Fight Is Promised at Polls," *San Antonio Light*, August 29, 1939.

2. Quoted in "Mob Storms Red Rally in S.A.," *San Antonio Light*, August 26, 1939.

3. Quoted in ibid.

4. Quoted in ibid. For details of the riot at Municipal Auditorium, see also "Communists Flee from 5,000 Texans," *New York Times*, August 26, 1939; and Alex N. Murphree, "Maverick Encounters Free-Speech Troubles," *New York Times*, September 3, 1939.

5. "Riots, Prayers Alternate in Parade to Alamo," *San Antonio Light*, August 26, 1939.

6. Quoted in ibid.

7. Ibid.

8. Alexander Boynton, quoted in "Recall of Maverick Is Sought," *San Antonio Light*, August 27, 1939. It is worth noting that running as a Republican for governor of Texas was little more than a symbolic gesture in the 1930s. Write-in candidates and Communists had as much chance of winning as Republicans.

9. Alexander Boynton, quoted in "Mob Storms Red Rally in S.A.," *San Antonio Light*, August 26, 1939.

10. Ibid.

CHAPTER 5

1. Menefee and Cassmore, *Pecan Shellers of San Antonio*, 28.

2. Blackwelder, *Women of the Depression*, 20.

3. Eckam, "Public Housing Day Comes to San Antonio," 570.

4. Quoted in Garcia, *Rise of the Mexican American Middle Class*, 75. For a profile of Tranchese and his work on the West Side, see George Sessions Perry, "Rumpled Angel of the Slums," *Saturday Evening Post*, August 21, 1948, 32–33, 43–44, 47.

5. Granneberg, "Maury Maverick's San Antonio."

6. American Public Welfare Association, *Public Welfare Survey of San Antonio*, 27.

7. Johnson, Booth, and Harris, *Politics of San Antonio*, 17; American Public Welfare Association, *Public Welfare Survey of San Antonio*, 96.

8. Secretaría de Relaciones Exteriores de México, *Apéndice a la memoria de la Secretaría de Relaciones Exteriores de agosto de 1931 a julio de 1932*, 979–80.

9. American Public Welfare Association, *Public Welfare Survey of San Antonio*, 29–30.

10. Ibid., 27.

11. Ibid., 86.

12. Ibid., 129.

13. Ibid., 132.

14. Caulfield, *Migration to Nowhere*. According to WorldCat, the only indexed copy of this pamphlet is located at the Central University Library at Southern Methodist University, where it is bound with two other mimeographed articles on migrant labor.

15. According to Linda and Theo Majka, the national agricultural wage index, with 1927 as the baseline of 100, dropped to 46 in 1933, the nadir of the Depression, and only recovered to 65 in 1939, when the looming war in Europe helped raise agricultural prices throughout the nation. Majka and Majka, *Farm Workers, Agribusiness, and the State*, 105.

16. Taylor, *American-Mexican Frontier*, 119–20.

17. McWilliams, *Ill Fares the Land*, 225.

18. Walter B. Ellis to Southwestern Land Company, September 12, 1932, Box D5D2, Folder 9, Unprocessed Collection, John H. Shary Collection, UTPA.

19. Menefee, *Mexican Migratory Workers of South Texas*, xiv.

20. Ibid.

21. Blackwelder, *Women of the Depression*, 83–84; Green, "ILGWU in Texas," 145; Menefee and Cassmore, *Pecan Shellers of San Antonio*.

22. Shapiro, "Pecan Shellers of San Antonio," 231. Shapiro provides the only claim that wages dropped this low, while four cents per pound seems to be the typical shelling wage during the Depression.

23. Menefee, *Mexican Migratory Workers of South Texas*, 38.

24. Secretaría de Relaciones Exteriores de México, *Memoria de la Secretaría de Relaciones Exteriores de agosto de 1931 a julio de 1932*, 319.

25. Secretaría de Relaciones Exteriores de México, *Apéndice de la Memoria de la Secretaría de Relaciones Exteriores de agosto de 1931 a julio de 1932*, 961–62.

26. Quoted in Garcia, *Rise of the Mexican American Middle Class*, 109–10.

27. See Mapes, *Sweet Tyranny*, 221.

28. Roland T. Diller to John J. Gleeson, December 27, 1930, File 170/6377, Box 218, Record Group 280, Department of Labor, USNA-CP.

29. John J. Gleeson to F. H. Hayne, August 5, 1931, File 170-6566, Box 224, RG 280, USNA-CP.

30. Thomas W. Lewis to John J. Gleeson, June 14, 1931, RG 280, USNA-CP.

31. George Wheeler to Chief of United States Immigration Commission, August 7, 1936, File 55854/100, RG 85, USNA-DC. Wheeler misspelled the last name of Representative Richard Kleberg.

32. McWilliams, "Getting Rid of the Mexican," 322–23.

33. McKay, "Texas Mexican Repatriation during the Great Depression," 125.

34. Ibid., 131.

35. A law passed on March 4, 1929, made the illegal entry of an individual a misdemeanor for the first time. Corwin, "Story of Ad Hoc Exemptions," 146.

36. Guerin-Gonzales, *Mexican Workers and American Dreams*, 77–82; Hoffman, *Unwanted Mexican Americans in the Great Depression*, 3–23; McKay, "Texas Mexican Repatriation during the Great Depression," 253–86; McWilliams,

"Getting Rid of the Mexican," 322–24; Taylor, "Mexican Labor in the United States: Migration Statistics, IV," 26–30.

37. Guerin-Gonzales, *Mexican Workers and American Dreams*, 93–94.

38. A large body of literature deals with efforts by the Mexican government to encourage emigrants to return from the United States during the decades after the Mexican Revolution. See Gamio, *Mexican Immigration to the United States*; Santibáñez, *Ensayo acerca de la inmigración mexicana en los Estados Unidos*; Martinez, *Mexican Emigration to the United States*; and Aguila, "Mexican/U.S. Immigration Policy prior to the Great Depression."

39. Secretaría de Relaciones Exteriores, *Memoria de la Secretaría de Relaciones Exteriores de agosto de 1929 a julio de 1930*, 1712. See also Walsh, *Building the Borderlands*, 45.

40. Gilbert, "Field Study in Mexico of the Mexican Repatriation Movement."

41. Walsh, *Building the Borderlands*, 63.

42. Guerin-Gonzales, *Mexican Workers and American Dreams*, 105; Walsh, *Building the Borderlands*, 63. Abraham Hoffman wrote that the Don Martín Colony was a success, though he did note that government expectations that large numbers of repatriates would be able to purchase their land rarely came true. See Hoffman, *Unwanted Mexican Americans in the Great Depression*, 145. Presumably, this is because he relied primarily on James Carl Gilbert's anthropological study of Mexican repatriates and simply assumed that the hopeful tone of the early days of the Don Martín Colony continued throughout the Depression.

43. Walsh, *Building the Borderlands*, 112–37.

44. González Navarro, *Los extranjeros en México y los mexicanos en el extranjero*, 300–302; Hoffman, *Unwanted Mexican Americans in the Great Depression*, 154; McKay, "Texas Mexican Repatriation during the Great Depression," 407–30. Balderrama and Rodriguez asserted that Beteta had little success in recruiting colonists. See Balderrama and Rodriguez, *Decade of Betrayal*, 146–58.

45. McKay, "Texas Mexican Repatriation during the Great Depression," 414.

46. "Origins and Problems, Texas Migratory Farm Labor," September 1940, Farm Placement Service, TSA, 78. "Mexico to Take 15,000 Families Back from United States," *Houston Chronicle*, April 18, 1939. The Farm Placement Service gave slightly different numbers, reporting, "In addition to these 4,451 Mexican agricultural workers who have returned permanently to Mexico as Repartitionists, immigration authorities have assisted 1,266 agricultural workers to return to Mexico from the Lower Valley alone." "Origins and Problems," 80.

47. Corwin, "¿Quién Sabe?," 117. See also Jones, *Mexican-American Labor Problems in Texas*, 7.

48. Guerin-Gonzales, *Mexican Workers and American Dreams*, 101, 109; Reisler, *By the Sweat of Their Brow*, 231.

49. The only study I have found that deals with these cries for renewed immigration from Mexico during the Depression is Ngai, *Impossible Subjects*, 137.

50. D. W. Brewster to District Director at Galveston, August 6, 1936, File 55854/100, RG 85, USNA-DC.

51. "Cotton Picker War Flares in Southwest Again," *Valley Morning Star*, July 31, 1936.

52. Ibid.

53. WPA Division of Social Research, "Summary of Reported Shortages of Cotton Pickers in Texas, August 1937," September 15, 1937, File 530/47/24/6, Record Group 174, Department of Labor, USNA-CP.

54. H. P. Drought to Nels Anderson, August 4, 1936, File 55854/100, RG 85, USNA-DC.

55. WPA Division of Social Research, "Investigation of Reported Shortages of Cotton Pickers in Texas, August 1937," September 15, 1937, File 530/47/24/6, Record Group 174, Department of Labor, USNA-CP; J. R. Steelman to Frances Perkins, March 24, 1938, File 530/47/24/6, Record Group 174, Department of Labor, USNA-CP.

56. Hahamovitch, *Fruits of Their Labor*, 153.

57. Linder, *Migrant Workers and Minimum Wages*, 137–41.

58. Coalson, *Development of the Migratory Farm Labor System in Texas*, 58.

59. See Volanto, *Texas, Cotton, and the New Deal*.

60. See Kester, *Revolt among the Sharecroppers*; Foley, *White Scourge*, 161–84; and Weber, *Dark Sweat, White Gold*, 112–36.

61. Blackwelder, *Women of the Depression*, 120.

62. McWilliams, *Ill Fares the Land*, 228.

63. Coalson, *Development of Migratory Farm Labor System in Texas*, 58.

64. Knippa, "San Antonio II," 70–71.

65. Ross Sterling to Reagan Houston et al., December (?) 1932, Box 2L50, Folder "Subject Correspondence—Diga Colony and Relief Work, Sept–Dec 1932," Maury Maverick, Sr., Papers, UT-CAH.

66. Balderrama and Rodriguez, *Decade of Betrayal*, 80.

67. American Public Welfare Association, *Public Welfare Survey of San Antonio*, 51.

68. In 1914 a reform coalition briefly wrested control from the machine dominated by Brian Callaghan, son of the machine's first boss and reputed to own most of San Antonio's thriving red light district, and created a commission government, but within a few years the machine took over the new city commission and dominated it through the 1930s. See Bridges, "Boss Tweed and V. O. Key in Texas," 64–65; and Johnson, Booth, and Harris, *Politics of San Antonio*, vii–x, 8–17.

69. See Blackwelder, *Women of the Depression*, 19–20.

70. White, "Machine Made," 32–33.

71. Granneberg, "Maury Maverick's San Antonio."

72. Ralph Bunche described Bellinger as "a Negro sportsman-gambler-racket boss" and a "great harm to Negro progress because of his unrepresentative stooges, who got positions of responsibility through his influence in city hall and the school board." Bunche also argued, "He was king of the lottery, allowed no competitors, and used his lottery kingdom to deliver votes for the candidates who would promise protection to this racket." Bunche, *Political Status of the Negro in the Age of FDR*, 73–74, 465.

73. Doyle, "Maury Maverick and Racial Politics in San Antonio," 199.

74. White, "Machine Made," 33.

75. Henderson, *Maury Maverick*, 50.

76. Ibid., 189.

77. Knippa, "San Antonio II," 84.

78. American Public Welfare Association, *Public Welfare Survey of San Antonio*, 42.

79. "San Antonio Relief Rolls to Be Slashed," *San Antonio Express*, August 7, 1937.

80. Ibid.

81. "Agricultural Workers on WPA to Be Available for Farm Jobs," *Corpus Christi Caller-Times*, April 14, 1942. See also Linder, *Migrant Workers and Minimum Wages*, 152–53.

82. Knippa, "San Antonio II," 75–76.

83. Ibid., 75–77.

84. See Weiss, "Maury Maverick and the Liberal Bloc," 880–95. For a serviceable chronology of Maverick's congressional career, see Davis, "Maury Maverick, Sr."

85. Blackwelder, *Women of the Depression*, 19.

86. For a contemporary view of Maverick and his allies in Congress, see High, "Neo–New Dealers," 10–11, 105–9.

87. In a letter to a journalist, Maverick described his opponent in the 1936 election as "a dumb (also damn), half-witted, silly, S.O.B., who has no brains and can't make a speech. He is backed by the Slick Oil Estate of Oklahoma and will probably spend such a prodigious amount that it would sound like bragging if I told you how much." Maury Maverick to Robert S. Allen, July 6, 1936, Box 2L22, Folder "General Correspondence May–Aug 1936," Maury Maverick, Sr., Papers, UT-CAH.

88. Quoted in Davis, "Maury Maverick, Sr.," 37–38.

89. Joseph Myers to J. R. Steelman, File 199/1189, Box 472, RG 280, Department of Labor, USNA-CP.

90. Davis, "Maury Maverick, Sr.," 47.

91. Henderson, *Maury Maverick*, 189.

92. Ibid., 191.

93. Quoted in Ibid., 192.

94. A full examination of the development of the so-called Mexican American generation and the emergence of LULAC lies beyond the scope of this study. Studies of this growing middle class in San Antonio and elsewhere include Buitron, *Quest for Tejano Identity in San Antonio*; García, *Mexican Americans*; Garcia, *Rise of the Mexican American Middle Class*; Gutiérrez, *Walls and Mirrors*; Kaplowitz, *LULAC, Mexican Americans, and National Policy*; Márquez, *LULAC*; and Sánchez, *Becoming Mexican American*.

95. Garcia, *Rise of the Mexican American Middle Class*, 213.

96. "Report of Emma Tenayuca to City Convention, Communist Party," July 6, 1939, Box 2L24, Folder "General Correspondence Jan–Jul 1939," Maury Maverick, Sr., Papers, UT-CAH.

97. This new police chief, Ray Ashworth, was in charge when the Municipal Auditorium riot occurred.

98. Garcia, *Rise of the Mexican American Middle Class*, 215.

99. Blackwelder, *Women of the Depression*, 117.

100. Granneberg, "Maury Maverick's San Antonio."

101. Public Housing Cost Chart, n.d., Document 95, Carmelo Tranchese Collection, St. Mary's University Special Collections, San Antonio, Texas. It is also worth noting that the housing projects were meant to be segregated. Alazán and Apache were for Mexicans and Mexican Americans, Wheatley and Lincoln Heights for African Americans, and Victoria for Anglos.

102. Nathan Straus to Eleanor Roosevelt, April 11, 1939, Document 126, Tranchese Collection.

103. Carmelo Tranchese to Eleanor Roosevelt, April 22, 1939, Document 128, Tranchese Collection.

104. Because of the activities of the West Side slumlords, the West Side projects cost far more to build than the East and South Side projects. Alazán cost $16,352 per acre, Apache $19,562, Victoria $14,018, Wheatley $5,346, and Lincoln Heights $6,700. See Public Housing Cost Chart, n.d, Document 95, Tranchese Collection.

105. Maverick, *Texas Iconoclast*, 39.

106. "Ouster of Maverick as Mayor Is Sought," *New York Times*, August 27, 1939; "Urges Maverick Recall," *New York Times*, September 1, 1939; Alex N. Murphree, "Maverick Encounters Free-Speech Troubles," *New York Times*, September 3, 1939.

107. Quoted in Henderson, *Maury Maverick*, 230.

108. Ibid., 231. While the machine was finally ousted for good in 1955, it was replaced by a new variety of machine called the Good Government League, which maintained control of the city until the 1970s.

CHAPTER 6

1. Quoted in "Testimony Ends in Strike Action," *San Antonio Express*, February 26, 1938.

2. "Chief Kilday Quells Outbreak with Fire Hose," *San Antonio Express*, February 26, 1938; George Lambert interviewed by George Green, November 1971, Oral History Collection, TLA; Mrs. M. M. Adams, Mrs. Hetty Browne, Mrs. Eron Dies, Mrs. Louise Warren, and Mrs. Cassie Jane Winfrey to C. K. Quin, Maury Maverick, and James Allred, March 5, 1938, File 530/47/24/6, Record Group 174, Department of Labor, USNA-CP.

3. Taylor, "Documentary History of the Strike of the Cotton Pickers in California 1933," in Taylor, *On the Ground in the Thirties*, 17.

4. Coalson, *Development of the Migratory Farm Labor System in Texas*, 61–62; Jamieson, *Labor Unionism in American Agriculture*, 271–72; Nelson-Cisneros, "UCAPAWA Organizing Activities in Texas," 73.

5. Rev. Charles Taylor, "To the Growers or Farmers of Crystal City," November 10, 1930, Series 3, Carton 12, Folder 30, PST.

6. Jamieson, *Labor Unionism in American Agriculture*, 272.

7. Coalson, *Development of the Migratory Farm Labor System in Texas*, 62; Jamieson, *Labor Unionism in American Agriculture*, 273.

8. José Jacobs to Senator Robert La Follette, May 5, 1936, Box 2E309, Folder 13, Labor Movement in Texas Collection, UT-CAH.

9. Jamieson, *Labor Unionism in American Agriculture*, 273.

10. José Jacobs interviewed by Ruth Allen, October 15, 1936, Box 2E309, Folder 12, Labor Movement in Texas Collection, UT-CAH.

11. Jamieson, *Labor Unionism in American Agriculture*, 273–74.

12. Francisco Hernández and Dionisio Rosales to Webb County Chamber of Commerce, March 29, 1935, File 182/326, Box 370, RG 280, Department of Labor, USNA-CP.

13. José Jacobs to Senator Robert La Follette, May 5, 1936, Box 2E309, Folder 13, Labor Movement in Texas Collection, UT-CAH.

14. Jamieson, *Labor Unionism in American Agriculture*, 274.

15. "Rangers, 1200 Onion Strikers Mill on Laredo Streets Today," *Laredo Times*, April 12, 1935.

16. Both the high and low numbers were given by Department of Labor conciliator J. R. Steelman for the same day, April 15, so it is difficult to say which is more accurate. Both estimates were also given in letters to the same man, H. L. Kerwin, director of conciliation for the Department of Labor. J. R. Steelman to H. L. Kerwin, April 15, 1935, File 182/326, Box 370, RG 280, Department of Labor, USNA-CP; J. R. Steelman to H. L. Kerwin, April 20, 1935, File 182/326, Box 370, RG 280, Department of Labor, USNA-CP.

17. J. R. Steelman to H. L. Kerwin, April 20, 1935, File 182/326, Box 370, RG 280, Department of Labor, USNA-CP.

18. J. R. Steelman to H. L. Kerwin, April 15, 1935, File 182/326, Box 370, RG 280, Department of Labor, USNA-CP; J. R. Steelman to H. L. Kerwin, April 20, 1935, File 182/326, Box 370, RG 280, Department of Labor, USNA-CP.

19. Vargas, *Labor Rights Are Civil Rights*, 118.

20. Quoted in "Judge Mullally Wires for Rangers in Onion Strike," *Laredo Times*, April 15, 1935.

21. "530 Strikers Back at Work," *Laredo Times*, April 16, 1935.

22. J. R. Steelman to H. L. Kerwin, April 20, 1935, File 182/326, Box 370, RG 280, Department of Labor, USNA-CP. None of those arrested remained in jail for more than a day: the police chief released them so they could go work in the fields.

23. J. R. Steelman to H. L. Kerwin, April 20, 1935, File 182/326, Box 370, RG 280, Department of Labor, USNA-CP.

24. See, for example, José Jacobs to Senator Robert La Follette, May 5, 1936, Box 2E309, Folder 13, Labor Movement in Texas Collection, UT-CAH.

25. "Onion Strike Off; Rangers Gone," *Laredo Times*, April 17, 1935.

26. Jamieson, *Labor Unionism in American Agriculture*, 275. Despite the seeming failure of this strike, the Asociación de Jornaleros was later given a charter by the AFL as the Agricultural Workers (Federal) Labor Union No. 20212, in an attempt to compete against the CIO's Texas Agricultural Workers Organizing Committee (AWOC) in 1937. The AWOC tried to establish locals throughout South Texas, and started to make some headway in the cotton fields of the Lower Valley, but it soon disappeared. See "CIO's on Job—Texas Cotton Pickers No Longer Slaves," *CIO News*, August 31, 1937.

27. F. H. Crockett to INS Commissioner, March 17, 1936, File 55854/100, RG 85, INS, USNA-DC.

28. Vargas, *Labor Rights Are Civil Rights*, 120–21.

29. Details of the organization founded in San Antonio are very sketchy, as is the role of Consul-General Hill in this episode. The confederation was founded "under sponsorship of the Mexican consulate general," but I could find little more about it. "Mexicans Form Labor Society," *San Antonio Express*, March 11, 1936; J. R. Steelman to Frances Perkins, March 26, 1936, File 195/349, Box 98, RG 280, Department of Labor, USNA-CP. It is also mentioned in a report from the INS inspector in charge in San Antonio, who wrote that the new labor organization was founded to counteract the activities of the company union established by Southern Pecan. W. W. Knopp to INS Headquarters, March 17, 1936, File 55854/100, RG 85, INS, USNA-DC.

30. Three pages of notes on March 13 meeting, File 55854/100, RG 85, INS, USNA-DC.

31. "Dies Says Consul Organizes Reds," *San Antonio Light*, March 23, 1936. Two years later Dies founded the House Un-American Activities Committee.

32. William Galligan to Cordell Hull, March 16, 1936, File 55854/100, RG 85, INS, USNA-DC.

33. González, *Mexican Consuls and Labor Organizing*, 47. The Secretariat of Foreign Relations made it very clear a few years earlier that the consular service should not take part in any strike activities or assume leadership roles in any labor organization. See Secretaría de Relaciones Exteriores de México, *Informe de la Secretaría de Relaciones Exteriores de agosto de 1933 a agosto 1 de 1934*, 411–12.

34. Quoted in J. R. Steelman to Frances Perkins, March 26, 1936, File 195/349, Box 98, RG 280, Department of Labor, USNA-CP.

35. Nelson-Cisneros, "UCAPAWA Organizing Activities in Texas." Though it focuses on California, the best survey of the UCAPAWA is Ruiz, *Cannery Women, Cannery Lives*.

36. Quoted in Zieger, *CIO*, 230.

37. For a more in-depth survey of the CIO's southern organizing campaigns, see Zieger, *CIO*, 227–41.

38. List of those who peeled shrimp on September 12, 1938, n.d., File 199/2425, Box 503, RG 280, Department of Labor, USNA-CP.

39. A. J. Holmes to Joseph Myers, n.d., File 199/867, Box 462, RG 280, Department of Labor, USNA-CP.

40. Summary of Shrimp Hullers Strike by Conciliation Service, September 28, 1938, File 199/2425, Box 503, RG 280, Department of Labor, USNA-CP.

41. Quoted in Summary of Shrimp Hullers Strike by Conciliation Service, September 28, 1938, File 199/2425, Box 503, RG 280, Department of Labor, USNA-CP.

42. See "UCAPAWA Yearbook" from Second National Convention, December 1938, Box 1, Folder 12, AR-36, Food, Tobacco, Agricultural, and Allied Workers Union of America Papers, TLA; Donald Henderson to UCAPAWA locals, n.d. (1941), Box 1, Folder 1, AR-36, TLA. Unlike in all of the other strikes dealt with in this chapter, the county sheriff's deputies and the Texas Rangers both served

impartially in Aransas Pass, standing guard over the picket lines to avoid another violent incident.

43. Summary of Shrimp Hullers Strike by Conciliation Service, September 28, 1938, File 199/2425, Box 503, RG 280, Department of Labor, USNA-CP.

44. Conciliation Service Progress Report, September 28, 1938, File 199/2425, Box 503, RG 280, Department of Labor, USNA-CP.

45. Ibid.

46. For more on the labor issues at Rice Brothers, see Rob Roy Rice Papers, UT-CAH, esp. Box 3M152, National Labor Relations Board Folder, and Box 3M177, Department of Labor Folder.

47. Vargas, *Labor Rights Are Civil Rights*, 121–22.

48. The labor movement in San Antonio is probably the only aspect of the Great Depression in South Texas that has a substantial historiography. The primary works, focused especially on the pecan shellers' strike, are Blackwelder, *Women of the Depression*, 67–150; Garcia, *Rise of the Mexican American Middle Class*, 61–108; Green, "ILGWU in Texas," 144–45; Jamieson, *Labor Unionism in American Agriculture*, 278–80; Menefee and Cassmore, *Pecan Shellers of San Antonio*; Shapiro, "Pecan Shellers of San Antonio," 229–44; and Vargas, *Labor Rights Are Civil Rights*, 81–143.

49. Blackwelder, *Women of the Depression*, 67, 83–84.

50. Blackwelder, "Texas Homeworkers in the 1930s," 75–90. One of the many public health measures passed by the Maverick administration was a ban on industrial homework in San Antonio. While the measure had as much to do with middle-class fears of purchasing products made in unsanitary environments as with any concerns over worker safety, it did help eliminate some of the worst features of the homework system.

51. MacLean, *Freedom Is Not Enough*, 117–54; Cobble, *Other Women's Movement*.

52. "San Antonio Exposed as City Where Labor Is Mistreated," *Weekly Dispatch*, January 19, 1934.

53. "San Antonio Shall Not Become Cesspool of Cheap Labor," *Weekly Dispatch*, September 28, 1934.

54. "Civic Leaders to Assist in Home Work Clean Up," *Weekly Dispatch*, January 15, 1937.

55. "Mr. E. Finck, in Cigar Strike Hearing, Refuses to Appear before Industrial Commission," *Weekly Dispatch*, December 6, 1935; Ruth Allen notes on Finck Cigar Strike, n.d., Box 2E309, Folder 13, Labor Movement in Texas Collection, UT-CAH.

56. Ruth Allen interview with Miss Gonzalez, October 7, 1936, Box 2E309, Folder 12, UT-CAH; Ruth Allen interview with Mrs. W. H. Ernst, October 8, 1936, Box 2E309, Folder 13, UT-CAH; "Mr. E. Finck, in Cigar Strike Hearing, Refuses to Appear before Industrial Commission," *Weekly Dispatch*, December 6, 1935.

57. Blackwelder, *Women of the Depression*, 133.

58. Mrs. W. H. Ernst interviewed by Ruth Allen, October 87, 1936, Box 2E309, Folder 13, Labor Movement in Texas Collection, UT-CAH; Blackwelder, *Women of the Depression*, 132–33.

59. The refusal to hire back the leaders of the first strike caused the NRA to revoke Finck's Blue Eagle, with Edward Finck declaring, "We will close the plant down before we put those four people back to work." "Finck Cigar Co. Returns Blue Eagle Rather than Comply with Labor Board Findings," *Weekly Dispatch*, September 28, 1934.

60. Vargas, *Labor Rights Are Civil Rights*, 81.

61. Mrs. W. H. Ernst interviewed by Ruth Allen, October 87, 1936, Box 2E309, Folder 13, Labor Movement in Texas Collection, UT-CAH; Blackwelder, *Women of the Depression*, 133–34.

62. Ruth Allen notes on Finck Cigar Strike, n.d., Box 2E309, Folder 13, Labor Movement in Texas Collection, UT-CAH; "Striking Cigarmakers Make Futile Gesture for Arbitration," *Weekly Dispatch*, April 26, 1935.

63. Blackwelder, *Women of the Depression*, 134–35.

64. "San Antonio 'Pauper Paid' Labor in Revolt," *Weekly Dispatch*, March 22, 1935.

65. Miss Gonzalez interview with Ruth Allen, October 7, 1936, Box 2E309, Folder 12, Labor Movement in Texas Collection, UT-CAH. Ernst stated that she and a number of other strikers could only find work with the WPA, and all worked together on a sewing project. See Mrs. W. H. Ernst interviewed by Ruth Allen, October 87, 1936, Box 2E309, Folder 13, Labor Movement in Texas Collection, UT-CAH. An interesting side note to the Finck Cigar episode is that the company still operates in San Antonio. A history on the company's website fails to mention the strikes of the 1930s. An Internet search for "Finck Cigar" turns up an endorsement of their products by Rush Limbaugh.

66. See Emma Tenayuca interviewed by Gerry Poyo, February 21, 1987, Oral History Collection, ITC; and Rips, "Living History," 7–15. In addition, the labor organization formed in San Antonio in 1936 with the help of the consul-general, mentioned above, included a number of former cigar strikers. Mrs. W. H. Ernst was president of the Confederation of Mexican and Mexican-American Laborers, while Tenayuca and other activists and workers involved with the Finck strikes held other positions in the short-lived labor organization. See "Mexicans Form Labor Society," *San Antonio Express*, March 11, 1936.

67. Blackwelder, *Women of the Depression*, 97.

68. Actually, workers claimed that some companies sent some work further south to Laredo, where wages were even lower. In addition, a contractor in Laredo farmed out work from a San Antonio factory to homeworkers across the border in Nuevo Laredo. This came to light only after the contractor was arrested multiple times for carrying the unassembled fabric across the border. See Blackwelder, *Women of the Depression*, 99–100.

69. "U.S. District Attorney W. R. Smith, Jr., Files Injunction against Juvenile Mfg. Co. Alleging Violation of Southern Code," *Weekly Dispatch*, September 7, 1934.

70. "San Antonio Shall Not Become Cesspool of Cheap Labor," *Weekly Dispatch*, September 28, 1934.

71. There is quite a bit of disagreement as to who deserves the credit for organizing ILGWU locals in San Antonio. Blackwelder credits ILGWU organizer Rebecca

Taylor, a San Antonio native, for recruiting garment workers, but a number of other activists and historians have cast doubt on Taylor's activities. Emma Tenayuca and Maria Solis Sager, two prominent Depression-era activists, claimed that Taylor was racist and condescending toward Mexican and Mexican American workers, and that she merely profited from the efforts of others in adding members to the ILGWU. While it is difficult to determine where exactly the truth lies in this situation, Taylor was conspicuous in decrying the pecan shellers' strike as an action led entirely by Communists. See Blackwelder, *Women of the Depression*, 135–36; Vargas, *Labor Rights Are Civil Rights*, 127–30; and Manuela Solis Sager interviewed by Debra McDonald, Phyllis McKenzie, and Sarah Massey, Oral History Collection, ITC.

72. "San Antonio Garment Workers Serve Time in County Jail," *Weekly Dispatch*, August 21, 1936.

73. Green, "ILGWU in Texas," 145.

74. Blackwelder, *Women of the Depression*, 138–39.

75. "Garment Union Pickets Plant," *San Antonio Express*, March 19, 1938; Meyer Perlstein to Ben Owens, April 5, 1940, Box 2E309, Folder 12, Labor Movement in Texas Collection, UT-CAH; Blackwelder, *Women of the Depression*, 139; González, *Mexican Consuls and Labor Organizing*, 198–99; Green, "ILGWU in Texas," 145.

76. Rips, "Living History," 10.

77. Tenayuca and Brooks, "Mexican Question in the Southwest," 262–63.

78. Vargas, *Labor Rights Are Civil Rights*, 130.

79. Cassie Jane Winfrey, "Gangster Police Methods Come to Texas," n.d., Box 2E189, Folder 5, Labor Movement in Texas Collection, UT-CAH.

80. Cassie Jane Winfrey, "Gangster Police Methods Come to Texas," n.d., Box 2E189, Folder 5, Labor Movement in Texas Collection, UT-CAH; "Riots Follow Sit-In Strike at WPA; Police Do the Rest," *San Antonio News*, June 30, 1937.

81. "Use of Axes by Police Rapped," *San Antonio Light*, June 30, 1937.

82. Ibid.

83. "Riots Follow Sit-In Strike at WPA; Police Do the Rest," *San Antonio News*, June 30, 1937.

84. Ibid.

85. "Use of Axes by Police Rapped," *San Antonio Light*, June 30, 1937.

86. Ibid.

87. Manaster, *Pecans*, 69.

88. Ibid., 72.

89. Menefee and Cassmore, *Pecan Shellers of San Antonio*, xv–xvi, 6–7; "Working Conditions of Pecan Shellers in San Antonio," *Monthly Labor Review* 48:3 (March 1939), 549–50. According to Jane Manaster, the Duerler Company shelled about 1,000 pounds of pecans a day in 1928. Manaster, *Pecans*, 73.

90. John Tedesco, "Freemans Linked to Labor Fight," *San Antonio Express-News*, November 7, 1999. Among other things, Joe Freeman has an arena, formerly the site of the San Antonio Stock Show and Rodeo, named after him. But Freeman remained a silent partner in Southern Pecan. Seligmann ran the day-to-day operations and was the sole face of the company in the ensuing strikes.

91. Shapiro, "Pecan Shellers of San Antonio," 229.

92. There is more than a passing resemblance between the practices of the sugar beet industry in the Upper Midwest during the 1920s and Southern Pecan in the 1930s. Both operations vertically integrated "agricultural" processes into a corporate structure, passing off the duties of employment to contractors restrained by the dictates of the company. And both relied on the migrant workers of South Texas.

93. Menefee and Cassmore, *Pecan Shellers of San Antonio*, 8–9; Shapiro, "Pecan Shellers of San Antonio," 229; "Working Conditions of Pecan Shellers in San Antonio," 549–50.

94. Menefee and Cassmore, *Pecan Shellers of San Antonio*, 5.

95. Southern Pecan proved this without a doubt in 1935 when Seligmann purchased almost the entire national surplus of the largest pecan crop in memory, 105 million pounds, for a fraction of their normal cost. He then put the surplus in storage for a year. When the 1936 harvest yielded only 40 million pounds, Seligmann sent his surplus nuts from the year before to smaller operators for twice what he had paid for them, making a profit of $500,000 from his speculation. See Menefee and Cassmore, *Pecan Shellers of San Antonio*, 8.

96. Jamieson, *Labor Unionism in American Agriculture*, 278; "Working Conditions of Pecan Shellers in San Antonio," 550.

97. A WPA study revealed that 17 percent of pecan shellers were San Antonio natives, a substantial majority came to San Antonio between 1911 and 1930, while only 10 percent came to the city during the 1930s. Most had spent several years working in the pecan industry. More than 40 percent first worked in pecan shelling before 1932, while only 11 percent began pecan work after 1936. More than two-thirds of women surveyed stated that they only worked in the pecan industry, while less than one-third of men worked only in the pecan sheds. Among those who held employment other than pecan shelling, almost all were either unskilled construction workers or migrant agricultural laborers. Menefee and Cassmore, *Pecan Shellers of San Antonio*, 3–5.

98. George Lambert interviewed by George Green, November 1971, Oral History Collection, TLA.

99. J. R. Steelman to Miss Jay (?), March 15, 1938, File 530/47/24/6, RG 174, Department of Labor, USNA-CP.

100. Menefee and Cassmore, *Pecan Shellers of San Antonio*, 28–29.

101. Quoted in ibid., 50.

102. Alberta Snid interviewed by Maria Flores and Glenn Scott, n.d., Oral History Collection, TLA.

103. Blackwelder, *Women of the Depression*, 104–5.

104. Richard Croxdale, "Pecan Shellers," 9.

105. Quoted in George Lambert, "Jersey City of the South," July 4, 1938, Box 1, Folder 6, AR-36, TLA; "America's Lowest Paid Workers," n.d., File 199/1189, Box 472, RG 280, Department of Labor, USNA-CP.

106. Menefee and Cassmore, *Pecan Shellers of San Antonio*, 15–16.

107. Shapiro, "Pecan Shellers of San Antonio," 233.

108. Menefee and Cassmore, *Pecan Shellers of San Antonio*, 16–17; Shapiro, "Pecan Shellers of San Antonio," 233.

109. Jamieson, *Labor Unionism in American Agriculture*, 279.

110. Rodriguez appears throughout the primary and secondary evidence, but he remains a shadowy figure. The only positive depiction I have ever seen is from Rubén Munguía, a labor supporter who ran a printing shop on the West Side. See Munguía, *Nuecero Spoke*. See also Herbert Henderson to Malcolm Bardwell, February 24, 1935, Document 77, Tranchese Collection, St. Mary's University Special Collections, San Antonio, Texas; Edward J. Shaughnessy to Senator Morris Sheppard, April 21, 1936, File 55854/100, RG 85, USNA-DC.

111. J. R. Steelman to Miss Jay (?), March 15, 1938, File 530/47/24/6, RG 174, Department of Labor, USNA-CP; Vargas, *Labor Rights Are Civil Rights*, 135.

112. See NLRB Official Report, Azar and Solomon vs. Pecan Workers Local No. 172, September 19, 1938, File 199/1189, Box 472, RG 280, Department of Labor, USNA-CP. The NLRB demanded that the contractor cease and desist from allowing Rodriguez to coerce employees to join his union during business hours.

113. See Maria Solis Sager interview, Oral History Collection, ITC; Emma Tenayuca interview, Oral History Collection, ITC.

114. Conciliation Service Official Summary of Pecan Strike, April 13, 1938, File 199/1189, Box 472, RG 280, Department of Labor, USNA-CP. Tenayuca was, in fact, a member of the Communist Party, but many of the other local leaders were not.

115. See John Crossland interviewed by George Green, November 1971, Oral History Collection, TLA George Lambert interview, Oral History Collection, TLA.

116. Conciliation Service Official Summary of Pecan Strike, April 13, 1938, File 199/1189, Box 472, RG 280, Department of Labor, USNA-CP.

117. George Lambert interview, Oral History Collection, TLA.

118. Ibid.

119. Joseph Myers to J. R. Steelman, February 12, 1938, File 199/1189, Box 472, RG 280, Department of Labor, USNA-CP.

120. Garcia, *Rise of the Mexican American Middle Class*, 107–8.

121. "Archbishop Drossaerts Praises Police Fight on Communism," *San Antonio Express*, February 19, 1938. As can be inferred from this quotation, Drossaerts did find conditions in the pecan shelling industry to be appalling, which the union used to its advantage. A number of UCAPAWA publications and statements featured his statement that "the Negro slaves before emancipation were a thousand times better off than these poor, defenseless people." See George Lambert, "Jersey City of the South," July 4, 1938, Box 1, Folder 6, AR-36, TLA; and "America's Lowest Paid Workers," n.d., File 199/1189, Box 472, RG 280, USNA-CP. Years later, when asked about the use of Drossaerts's statement, George Lambert said, "I believe this was sort of a tongue-in-cheek pickup." Lambert interview, Oral History Collection, TLA.

122. Quoted in "Officers Declare Strike in Shelling Plants Does in Fact Exist," *San Antonio News*, February 4, 1938.

123. "America's Lowest Paid Workers," n.d, File 199/1189, Box 472, RG 280, USNA-CP.

124. "Soup Kitchen Closing Ires Crowd," *San Antonio Light*, February 12, 1938.

125. The picture's caption read, "R. DeBona is shown with some of the clubs, all two and one-half feet long and heavier than old clubs." "Police Get Clubby," *San Antonio Light*, February 14, 1938.

126. Joseph Myers to J. R. Steelman, February 11, 1938, File 199/1189, Box 472, RG 280, USNA-CP.

127. Ibid.

128. Conciliation Service Official Summary of Pecan Strike, April 13, 1938, File 199/1189, Box 472, RG 280, Department of Labor, USNA-CP.

129. Stanley White to J. R. Steelman, March 29, 1938, File 199/1189, Box 472, RG 280, Department of Labor, USNA-CP.

130. Joseph Myers to J. R. Steelman, April 2, 1938, File 199/1189, Box 472, RG 280, Department of Labor, USNA-CP.

131. "Report of the Board of Arbitration in San Antonio Pecan Controversy," April 13, 1938, File 199/1189, Box 472, RG 280, Department of Labor, USNA-CP.

132. "Decision of Board of Arbitration in San Antonio Pecan Strike," April 13, 1938, Box 1, Folder 4, AR-36, TLA.

133. Menefee and Cassmore, *Pecan Shellers of San Antonio*, 18.

134. George Lambert open letter, November 1, 1938, File 199/1189, Box 472, RG 280, Department of Labor, USNA-CP.

135. Conciliation Service Report on Threatened Strike, May 20, 1939, File 199/3673, Box 536, RG 280, Department of Labor, USNA-CP.

136. A thorough examination of Southern Pecan's efforts to gain exemption from the FLSA can be found in the twenty-three-page report prepared by the Wage and Hour Division of the Department of Labor in 1939. Merle D. Vincent, January 23, 1939, Box 2E189, Folder 15, Labor Movement in Texas Collection, UT-CAH.

137. Meyers, *Economics of Labor Relations*, 409–10.

138. Ibid., 410n.

139. Shapiro, "Pecan Shellers of San Antonio," 243. Menefee and Cassmore reported that a large number of former pecan shellers left for sugar beet work in 1939 intent on not returning to San Antonio. Menefee and Cassmore, *Pecan Shellers of San Antonio*, 58.

140. For more on the failure of New Deal policymakers to deal with the issues of agricultural labor, see Hahamovitch, *Fruits of Their Labor*; and Daniel, *Bitter Harvest*.

141. The exception was the continued presence of the ILGWU in San Antonio, which actually carried on a strike that lasted for several years in the late 1950s and early 1960s. See International Ladies Garment Workers Union Local 180 Collection, AR-30, TLA.

PART IV

1. Quoted in Martin, "Guest Workers," 889.

2. On the H-2 guest worker program, see Hahamovitch, *No Man's Land*.

3. Martin, "Guest Workers," 889–90.

4. Henry B. Gonzalez to John Bryant, March 13, 1996, Box 2004-127/393, Henry B. Gonzalez Papers, UT-CAH.

5. Press release from Office of Congressman Henry B. Gonzalez, September 4, 1963, Box 2004-127/393, Bracero Program Folder, Henry B. Gonzalez Papers, UT-CAH.

6. Henry B. Gonzalez, "At the Bottom of the Chasm" (unpublished manuscript), September 20, 1969, Box 2004-127/58, Migrant Workers 1969 Folder, Henry B. Gonzalez Papers, UT-CAH.

CHAPTER 7

1. Clifford Parliman to Allan Shivers, February 6, 1952, File 1977/81-157, Allan Shivers Gubernatorial Papers, TSA.

2. Mrs. John H. Schmidt to Congressman Paul B. Dague (D-PA), March 9, 1953, in U.S. Congress, House Committee on Agriculture, *Extension of Mexican Farm Labor Program*, 10–14.

3. The scope of this study does not allow for a complete history of the Bracero Program. Instead, I will focus on the ways the conditions and practices of agricultural labor relations in South Texas affected the contract labor program throughout its twenty-two years of existence. For surveys of the Bracero Program and in-depth analyses of the diplomatic and political underpinnings of the agreement, see Rasmussen, *History of the Emergency Farm Labor Supply Program*; Galarza, *Merchants of Labor*; Craig, *Bracero Program*; Kirstein, *Anglo over Bracero*; Calavita, *Inside the State*; Cohen, *Braceros*; and Mitchell, *They Saved the Crops*.

4. Rasmussen, *History of the Emergency Farm Labor Supply Program*, 14.

5. Vargas, *Labor Rights Are Civil Rights*, 238.

6. Scruggs, "Evolution of the Mexican Farm Labor Agreement of 1942," 140–41.

7. Ibid.; Vargas, *Labor Rights Are Civil Rights*, 238–39.

8. Scruggs, "Evolution of Mexican Farm Labor Agreement of 1942," 141. The California State Federation of Labor sent a telegram to Governor Culbert Olson in August 1941 complaining that requests by agricultural and railroad interests in the state for 30,000 Mexican workers were unnecessary as an investigation "reveals no acute shortage of this class of workers but only reason jobs are not filled is the inadequate rates of pay which range in the western states from 36 cents to 43 cents per hour." California State Federation of Labor to Culbert Olson, August 29, 1941, Series 5, Carton 39, Folder 13, PST.

9. "Supplement to Origins and Problems, Texas Migratory Farm Labor," November 1941, Farm Placement Service Papers, TSA, 83–84.

10. "Campaign to Secure Adequate Farm Labor May Be Endangered by Snipers," *Corpus Christi Caller-Times*, February 27, 1942.

11. Vargas, *Labor Rights Are Civil Rights*, 240.

12. Hahamovitch, *No Man's Land*, 23–37; Scruggs, "United States, Mexico, and the Wetbacks," 150; Vargas, *Labor Rights Are Civil Rights*, 238–39.

13. Before the outlines of the Bracero Program emerged from the negotiation between the governments of the United States and Mexico, however, groups like the Texas Farm Bureau and the South Texas Chamber of Commerce had already begun to gauge Mexico's willingness to allow workers into the United States through a privately managed guest worker program. These negotiations obviously never went anywhere, but they do exhibit an interesting tension between growers' desire to have unfettered access to Mexican labor and their fear that a guest worker program

run from Washington could introduce a new regime of government regulation in agricultural labor relations. See "Campaign to Secure Adequate Farm Labor May Be Endangered by Snipers," *Corpus Christi Caller-Times*, February 27, 1942; "Robstown Farm Leaders Ask for Mexican Labor," *Corpus Christi Caller-Times*, April 16, 1942; E. O. Taulbee to Coke Stevenson, May 24, 1942, Box 4-14/183, Labor Immigration Folder, Coke Stevenson Gubernatorial Papers, TSA; and "Application for the Importation of Mexican Nationals for Temporary Employment in the 1942 Fall Harvest in Texas," May 23, 1942, Box 4-14/183, Labor Immigration Folder, Coke Stevenson Gubernatorial Papers, TSA.

14. Cross and Sandos, *Across the Border*, 18.

15. Bartra, *Agrarian Structure and Political Power in Mexico*, 38.

16. In part because of this increased internal migration and the underemployment that came along with it, wage levels in Mexico City plummeted during these years. From an index of 100 in 1938 real wages in Mexico City fell to a low of 46.6 in 1947, and did not regain the 1938 levels until 1971. Cited in Niblo, *Mexico in the 1940s*, 4.

17. Cross and Sandos, *Across the Border*, 35; Simpson, *Ejido*. A number of scholars have debated the degree to which the agrarian reform has affected patterns of migration. See González Navarro, *Los extranjeros en México y los mexicanos en el extranjero, 1821–1970*, vol. 3; Bartra, *Agrarian Structure and Political Power in Mexico*; and Cross and Sandos, *Across the Border*.

18. Scruggs, "Evolution of the Mexican Farm Labor Agreement of 1942," 143–44.

19. Quoted in "Supplement to Origins and Problems, Texas Migratory Farm Labor," November 1941, Farm Placement Service Papers, TSA.

20. Craig, *Bracero Program*, 23.

21. Secretaría de Relaciones Exteriores de México, *Memoria de la Secretaría de Relaciones Exteriores, septiembre de 1943 a agosto de 1944*, 115.

22. Growers especially disliked this prevailing wage clause, since keeping wages from rising was their entire reason for demanding Mexican labor in the first place. For the first few months of the program many of the growers' worst fears seemed to be coming true under the Farm Security Administration, which tried to extend some of the guarantees of the Bracero Program to domestic farmworkers. These efforts to finally extend the New Deal to agricultural labor brought a fierce backlash from farming interests and led to the shifting of supervision of the program from the Farm Security Administration to the War Food Administration, which growers considered a much more reliable ally in their fight to keep their workers from gaining the rights industrial workers had secured during the previous decade. See Calavita, *Inside the State*, 20–22.

23. Hahamovitch, *No Man's Land*, 133.

24. See McWilliams, *North from Mexico*, 221–31; and Obregón Pagán, *Murder at the Sleepy Lagoon*.

25. See File 1989/59-19, Good Neighbor Commission Collection, TSA.

26. Reproduced in Perales, *Are We Good Neighbors?*, 121.

27. The state government did establish the Good Neighbor Commission, as will be discussed at length below, but this was never more than a public relations agency that tried to muffle publicity of discrimination rather than eliminate it.

28. Stilwell, "Good Neighbors and Band Music," 3.

29. See, for instance, Cullen W. Briggs to Coke Stevenson, July 8, 1943, Box 4-14/156, Inter-American Affairs 1943 Folder, Coke Stevenson Gubernatorial Papers, TSA.

30. Zamora, *Claiming Rights and Righting Wrongs in Texas*, 89.

31. Green, *Establishment in Texas Politics*, 81.

32. Coke Stevenson to Ezequiel Padilla, July 12, 1943, and Ezequiel Padilla to Coke Stevenson, July 20, 1943, in Padilla and Stevenson, "Good Neighbor Policy and Mexicans in Texas."

33. Stevenson only authorized the creation of the commission after he found out that funding for it would come from the State Department's Office of Inter-American Affairs. Scruggs, "Texas and the Bracero Program," 257.

34. Pauline Kibbe to Good Neighbor Commission, December 29, 1944, File 1990/16-1, Good Neighbor Commission Collection, TSA.

35. Glenn Garrett, "The Good Neighbor Commission of Texas and Problems in Human Relations between the Anglo and Latin American Citizens of Texas," January 26, 1959, File 1990/16-1, Good Neighbor Commission Collection, TSA; emphasis added.

36. George Sanchez to Senator Ralph Yarborough, April 12, 1954, Box 3, Folder 4, Ed Idar Papers, UT-Benson.

37. Zamora, *Claiming Rights and Righting Wrongs in Texas*, 87–88.

38. Patrick Carroll seems to indicate that Longoria enlisted and was not drafted, but that point is not absolutely clear. See Carroll, *Felix Longoria's Wake*.

39. Ibid., 53.

40. "Report on Schools in Sandia, Texas," April 11, 1948, reported that school-children were forced to use open-air toilets in shockingly filthy condition, and that the small segregated school in this town "should be condemned and torn down and lumber sold for firewood." Box 21, Folder 8, Hector Garcia Papers, Texas A&M University–Corpus Christi. The conditions at the labor camps in the region almost defy belief, with almost every one inspected by Garcia unsuitable for livestock, much less humans. Almost all of them lacked water, had toilets overflowing with feces, and suffered from epidemic rates of dysentery. "Labor Camp Investigation and Report," April 22, 1948, Box 91, Folder 59, Garcia Papers. The only attention that these reports seemed to garner came from the State Bureau of Sanitary Engineering, which traveled to the same labor camps as Garcia and found that "sanitation was found to be almost exactly as reported by Dr. Hector P. Garcia and extremely unsatisfactory." An engineer from the Bureau of Sanitary Engineering concluded that the "camps are entirely inadequate and unsanitary to the extent that they are not fit for human habitation" and that they "should be abandoned and torn down inasmuch as they are not subject to prac-tical improvements and are a definite public health menace to occupants and neighbors." N. E. Davis and J. W. Wilson to George Cox, May 28, 1948, Box 47, Folder 55, Garcia Papers.

41. Good Neighbor Commission official memorandum, February 11, 1949, File 1989/59-17, Good Neighbor Commission Collection, TSA.

42. Patrick Carroll paints the commission in a much more positive light, calling it a "well-intentioned mediator," but I think he overstates its intentions of doing anything but covering up discrimination. See Carroll, *Felix Longoria's Wake*, 176.

43. Neville G. Penrose to Vaughan Bryant, August 14, 1952, File 1989/59-19, Good Neighbor Commission Collection, TSA.

44. Carter Wheelock to Eagle Pass Human Relations Council, June 16, 1952, File 1989/59-18, Good Neighbor Commission Collection, TSA.

45. The law also erased the possibility of the Bracero Program's allowing for a backdoor application of wage and hour standards to domestic farmworkers, adding a statutory basis to the removal of the program from the oversight of the Farm Security Administration. See Hahamovitch, *Fruits of Their Labor*, 173–74.

46. Calavita, *Inside the State*, 20–23. According to Rasmussen, "Hostilities actually ceased August 14, 1945. However, official determination of this cessation was not made during the year and an appropriate sentence was inserted in the 1946 appropriation bill, extending the authority to admit laborers under Section 5 (g) of the Farm Labor Supply Appropriation Act, 1944, for the continuance of the program." Rasmussen, *History of the Emergency Farm Labor Supply Program*, 227.

47. Galarza, *Merchants of Labor*, 52–53; Craig, *Bracero Program*, 50.

48. Craig, *Bracero Program*, 50.

49. President's Commission on Migratory Labor, *Migratory Labor in American Agriculture*, 55.

50. Quoted in Gutiérrez, *Walls and Mirrors*, 139–40.

51. Scruggs, "United States, Mexico, and the Wetbacks," 152.

52. Quoted in ibid.

53. According to Ernesto Galarza, "Notwithstanding the views of the Department, some employers continued to plead an acute need for braceros and it was on their behalf that recruitment was extended through 1949. This was done on the basis of permits granted by the Department of Justice under provisions of the 1917 immigration law." Galarza, *Merchants of Labor*, 48.

54. Corwin, "Story of Ad Hoc Exemptions," 151.

55. Kirstein, *Anglo over Bracero*, 55–56.

56. Saunders and Leonard, *Wetback in the Lower Rio Grande Valley of Texas*, 72–73.

57. Ibid., 79–80.

58. Corwin, "Mexican Policy and Ambivalence toward Labor Emigration to the United States," 184–85.

59. President's Commission, *Migratory Labor in American Agriculture*, 53.

60. Calavita, *Inside the State*, 29–30.

61. Ibid., 29–30.

62. Don Larin, quoted in Galarza, *Merchants of Labor*, 50.

63. Ibid., 49–50.

64. Quoted in Kirstein, *Anglo over Bracero*, 69.

65. Quoted in ibid. Kirstein also noted, "It seems certain that no direct order emanated from the White House to open the border, for the president was critical of USES and INS laxity in honoring international agreements."

66. Quoted in Galarza, *Merchants of Labor*, 50.

67. Galarza, *Merchants of Labor*, 49–50.

68. Calavita, *Inside the State*, 29–30; Kirstein, *Anglo over Bracero*, 70.

69. International Executive Agreement, July 29, 1949, Box 3C38, Folder 8, Texas State Federation of Labor Papers, UT-CAH.

70. Saunders and Leonard, *Wetback in the Lower Rio Grande Valley of Texas*, 56. Two of the major complaints of Valley growers were eliminated in 1950 with the beginning of border contracting and the elimination of a requirement that all contracts last at least four months (Valley growers only wanted braceros for a few weeks at a time).

71. Whalen, "Wetback Problem in Southeast Texas," 104. Whalen claimed that "255,424 wetbacks were apprehended in this district during the past fiscal year" and that these numbers surely would have been much higher if not for the Bracero Program.

72. Calavita, *Inside the State*, 35–38; Saunders and Leonard, *Wetback in the Lower Rio Grande Valley of Texas*, 56.

73. President's Commission on Migratory Labor, *Migratory Labor in American Agriculture*, 55.

74. Galarza, *Merchants of Labor*, 63.

75. Hahamovitch, *No Man's Land*, 90.

76. Ibid., 112–13.

77. President's Commission on Migratory Labor, *Migratory Labor in American Agriculture*, 17.

78. Ibid., 53.

79. Ibid., 78–81.

80. Ibid., 178.

81. Andy McClellan to J. J. Hickman, July 16, 1951, Box 3C38, Folder 7, Texas State Federation of Labor Papers, UT-CAH.

82. See Bureau of Employment Security, Department of Labor, "Basic Requirements for Certification of Foreign Workers," n.d., Box 3C38, Folder 7, Texas State Federation of Labor Papers, UT-CAH.

83. Calavita, *Inside the State*, 46; Hahamovitch, *Fruits of Their Labor*, 151–81; Hahamovitch, *No Man's Land*, 86–109.

84. Galarza, *Farm Workers and Agri-business in California*, 205.

85. Calavita, *Inside the State*, 65–66; Galarza, *Merchants of Labor*, 66.

86. Lázaro Salinas, *La emigración de braceros*, 12.

87. Jim Griffin quoted in "Wetbacks More than Illegal Aliens to Texans at Hearing," *Corpus Christi Caller*, December 12, 1952.

88. McBride, *Vanishing Bracero*, 3.

89. On South Texas growers' rhetorical campaign against the Border Patrol and INS in the 1950s, see Hernández, *Migra*, 159–64.

90. Calavita, *Inside the State*, 29–30. In June 1952, John Rooney, a congressman from New York, charged on the floor of the U.S. House of Representatives that Shivers employed illegal labor on his Sharyland Farm.

91. Galarza, *Merchants of Labor*, 61.

92. Willard Kelly as quoted in Hernández, *Migra!*, 164.

93. García, *Operation Wetback*, 112.

94. My interpretation obviously owes a lot to the reinterpretation of Operation Wetback in Hernández, *Migra!*, 171–95.

95. Quoted in Calavita, *Inside the State*, 52.

96. Calavita, *Inside the State*, 54.

97. García, *Operation Wetback*, 208.

98. Quoted in García, *Operation Wetback*, 208–9.

99. Andy McClellan to Jerry Holleman, June 28, 1954, Box 1, Folder 2, Series 7, Texas AFL-CIO Collection (AR-110), TLA.

100. García, *Operation Wetback*, 210–12. Rather than return them to Mexico at nearby border towns, however, the INS shipped the vast majority of the deportees to Presidio and El Paso in West Texas, approximately 750 miles from the Lower Rio Grande Valley. Not only did this mean that the deportees could not quickly cross the border and return to the same employer, but it also meant that the Mexican government had to cover the transportation of tens of thousands of repatriates from Ojinaga and Ciudad Juárez to their homes. See "US Wetback Plan Puzzles Mexico, Too," *Laredo Times*, July 16, 1954; and "Details of Work Secret," *Hidalgo County News* (Edinburg), July 15, 1954.

101. "Wetbacks Combed from Cotton Fields by Border Army: Housemaids Taken," *San Benito News*, July 15, 1954.

102. "Editorial: Even Border Patrolmen Are Getting Self-Conscious about Their Activities," *Weslaco News*, July 29, 1954.

103. "Here's Our Side of the Wetback Argument," *Valley Monitor*, July 18, 1954.

104. McBride, *Vanishing Bracero*, 6–9.

105. García, *Operation Wetback*, 227–32.

106. "Wetback Halt Raises Legal Labor Need," *Corpus Christi Caller*, July 15, 1954.

107. Kirstein, *Anglo over Bracero*, 103; Galarza, *Merchants of Labor*, 79.

108. Galarza, *Merchants of Labor*, 69, 71. See also "Down in the Valley: A Supplementary Report on Developments in the Wetback and Bracero Situation of the Lower Rio Grande Valley of Texas since Publication of 'What Price Wetbacks?,'" n.d., Box 65, Folder 14, Garcia Papers, TAMU-CC.

109. Hernández, *Migra!*, 171.

110. The best study of the essential illusion of border control and the instrumental value of image crafting in border enforcement is Andreas, *Border Games*.

111. Andrew C. McClellan, Subcommittee on Equipment, Supplies and Manpower of the House Committee on Agriculture, March 21, 1955, Box 1, Folder 3, Series 7, AR-110, TLA.

112. "Down in the Valley: A Supplementary Report on Developments in the Wetback and Bracero Situation of the Lower Rio Grande Valley of Texas since Publication of 'What Price Wetbacks?,'" n.d., Box 65, Folder 14, Garcia Papers, TAMU-CC; Ngai, *Impossible Subjects*, 143.

113. Ngai, *Impossible Subjects*, 147.

114. Ibid., 144.

115. Calavita, *Inside the State*, 144, 218. See also Press Release, Office of Congressman Henry B. Gonzalez, September 4, 1963, Box 2004-127/393, Bracero Program Folder, Henry B. Gonzalez Papers, UT-CAH.

116. Department of Agriculture, "Termination of the Bracero Program: Some Effects on Farm Labor and Migrant Housing Needs," June 1965, File 1989/59-42, Good Neighbor Commission Papers, TSA.

117. Calavita, *Inside the State*, 144.

118. Good Neighbor Commission, "Mechanization and the Texas Migrant, 1966," March 1967, "Migrant Labor" Vertical File, UT-CAH.

119. "Texans Show Small Concern at Bracero Program's End," *Dallas Times Herald*, May 31, 1963.

120. "Farmers Themselves Actually Killed the Mexican Contract Worker Program," *Corpus Christi Caller*, June 9, 1963. See also the testimony of South Texas grower Othal Brand in U.S. Congress, Senate Committee on Labor and Public Welfare, *Amending Migratory Labor Laws*, 798–800.

121. Statement of Henry Muñoz before U.S. Department of Labor Hearings on Immigration and Nationality Act of 1952, December 4, 1964, Box 5, Folder 6, Series 7, AR-110, UTA. See also Testimony of Thomas L. Pitts before the Senate Committee on Agriculture, January 16, 1965, Box 2004-127/58, Bracero Program Folder, Henry B. Gonzalez Papers, UT-CAH.

122. Council of California Growers News Letter, Issue Number 71, October 14, 1963, Box 2004-127/393, Bracero Program Folder, Henry B. Gonzalez Papers, UT-CAH.

123. Wirtz, *Year of Transition*, 2.

124. One other important factor in the final end of the Bracero Program was an accident that occurred in California in September 1963, when a train struck a truck hauling fifty-six braceros and one undocumented Mexican worker, killing thirty-one. The crash revealed many of the problems inherent in the Bracero Program and served as a rallying point for those who sought to end it. For more on this event see Flores, "Town Full of Dead Mexicans," 125–43.

125. Coalson, *Development of the Migratory Farm Labor System in Texas*, 107; Unitarian Service Committee, "Border Trends," October 1948, Box 55, Folder 64, Hector Garcia Papers, TAMU-CC.

126. Gus Garcia to Robert Jackson, December 9, 1954, Box 1, Folder 1, Gus Garcia Papers, UT-Benson.

127. President's Commission on Migratory Labor, *Migratory Labor in American Agriculture*, 2.

128. Anonymous, quoted in Saunders and Leonard, *Wetback in the Lower Rio Grande Valley of Texas*, 66–67.

129. Anonymous, quoted in ibid., 67–68.

130. Willard Wirtz to Bill Moyers, January 21, 1966, LA5, Box 17, Folder "6/3/65-1/21/66," White House Central Files, Subject Files, Lyndon Baines Johnson Presidential Library, Austin, TX.

131. Ruth Graves (Research Director of Texas Committee on Migrant Farm Workers), "Research Summary on Effects of the Bracero Program," January 11, 1961, Box 3, Folder 8, Series 11, AR-278, UTA.

132. Texas Council on Migrant Labor, "Trends in Total Migration, 1962–1963," March 1964, Box 6, Folder 2, Jacob I. Rodriguez Papers, UT-Benson.

133. Texas Council on Migrant Labor, "Texas Migrant Workers—1961: Summary of Data," Box 9, Folder 5, AR-46, UTA.

134. Texas Council on Migrant Labor, "Trends in Total Migration, 1962–1963, March 1964," Box 6, Folder 2, Jacob I. Rodriguez Papers, UT-Benson.

135. Good Neighbor Commission, "Texas Migrant Labor, the 1965 Migration," May 1966, Box 137, Folder 45, Garcia Papers, TAMU-CC.

136. Good Neighbor Commission, "Trends in Migration, 1965–1966," February 1967, "Migrant Labor" Vertical Files, UT-CAH.

137. Corwin and Fogel, "Shadow Labor Force," 258.

138. Good Neighbor Commission, "Texas Migrant Labor, the 1965 Migration," May 1966, Box 137, Folder 45, Garcia Papers, TAMU-CC. See also Norris, *North for the Harvest*, 149.

139. Southwestern growers tried for several more years to receive Mexican contract workers through the H-2 program, but they were unsuccessful. In 1968, for instance, the Texas Citrus Mutual, a Rio Grande Valley farmers' association, requested workers directly from the Mexican government to alleviate a shortage they claimed would threaten the upcoming grapefruit harvest. They proposed that the workers be allowed in under Public Law 414. Secretaría de Relaciones Exteriores de México, *Memoria de la Secretaría por el periodo comprendido de 1 de septiembre de 1967 al 31 de agosto de 1968*, 101.

140. Hahamovitch, "Creating Perfect Immigrants," 84. For a theoretical and comparative perspective on migrant labor and guest workers, see Burawoy, "Functions and Reproduction of Migrant Labor," 1050–87.

141. The report of the President's Commission on Migratory Labor stated, "Beyond wanting migrants to be available when needed and to be gone when not needed, they are expected to work under conditions no longer typical or characteristic of the American standard of life." President's Commission on Migratory Labor, *Migratory Labor in American Agriculture*, 16.

142. Agricultural Workers Organizing Committee, AFL-CIO, "The Future Disposition of Public Law 78," August 30, 1959, File 1989/59-49, Good Neighbor Commission Papers, TSA.

143. The best sources on the global nature of guest worker programs are Hahamovitch, "Creating Perfect Immigrants," 69–94; and Hahamovitch, *No Man's Land*.

144. Hahamovitch, *No Man's Land*, 8–9.

145. Hahamovitch, "Creating Perfect Immigrants," 72–73.

146. Calavita, *Inside the State*, 21–22.

147. Majka and Majka, *Farm Workers, Agribusiness, and the State*, 137.

148. Ngai, *Impossible Subjects*, 139.

149. Galarza, *Merchants of Labor*, 258.

150. Agricultural Workers Organizing Committee, AFL-CIO, "The Future Disposition of Public Law 78," August 30, 1959, File 1989/59-49, Good Neighbor Commission Papers, TSA.

151. Hahamovitch, "Creating Perfect Immigrants," 93.

152. Cross and Sandos, *Across the Border*, 43.

153. For a recent perspective on guest workers and their impact on labor relations and labor conditions, see Ness, *Guest Workers and Resistance to U.S. Corporate Despotism*.

EPILOGUE

1. *Guadalupe Sosa, et al., V. Wailuku Agribusiness Co., Inc., Agricultural Labor Services of Hawaii, Inc., and Cristobal Gomez*, Civil Action No. M-92-129, United States District Court, Southern District of Texas, McAllen Division. Some additional details about the case came from conversations with Michael Kirkpatrick, the lawyer who tried the case for TRLA, and David Hall, TRLA's executive director.

2. Joint Pre-Trial Order, January 26, 1993; Plaintiff's First Amended Complaint, Item 37, February 4, 1993; Settlement Agreement, Item 85, January 24, 1994. Quotation from Settlement Agreement. The only mention of this case I have seen anywhere appeared in Plascencia, Glover, and Craddock, "Case Study of the Agricultural Labor Market in South Texas Winter Vegetable Production," 546.

3. On Hawaii's twentieth-century labor history, see Beechert, *Working in Hawaii*; Jung, *Reworking Race*; Horne, *Fighting in Paradise*; and Valdés, *Organized Agriculture and the Labor Movement before the UFW*, 107–68.

4. Deposition of Stephen W. Knox (president of Wailuku Agribusiness Corporation), Exhibit A, October 19–20, 1992; Joint Pre-Trial Order, January 26, 1993.

5. See Hitch, *Islands in Transition*, 194–95.

6. See also *Daniel Reyes, et al., v. Remington Hybrid Seed Company, Inc., et al.*, 495 F. 3d 403 (7th Cir. 2007). This case is almost exactly the same as *Sosa v. Wailuku*, with workers recruited from South Texas to Indiana under false promises by a contractor. Promised more than seventy hours of work each week, the migrants instead received barely twenty hours per week and were not even given their wages for that limited amount of work.

7. Plaintiff's Response to Defendant Wailuku Agribusiness Co.'s Second Amended Motion to Dismiss, Item 13, August 10, 1992; Brief in Support of Plaintiff's Motion for Partial Summary Judgment, Item 29, December 23, 1992.

8. See Hahamovitch, "Creating Perfect Immigrants," 69–94.

9. Andradet, "Biting the Hand That Feeds You," 620.

10. On early utility of contractor system, see Way, *Common Labor*, 51–150.

11. *Hodgson v. Griffin and Brand of McAllen, Inc.*, 471 F. 2d 235.

12. Linder, *Migrant Workers and Minimum Wages*, 179.

13. Ibid. A great example of the courts' nonresponsiveness to these sorts of issues can be found in Hahamovitch, *No Man's Land*, 172–226.

14. The Microsoft Corporation has done the same with many employees, claiming that they worked for wholly owned subsidiaries of Microsoft but were not eligible for things like the corporate retirement plan. See *Vizcaino, et al., v. Microsoft Corporation*, 97 F.3d 1187 (9th Cir. 1995) and 120 F.3d 1006 (9th Cir. 1997).

15. Ruckelshaus, "Labor's Wage War," 379–80.

16. VanderVelde, "Wal-Mart as a Phenomenon in the Legal World," 127.

17. Harold Meyerson, "Wal-Mart's Strategy of Deniability for Workers' Safety," *Washington Post*, November 27, 2012.

18. Schlosser, *Reefer Madness*, 216.

19. Tanger, "Enforcing Corporate Responsibility for Violations of Workplace Immigration Laws," 59.

20. Ibid., 73–74.

21. Compa, *Blood, Sweat, and Fear*, 114.

22. For a more complete picture of the chicken processing industry, see Striffler, *Chicken*.

23. Compa, *Blood, Sweat, and Fear*.

24. Ibid., 15–16.

25. Davis, foreword to Nevins, *Operation Gatekeeper*, x.

26. Davidson, *Race and Class in Texas Politics*, 113–17; Majka and Majka, *Farm Workers, Agribusiness, and the State*, 167; Martin, *Promise Unfulfilled*.

27. See Chavez, *Latino Threat*.

28. See Davis, *Magical Urbanism*, 59–65. Davis uses the notion of the "third border" to conceptualize the taint of illegality that follows Latino communities throughout the nation.

Bibliography

MANUSCRIPT COLLECTIONS

Arlington, Texas
    University of Texas–Arlington Special Collections, Texas Labor Archives
        Oral History Collection
        AR-7—Amalgamated Transit Union, Local 694, San Antonio, Texas
        AR-30—International Ladies' Garment Workers Union, Local 180, San
            Antonio, Texas
        AR-31—Ruth Allen Papers
        AR-36—Food, Tobacco, Agricultural, and Allied Workers Union of America
            Papers
        AR-46—Mexican-American Farm Workers' Movement Papers
        AR-49—International Brotherhood of Electrical Workers, Local 278,
            Corpus Christi, Texas
        AR-110—Texas AFL-CIO
        AR-127—George Lambert Papers
        AR-278—Texas AFL-CIO
Austin, Texas
    Lyndon Baines Johnson Presidential Library, Austin, Texas
        Connally, John, Papers
        White House Central Files
    Texas State Archives, Austin, Texas
        Adjutant General Department Records
        Adjutant General Annual and Biennial Reports
        Bureau of Labor Statistics Records
        Bureau of Labor Statistics Biennial Reports
        Colquitt, Oscar B., Gubernatorial Papers
        Farm Placement Service Records
        Farm Placement Service Annual Reports
        Ferguson, Miriam Amanda, Gubernatorial Papers
        Davenport, Harbert, Collection
        Good Neighbor Commission Records
        King Family Papers
        Moody, Dan, Gubernatorial Papers
        O'Daniel, W. Lee, Gubernatorial Papers
        Shivers, Allan, Gubernatorial Papers
        Stevenson, Coke, Gubernatorial Papers
    University of Texas–Austin, Benson Latin American Collection
        Buckley, William F., Sr., Papers

Castañeda, Carlos, Papers
de la Luz Sáenz, Jóse, Papers
de Luna, Andres, Papers
Flores, Maria G., Papers
Flores, William, Papers
Garcia, Gus, Papers
González, Manuel C., Papers
Idar, Ed, Papers
Munguía, Rómulo, Papers
Rodríguez, Jacob I., Papers
Sanchez, George I., Papers
Weeks, Oliver Douglas, Papers
University of Texas–Austin, Dolph Briscoe Center for American History
Allen, Ruth, Papers
Bentsen, Lloyd M., Jr., Papers
Colquitt, Oscar, Papers
Garner, John Nance, Papers
Gonzalez, Henry B., Papers
Labor Movement in Texas Collection
Maverick, Maury, Sr., Papers
Rayburn, Sam, Papers
Rice, Rob Roy, Papers
San Antonio Papers
Texas State Federation of Labor Papers
Vertical Files
Allee, A.Y.
Corpus Christi, Texas
Corpus Christi, Texas—History
Farm Workers
Harlingen, Texas
Labor and Laboring Classes
Labor Unions
Laredo, Texas
Laredo, Texas—Economic Conditions
Laredo, Texas—History
McAllen, Texas
Migrant Labor
Munguía, Rómulo
Rainey Controversy
San Antonio, Texas—Economic Conditions
San Antonio, Texas—Growth and Population
San Antonio, Texas—HemisFair
San Antonio, Texas—History
San Benito, Texas

Weslaco, Texas
Berkeley, California
   University of California, Berkeley, Bancroft Library
      Taylor, Paul S., Collection
College Park, Maryland
   National Archives and Records Administration
      Record Group 43, Records of International Conferences, Commissions, and
         Expositions
      Record Group 59, Central Files of the Department of State
      Record Group 60, General Records of the Department of Justice
      Record Group 76, Records of Boundary and Claims Commissions and
         Arbitrations
      Record Group 174, General Records of the Department of Labor
      Record Group 280, Records of the Federal Mediation and Conciliation
         Service
Corpus Christi, Texas
   Texas A&M University–Corpus Christi Archives
      Garcia, Hector, Papers
Edinburg, Texas
   University of Texas–Pan American Library Special Collections
      Shary, John H., Collection
Kingsville, Texas
   Texas A&M University–Kingsville, South Texas Archives
      Canales, J. T., Estate Collection
      Coalson, George Otis, Collection
      McNeil, Norman L., Music Collection
      Quarters Project Collection
San Antonio, Texas
   Institute of Texan Cultures Library, San Antonio, Texas, Oral History
         Collection
      Vertical Files
         Mexican
   Saint Mary's University Special Collections
      Carmelo Tranchese Collection
   University of Texas–San Antonio Archives
      Pan-American Round Table of San Antonio Collection
      San Antonio Fair, Inc., Collection
Washington, D.C.
   National Archives and Records Administration
      Record Group 85, Records of the Immigration and Naturalization Service
Williamsburg, Virginia
   Swem Library, College of William and Mary
      United States Department of Justice Peonage Files, 1901–1945
         (microfilm)

NEWSPAPERS

Carrizo Springs Javelin
Chicago Record-Herald
Chicano Times (San Antonio)
CIO News
Corpus Christi Caller-Times
Dallas News
Dallas Times-Herald
Denver Weekly
El Malcriado (Delano, California)
El Malcriado (McAllen)
El Paso Evening Post
El Pueblo (Mexico City)
El Rejidor (San Antonio)
Hidalgo County News (Edinburg)
Houston Chronicle
Houston Post

Laredo Times
La Voz de Esperanza (San Antonio)
London Times
New Orleans Times-Democrat
New York Times
San Antonio Express-News
San Antonio Light
San Antonio News
San Benito News
Saturday Evening Post
Texas Argus (San Antonio)
Valley Monitor (McAllen)
Valley Morning Star (Harlingen)
Washington Post
Weekly Dispatch (San Antonio)
Weslaco News

COURT CASES

Hodgson v. Griffin and Brand of McAllen, Inc., 471 F. 2d 235.

Reyes, Daniel, et al., v. Remington Hybrid Seed Company, Inc., et al. 495 F. 3d 403 (7th Cir. 2007).

Sosa, Guadalupe, et al., v. Wailuku Agribusiness Co., Inc., Agricultural Labor Services of Hawaii, Inc., and Cristobal Gomez. Civil Action No. M-92-129, United States District Court, Southern District of Texas, McAllen Division.

Vizcaino, et al., v. Microsoft Corporation. 97 F.3d 1187 (9th Cir. 1995) and 120 F.3d 1006 (9th Cir. 1997).

DISSERTATIONS AND THESES

Davis, Ronnie C., Sr. "Maury Maverick, Sr.: The Rise and Fall of a National Congressman." M.A. thesis, St. Mary's University, 1966.

DeStefanis, Anthony Roland. "Guarding Capital: Soldier Strikebreakers on the Long Road to the Ludlow Massacre." Ph.D. diss., College of William and Mary, 2004.

Gilbert, James Carl. "A Field Study in Mexico of the Mexican Repatriation Movement." M.A. thesis, University of Southern California, 1934.

Ledesma, Irene. "The New Deal Public Works Programs and Mexican-Americans in McAllen, Texas, 1933–36." M.A. thesis, Pan American University, 1977.

McKay, R. Reynolds. "Texas Mexican Repatriation during the Great Depression." Ph.D. diss., University of Oklahoma, Norman, 1982.

Meyers, William K. "Interest Group Conflict and Revolutionary Politics: A Social History of La Comarca Lagunera, 1888–1911." Ph.D. diss., University of Chicago, 1980.

Pastrano, José Guillermo. "Industrial Agriculture in the Peripheral South: State, Race, and the Politics of Migrant Labor in Texas, 1890–1930." Ph.D. diss., University of California, Santa Barbara, 2006.

Quezada, Juan Gilberto. "Father Carmelo Antonio Tranchese, S.J.: A Pioneer Social Worker in San Antonio, Texas, 1932–1953." M.A. thesis, St. Mary's University, 1972.

Ribb, Richard Henry. "José Tomás Canales and the Texas Rangers: Myth, Identity, and Power in South Texas, 1900–1920." Ph.D. diss., University of Texas, Austin, 2001.

Rodriguez, Marc Simon. "*Obreros Unidos*: Migration, Migrant Farm Worker Activism, and the Chicano Movement in Wisconsin and Texas, 1950–1980." Ph.D. diss., Northwestern University, 2000.

Sandos, James Anthony. "The Mexican Revolution and the United States, 1915–1917: The Impact of Conflict in the Tamaulipas-Texas Frontier upon the Emergence of Revolution." Ph.D. diss., University of California, Berkeley, 1978.

BOOKS, ARTICLES, ESSAYS, AND PAPERS

Acuña, Rodolfo. *Occupied America: A History of Chicanos*. 3rd ed. New York: Harper Collins, 1988.

Adelman, Jeremy, and Stephen Aron. "From Borderlands to Borders: Empires, Nation-States, and the Peoples in between in North American History." *American Historical Review* 104, no. 3 (June 1999): 814–41.

Aguila, Jaime R. "Mexican/U.S. Immigration Policy prior to the Great Depression." *Diplomatic History* 31, no. 2 (April 2007): 207–25.

Aguilar Camín, Héctor, and Lorenzo Meyer. *In the Shadow of the Mexican Revolution: Contemporary Mexican History, 1910–1989*. Austin: University of Texas Press, 1993.

Albro, Ward S. *Always a Rebel: Ricardo Flores Magón and the Mexican Revolution*. Fort Worth: Texas Christian University Press, 1992.

———. *To Die on Your Feet: The Life, Times, and Writings of Praxedis G. Guerrero*. Fort Worth: Texas Christian University Press, 1996.

Allen, Ruth A. *Chapters in the History of Organized Labor in Texas*. Austin: University of Texas Press, 1941.

Alonzo, Armando C. *Tejano Legacy: Rancheros and Settlers in South Texas, 1734–1900*. Albuquerque: University of New Mexico Press, 1998.

American Public Welfare Association. *Public Welfare Survey of San Antonio, Texas: A Study of a Local Community*. Chicago: American Public Welfare Association, 1940.

Anders, Evan. *Boss Rule in South Texas: The Progressive Era*. Austin: University of Texas Press, 1982.

Anderson, Benedict. *Imagined Communities: Reflection on the Origin and Spread of Nationalism*. New York: Verso, 1991.

Andradet, Sean A. "Biting the Hand That Feeds You: How Federal Law Has Permitted Employers to Violate the Basic Rights of Farmworkers and How This

Has Begun to Impact Other Industries." *University of Pennsylvania Journal of Labor and Employment Law* 4, no. 3 (2002): 601–21.

Andreas, Peter. *Border Games: Policing the U.S.-Mexico Divide*. Ithaca: Cornell University Press, 2000.

Andrews, Gregg. *Shoulder to Shoulder? The American Federation of Labor, the United States, and the Mexican Revolution, 1910–1924*. Berkeley: University of California Press, 1991.

Ankerson, Dudley. "Saturnino Cedillo, a Traditional Caudillo in San Luis Potosi, 1890–1938." In *Caudillo and Peasant in the Mexican Revolution*, edited by D. A. Brading, 140–68. New York: Cambridge University Press, 1980.

Arreola, Daniel D. *Tejano South Texas: A Mexican American Cultural Province*. Austin: University of Texas Press, 2002.

Bailey, David C. *Viva Cristo Rey: The Cristero Rebellion and the Church-State Conflict in Mexico*. Austin: University of Texas Press, 1974.

Balderrama, Francisco E., and Raymond Rodriguez. *Decade of Betrayal: Mexican Repatriation in the 1930s*. Albuquerque: University of New Mexico Press, 1995.

Barton, Josef. "Borderland Discontents: Mexican Migration in Regional Contexts, 1880–1930." In *Repositioning North American Migration History: New Directions in Modern Continental Migration, Citizenship, and Community*, edited by Marc S. Rodriguez, 141–205. Rochester, N.Y.: University of Rochester Press, 2004.

Bartra, Roger. *Agrarian Structure and Political Power in Mexico*. Baltimore: Johns Hopkins University Press, 1993.

Becker, Marjorie. *Setting the Virgin on Fire: Lázaro Cárdenas, Michoacán Peasants, and the Redemption of the Mexican Revolution*. Berkeley: University of California Press, 1995.

Beechert, Edward D. *Working in Hawaii: A Labor History*. Honolulu: University of Hawai'i Press, 1985.

Beezley, William H. *Judas at the Jockey Club and Other Episodes of Porfirian Mexico*. Lincoln: University of Nebraska Press, 1987.

———. "New Celebrations of Independence: Puebla (1869) and Mexico City (1883)." In *Viva Mexico, Viva la Independencia: Celebrations of September 16*, edited by William H. Beezley and David E. Lorey, 131–40. Wilmington, Del.: Scholarly Resources, 2001.

Beezley, William H., and David E. Lorey, eds. "Introduction: The Functions of Patriotic Ceremony in Mexico." In *Viva Mexico, Viva la Independencia: Celebrations of September 16*, edited by William H. Beezley and David E. Lorey, ix–xviii. Wilmington, Del.: Scholarly Resources, 2001.

———. *Viva Mexico, Viva la Independencia: Celebrations of September 16*. Wilmington, Del.: Scholarly Resources, 2001.

Benjamin, Thomas. "Introduction: Approaching the Porfiriato." In *Other Mexicos: Essays on Regional Mexican History, 1876–1911*, edited by Thomas Benjamin and William McNellie, 3–25. Albuquerque: University of New Mexico Press, 1984.

———. "Laboratories of the New State, 1920–1929: Regional Social Reform and Experiments in Mass Politics." In *Provinces of the Revolution: Essays on Regional Mexican History, 1910–1929*, edited by Thomas Benjamin and Mark Wasserman, 71–90. Albuquerque: University of New Mexico Press, 1990.

———. "Regionalizing the Revolution: The Many Mexicos in Revolutionary Historiography." In *Provinces of the Revolution: Essays on Regional Mexican History, 1910–1929*, edited by Thomas Benjamin and Mark Wasserman, 319–57. Albuquerque: University of New Mexico Press, 1990.

———. *La Revolución: Mexico's Great Revolution as Memory, Myth, and History.* Austin: University of Texas Press, 2000.

Benjamin, Thomas, and William McNellie, eds. *Other Mexicos: Essays on Regional Mexican History, 1876–1911.* Albuquerque: University of New Mexico Press, 1984.

Benjamin, Thomas, and Mark Wasserman, eds. *Provinces of the Revolution: Essays on Regional Mexican History, 1910–1929.* Albuquerque: University of New Mexico Press, 1990.

Benton-Cohen, Katherine. *Borderline Americans: Racial Division and Labor War in the Arizona Borderlands.* Cambridge: Harvard University Press, 2009.

Bethell, Leslie, ed. *Mexico since Independence.* New York: Cambridge University Press, 1991.

Blackwelder, Julia Kirk. "Texas Homeworkers in the 1930s." In *Homework: Historical and Contemporary Perspectives on Paid Labor at Home*, edited by Eileen Boris and Cynthia R. Daniels, 75–90. Urbana: University of Illinois Press, 1989.

———. *Women of the Depression: Caste and Culture in San Antonio, 1929–1939.* College Station: Texas A&M University Press, 1984.

Bodnar, John. *The Transplanted: A History of Immigrants in Urban America.* Bloomington: Indiana University Press, 1985.

Boris, Eileen, and Cynthia R. Daniels, eds. *Homework: Historical and Contemporary Perspectives on Paid Labor at Home.* Urbana: University of Illinois Press, 1989.

Boyer, Christopher R. *Becoming Campesinos: Politics, Identity, and Agrarian Struggle in Postrevolutionary Michoacan, 1920–1935.* Stanford, Calif.: Stanford University Press, 2003.

Brading, D. A., ed. *Caudillo and Peasant in the Mexican Revolution.* New York: Cambridge University Press, 1980.

Braverman, Harry. *Labor and Monopoly Capital: The Degradation of Work in the Twentieth Century.* New York: Monthly Review Press, 1974.

Bridges, Amy. "Boss Tweed and V. O. Key in Texas." In *Urban Texas: Politics and Development*, edited by Char Miller and Heywood T. Sanders, 58–71. College Station: Texas A&M University Press, 1990.

Briggs, Vernon M., Jr., Walter Fogel, and Fred H. Schmidt. *The Chicano Worker.* Austin: University of Texas Press, 1977.

Brinkley, Alan. *Voices of Protest: Huey Long, Father Coughlin, and the Great Depression.* New York: Vintage, 1982.

Britton, John A. *Revolution and Ideology: Images of the Mexican Revolution in the United States*. Lexington: University Press of Kentucky, 1995.

Brunn, Stanley D., ed. *Wal-Mart World: The World's Biggest Corporation in the Global Economy*. New York: Routledge, 2006.

Buitron, Richard A., Jr. *The Quest for Tejano Identity in San Antonio, Texas, 1913–2000*. New York: Routledge, 2004.

Bunche, Ralph J. *The Political Status of the Negro in the Age of FDR*. Chicago: University of Chicago Press, 1973.

Burawoy, Michael. "The Functions and Reproduction of Migrant Labor: Comparative Material from Southern Africa and the United States." *American Journal of Sociology* 81, no. 5 (1976): 1050–87.

Cahill, Kevin J. "The U.S. Bank Panic of 1907 and Mexican Depression of 1908–1909." *Historian* 60, no. 4 (June 1998): 795–811.

Calavita, Kitty. *Inside the State: The Bracero Program, Immigration, and the I.N.S.* New York: Routledge, 1992.

Calderon, Roberto R. *Mexican Coal Mining Labor in Texas and Coahuila, 1880–1930*. College Station: Texas A&M University Press, 2000.

Campbell, Randolph B. *Gone to Texas: A History of the Lone Star State*. New York: Oxford University Press, 2003.

Cannadine, David. "The Context, Performance and Meaning of Ritual: The British Monarchy and the 'Invention of Tradition,' c. 1820–1977." In *The Invention of Tradition*, edited by Eric Hobsbawm and Terence Ranger, 101–64. New York: Cambridge University Press, 1983.

Cardoso, Lawrence. *Mexican Emigration to the United States, 1897–1931: Socio-economic Patterns*. Tucson: University of Arizona Press, 1980.

Carr, Barry. "The Peculiarities of the Mexican North, 1880–1928: An Essay in Interpretation." University of Glasgow, Institute of Latin-American Studies Occasional Papers no. 4, 1971.

Carroll, Patrick J. *Felix Longoria's Wake: Bereavement, Racism, and the Rise of Mexican American Activism*. Austin: University of Texas Press, 2003.

Caulfield, John H. *Migration to Nowhere: FSA Labor Camps in South Texas Mark Breakdown of Small Farm System*. Washington, D.C.: Farm Security Administration, 1939.

Chavez, Leo R. *The Latino Threat: Constructing Immigrants, Citizens, and the Nation*. Stanford, Calif.: Stanford University Press, 2008.

Clark, John E. *The Fall of the Duke of Duval: A Prosecutor's Journal*. Austin, Tex.: Eakin, 1995.

Clark, John W., Jr., and Ana Maria Juarez. *Urban Archaeology: A Culture History of a Mexican-American Barrio in Laredo, Webb County, Texas*. Austin: Texas State Department of Highways and Public Transportation, 1986.

Coalson, George O. *The Development of the Migratory Farm Labor System in Texas: 1900–1954*. San Francisco: R&E Research Associates, 1977.

Cobble, Dorothy Sue. *The Other Women's Movement: Workplace Justice and Social Rights in Modern America*. Princeton, N.J.: Princeton University Press, 2004.

Cockcroft, James D. *Intellectual Precursors of the Mexican Revolution, 1900–1913*. Austin: University of Texas Press, 1968.

———. *Mexico: Class Formation, Capital Accumulation, and the State*. New York: Monthly Review Press, 1983.

Coerver, Don M., and Linda B. Hall. *Texas and the Mexican Revolution: A Study in State and National Border Policy, 1910–1920*. San Antonio, Tex.: Trinity University Press, 1984.

Cohen, Deborah. *Braceros: Migrant Citizens and Transnational Subjects in the Postwar United States and Mexico*. Chapel Hill: University of North Carolina Press, 2011.

Cohen, Lizabeth. *Making a New Deal: Industrial Workers in Chicago, 1919–1939*. New York: Cambridge University Press, 1990.

Cohn, Bernard S. "Representing Authority in Victorian India." In *The Invention of Tradition*, edited by Eric Hobsbawm and Terence Ranger, 165–209. New York: Cambridge University Press, 1983.

Compa, Lance. *Blood, Sweat, and Fear: Workers' Rights in U.S. Meat and Poultry Plants*. Washington, D.C.: Human Rights Watch, 2004.

Cornelius, Wayne A., Takeyuki Tsuda, Philip L. Martin, and James L. Hollifield, eds. *Controlling Immigration: A Global Perspective*. 2nd ed. Stanford, Calif.: Stanford University Press, 2004.

Corwin, Arthur F. "Early Mexican Labor Migration: A Frontier Sketch, 1848–1900." In *Immigrants—and Immigrants: Perspectives on Mexican Labor Migration to the United States*, edited by Arthur F. Corwin, 25–37. Westport, Conn.: Greenwood, 1978.

———. *Immigrants—and Immigrants: Perspectives on Mexican Labor Migration to the United States*. Westport, Conn.: Greenwood, 1978.

———. "Mexican Policy and Ambivalence toward Labor Emigration to the United States." In *Immigrants—and Immigrants: Perspectives on Mexican Labor Migration to the United States*, edited by Arthur F. Corwin, 176–224. Westport, Conn.: Greenwood, 1978.

———. "¿Quién Sabe? Mexican Migration Statistics." In *Immigrants—and Immigrants: Perspectives on Mexican Labor Migration to the United States*, edited by Arthur F. Corwin, 108–35. Westport, Conn.: Greenwood, 1978.

———. "A Story of Ad Hoc Exemptions: American Immigration Policy toward Mexico." In *Immigrants—and Immigrants: Perspectives on Mexican Labor Migration to the United States*, edited by Arthur F. Corwin, 136–75. Westport, Conn.: Greenwood, 1978.

———. "The Study and Interpretation of Mexican Labor Migration: An Introduction." In *Immigrants—and Immigrants: Perspectives on Mexican Labor Migration to the United States*, edited by Arthur F. Corwin, 3–24. Westport, Conn.: Greenwood, 1978.

Corwin, Arthur F., and Lawrence A. Cardoso. "Vamos al Norte: Causes of Mass Mexican Migration to the United States." In *Immigrants—and Immigrants: Perspectives on Mexican Labor Migration to the United States*, edited by Arthur F. Corwin, 38–66. Westport, Conn.: Greenwood, 1978.

Corwin, Arthur F., and Walter A. Fogel. "Shadow Labor Force: Mexican Workers in the American Economy." In *Immigrants—and Immigrants: Perspectives on Mexican Labor Migration to the United States*, edited by Arthur F. Corwin, 257–304. Westport, Conn.: Greenwood, 1978.

Corwin, Arthur F., and Johnny M. McCain. "Wetbackism since 1964: A Catalogue of Factors." In *Immigrants—and Immigrants: Perspectives on Mexican Labor Migration to the United States*, edited by Arthur F. Corwin, 67–107. Westport, Conn.: Greenwood, 1978.

Cosio Villegas, Daniel. *American Extremes*, translated by Américo Paredes. Austin: University of Texas Press, 1964.

Council on Foreign Relations. *Survey of American Foreign Relations*. Vol. 4. New Haven, Conn.: Yale University Press, 1931.

Craig, Richard B. *The Bracero Program: Interest Groups and Foreign Policy*. Austin: University of Texas Press, 1971.

Cross, Harry E., and James A. Sandos. *Across the Border: Rural Development in Mexico and Recent Migration to the United States*. Berkeley: University of California Institute of Governmental Studies, 1981.

Croxdale, Richard. "Pecan Shellers." *Texas Humanist*, April 1979, 1, 8–9.

Daniel, Cletus E. *Bitter Harvest: A History of California Farmworkers, 1870–1945*. Chapel Hill: University of North Carolina Press, 1981.

Davidson, Chandler. *Race and Class in Texas Politics*. Princeton, N.J.: Princeton University Press, 1990.

Davis, Mike. *Ecology of Fear: Los Angeles and the Imagination of Disaster*. New York: Vintage, 1998.

———. Foreword to Joseph Nevins, *Operation Gatekeeper: The Rise of the "Illegal Alien" and the Making of the U.S.-Mexico Boundary*. New York: Routledge, 2002.

———. *In Praise of Barbarians: Essays against Empire*. Chicago: Haymarket, 2007.

———. *Late Victorian Holocausts: El Niño Famines and the Making of the Third World*. New York: Verso, 2002.

———. *Magical Urbanism: Latinos Reinvent the U.S. City*. New York: Verso, 2000.

———. *Planet of Slums*. New York: Verso, 2006.

de la Garza, Beatriz. *A Law for the Lion: A Tale of Crime and Injustice in the Borderlands*. Austin: University of Texas Press, 2003.

de León, Arnoldo. *In Re Ricardo Rodríguez: An Attempt at Chicano Disfranchisement in San Antonio, 1896–1897*. San Antonio, Tex.: Caravel, 1979.

———. *The Tejano Community, 1836–1890*. Albuquerque: University of New Mexico Press, 1982.

———. *They Called Them Greasers: Anglo Attitudes toward Mexicans in Texas, 1821–1900*. Austin: University of Texas Press, 1983.

de León, Arnoldo, and Kenneth L. Stewart. *Not Room Enough: Mexicans, Anglos, and Socioeconomic Change in Texas, 1850–1900*. Albuquerque: University of New Mexico Press, 1993.

Deutsch, Sarah. *No Separate Refuge: Culture, Class, and Gender on an Anglo-Hispanic Frontier in the American Southwest, 1880-1940*. New York: Oxford University Press, 1987.

Doyle, Judith Kaaz. "Maury Maverick and Racial Politics in San Antonio, Texas, 1938-1941." *Journal of Southern History* 53, no. 2 (May 1987): 194-224.

Driscoll, Barbara A. *The Tracks North: The Railroad Bracero Program of World War II*. Austin: University of Texas Press, 1999.

Eckam, Tad. "Public Housing Day Comes to San Antonio." *America*, August 31, 1940, 570-71.

Falcón, Romana. "Force and the Search for Consent: The Role of the *Jefaturas Políticas* of Coahuila in National State Formation." In *Everyday Forms of State Formation: Revolution and the Negotiation of Rule in Modern Mexico*, edited by Gilbert M. Joseph and Daniel Nugent, 107-34. Durham, N.C.: Duke University Press, 1994.

———. "San Luis Potosi: Confiscated Estates—Revolutionary Conquests or Spoils?" In *Provinces of the Revolution: Essays on Regional Mexican History, 1910-1929*, edited by Thomas Benjamin and Mark Wasserman, 133-62. Albuquerque: University of New Mexico Press, 1990.

Fehrenbach, T. R. *Lone Star: A History of Texas and the Texans*. New York: Collier, 1968.

Fitzgerald, Deborah. *Every Farm a Factory: The Industrial Ideal in American Agriculture*. New Haven, Conn.: Yale University Press, 2003.

Flores, Lori. "A Town Full of Dead Mexicans: The Salinas Valley Tragedy of 1963, the End of the Bracero Program, and the Evolution of California's Chicano Movement." *Western Historical Quarterly* 44 (Summer 2013): 125-43.

Flores Magón, Ricardo. *Land and Liberty: Anarchist Influences in the Mexican Revolution*. Sanday, U.K.: Cienfuegos, 1977.

Flores Magón, Ricardo, et al. *Obras completas: Correspondencia*. 2 vols. Mexico City: Consejo Nacional para la Cultura y las Artes, 2000.

———. *Regeneración, 1900-1918: La corriente más radical de la Revolución mexicana de 1910 a través de su periódico de combate*. Mexico City: Era, 1977.

Foerster, Robert F. *The Racial Problems Involved in Immigration from Latin America and the West Indies to the United States: A Report Submitted to the Secretary of Labor*. Washington, D.C.: Government Printing Office, 1925.

Foley, Douglas E., et al. *From Peones to Politicos: Class and Ethnicity in a South Texas Town, 1900-1987*. Austin: University of Texas, 1988.

Foley, Neil. "Mexicans, Mechanization, and the Growth of Corporate Cotton Culture in South Texas: The Taft Ranch, 1900-1930." *Journal of Southern History* 62, no. 2 (May 1996): 275-302.

———. *The White Scourge: Mexicans, Blacks, and Poor Whites in Texas Cotton Culture*. Berkeley: University of California Press, 1997.

Friedrich, Paul. *Agrarian Revolt in a Mexican Village*. Chicago: University of Chicago Press, 1977.

Fuentes, Carlos. *A New Time for Mexico*. New York: Farrar, Straus, and Giroux, 1996.

Gabaccia, Donna R. "Constructing North America: Railroad Building and the Rise of Continental Migrations, 1850–1914." In *Repositioning North American Migration History: New Directions in Modern Continental Migration, Citizenship, and Community*, edited by Marc S. Rodriguez, 27–53. Rochester, N.Y.: University of Rochester Press, 2004.

Galarza, Ernesto. *Barrio Boy*. Notre Dame, Ind.: University of Notre Dame Press, 1971.

———. *Farm Workers and Agri-business in California, 1947–1960*. Notre Dame, Ind.: University of Notre Dame Press, 1977.

———. *Man of Fire: Selected Writings*. Edited by Armando Ibarra and Rodolfo D. Torres. Urbana: University of Illinois Press, 2013.

———. *Merchants of Labor: The Mexican Bracero Story*. Santa Barbara: McNally and Loftin, 1964.

———. *Strangers in our Fields*. 2nd ed. Washington, D.C.: Joint United States–Mexico Trade Union Committee, 1956.

Gamio, Manuel. *The Life Story of the Mexican Immigrant*. New York: Dover, 1971 [1931].

———. *Mexican Immigration to the United States: A Study of Human Migration and Adjustment*. New York: Dover, 1971 [1930].

Gamio, Manuel, and José Vasconcelos. *Aspects of Mexican Civilization*. Chicago: University of Chicago Press, 1926.

García, Ignacio M. *United We Win: The Rise and Fall of La Raza Unida Party*. Tucson: University of Arizona Press, 1989.

García, Juan Ramón. *Operation Wetback: The Mass Deportation of Mexican Undocumented Workers in 1954*. Westport, Conn.: Greenwood, 1980.

García, Mario T. *Mexican Americans: Leadership, Ideology, and Identity, 1930–1960*. New Haven, Conn.: Yale University Press, 1989.

Garcia, Richard A. *Rise of the Mexican American Middle Class: San Antonio, 1929–1941*. College Station: Texas A&M University Press, 1991.

García Tellez, Ignacio. *La migración de braceros a los Estados Unidos de Norteamérica*. Mexico City: n.p., 1955.

Gilly, Adolfo. *The Mexican Revolution*. New York: New Press, 2005.

Gledhill, John. *Casi Nada: A Study of Agrarian Reform in the Homeland of Cardenismo*. Austin: University of Texas Press, 1991.

Gómez-Quiñones, Juan. *Chicano Politics: Reality and Promise, 1940–1990*. Albuquerque: University of New Mexico Press, 1990.

———. *Development of the Mexican Working Class North of the Rio Bravo: Work and Culture among Laborers and Artisans, 1600–1900*. Los Angeles: Chicano Studies Research Center Publications, University of California, Los Angeles, 1982.

González, Gilbert G. *Mexican Consuls and Labor Organizing: Imperial Politics in the American Southwest*. Austin: University of Texas Press, 1999.

Gonzalez, Gilbert G., and Raul A. Fernandez. *A Century of Chicano History: Empire, Nations, and Migration*. New York: Routledge, 2003.

González Navarro, Moisés. *Los extranjeros en México y los mexicanos en el extranjero, 1821–1970*. Vol. 3. Mexico City: Colegio de México, 1994.

———. *México: El capitalismo nacionalista*. Guadalajara: Universidad de Guadalajara, 2003.

———. *Mexico: The Lop-sided Revolution*. London: Oxford University Press, 1965.

Granneberg, Audrey. "Maury Maverick's San Antonio." *Survey Graphic* 28, no. 7 (July 1939), 421–266.

Green, George Norris. *The Establishment in Texas Politics: The Primitive Years, 1938–1957*. Norman: University of Oklahoma Press, 1979.

———. "ILGWU in Texas, 1930–1970." *Journal of Mexican-American History*, Spring 1971, 144–69.

Guerin-Gonzales, Camille. *Mexican Workers and American Dreams: Immigration, Repatriation, and California Farm Labor, 1900–1939*. New Brunswick, N.J.: Rutgers University Press, 1994.

Gutiérrez, David G. *Walls and Mirrors: Mexican Americans, Mexican Immigrants, and the Politics of Ethnicity*. Berkeley: University of California Press, 1995.

Gutiérrez, José Angel. *The Making of a Chicano Militant: Lessons from Cristal*. Madison: University of Wisconsin Press, 1998.

Gutman, Herbert G. *Work, Culture, and Society in Industrializing America: Essays in American Working-Class and Social History*. New York: Knopf, 1976.

Hahamovitch, Cindy. "Creating Perfect Immigrants: Guestworkers of the World in Historical Perspective." *Labor History* 44, no. 1 (2003): 69–94.

———. *The Fruits of Their Labor: Atlantic Coast Farmworkers and the Making of Migrant Poverty, 1870–1945*. Chapel Hill: University of North Carolina Press, 1997.

———. *No Man's Land: Jamaican Guestworkers in America and the Global History of Deportable Labor*. Princeton, N.J.: Princeton University Press, 2011.

Hahamovitch, Cindy, and Rick Halpern. "Not a 'Sack of Potatoes': Why Labor Historians Need to Take Agriculture Seriously." *International Labor and Working-Class History* 65 (Spring 2004): 3–10.

Hale, Charles A. *The Transformation of Liberalism in Late Nineteenth-Century Mexico*. Princeton, N.J.: Princeton University Press, 1989.

Hamilton, Nora. *The Limits of State Autonomy: Post-revolutionary Mexico*. Princeton, N.J.: Princeton University Press, 1982.

Hancock, Richard H. *The Role of the Bracero in the Economic and Cultural Dynamics of Mexico: A Case Study of Chihuahua*. Stanford, Calif.: Hispanic American Society, 1959.

Handlin, Oscar. *The Uprooted: The Epic Story of the Great Migrations That Made the American People*. Boston: Little, Brown, 1951

Hansen, Roger D. *The Politics of Mexican Development*. Baltimore: Johns Hopkins University Press, 1974.

Harris, Charles H., III, and Louis R. Sadler. *The Texas Rangers and the Mexican Revolution: The Bloodiest Decade, 1910–1920*. Albuquerque: University of New Mexico Press, 2004.

Hart, John Mason. *Empire and Revolution: The Americans in Mexico since the Civil War*. Berkeley: University of California Press, 2002.

———. "The Evolution of the Mexican and Mexican-American Working Classes." In *Border Crossings: Mexican and Mexican-American Workers*, edited by John Mason Hart, 1–26. Wilmington, Del.: Scholarly Resources, 1998.

———. *Revolutionary Mexico: The Coming and Process of the Mexican Revolution.* 10th anniversary ed. Berkeley: University of California Press, 1997.

———, ed. *Border Crossings: Mexican and Mexican-American Workers.* Wilmington, Del.: Scholarly Resources, 1998.

HemisFair 1968 Official Souvenir Guidebook. Dallas: A. H. Belo, 1968.

Henderson, Richard B. *Maury Maverick: A Political Biography.* Austin: University of Texas Press, 1970.

Hernández, Kelly Lytle. *Migra! A History of the U.S. Border Patrol.* Berkeley: University of California Press, 2010.

Hietala, Thomas R. *Manifest Design: Anxious Aggrandizement in Late Jacksonian America.* Ithaca, N.Y.: Cornell University Press, 1985.

Higbie, Frank Tobias. *Indispensable Outcasts: Hobo Workers and Community in the American Midwest, 1880–1930.* Urbana: University of Illinois Press, 2003.

High, Stanley. "The Neo–New Dealers." *Saturday Evening Post,* May 22, 1937, 10–11, 105–9.

Higham, John. *Strangers in the Land: Patterns of American Nativism, 1860–1925.* New Brunswick, N.J.: Rutgers University Press, 1955.

Hitch, Thomas Kemper. *Islands in Transition: The Past, Present, and Future of Hawaii's Economy.* Honolulu: First Hawaiian Bank, 1992.

Hobsbawm, Eric. "Introduction: Inventing Traditions." In *The Invention of Tradition,* edited by Eric Hobsbawm and Terence Ranger, 1–14. New York: Cambridge University Press, 1983.

———. "Mass-Producing Traditions: Europe, 1870–1914." In *The Invention of Tradition,* edited by Eric Hobsbawm and Terence Ranger, 263–307. New York: Cambridge University Press, 1983.

Hobsbawm, Eric, and Terence Ranger, eds. *The Invention of Tradition.* New York: Cambridge University Press, 1983.

Hodgdon, A. Dana. "Extension of Administrative Authority in Immigration Regulation." *American Foreign Service Journal* 8, no. 2 (February 1931): 45–49, 84–86.

Hoffman, Abraham. *Unwanted Mexican Americans in the Great Depression: Repatriation Pressures, 1929–1939.* Tucson: University of Arizona Press, 1974.

Holmesly, Sterlin. *HemisFair '68 and the Transformation of San Antonio.* San Antonio, Tex.: Maverick, 2003.

Horne, Gerald. *Black and Brown: African Americans and the Mexican Revolution, 1910–1920.* New York: New York University Press, 2005.

———. *Fighting in Paradise: Labor Unions, Racism, and Communists in the Making of Modern Hawaii.* Honolulu: University of Hawai'i Press, 2011.

Jacobson, Matthew Frye. *Barbarian Virtues: The United States Encounters Foreign Peoples at Home and Abroad, 1876–1917.* New York: Hill and Wang, 2000.

Jamieson, Stuart. *Labor Unionism in American Agriculture.* U.S. Department of Labor, Bureau of Labor Statistics Bulletin, no. 836. Washington, D.C.: Government Printing Office, 1945.

Johns, Michael. *The City of Mexico in the Age of Díaz.* Austin: University of Texas Press, 1997.

Johnson, Benjamin Heber. *Revolution in Texas: How a Forgotten Rebellion and Its Bloody Suppression Turned Mexicans into Americans.* New Haven, Conn.: Yale University Press, 2003.

Johnson, David R. "Frugal and Sparing: Interest Groups, Politics, and City Building in San Antonio, 1870–85." In *Urban Texas: Politics and Development,* edited by Char Miller and Heywood T. Sanders, 33–57. College Station: Texas A&M University Press, 1990.

Johnson, David R., John A. Booth, and Richard J. Harris. *The Politics of San Antonio: Community, Progress, and Power.* Lincoln: University of Nebraska Press, 1983.

Jones, Lamar Babington. *Mexican-American Labor Problems in Texas.* San Francisco: R&E Research Associates, 1971.

Jordan, Terry G. *North American Cattle-Ranching Frontiers: Origins, Diffusion, and Differentiation.* Albuquerque: University of New Mexico Press, 1993.

Joseph, Gilbert M. "On the Trail of Latin American Bandits: A Reexamination of Peasant Resistance." *Latin American Research Review* 25, no. 3 (1990): 7–53.

———. "Popular Culture and State Formation in Revolutionary Mexico." In *Everyday Forms of State Formation: Revolution and the Negotiation of Rule in Modern Mexico,* edited by Gilbert M. Joseph and Daniel Nugent, 3–23. Durham, N.C.: Duke University Press, 1994.

———, ed. *Reclaiming the Political in Latin American History: Views from the North.* Durham, N.C.: Duke University Press, 2001.

Joseph, Gilbert M., and Timothy J. Henderson, eds. *The Mexico Reader: History, Culture, Politics.* Durham, N.C.: Duke University Press, 2002.

Joseph, Gilbert M., Catherine C. LeGrand, and Ricardo D. Salvatore, eds. *Close Encounters of Empire: Writing the Cultural History of U.S.-Latin American Relations.* Durham, N.C.: Duke University Press, 1998.

Joseph, Gilbert M., and Daniel Nugent, eds. *Everyday Forms of State Formation: Revolution and the Negotiation of Rule in Modern Mexico.* Durham, N.C.: Duke University Press, 1994.

Joseph, Gilbert M., and Allen Wells. *Summer of Discontent, Seasons of Upheaval: Elite Politics and Rural Insurgency in Yucatán, 1876–1915.* Stanford, Calif.: Stanford University Press, 1996.

Jung, Moon-Kie. *Reworking Race: The Making of Hawaii's Interracial Labor Movement.* New York: Columbia University Press, 2006.

Kanstroom, Daniel. *Deportation Nation: Outsiders in American History.* Cambridge: Harvard University Press, 2007.

Kaplowitz, Craig A. *LULAC, Mexican Americans, and National Policy.* College Station: Texas A&M University Press, 1993.

Katz, Friedrich. "The Liberal Republic and the Porfiriato, 1867–1910." In *Mexico since Independence*, edited by Leslie Bethell, 49–124. New York: Cambridge University Press, 1991.

——."Pancho Villa, Peasant Movements, and Agrarian Reform in Northern Mexico." In *Caudillo and Peasant in the Mexican Revolution*, edited by D. A. Brading, 59–75. New York: Cambridge University Press, 1980.

——. *The Secret War in Mexico: Europe, the United States, and the Mexican Revolution*. Chicago: University of Chicago Press, 1981.

Kelley, Robin D. G. *Race Rebels: Culture, Politics, and the Black Working Class*. New York: Free Press, 1994.

Kelly, Brian. *Race, Class, and Power in the Alabama Coalfields, 1908–1921*. Urbana: University of Illinois Press, 2001.

Kessler-Harris, Alice. *Out to Work: A History of Wage-Earning Women in the United States*. New York: Oxford University Press, 1982.

Kester, Howard. *Revolt among the Sharecroppers*, edited by Alex Lichtenstein. Knoxville: University of Tennessee Press, 1997 [1936].

Kirstein, Peter R. *Anglo over Bracero: A History of the Mexican Worker in the United States from Roosevelt to Nixon*. San Francisco: R&E Research Associates, 1977.

Knight, Alan. *The Mexican Revolution*. Vol. 1, *Porfirians, Liberals, and Peasants*. New York: Cambridge University Press, 1986.

——. *The Mexican Revolution*. Vol. 2, *Counter-revolution and Reconstruction*. Lincoln: University of Nebraska Press, 1986.

——. "Peasant and Caudillo in Revolutionary Mexico, 1910–1917." In *Caudillo and Peasant in the Mexican Revolution*, edited by D. A. Brading, 17–58. New York: Cambridge University Press, 1980.

——. "Revolutionary Project, Recalcitrant People: Mexico, 1910–1940." In *The Revolutionary Process in Mexico: Essays on Political and Social Change, 1880–1940*, edited by Jaime E. Rodriguez, 227–64. Los Angeles: UCLA Latin American Center Publications, 1990.

——. "The Rise and Fall of Cardenismo, c.1930–c.1946." In *Mexico since Independence*, edited by Leslie Bethell, 241–320. New York: Cambridge University Press, 1991.

——. "The United States and the Mexican Peasantry, circa 1880–1940." In *Rural Revolt in Mexico: U.S. Intervention and the Domain of Subaltern Politics*, edited by Daniel Nugent, 25–63. Durham, N.C.: Duke University Press, 1998.

——. "Weapons and Arches in the Mexican Revolutionary Landscape." In *Everyday Forms of State Formation: Revolution and the Negotiation of Rule in Modern Mexico*, edited by Gilbert M. Joseph and Daniel Nugent, 24–66. Durham, N.C.: Duke University Press, 1994.

Knippa, Lyndon Gayle. "San Antonio II: The Early New Deal." In *Texas Cities and the Great Depression*, 69–90. Austin: Texas Memorial Museum, 1973.

LaFeber, Walter. *The New Empire: An Interpretation of American Expansion, 1860–1898*. Ithaca, N.Y.: Cornell University Press, 1998 [1963].

LaFrance, David. "Many Causes, Movements, Failures, 1910–1913: The Regional Nature of Maderismo." In *Provinces of the Revolution: Essays on Regional Mexican History, 1910–1929*, edited by Thomas Benjamin and Mark Wasserman, 17–40. Albuquerque: University of New Mexico Press, 1990.

Lamar, Howard R. *Texas Crossings: The Lone Star State and the American Far West, 1836–1986*. Austin: University of Texas Press, 1991.

Langham, Thomas C. *Border Trials: Ricardo Flores Magón and the Mexican Liberals*. El Paso, Tex.: Texas Western Press, 1981.

Langston, William Stanley. "Coahuila: Centralization against State Autonomy." In *Other Mexicos: Essays on Regional Mexican History, 1876–1911*, edited by Thomas Benjamin and William McNellie, 55–76. Albuquerque: University of New Mexico Press, 1984.

Lázaro Salinas, José. *La emigración de braceros: Visión objetiva de un problema mexicano*. Mexico City: Cuauhtémoc, 1955.

Limerick, Patricia Nelson. *The Legacy of Conquest: The Unbroken Past of the American West*. New York: Norton, 1987.

Linder, Marc. *Migrant Workers and Minimum Wages: Regulating the Exploitation of Agricultural Labor in the United States*. Boulder, Colo.: Westview, 1992.

Lloyd, Jane-Dale. "Rancheros and Rebellion: The Case of Northwestern Chihuahua, 1905–1909." In *Rural Revolt in Mexico: U.S. Intervention and the Domain of Subaltern Politics*, edited by Daniel Nugent, 107–33. Durham, N.C.: Duke University Press, 1998.

Lorey, David E. *United States–Mexico Border Statistics since 1900: 1990 Update*. Los Angeles: UCLA Latin American Center Publications, 1993.

———. *The U.S.-Mexican Border in the Twentieth Century*. Wilmington, Del.: Scholarly Resources, 1999.

Maciel, David. *La clase obrera en la historia de México*. Vol. 17, *Al norte del Rio Bravo (pasado inmediato) (1930–1981)*. Mexico City: Siglo Veintiuno, 1981.

MacLachlan, Colin M. *Anarchism and the Mexican Revolution: The Political Trials of Ricardo Flores Magón in the United States*. Berkeley, Calif.: University of California Press, 1991.

MacLean, Nancy. *Freedom Is Not Enough: The Opening of the American Workplace*. Cambridge: Harvard University Press, 2006.

Madsen, William. *Mexican-Americans of South Texas*. New York: Holt, Rinehart and Winston, 1964.

Majka, Linda C., and Theo J. Majka. *Farm Workers, Agribusiness, and the State*. Philadelphia: Temple University Press, 1982.

Mallon, Florencia E. *Peasant and Nation: The Making of Postcolonial Mexico and Peru*. Berkeley: University of California Press, 1995.

Manaster, Jane. *Pecans: The Story in a Nutshell*. Lubbock: Texas Tech University Press, 2008.

Mapes, Kathleen. "'A Special Class of Labor': Mexican (Im)migrants, Immigration Debate, and Industrial Agriculture in the Rural Midwest." *Labor: Studies in Working-Class History of the Americas* 1, no. 2 (2004): 65–88.

———. *Sweet Tyranny: Migrant Labor, Industrial Agriculture, and Imperial Politics*. Urbana: University of Illinois Press, 2009.

Maril, Robert Lee. *Poorest of Americans: The Mexican-Americans of the Lower Rio Grande Valley of Texas*. Notre Dame, Ind.: University of Notre Dame Press, 1989.

Márquez, Benjamin. *LULAC: The Evolution of a Mexican American Political Organization*. Austin: University of Texas Press, 1993.

Martin, Philip L. "Guest Workers: Past and Present." In *Migration Between Mexico and the United States: Binational Study*, 3:877–95. Washington, D.C.: U.S. Commission on Immigration Reform, 1998.

———. *Promise Unfulfilled: Unions, Immigration, and the Farm Workers*. Ithaca, N.Y.: Cornell University Press, 2003.

———. "The United States: The Continuing Immigration Debate." In *Controlling Immigration: A Global Perspective*, edited by Wayne A. Cornelius, Takeyuki Tsuda, Philip L. Martin, and James L. Hollifield, 2nd ed., 51–85. Stanford, Calif.: Stanford University Press, 2004.

Martin, Philip L., Manolo Abella, and Christiane Kuptsch. *Managing Labor Migration in the Twenty-First Century*. New Haven, Conn.: Yale University Press, 2006.

Martinez, John Ramon. *Mexican Emigration to the United States, 1910–1930*. San Francisco: R&E Research Associates, 1971.

Martínez, Oscar J. *Border People: Life and Society in the U.S.-Mexico Borderlands*. Tucson: University of Arizona Press, 1994.

———. *Troublesome Border*. Tucson: University of Arizona Press, 1988.

Matthiessen, Peter. *Sal Si Puedes (Escape If You Can): Cesar Chavez and the New American Revolution*. Berkeley: University of California Press, 2000 [1969].

Maverick, Maury. *A Maverick American*. New York: Covici Friede, 1937.

Maverick, Maury, Jr. *Texas Iconoclast*. Fort Worth: Texas Christian University Press, 1997.

Mazón, Mauricio. *The Zoot-Suit Riots: The Psychology of Symbolic Annihilation*. Austin: University of Texas Press, 1984.

McBride, John. *Vanishing Bracero: Valley Revolution*. San Antonio, Tex.: Naylor, 1963.

McKiernan-González, John. *Fevered Measures: Public Health and Race at the Texas-Mexico Border, 1848–1942*. Durham, N.C.: Duke University Press, 2012.

McWilliams, Carey. *Factories in the Field: The Story of Migratory Farm Labor in California*. Berkeley: University of California Press, 1939.

———. "Getting Rid of the Mexican." *American Mercury* 28 (March 1933): 322–24.

———. *Ill Fares the Land: Migrants and Migratory Labor in the United States*. New York: Barnes and Noble, 1967 [1942].

———. *North from Mexico: The Spanish-Speaking People of the United States*. New York: Praeger, 1948.

Meinig, D. W. *Imperial Texas: An Interpretive Essay in Cultural Geography*. Austin: University of Texas Press, 1969.

Menchaca, Martha. *The Mexican Outsiders: A Community History of Marginalization and Discrimination in California*. Austin: University of Texas Press, 1995.

Menefee, Selden. *Mexican Migratory Workers of South Texas*. Washington, D.C.: Government Printing Office, 1941.

Menefee, Selden C., and Orin C. Cassmore. *The Pecan Shellers of San Antonio: The Problem of Underpaid and Unemployed Mexican Labor*. Washington, D.C.: Government Printing Office, 1940.

Meyer, Jean A. *The Cristero Rebellion: The Mexican People between Church and State, 1926–1929*, translated by Richard Southern. New York: Cambridge University Press, 1976.

———. "Revolution and Reconstruction in the 1920s." In *Mexico since Independence*, edited by Leslie Bethell, 201–40. New York: Cambridge University Press, 1991.

Meyers, Frederic. *Economics of Labor Relations*. Chicago: Richard D. Irwin, 1951.

Meyers, William K. "La Comarca Lagunera: Work, Protest, and Popular Mobilization in North Central Mexico." In *Other Mexicos: Essays on Regional Mexican History, 1876–1911*, edited by Thomas Benjamin and William McNellie, 243–74. Albuquerque: University of New Mexico Press, 1984.

———. *Forge of Progress, Crucible of Revolt: The Origins of the Mexican Revolution in La Comarca Lagunera, 1880–1911*. Albuquerque: University of New Mexico Press, 1994.

Michaels, Albert L. "The Crisis of Cardenismo." *Journal of Latin American Studies* 2, no. 1 (May 1970): 51–79.

Middlebrook, Kevin J. *The Paradox of Revolution: Labor, the State, and Authoritarianism in Mexico*. Baltimore: Johns Hopkins University Press, 1995.

Miller, Char. *Deep in the Heart of San Antonio: Land and Life in South Texas*. San Antonio, Tex.: Trinity University Press, 2004.

———, ed. *On the Border: An Environmental History of San Antonio*. Pittsburgh: University of Pittsburgh Press, 2001.

Miller, Char, and David R. Johnson. "The Rise of Urban Texas." In *Urban Texas: Politics and Development*, edited by Char Miller and Heywood T. Sanders, 3–29. College Station: Texas A&M University Press, 1990.

Miller, Char, and Heywood T. Sanders. "Olmos Park and the Creation of a Suburban Bastion, 1927–39." In *Urban Texas: Politics and Development*, edited by Char Miller and Heywood T. Sanders, 113–27. College Station: Texas A&M University Press, 1990.

———, eds. *Urban Texas: Politics and Development*. College Station: Texas A&M University Press, 1990.

Miller, Tom. *On the Border: Portraits of America's Southwestern Frontier*. Tucson: University of Arizona Press, 1981.

Mitchell, Don. *The Lie of the Land: Migrant Workers and the California Landscape*. Minneapolis: University of Minnesota Press, 1996.

———. *They Saved the Crops: Labor, Landscape, and the Struggle over Industrial Farming in Bracero-Era California*. Athens: University of Georgia Press, 2012.

Molina, Natalia. *Fit to Be Citizens? Public Health and Race in Los Angeles, 1879–1939*. Berkeley: University of California Press, 2006.

Moloney, Deirdre M. *National Insecurities: Immigrants and U.S. Deportation Policy since 1882*. Chapel Hill: University of North Carolina Press, 2012.

Montejano, David. *Anglos and Mexicans in the Making of Texas, 1836–1986*. Austin: University of Texas Press, 1987.

———. "Is Texas Bigger than the World-System?" *Review* 4, no. 3 (Winter 1981): 597–628.

———. *Race, Labor Repression, and Capitalist Agriculture: Notes from South Texas, 1920–1930*. Berkeley: Institute for the Study of Social Change, 1977.

Montgomery, David. *Workers' Control in America: Studies in the History of Work, Technology, and Labor Struggles*. New York: Cambridge University Press, 1979.

Mora-Torres, Juan. *The Making of the Mexican Border: The State, Capitalism, and Society in Nuevo Leon, 1848–1910*. Austin: University of Texas Press, 2001.

Munguía, Ruben. *The Nuecero Spoke*. N.p., 1982.

Navarro, Armando. *Mexican American Youth Organization: Avant-Garde of the Chicano Movement in Texas*. Austin: University of Texas Press, 1995.

Nelson-Cisneros, Victor B. "UCAPAWA Organizing Activities in Texas, 1932–1950." *Aztlán* 9 (1979): 71–84.

Ness, Immanuel. *Guest Workers and Resistance to U.S. Corporate Despotism*. Urbana: University of Illinois Press, 2011.

Ngai, Mae M. *Impossible Subjects: Illegal Aliens and the Making of Modern America*. Princeton, N.J.: Princeton University Press, 2004.

Niblo, Stephen R. *Mexico in the 1940s: Modernity, Politics, and Corruption*. Wilmington, Del.: Scholarly Resources, 1999.

Norris, Jim. *North for the Harvest: Mexican Workers, Growers, and the Sugar Beet Industry*. St. Paul: Minnesota Historical Society, 2009.

Nugent, Daniel. *Spent Cartridges of Revolution: An Anthropological History of Namiquipa, Chihuahua*. Chicago: University of Chicago Press, 1993.

———, ed. *Rural Revolt in Mexico: U.S. Intervention and the Domain of Subaltern Politics*. Durham, N.C.: Duke University Press, 1998.

Obregón Pagán, Eduardo. *Murder at the Sleepy Lagoon: Zoot Suits, Race, and Riot in Wartime L.A.* Chapel Hill: University of North Carolina Press, 2003.

Paredes, Américo. *"With His Pistol in His Hand": A Border Ballad and Its Hero*. Austin: University of Texas Press, 1958.

Paz, Octavio. *The Labyrinth of Solitude and Other Writings*. New York: Grove, 1985.

Peck, Gunther. *Reinventing Free Labor: Padrones and Immigrant Workers in the North American West, 1880–1930*. New York: Cambridge University Press, 2000.

Pegler-Gordon, Anna. *In Sight of America: Photography and the Development of U.S. Immigration Policy*. Berkeley: University of California Press, 2009.

Perales, Alonso S. *Are We Good Neighbors?* New York: Arno, 1974 [1948].

Piccato, Pablo. *City of Suspects: Crime in Mexico City, 1900–1931*. Durham, N.C.: Duke University Press, 2001.

Plascencia, Luis F. B., Robert W. Glover, and Brian Craddock. "A Case Study of the Agricultural Labor Market in South Texas Winter Vegetable Production." In *Report of the Commission on Agricultural Workers*, Appendix 1: "Case Studies and Research Reports Prepared for the Commission on Agricultural Workers, 1989–1993, to Accompany the Report of the Commission," 523–71. Washington, D.C.: Government Printing Office, 1993.

Plumb, J. H. *The Death of the Past.* London: Macmillan, 1969.

President's Commission on Migratory Labor. *Migratory Labor in American Agriculture.* Washington, D.C.: Government Printing Office, 1951.

Raat, W. Dirk. *Revoltosos: Mexico's Rebels in the United States, 1903–1923.* College Station: Texas A&M University Press, 1981.

Ranger, Terence. "The Invention of Tradition in Colonial Africa." In *The Invention of Tradition*, edited by Eric Hobsbawm and Terence Ranger, 211–62. New York: Cambridge University Press, 1983.

Rasmussen, Wayne D. *A History of the Emergency Farm Labor Supply Program, 1943–1947.* Bureau of Agricultural Economics no. 13. Washington, D.C.: U.S. Government Printing Office, 1951.

Reed, John. *Insurgent Mexico.* New York: International, 1969 [1914].

Reimers, David M. *Still the Golden Door: The Third World Comes to America.* New York: Columbia University Press, 1992.

Reisler, Mark. *By the Sweat of Their Brow: Mexican Immigrant Labor in the United States, 1900–1940.* Westport, Conn.: Greenwood, 1976.

Reynolds, Lloyd G. *Labor Economics and Labor Relations.* Englewood Cliffs, N.J.: Prentice-Hall, 1959.

Rips, Geoffrey. "Living History: Emma Tenayuca Tells Her Story." *Texas Observer*, October 28, 1983, 7–15.

Rodriguez, Jaime E., ed. *The Revolutionary Process in Mexico: Essays on Political and Social Change, 1880–1940.* Los Angeles: UCLA Latin American Center Publications, 1990.

Rodriguez, Marc S. *The Tejano Diaspora: Mexican Americanism and Ethnic Politics in Texas and Wisconsin.* Chapel Hill: University of North Carolina Press, 2011.

———, ed. *Repositioning North American Migration History: New Directions in Modern Continental Migration, Citizenship, and Community.* Rochester, N.Y.: University of Rochester Press, 2004.

Roediger, David R. *The Wages of Whiteness: Race and the Making of the American Working Class.* New York: Verso, 1991.

Ronfeldt, David. *Atencingo: The Politics of Agrarian Struggle in a Mexican Ejido.* Stanford, Calif.: Stanford University Press, 1973.

Rosales, F. Arturo. *Pobre Raza: Violence, Justice, and Mobilization among Mexico Lindo Immigrants, 1900–1936.* Austin: University of Texas Press, 1999.

Rosales, Rodolfo. *The Illusion of Inclusion: The Untold Political Story of San Antonio.* Austin: University of Texas Press, 2000.

Rouse, Roger. "Mexican Migration and the Social Space of Postmodernism." In *Between Two Worlds: Mexican Immigrants in the United States*, edited by David G. Gutiérrez, 247–63. Wilmington, Del.: Scholarly Resources, 1996.

Ruckelshaus, Catherine. "Labor's Wage War." *Fordham Urban Law Journal* 35 (February 1, 2008): 373–407.

Ruiz, Ramón Eduardo. *On the Rim of Mexico: Encounters of the Rich and Poor.* Boulder, Colo.: Westview, 2000.

Ruiz, Vicki L. *Cannery Women, Cannery Lives: Mexican Women, Unionization, and the California Food Processing Industry, 1930–1950.* Albuquerque: University of New Mexico Press, 1987.

———. *From Out of the Shadows: Mexican Women in Twentieth-Century America.* New York: Oxford University Press, 1998.

Salamini, Heather Fowler. "Tamaulipas: Land Reform and the State." In *Provinces of the Revolution: Essays on Regional Mexican History, 1910–1929*, edited by Thomas Benjamin and Mark Wasserman, 185–217. Albuquerque: University of New Mexico Press, 1990.

Samora, Julian, Joe Bernal, and Albert Peña. *Gunpowder Justice: A Reassessment of the Texas Rangers.* Notre Dame, Ind.: University of Notre Dame Press, 1979.

Sánchez, George J. *Becoming Mexican American: Ethnicity, Culture and Identity in Chicano Los Angeles, 1900–1945.* New York: Oxford University Press, 1993.

Sanders, Heywood T. "Building a New Urban Infrastructure: The Creation of Postwar San Antonio." In *Urban Texas: Politics and Development*, edited by Char Miller and Heywood T. Sanders, 154–73. College Station: Texas A&M University Press, 1990.

Sandos, James A. *Rebellion in the Borderlands: Anarchism and the Plan of San Diego, 1904–1923.* Norman, Okla.: University of Oklahoma Press, 1992.

San Miguel, Guadalupe. *"Let All of Them Take Heed": Mexican Americans and the Campaign for Education Equality in Texas, 1910–1981.* Austin: University of Texas Press, 1987.

Santibáñez, Enrique. *Ensayo acerca de la inmigración mexicana en los Estados Unidos.* San Antonio, Tex.: Clegg, 1930.

Saunders, Lyle, and Olen E. Leonard. *The Wetback in the Lower Rio Grande Valley of Texas.* Inter-American Education Occasional Papers 7. Austin: University of Texas Press, 1951.

Schlosser, Eric. *Reefer Madness: Sex, Drugs, and Cheap Labor in the American Black Market.* New York: Houghton Mifflin, 2003.

Scott, James C. *Domination and the Arts of Resistance: Hidden Transcripts.* New Haven, Conn.: Yale University Press, 1990.

———. *Weapons of the Weak: Everyday Forms of Peasant Resistance.* New Haven, Conn.: Yale University Press, 1985.

Scruggs, Otey M. "Evolution of the Mexican Farm Labor Agreement of 1942." *Agricultural History* 34 (July 1960): 140–49.

———. "Texas and the Bracero Program, 1942–1947." *Pacific Historical Review* 32 (1963): 251–64.

———. "The United States, Mexico, and the Wetbacks, 1942–1947." *Pacific Historical Review* 30 (May 1961): 149–64.

Secretaría de Relaciones Exteriores de México. *Memoria de la Secretaría de Relaciones Exteriores de agosto de 1929 a julio de 1930, presentada al H. Congreso de la Unión por Genaro Estrada, secretario de relaciones exteriores.* Vol 2. Mexico City: Imprenta de la Secretaría de Relaciones Exteriores, 1930.

———. *Memoria de la Secretaría de Relaciones Exteriores de agosto de 1930 a julio de 1931, presentada al H. Congreso de la Unión por Genaro Estrada, secretario de relaciones exteriores.* Vol 2. Mexico City: Imprenta de la SRE, 1931.

———. *Memoria de la Secretaría de Relaciones Exteriores de agosto de 1931 a julio de 1932, presentada al H. Congreso de la Unión por el C. Manuel C. Téllez, secretario de relaciones exteriores.* Mexico City: Imprenta de la SRE, 1932.

———. *Apéndice a la memoria de la Secretaría de Relaciones Exteriores de agosto de 1931 a julio de 1932, presentada a H. Congreso de la Unión por el C. Manuel C. Téllez, secretario de relaciones exteriores.* Mexico City: Imprenta de la SRE, 1932.

———. *Informe de la Secretaría de Relaciones Exteriores de agosto de 1933 a agosto 1 de 1934, presentada al H. Congreso de la Unión por el C. Dr. José Manuel Puig Casauranc, secretario de relaciones exteriores.* Mexico City: Imprenta de la SRE, 1934.

———. *Memoria de la Secretaría de Relaciones Exteriores, septiembre de 1943 a agosto de 1944.* Mexico City: Talleres Gráficos de la Nación, 1944.

———. *Memoria de la Secretaría de Relaciones Exteriores, septiembre de 1945 a agosto de 1946.* Mexico City: Talleres Gráficos de la Nación, 1946.

———. *Memoria de la Secretaría de Relaciones Exteriores, enero a diciembre de 1954, presentada al H. Congreso de la Unión por el Lic. Luis Padilla Nervo, secretario del ramo.* Mexico City: Talleres Gráficos de la Nación, 1955.

———. *Memoria de la Secretaría de Relaciones Exteriores, enero a diciembre de 1955, presentada al H. Congreso de la Unión por el C. Lic. Luis Padilla Nervo, secretario del ramo.* Vol 2. Mexico City: Talleres Gráficos de la Nación, 1956.

———. *Memoria de la Secretaría de Relaciones Exteriores, por el periodo comprendido del 1 de septiembre de 1964 al 31 de agosto de 1965.* Mexico City: Talleres Gráficos de la Nación, 1965.

———. *Memoria de la Secretaría de Relaciones Exteriores por el periodo comprendido de 1 de septiembre de 1967 al 31 de agosto de 1968.* Tlatelolco, Mexico: Talleres Gráficos de la Nación, 1968.

Senior, Clarence. *Democracy Comes to a Cotton Kingdom: The Story of Mexico's La Laguna.* Mexico City: Centro de Estudios Pedagógicos e Hispanoamericanos, 1940.

Sepúlveda, Juan A., Jr. *The Life and Times of Willie Velásquez: Su Voto Es Su Voz.* Houston: Arte Público, 2003.

Shapiro, Harold. "The Pecan Shellers of San Antonio, Texas." *Southwestern Social Science Quarterly* 32, no. 4 (March 1952): 229–44.

Shostack, Albert. *Hired Farm Workers in the United States.* Washington, D.C.: Bureau of Employment Security, 1961.

Siciliano, Rocco C. *Walking on Sand: The Story of an Immigrant Son and the Forgotten Art of Public Service.* Salt Lake City: University of Utah Press, 2004.

Simpson, Eyler Newton. *The Ejido, Mexico's Way Out*. Chapel Hill: University of North Carolina Press, 1937.

Simpson, Lesley Byrd. *Many Mexicos*. 4th ed. Berkeley: University of California Press, 1969.

Starr, Kevin. *Endangered Dreams: The Great Depression in California*. New York: Oxford University Press, 1996.

———. *Inventing the Dream: California through the Progressive Era*. New York: Oxford University Press, 1985.

———. *Material Dreams: Southern California through the 1920s*. New York: Oxford University Press, 1990.

Sterling, William Warren. *Trails and Trials of a Texas Ranger*. N.p., 1959.

Stevenson, Coke R., and Ezequiel Padilla. "The Good Neighbor Policy and Mexicans in Texas." In *The Mexican American and Law*. New York: Arno, 1974.

Stilwell, Hart. "Good Neighbors and Band Music." *Texas Spectator*, October 11, 1946, 3.

Striffler, Steve. *Chicken: The Dangerous Transformation of America's Favorite Food*. New Haven, Conn.: Yale University Press, 2005.

Tanger, Stephanie E. "Enforcing Corporate Responsibility for Violations of Workplace Immigration Laws: The Case of Meatpacking." *Harvard Latino Law Review* (Spring 2006): 59–89.

Taylor, Paul Schuster. "Again the Covered Wagon." *Survey Graphic* 24, no. 7 (July 1935): 348.

———. *An American-Mexican Frontier: Nueces County, Texas*. New York: Russell and Russell, 1971 [1934].

———. "Mexican Labor in the United States: Bethlehem, Pennsylvania." *University of California Publications in Economics* 7, no. 1 (1931): ix, 1–24.

———. "Mexican Labor in the United States: Chicago and the Calumet Region." *University of California Publications in Economics* 7, no. 2 (1932): vii, 25–284.

———. "Mexican Labor in the United States: Dimmit County, Winter Garden District, South Texas." *University of California Publications in Economics* 6, no. 5 (1930): 293–464.

———. "Mexican Labor in the United States: Imperial Valley." *University of California Publications in Economics* 6, no. 1 (1928): 1–94.

———. "Mexican Labor in the United States: Migration Statistics." *University of California Publications in Economics* 6, no. 3 (1929): 237–55.

———. "Mexican Labor in the United States: Migration Statistics, II." *University of California Publications in Economics* 12, no. 1 (1933): 1–10.

———. "Mexican Labor in the United States: Migration Statistics, III." *University of California Publications in Economics* 12, no. 2 (1933): 11–22.

———. "Mexican Labor in the United States: Migration Statistics, IV." *University of California Publications in Economics* 12, no. 3 (1934): 23–50.

———. "Mexican Labor in the United States: Valley of the South Platte, Colorado." *University of California Publications in Economics* 6, no. 2 (1929): 95–235.

———. *On the Ground in the Thirties*. Salt Lake City: Peregrine Smith, 1983.

———. *A Spanish-Mexican Peasant Community: Arandas in Jalisco, Mexico*. Berkeley: University of California Press, 1933.

Tenayuca, Emma, and Homer Brooks. "The Mexican Question in the Southwest." *Communist*, March 1939, 257–68.

Tenorio Trillo, Mauricio. "1910 Mexico City: Space and Nation in the City of the Centenario." In *Viva Mexico, Viva la Independencia: Celebrations of September 16*, edited by William H. Beezley and David E. Lorey, 167–97. Wilmington, Del.: Scholarly Resources, 2001.

Texas Advisory Committee to the United States Commission on Civil Rights. *Employment Practices at Kelly Air Force Base, San Antonio, Texas: A Report of the Texas Advisory Committee to the United States Commission on Civil Rights.* Washington, D.C.: Government Printing Office, 1968.

Thompson, Jerry D., ed. *Juan Cortina and the Texas-Mexico Frontier, 1859–1877.* El Paso: Texas Western Press, 1994.

Tijerina, Andrés. *Tejano Empire: Life on the South Texas Ranchos.* College Station: Texas A&M University Press, 1998.

Tiller, James Weeks, Jr. *The Texas Winter Garden: Commercial Cool-Season Vegetable Production.* Research Monograph no. 33. Austin: Bureau of Business Research at the University of Texas at Austin, 1971.

Trachtenberg, Alan. *The Incorporation of America: Culture and Society in the Gilded Age.* New York: Hill and Wang, 1982.

Trevor-Roper, Hugh. "The Invention of Tradition: The Highland Tradition of Scotland." In *The Invention of Tradition*, edited by Eric Hobsbawm and Terence Ranger, 15–41. New York: Cambridge University Press, 1983.

Truett, Samuel, and Elliott Young, eds. *Continental Crossroads: Remapping U.S.-Mexico Borderlands History.* Durham, N.C.: Duke University Press, 2004.

Tutino, John. *From Insurrection to Revolution in Mexico: Social Bases of Agrarian Violence, 1750–1940.* Princeton, N.J.: Princeton University Press, 1986.

———. "Revolutionary Confrontation, 1913–1917: Regional Factions, Class Conflicts, and the New National State." In *Provinces of the Revolution: Essays on Regional Mexican History, 1910–1929*, edited by Thomas Benjamin and Mark Wasserman, 41–70. Albuquerque: University of New Mexico Press, 1990.

U.S. Bureau of the Census. *Thirteenth Census of the United States: 1910.* Washington, D.C.: Government Printing Office, 1913.

———. *Fifteenth Census of the United States: 1930.* Washington, D.C.: Government Printing Office, 1932.

———. *United States Census of Agriculture: 1925.* Washington, D.C.: Government Printing Office, 1928.

U.S. Commission on Industrial Relations. *Final Report and Testimony Submitted to Congress by the Commission on Industrial Relations.* Vol. 10. Washington, D.C.: Government Printing Office, 1916.

U.S. Congress. House. Committee on Agriculture. *Extension of Mexican Farm Labor Program.* H.R. 3480, 83rd Cong., 1st sess. Washington, D.C.: Government Printing Office, 1953.

———. House. Committee on Agriculture, Subcommittee on Equipment, Supplies, and Manpower. *Farm Labor.* 85th Cong., 2nd sess. Washington, D.C.: Government Printing Office, 1958.

———. House. Committee on Immigration and Naturalization. *Seasonal Agricultural Laborers from Mexico*. 69th Cong., 1st sess. Washington, D.C.: Government Printing Office, 1926.

———. Senate. Committee on Immigration. *Admission of Mexican Agricultural Laborers*. 66th Cong., 2nd sess. Washington, D.C.: Government Printing Office, 1920.

———. Senate. Committee on Immigration. *Restriction of Western Hemisphere Immigration*. 70th Cong., 1st sess. Washington, D.C.: Government Printing Office, 1928.

———. Senate. Committee on Labor and Public Welfare. *Amending Migratory Labor Laws: Hearings before the Subcommittee on Migratory Labor of the Committee on Labor and Public Welfare, United States Senate, Eighty-Ninth Congress, First and Second Sessions on S. 1864, S. 1865, S. 1866, S. 1867, and S. 1868, Bills to Amend Migratory Labor Legislation Relating to Migrant Workers*. Washington, D.C.: Government Printing Office, 1966.

U.S. Department of Labor. Bureau of Immigration. *Annual Report of the Commissioner General of Immigration to the Secretary of Labor: Fiscal Year Ended June 30, 1915*. Washington, D.C.: Government Printing Office, 1915.

———. *Annual Report of the Commissioner General of Immigration to the Secretary of Labor: Fiscal Year Ended June 30, 1927*. Washington, D.C.: Government Printing Office, 1927.

———. *Annual Report of the Commissioner General of Immigration to the Secretary of Labor: Fiscal Year Ended June 30, 1929*. Washington, D.C.: Government Printing Office, 1929.

Utley, Robert M. *Lone Star Justice: The First Century of the Texas Rangers*. New York: Oxford University Press, 2002.

Valdés, Dennis Nodin. *Al Norte: Agricultural Workers in the Great Lakes Region, 1917–1970*. Austin: University of Texas Press, 1991.

———. *Organized Agriculture and the Labor Movement before the UFW: Puerto Rico, Hawaii, California*. Austin: University of Texas Press, 2011.

VanderVelde, Lea. "Wal-Mart as a Phenomenon in the Legal World: Matters of Scale, Scale Matters." In *Wal-Mart World: The World's Biggest Corporation in the Global Economy*, edited by Stanley D. Brunn, 115–40. New York: Routledge, 2006.

Vanderwood, Paul J. *Disorder and Progress: Bandits, Police, and Mexican Development*. Lincoln: University of Nebraska Press, 1981.

———. *The Power of God against the Guns of Government*. Stanford, Calif.: Stanford University Press, 1998.

Vargas, Zaragoza. *Labor Rights Are Civil Rights: Mexican American Workers in Twentieth-Century America*. Princeton, N.J.: Princeton University Press, 2005.

———. *Proletarians of the North: A History of Mexican Industrial Workers in Detroit and the Midwest, 1917–1933*. Berkeley: University of California Press, 1993.

Volanto, Keith J. *Texas, Cotton, and the New Deal*. College Station: Texas A&M University Press, 2005.

Voss, Stuart F. "Nationalizing the Revolution: Culmination and Circumstance." In *Provinces of the Revolution: Essays on Regional Mexican History, 1910-1929*, edited by Thomas Benjamin and Mark Wasserman, 273-317. Albuquerque: University of New Mexico Press, 1990.

Walsh, Casey. *Building the Borderlands: A Transnational History of Irrigated Cotton along the Mexico-Texas Border*. College Station: Texas A&M University Press, 2008.

Warburton, Amber Arthur, Helen Wood, and Marian M. Crane. *The Work and Welfare of Children of Agricultural Laborers in Hidalgo County, Texas*. United States Department of Labor, Children's Bureau Publication 298. Washington, D.C.: Government Printing Office, 1943.

Wasserman, Mark. "Chihuahua: Family Power, Foreign Enterprise, and National Control." In *Other Mexicos: Essays on Regional Mexican History, 1876-1911*, edited by Thomas Benjamin and William McNellie, 3-54. Albuquerque: University of New Mexico Press, 1984.

———. "Chihuahua: Politics in an Era of Transition." In *Provinces of the Revolution: Essays on Regional Mexican History, 1910-1929*, edited by Thomas Benjamin and Mark Wasserman, 219-35. Albuquerque: University of New Mexico Press, 1990.

———. *Persistent Oligarchs: Elites and Politics in Chihuahua, Mexico, 1910-1940*. Durham, N.C.: Duke University Press, 1993.

———. "Provinces of the Revolution: An Introduction." In *Provinces of the Revolution: Essays on Regional Mexican History, 1910-1929*, edited by Thomas Benjamin and Mark Wasserman, 1-14. Albuquerque: University of New Mexico Press, 1990.

Watkins, T. H. *The Hungry Years: A Narrative History of the Great Depression in America*. New York: Holt, 1999.

Way, Peter. *Common Labor: Workers and the Digging of North American Canals, 1780-1860*. Baltimore: Johns Hopkins University Press, 1993.

Webb, Walter Prescott. *The Texas Rangers: A Century of Frontier Defense*. Austin: University of Texas Press, 1935.

Weber, David J. *Myth and the History of the Hispanic Southwest*. Albuquerque: University of New Mexico Press, 1988.

Weber, Devra. *Dark Sweat, White Gold: California Farm Workers, Cotton, and the New Deal*. Berkeley: University of California Press, 1994.

Weeks, Oliver Douglas. "The League of United Latin-American Citizens: A Texas-Mexican Civic Organization." *Southwestern Political and Social Science Quarterly* 10, no. 3 (December 1929): 257-78.

———. "The Texas-Mexican and the Politics of South Texas." *American Political Science Review* 24, no. 3 (August 1930): 606-27.

Weiss, Stuart L. "Maury Maverick and the Liberal Bloc." *Journal of American History* 57, no. 4 (March 1971): 880-95.

Whalen, William A. "The Wetback Problem in Southeast Texas." Immigration and Naturalization Service. *Monthly Review* 8, no. 8 (February 1951): 103-4.

White, Owen P. "Machine Made." *Collier's*, September 18, 1937, 32-33.

Willard, Rex E. *Status of Farming in the Lower Rio Grande Irrigated District of Texas*. U.S. Department of Agriculture Bulletin, no. 665. Washington, D.C.: Government Printing Office, 1918.

Wirtz, W. Willard. *Year of Transition: Seasonal Farm Labor—1965*. Washington, D.C.: Government Printing Office, 1966.

Wolf, Eric R. *Sons of the Shaking Earth*. Chicago, University of Chicago Press, 1959.

Womack, John, Jr. "The Mexican Revolution, 1910–1920." In *Mexico since Independence*, edited by Leslie Bethell, 125–200. New York: Cambridge University Press, 1991.

———. *Zapata and the Mexican Revolution*. New York: Vintage, 1968.

Wood, Andrew Grant. *Revolution in the Street: Women, Workers, and Urban Protest in Veracruz, 1870–1927*. Wilmington, Del.: Scholarly Resources, 2001.

"Working Conditions of Pecan Shellers in San Antonio." *Monthly Labor Review* 48, no. 3 (March 1939): 549–51.

Worster, Donald. *Rivers of Empire: Water, Aridity, and the Growth of the American West*. New York: Oxford University Press, 1985.

Young, Elliott. *Catarino Garza's Revolution on the Texas-Mexico Border*. Durham, N.C.: Duke University Press, 2004.

———. "Deconstructing *La Raza*: Identifying the *Gente Decente* of Laredo, 1904–1911." *Southwestern Historical Quarterly* 98 (October 1994): 227–59.

———. "Red Men, Princess Pocahontas, and George Washington: Harmonizing Race Relations in Laredo at the Turn of the Century." *Western Historical Quarterly* 29 (Spring 1998): 48–85.

Zamora, Emilio. *Claiming Rights and Righting Wrongs in Texas: Mexican Workers and Job Politics during World War II*. College Station: Texas A&M University Press, 2009.

———. "Labor Formation, Community, and Politics: The Mexican Working Class in Texas, 1900–1945." In *Border Crossings: Mexican and Mexican-American Workers*, edited by John Mason Hart, 139–62. Wilmington, Del.: Scholarly Resources, 1998.

———. *The World of the Mexican Worker in Texas*. College Station: Texas A&M University Press, 1993.

Zieger, Robert H. *The CIO, 1935–1955*. Chapel Hill: University of North Carolina Press, 1995.

Zolberg, Aristide. *A Nation by Design: Immigration Policy in the Fashioning of America*. Cambridge: Harvard University Press, 2006.

Index

African Americans, 32, 53, 67–68, 83, 86–87, 89, 111, 125, 146, 149. *See also* Charlie Bellinger

Agricultural Adjustment Act, 143

Agricultural Workers Protection Act, 224

Agriculture: and growth of agribusiness, 52, 53, 57–58, 70, 78, 228; and land values, 19, 28–29; and market consolidation, 51; mechanization of, 56–57; in South Texas, 16, 19, 27–28, 42–44, 46–47, 103; and South Texas crops, 51–52;. *See also* Great Depression; Growers; Labor/ Laborers: agricultural

Alamo Cement Company, 93

Allred, James, 178

American Beet Sugar Company, 60

American Federation of Labor, 97, 115–16, 150, 155, 163, 165, 214–15, 219

American G.I. Forum, 197

American Legion, 125–26, 142

American Public Welfare Association, 131–32

Anders, Evan, 18

Austin, A. L., 36

Banditry, 11, 13, 15, 21, 30–31, 37. *See also* Mexican Cotton Pickers

Bellinger, Charlie, 146, 262 (n. 72)

Beteta, Ramón, 139, 261 (n. 44)

Bethlehem Steel, 67

Bexar County Board of Welfare and Employment, 148

Border Patrol, 73, 112, 120–22, 201, 204–5, 210–11, 230

Border Raids, 15, 29, 38, 241 (n. 66)

Border War of 1915, 32–40, 43, 240 (n. 63), 242 (n. 71), 243 (nn. 87, 103)

Boynton, Alexander, 127

Bracero Program, 184, 187, 201, 273 (n. 13); and Border Patrol collusion, 209–10; and civil rights, 215; and discrimination, 198; evolution of 200–202; and exclusion of Texas, 194–96, 199, 201; and growers, 188–89, 199, 204, 206–7, 210–11, 218; and legalization of immigrants, 202–4, 206, 209; and Mexican Americans, 214–16; and Mexico, 192, 196, 202, 205, 207–8, 213; and number of braceros, 200, 205–6, 212, 215, 217; and Operation Wetback, 210–12, 213, 230, 277 (n. 71); opposition to, 184, 188, 277 (n. 70); and organized labor, 214–15; restrictions on, 189; and wages, 218, 221, 274 (n. 22); and worker rights, 193–94. *See also* Guest worker programs

Bricklayers and Masons International Union, 135

Brownsville, Tex., 25, 27, 32, 35, 37, 55–56, 59, 107, 119, 141; and Border Patrol raids, 120; and Great Depression, 131; segregation, 88; as transshipment point, 15, 17–18; violence in, 15, 33–34

Bryant, John, 184

Bureau of Agricultural Economics, 189

California: and agriculture, 12, 50, 52; and guest worker programs, 200, 205, 212, 214, 279 (n. 124); and immigration, 46, 104, 210, 258 (n. 70); and irrigation, 245 (n. 25); and laborers, 7, 67,

183–84, 188, 190, 252 (n. 53), 253 (n. 62), 273 (n. 8); migration to, 70, 234 (n. 16), 244 (n. 15)

Cárdenas, Lázaro, 139, 159, 191

Carranza, Venustiano, 21, 23, 33, 241 (nn. 66, 68)

Cart War, 236 (n. 3)

Catholic Women's Organization, 145

Catholic Workers Union, 155Caucasian Race Resolution, 195–96

Chambers, C. M., 146

Chambers of Commerce, 48, 73–74, 97, 105, 110, 141, 156–57, 255 (n. 14), 273 (n. 13)

Chicago, Ill., 1, 66–70, 109, 145, 248 (n. 108)

Chinese, 12, 24, 45, 106. *See also* Immigrants/immigration

Chinese Exclusion Act, 27, 104

Cigar industry 134, 162–69, 176. *See also* Labor/laborers: industrial

Cigar Makers' International Union, 165–66

Civil Rights Act of 1964, 216, 224

Clarich, Christopher, 161

Collective Bargaining, 57, 142, 156, 158, 161, 176. *See also* Labor/laborers: militancy of

Colorado, 12, 32, 60–62, 70, 217

Colquitt, Oscar, 30, 238 (n. 44), 240 (n. 57)

Columbia Sugar Company, 61

Communist Party/Communism, 125–28, 149–50, 152, 157, 159, 170, 175, 177–78, 181, 209

Confederation of Mexican and Mexican-American Laborers, 158

Congress of Industrial Organizations, 155, 159–60, 173, 176, 211, 214, 219

Contractors, 55–56, 58, 60, 93, 95–96, 171, 223; straw contractors, 223–27. *See also* Growers

Cotton industry: and Bracero Program, 187, 244; and labor, 54, 56, 60, 88, 108, 140, 155, 190, 204, 209;

mechanization of, 57, 209, 214; and migration, 69–70, 133–34, 147; production of, 11, 56, 143; and wages, 12, 56, 58, 93–94, 133, 141, 172–73, 203–4; and work conditions, 77. *See also* Labor/ laborers: agricultural

Council of Garment Workers, 168

Councils of Defense, 105

Cristero Rebellion, 21

Cross, Harry, 192, 222

Culberson, Charles, 105

Davis, James, 117

De la Huerta, Adolfo, 21

De la Rosa, Luis, 35–36, 243 (n. 87)

Democratic Party of Texas, 80–81, 83, 122, 128, 148–49, 184

Denver, Colo., 70, 145

Deportation, 118, 205, 231, 255 (n. 2), 278 (n. 100); immigrant response to, 102–4, 112, 119, 138, 153, 155–57, 181, 211; and law enforcement campaigns, 104, 109, 111, 119–23, 128, 130, 135–37, 141, 155, 169, 177, 205, 212, 228, 239 (n. 47), 248 (n. 108), 258 (nn. 67, 70); protests against, 73; voluntary 137, 138, 139, 211. *See also* Immigrants/immigration; Nativism

Díaz, Porfirio, 12, 15, 20, 22, 34, 67, 236 (n. 2), 239 (n. 50), 249 (n. 9)

Dies, Martin, 159

Don Martín Colony, 138–39, 261 (n. 42)

Dorothy Frocks Company, 167

Drossaerts, Arthur, 125, 177, 271 (n. 121)

Duerler, Gustave, 171

18 de marzo colony, 139–40. *See also* Deportation; Immigrants/ immigration: repatriation of

Eisenhower, Dwight D., 210

El Paso, Tex., 21, 29, 58–59, 77, 107, 120, 145, 203–4, 244 (n. 7), 278 (n. 100)

Emigrant Labor Agency Law (1929), 97–101, 190

Employers. *See* Growers; Labor/
    laborers
Ernst, Mrs. W. H., 165

Fair Labor Standards Act, 142,
    179–80, 224
Farmers. *See* Growers
Farmers Association, 49
Farming. *See* Agriculture
Farm Placement Service, 96, 191, 204
Farm Security Administration, 99, 132,
    274 (n. 22)
Federal Emergency Relief Administra-
    tion, 142, 147
Ferguson, James, 34, 80–82, 240 (n. 57)
Ferguson, Miriam, 148
Finck Cigar Company, 167, 180,
    268 (n. 65)
Flores, Emilio, 53
Foerster, Robert, 114
Foley, Neil, 4, 57
Foran Act, 25, 104
Ford Motor Company, 69, 129
Fort Worth, Tex., 70, 141, 148
Frankfurter, Felix, 107
Freeman, Joe, 171, 269 (n. 90)

Galarza, Ernesto, 24, 204, 208, 210,
    213, 221, 258 (n. 71)
Gallegly, Elton, 183
Garcia, Gus, 216
Garcia, Hector, 197–98, 275 (n. 40)
Garcia, Richard, 177
Garment industry, 134, 162–64,
    166–69, 174–75, 269 (n. 71).
    See also Labor/laborers: industrial
Garner, John Nance, 73–74, 110,
    119, 135
Garza Rebellion, 236 (n. 2)
General Motors, 69
Glasscock, D. W., 82
Goethe, C. M., 116
Gómez, Cristobal, 223–25
Gompers, Samuel, 106, 115
Gonzalez, Henry B., 183–85, 215

Good Neighbor Commission, 196–99,
    214, 218
Good Neighbor Policy, 192, 194
Great Depression, 120–23, 141, 145,
    147, 153, 172, 181, 189; and eco-
    nomic decline, 51, 128, 130, 133,
    135; and employment, 131, 135;
    and government, 9, 145, 153; and
    immigration, 103–4 , 130, 136–37,
    140, 192; and labor 133, 154, 155,
    161, 181, 188, 190, 246 (n. 52); and
    living conditions, 129, 131, 134; and
    migration, 67, 70, 132, 138; and
    wages, 133, 147; and working con-
    ditions, 155. *See also* Deportation;
    Growers; Labor/laborers
Great Western Sugar Company, 60, 62
Griffin and Brand of McAllen Inc., 226
Growers: associations of, 54; during
    Great Depression, 130, 133, 135,
    140; hiring practices of, 12–13, 54;
    and immigration restriction laws,
    73–75, 103–5, 107–8, 110, 112–13,
    115; and labor control, 92–101; and
    labor demands, 189–91; and lab-
    orers' rights, 44; labor recruitment
    practices of, 54–55, 141, 223; during
    Mexican Revolution, 28–29; and
    New Deal 143, 147; political power
    of, 78–101; and protective legisla-
    tion, 95–99; and wages, 48, 64, 96,
    106, 141; and worker mobility, 11,
    73–75, 78, 92, 95, 97, 190. *See also*
    Labor/laborers: militancy of
Guerra, Manuel, 80
Guest worker/guest worker programs,
    183–85; and Emergency Farm
    Labor Supply Program, 193; in
    Germany, 113–14; H-1 Program,
    222; H-2A Program, 183, 222,
    280 (n. 139); Jamaican, 183;
    Mexican, 183; opposition to, 114–15;
    in South Africa, 220. *See also*
    Bracero Program; Labor/laborers
Gutiérrez, David, 4

Hahamovitch, Cindy, 4, 143, 194, 206, 220, 222
Hanson, W. M., 80, 243 (n. 84), 249 (n. 9)
Harley, James, 80, 82
Harris, William, 116
HemisFair, 1–3, 6, 10
Henderson, Donald, 175
Hernández, Kelly Lytle, 4
Hernández, Nicolas, 21
Hidalgo County, Tex., 18, 27, 33, 42, 44, 47, 52, 80, 102, 187, 212, 236 (n. 5), 250 (n. 16)
Hill, Benjamin, 158
Hobby, William, 80–83, 240 (n. 57)
Hobby Loyalty Act, 81
Hodgson v. Griffin and Brand, 226
Hoover, Herbert, 107–8, 142
Houston, Tex., 30, 34, 48
Huerta, Victoriano, 20–22, 29
Hull, Cordell, 159
Human Rights Watch, 228

Illinois, 68, 70, 74
Immigrants/immigration, 11; from Asia 24, 111, 238 (n. 28); decline of during WWI, 118, 241 (n. 68); from Europe 24, 111; illegal, 104, 111–12, 121–22, 137–38, 140, 201–2, 204, 206, 211, 222, 227–28, 230; and Great Depression, 140; and lack of regulation, 24–25; legislation concerning, 104–6, 109, 111–12, 121, 184; and Mexican Revolution, 5, 12, 14, 16, 22, 25–27; from Mexico, 38–39, 42–44, 46–47, 73–74, 77, 100, 105, 107, 109–10, 117, 192, 197; from Middle East, 24; and quotas, 116, 118, 258 (n. 71); and race, 114–16; as refugees, 38–39, 43, 109; repatriation of, 137–39, 181, 261 (n. 46); restrictions on, 103–23, 136, 190–91; and restrictive exemptions, 106–8; and union opposition, 115. *See also* Deportation

Immigration Act of 1917, 104–9, 111, 121
Immigration Act of 1921, 109, 121
Immigration Act of 1924, 102–3, 109, 112, 118, 120–21
Immigration Study Commission, 116
International Ladies Garment Workers Union, 167
International Workers of the World, 31
Irrigation/irrigation companies, 11, 27–29, 36–37, 39, 41, 43, 47, 245 (n. 25)

Japanese, 24, 32, 45
Johnson, A. P., 97, 115–16
Johnson, Benjamin, 4–5, 39
Johnson, Lyndon Baines, 179, 198, 215

Kellogg, Frank, 117–18
Kelly, W. F., 201
Kelly, Willard, 210
Kenedy, Mifflin, 17
Kennedy, John F., 215
Kennerly, F. M., 137
Kibbe, Pauline, 196
Kilday, Owen, 149, 154, 165–66, 170, 176–78
Kilday, Paul, 149
King, Martin Luther, Jr., 1
King, Richard, 17
King Ranch, 33, 36, 136
Knights of Columbus, 125
Knopp, W. W., 176
Kreutzer, George C., 117
Ku Klux Klan, 125–26, 128

Labor/Laborers:
—agricultural: and children, 65, 77, 155, 226; control of, 43, 92–101; and families, 48, 62, 65, 69, 77, 110; and Great Depression, 132–33, 140; and mobility of, 11–12, 42–43, 46, 53–54, 66, 73–75, 92, 95, 97–98, 129, 190; and New Deal, 143; racialization of 53–54, 57–58, 85, 99; recruitment of, 54–55, 58–63, 67, 155, 223,

225–26, 228; relations with growers, 44; seasonal/temporary, 43,
55–57, 133–34, 143, 156, 160, 169,
188; tenant, 43, 53, 86–87, 100, 143,
246 (n. 52); treatment of, 46, 55,
62, 223, 226; wage labor, 12, 29, 43,
62–66, 133, 190–91; wages of, 12,
14, 44, 46–48, 53, 56–57, 85–86, 96,
130, 155–56, 184, 226, 260 (n. 15),
274 (n. 16); and working conditions,
62–63, 65, 66, 155–56, 184, 223
—deportation of, 102, 104, 109–10,
112, 118–22
—industrial: 46, 53, 57–58, 66–70,
161–62, 173; and family labor,
173–74; and homework, 162–64;
and New Deal, 143; racialization
of, 135–36, 173; recruitment of, 67,
171; wages of, 63, 134, 160, 164,
166–68, 170, 172, 174, 176, 178–79,
227, 228; working conditions of, 68,
154, 162–63, 165–66, 172, 174, 178,
227–28, 271 (n. 121)
—militancy of: and arbitration, 166,
178–79; employer response to, 155,
157–61, 166–68, 175, 224–25, 268
(n. 59); law-enforcement response
to, 157, 165–70, 176–78, 195; and
protests/walkouts, 154–56, 160, 165,
169; and strikes, 127, 129, 155–59,
161, 164–69, 171, 175–77, 223–24;
unionizing/organizing, 57, 127,
136, 155–56, 158–59, 161–62, 164,
166–69, 174–76, 180–82, 227,
268 (n. 66)
—protective legislation, 155, 158, 166,
187, 224, 226; and exclusion of agricultural labor 142–43, 161
—ranching, 6, 9, 19–20, 46. *See also*
Growers; Immigrants/immigration;
Migration
Laguna, Mexico, 11–13, 235 (nn. 2, 8)
Lambert, George, 173, 176
Land Companies, 41–42, 47– 50
Land Speculation, 16–17, 41, 120

Laredo, Tex., 17, 25, 27, 38, 43–44, 53,
55, 68, 70, 77, 88–89, 93, 96, 107,
133, 137–38, 156–59
Larin, Don, 204
Law and Order League, 36
League of United Latin American
Citizens, 150
Longoria, Felix, 197–98, 275 (n. 38)
Los Tulitos Ranch, 35–36
Lower Rio Grande Valley:
agricultural development of, 43,
52; and irrigation, 28–29, 47; and
labor, 88, 94, 135, 140, 161, 188,
210, 217, 224; and migration, 54,
56, 102; and railroads, 17, 27.
See also Agriculture; Deportation;
Immigrants/immigration; Labor;
South Texas
Loyalty Ranger Force, 80–83
Lynching, 34–38

Maderista Revolution, 20
Madero, Francisco, 20, 22, 29
Mapes, Kathleen, 62, 68
Maverick, Maury, Sr., 125–28, 148–53,
162, 176–77, 262 (n. 87), 267 (n. 50)
McClellan, Andrew, 207, 213
McWilliams, Carey, 50, 52, 59–60, 66,
71, 98, 136, 253 (n. 62)
Meat processing industry, 10, 143,
227–28, 230. *See also* Labor/
laborers: industrial
Medina Dam and Irrigation Company,
93–94, 253 (n. 59)
Mexican Americans: and beet industry,
61–62, 65; and Border War of
1915, 39; changing definition of,
45; citizenship of, 87, 121–23, 136,
182; demographic representation
of, 46, 70–71; depictions of in
white society, 8, 86, 87, 104,
110–12, 114–15, 118–19, 121–22,
231, 234 (n. 7); and deportations,
119–20, 139; and education, 87–88;
and Great Depression/New Deal,

121, 131, 132, 134–35, 152–53; and
immigration reform, 75, 104; as
landowners 16–17; and middle class,
176–77; and political machines, 18,
78–84; and public utilities, 89; and
rights 18, 78–85, 163, 194, 198; and
social marginalization, 45, 49.
See also Labor/laborers; Segregation
Mexican Cotton Pickers, 13, 236 (n. 16)
Mexican Federation of Workers, 158
Mexican Protective Association, 53
Mexican Revolution, 8, 15, 20–21;
catalysts for, 13–14; and
Constitutionalist alliance, 20;
and Conventionists, 20; and
demographic shifts, 20, 23;
and economic collapse, 22; and
impressment, 22; and migrant
workers, 14; and migration, 16,
21–27, 38–39, 42, 237 (n. 23); and
refugees, 25–26, 32, 38–40, 43;
and trade, 23; and transportation
disruption, 23; and U.S., 14, 15,
20–22, 29–40, 71, 80, 117
Mexicans: and beet industry, 61–62,
65; depictions of in white society,
8, 86, 104, 110–12, 114–15, 118–19,
121–22, 231, 234 (n. 7); and Great
Depression/New Deal, 121, 131,
134–35, 152–53; and immigration
reform, 75; as landowners, 16–17;
and legal rights, 78–85, 185, 194;
and legal status, 111, 121–23, 136; as
a "race," 110–23; and repatriation
colonies, 139; social marginalization
of, 45. *See also* Growers;
Immigrants/immigration; Labor/
laborers; Mexico
Mexican War, 17
Mexico, 2; agricultural development of,
192; and border with Texas, 3, 14, 17,
29–31; and chamber of commerce,
176; and demographic shifts, 12;
during Great Depression/New Deal,
138–39, 191; and land consolidation,

12, 19, 237 (n. 5); during Mexican
Revolution, 11, 14; and migrant
rights, 67, 159, 189, 192–93; during
the Porfiriato, 13, 15, 19–20; and
repatriation colonies, 138–39; and
Skinning War, 15; during WWI,
50. *See also* Growers; Immigrants/
immigration; Deportation
Mexico City, 1, 11, 91, 192, 194, 198, 207,
274 (n. 16)
Michigan, 59–62, 65, 69–70, 74,
96–97, 214
Michigan Sugar Company, 60
Migrants/migration: and Great
Depression, 130, 132–33; internal
U.S. migration, 39, 41–42, 58–60,
67–70, 141, 185, 216; to Mexico, 15,
140; out of Texas 58–60, 67–70.
See also Labor/laborers
Mining industry, 11–13, 23, 57, 105,
236 (n. 14). *See also* Labor/laborers:
industrial
Minnesota, 68, 70
Mitchell, Don, 92
Montejano, David, 4, 17–18, 84–85, 92,
237 (n. 5)
Moore, C. B., 117
Mullally, J. F., 96, 157
Muñoz, Adolfo, 34–35, 242 (nn. 79, 80)
Muñoz, Henry, 215
Myers, Joseph, 176, 178

Nafarrate, Emiliano, 32, 241 (n. 66)
National Council of Agricultural
Employers, 183
National Industrial Recovery Act, 142
National Labor Relations Act. *See*
Wagner Act
National Labor Relations Board,
142–43, 160–61, 168
National Pecan Shellers' Association, 174
National Relief Administration, 162,
165–68, 174–75
National Youth Administration, 147–48
Nativism, 102, 103–23, 135–36, 213

Navasota Cooperage Company, 115
Nebraska Beef, 227–28
New Deal, 128, 147; and agricultural labor, 130, 142–44, 155, 158–59, 274 (n. 22); and agricultural programs, 130; and relief, 151, 181, 229; and Texas response, 130, 141, 144, 149, 152
New Orleans, La., 22, 29, 91
New York, N.Y., 13, 51, 68, 70, 131, 167
Ngai, Mae, 4, 109, 112, 123, 221
Nueces County, Tex., 15, 52, 55–57, 80, 86–88, 93, 98, 116, 129, 134
Nuevo Laredo, Mexico, 32, 268 (n. 68)

Obregón, Alvaro, 21, 257 (n. 53)
Orozco, Pascual, 29

Padilla, Ezequiel, 196
Paris, France, 1, 131
Parr, Archie, 82–83
Pecan industry, 129, 172; and labor, 163–64, 166, 170–76, 180–81, 269 (n. 71), 270 (n. 97); mechanization of, 167, 171, 180; and operators, 171–72, 179, 270 (nn. 92, 95) and wages, 134, 172–73, 175; and working conditions, 154, 162, 174, 179. See also Labor/laborers: industrial
Pecan Shelling Workers Union, 175
Pecan Workers Local No. 172, 176
Peck, Gunther, 4
Pennsylvania, 67–68, 70
Penrose, Neville, 198
Perales, Alonso, 195
Piedras Negras, Mexico, 26
Pizaña, Aniceto, 35–36, 242 (n. 84), 243 (nn. 87, 97)
Plan de San Diego, 32–40, 42–43, 155, 240 (n. 63), 241 (nn. 65, 66, 68), 242 (n. 71), 243 (n. 85), 250 (n. 9)
Polin Tapia, Francisco, 193–94
Pombo, Richard, 183
Prague, Czech Republic, 1

President's Commission on Migratory Labor, 200, 206, 217, 280 (n. 141)
Public Law 45, 199
Public Law 78, 208, 215
Public Law 414, 280 (n. 139)

Quin, C. K., 146–47, 149, 150, 152, 166, 169, 178–79

Railroads, 11, 16–17, 19, 27–28, 58; and Border War of 1915, 36–37; Corpus Christi–Laredo, 18; and development of South Texas, 41–43, 47, 52; and dispossession of land-holders, 16–17; and Immigration Act of 1917, 105; International and Great Northern, 17; and labor practices, 57, 236 (n. 14); St. Louis, Brownsville, and Mexico Railway, 28, 33; Southern Pacific, 16
Ramos, Basilio, 32–33, 36
Ranching, 16–17, 19, 27–29, 46–47, 80. See also Labor/laborers
Ransom, Harry, 34, 36–37
Raymondville Peonage Cases, 94
Reconstruction Finance Corporation, 142
Regional Labor Relations Board, 163
Reyes, Bernardo 29, 238 (n. 44)
Ribb, Richard, 37
Rice Brothers Cannery, 160
Richer, Juan, 158–59
Rio Grande Valley. See Lower Rio Grande Valley
Riots, 125–27, 152, 177, 181, 194. See also Nativism
Robertson, Sam, 47, 120, 135
Rodríguez, Magdaleno, 175, 271 (nn. 110, 112)
Roosevelt, Eleanor, 151
Roosevelt, Franklin Delano, 73, 98, 142, 144, 151, 162, 191
Root, Elihu, 24

Sager, María Solis, 175, 269 (n. 71)
St. Louis, Mo., 68, 70, 171, 174

Salinas, José Lázaro, 209

Samuels, H. G., 157

San Antonio, Tex.: and agricultural development, 43; and disasters, 89–91, 252 (n. 46); and Great Depression/New Deal, 144, 146–47, 151–52, 173; and labor, 55–56, 70, 129–30, 132, 134, 143, 163–64, 167, 171–74, 178, 181, 253 (n. 59), 270 (n. 97); and labor activism, 154, 158, 162, 165–70, 175–76, 266 (n. 29); and labor recruitment, 58, 61, 93–94, 98; and living conditions, 129, 131–32, 135, 153; and Mexican Revolution, 20, 29, 31, 81; and migration, 54, 59, 67, 69, 77; and politics, 89, 128, 146, 148–50, 238 (n. 44), 252 (n. 48), 262 (n. 68), 267 (n. 50), 268 (n. 66); and segregation, 88–89; and transportation networks, 15–17; violence in, 125–26, 195, 236 (n. 3); and World's Fair, 1–3. See also South Texas

San Antonio Express-News, 2–3, 119, 147, 170

San Antonio Light, 38, 152, 170, 177–78, 243 (n. 98, 100, 101), 258–59 (n. 1–3, 5–10), 266 (n. 31), 269 (n. 81–82, 85–86), 271 (n. 124–25)

San Antonio Trades Council, 163

San Benito, Tex., 34–35, 47

Sanchez, Amador, 239 (n. 44)

Sánchez, George I., 197

Sandos, James, 28, 222

Santibáñez, Enrique, 135

Segregation, 75, 85, 92, 100–101, 113, 123, 146, 194–95, 196; and education, 87–89, 275 (n. 40); and housing, 87, 89–91, 275 (n. 40); and Jim Crow laws, 53, 62, 68. See also Labor/laborers: agricultural, racialization of

Seligmann, Julius, 171, 173–75, 179, 269 (n. 90), 270 (n. 95)

Shapiro, Harold, 171

Sharecropping, 43, 53, 56, 100, 130, 143, 246 (n. 52), 252 (n. 55). See also Labor/laborers: agricultural

Shary, John, 48, 50, 133, 244 (n. 1)

Shivers, Allan, 187, 198, 210–11, 216

Shrimp industry, 160, 180

Skinning War, 15

Southern Pecan Shelling Company, 171–76, 178–80, 269 (n. 90), 270 (nn. 92, 95), 272 (n. 136)

South Texas: and Border War of 1915, 32–40; and border with Mexico, 14, 15, 19; demographic makeup of, 45, 66; geographic definition of, 4; and Great Depression, 9, 130–31, 132, 140, 145; and guest worker programs, 184; and labor legislation, 78; and land consolidation 19, 78; and Mexican Revolution, 9, 28–40; migration to, 7–8, 15–16, 38–39, 41–42; as a model for national labor practices, 42, 58, 60–62, 99, 185, 229; and New Deal, 141–42, 147–49, 151; and political machines, 18, 78–84, 150–53, 250 (n. 16), 252 (n. 48), 262 (n. 68); and political reform, 148–53; political restructuring of, 78–84; during Porfiriato, 15–19, 27; and poverty, 49, 162; and race violence, 32–40, 84; racialization of, 49, 50; social caste system in, 8, 18, 49, 53, 61, 84, 99, 102, 123, 162; and unions, 162; and WWI era, 41–42, 50. See also Agriculture; Border War of 1915; Plan de San Diego; Segregation

South Texas Cotton Growers' Association, 108

Southwestern Land Company, 41, 48–50, 133

Spain, 2

Special Rangers, 243 (n. 103). See also Labor/laborers: militancy of; South

Texas: and race violence; Texas: mythology of

Starr County, Tex., 18

Steel industry, 57, 62, 66–70

Steelman, J. R., 98, 157–59

Sterling, Ross, 145

Sterling, William Warren, 239 (n. 50)

Stevenson, Coke, 196, 275 (n. 33)

Stilwell, Hart, 195

Strauss, Nathan, 151

Strauss, Oscar, 24

Sugar beet industry, 59, 92, 99, 227, 229, 277; and labor, 60–62, 66, 68, 108, 110, 113, 121; and migration, 70, 133, 176, 272 (n. 139); and recruitment, 61, 63, 69, 97–98; and wages, 64–65, 134, 172, 253 (n. 73). *See also* Labor/laborers: agricultural

Sugar industry, 60, 224

Swing, Joseph, 210–13

Taft, William Howard, 30

Taft Ranch, 57, 60, 83

Tamaulipas, Mexico, 28, 32, 33, 44, 102, 139–40

Taylor, Charles, 155

Taylor, Edward, 113

Taylor, Paul, 54, 56, 69–70, 84–85, 87–88, 96, 98, 155, 246 (n. 52)

Taylor, Rebecca, 268 (n. 71)

Teamsters, 4, 15, 236 (n. 3). *See also* Labor/laborers

Tenayuca, Emma, 125–27, 150, 152, 169, 170, 175, 268 (n. 66), 269 (n. 71)

Texas: and border with Mexico, 3–4, 11, 14, 17, 19, 29, 33, 44; demographic makeup of, 195; and Great Depression, 130, 145; mythology of, 2–3, 39, 127, 187; and New Deal, 130, 144, 145; and Spanish heritage, 3; and State Industrial Commission, 178; and Texas Revolution, 30. *See also* Agriculture; Growers; Immigration; Labor; Mexican Revolution: and U.S.; South Texas

Texas Farm Placement Service, 96, 190–91

Texas Infant Manufacturing Company, 168

Texas Labor Bureau, 55

Texas Pioneers Association, 125

Texas Railroad Commission, 99

Texas Rangers, 18, 29–31, 34–35, 37–39, 80–83, 155, 157, 239 (n. 56), 240 (nn. 57, 68), 266 (n. 42). *See also* Texas: mythology of

Textile industry, 11, 48, 163. *See also* Labor/laborers: industrial

Tijerina, Andrés, 4

Tobin, John, 146

Torreón, Mexico, 11, 13, 20, 22

Tuxtepec rebellion, 15

Tyson Foods, 227–29. *See also* Labor/laborers: industrial

Unión de Nueceros Unidos, 175

United Cannery, Agricultural, Packing, and Allied Workers of America, 159

United Farm Workers, 162, 229

U.S. Army, 30–31, 37

U.S. Bureau of Agricultural Economics, 58, 189

U.S. Congress, 96–97, 103, 109, 113–14, 116, 183–84. *See also* Labor/laborers: protective legislation

U.S. Department of Agriculture, 117, 179, 191

U.S. Department of the Interior, 117

U.S. Department of Justice, 93–94, 228

U.S. Department of Labor, 24, 118

U.S. Department of State, 117, 199, 210

U.S. Department of War, 136

U.S. Employment Service, 99, 106, 188, 199, 204–5

U.S. Food Administration, 107–8

U.S. Housing Authority, 151

U.S. Immigration Service, 24–26, 73, 102, 104–6, 108, 118–19, 121, 136. *See also* Immigrants/immigration; Deportation

Vahlsing, Fred, 51
Valdés, Dennis, 65
Valenta, M. A., 126–27
Valls, John, 157
Vargas, Zaragoza, 4, 58, 66, 248 (n. 108)
Veterans of Foreign Wars, 145
Viesca, Mexico, 13, 236 (nn. 16, 18)
Villa, Pancho, 20–21, 23

Wagner Act, 142, 166, 168
Wailuku Agribusiness Corporation, 223–26
Wallace, Henry, 189
Walmart, 227, 229
War Manpower Commission, 99
Weber, Devra, 46
Wells, James, 18, 78, 80, 82–83, 131, 250 (n. 11)
White Man's Primary Association, 79
Wilmoth, Grover, 204
Willson, John, 73–75
Wilson, William B., 105–9
Wilson, Woodrow, 107, 241 (n. 66)
Winter Garden, 45, 79, 87, 97; and agriculture, 44, 50–52, 56; and growers, 97; and labor, 54, 62, 247 (n. 52); and mechanization, 57; and migration, 70, 134, 217; and wages, 133. *See also* Agriculture; South Texas
Wirtz, Willard, 215, 217
Workers. *See* Laborers
Workers Alliance, 168–70, 175
Works Progress Administration, 133, 142, 147, 149, 169, 176, 270 (n. 97)
World's Fair (1968). *See* HemisFair
World War I, 50, 58, 62, 105, 108–9, 113, 127, 190, 192, 241 (n. 68)
World War II, 10, 99, 182, 184–85, 189–90, 192, 194, 197, 201, 216, 219, 221
Wynhoven, Peter, 163

Young, Elliot, 4

Zamora, Emilio, 4, 99, 197
Zapata, Emiliano, 20–21
Zavala County, Tex., 42, 45, 51
Zimmerman Telegram, 241 (n. 68)
Zoot Suit Riots, 194